The Cumulated
Dickens Checklist
1970 - 1979

"Boz" in his Study

George Sala's frontispiece to Thomas O'Keefe's
The Battle of London Life; or, Boz and His Secretary
(1849)

The Cumulated
Dickens Checklist
1970 - 1979

Alan M. Cohn
&
K. K. Collins

The Whitston Publishing Company
Troy, New York
1982

To

George Michael Collins

CONTENTS

Acknowledgments

During most of the years that "The Dickens Checklist" has appeared in the *Dickens Studies Newsletter,* founded by our colleague Robert B. Partlow, Jr., the Department of English at Southern Illinois University at Carbondale provided Alan Cohn with the following research assistants, who appeared as co-compilers: Kenneth Denning, William D. Faulhaber, J. E. Kasel, George V. Griffith, and James T. Jones.

For help with this cumulation, Southern Illinois University's Office of Research Development and Administration, Michael R. Dingerson, Director, funded research assistantships ably filled by Thomas K. Pasch, who provided both literary and computational skills; by Julie Sollman, who co-read hundreds of scholarly items; and by Nancy Buss, who typed countless index tags.

Our Office of Academic Computing, Philip Spielmacher, Director, supplied invaluable help. Thanks are due to Janice A. Bartleson and to Albert A. Allen. To Laurie Straub and Daniel E. Seaman, who spent many late hours creating and perfecting the complex program that made our index work, we are especially grateful.

David T. Ray and James S. Chervinko were particularly helpful with the more exotic languages, Hensley C. Woodbridge with the less.

Betty J. Hutton and Thyra K. Russell of the Morris Library Order Department got things for us fast, as did Thomas L. Kilpatrick and the interlibrary loan crew.

Duane DeVries, the current editor of *DSN,* has given us permission on behalf of the journal to recycle material from the checklists, as has Deborah Thomas on behalf of the sponsoring Dickens Society.

We are indebted to many for bringing items to our attention.

God bless You, Every One!

Drawing by John Leech
(coll. AMC)

Introduction

"Well—nobody's perfect."
Osgood Fielding III in
Billy Wilder's *Some Like It Hot*

The present bibliography is based on the quarterly checklists that have appeared in the *Dickens Studies Newsletter* beginning with its second issue in September 1970. Despite the dates of coverage given in our title, works published in 1969 and in 1980 are included. Since we consider our compilation an extension of Joseph Gold's *The Stature of Dickens: A Centenary Bibliography* (1971), which officially cuts off with 1968 but which includes 1969 "as far as possible," it seemed proper that we go back and gather items from 1969 not in Gold. In like manner, we thought it wasteful to omit material from 1980 in hand before the final cumulation. Some pre-1970 entries in Gold's bibliography reappear here, in abbreviated form within parentheses, because they were reviewed in 1970 or later.

This work is comprised of five consecutively numbered, alphabetically arranged bibliographical registers, an appendix, addenda, and an index. The registers are devoted to publications of Dickens's works (#1-#106); critical, scholarly, and biographical publications about him (#107-#2239); reprints (#2240-#2446); doctoral dissertations (#2447-#2776); and a selection of miscellanea (#2777-#2972).

Reviews are cited throughout the registers directly under the work reviewed. The exceptions are reviews of four or more items, which appear under the reviewers' names with cross-references there and under the items reviewed. (A few such reviews are so comprehensive that they are cross-referenced only at the items reviewed.) Reviews of an entry not solely or chiefly about Dickens are cited if they appear in the *Dickens Studies Newsletter* or in the *Dickensian,* or are part of a cross-referenced review. Unless otherwise noted, reviews marked with an asterisk are available on NewsBank microfiche.

Other closely related materials are also cited or cross-referenced under an entry: letters to editors or articles in response or rebuttal; earlier editions or versions of the item (e.g., dissertations); previously published articles incorporated into the entry; selections from the item reprinted in other entries; and so forth.

Annotations are light and informative rather than judgmental. We have added titles of Dickens's works only if an entry does not sufficiently indicate the titles it treats. Such an annotation has been omitted for items of broad, general coverage.

The first register, "Dickens's Works," is limited to the English language. The inaccessibility of most translations and the magnitude of the problems attending them exceed the capacities of the present bibliographers.

The second register, "Secondary Sources," is meant—despite the sentiment of our epigraph—to be as inclusive, comprehensive, and polyglot as possible. Titles in non-Latin alphabets have been translated and surrounded by brackets, except those in Cyrillic, which have been transliterated. To save space, each item from a collection of essays or a special issue of a journal has been entered in short form and cross-referenced to a full entry elsewhere, usually under the editor's name. Unsigned entries appear at the end of the register.

The third register, "Reprints," lists pre-1970 books by or about Dickens that have been reprinted in our decade. We have defined a reprinted book (as distinct from a later edition) as one reproduced by photo-facsimile process.

The fourth register, "Doctoral Dissertations," is an international list made as complete as our reference sources have allowed. We have grouped dissertations in a separate section for two reasons: graduate students must review such a list, but other users may wish to be spared being frequently referred to dissertations (there are over 300 entered). Those wanting to detour around dissertations may therefore skip over the numbers in the index encompassed by this section (#2447-

#2776).

The fifth and final register, "Miscellaneous," lists such materials as audio-visual aids, theatrical and film adaptations based on Dickens's life and works, and recordings. Here again we have had to be selective. The dozens of productions of *A Christmas Carol* alone which tread the boards each holiday season would have swelled this section to monstrous girth. But we hope at least to have included items of national importance—though we are chagrined to have had to omit reference to the 1977 Leningrad production of *Pickwick Papers* for want of time to run down full particulars (see *International Theatre Yearbook '78*, p. 139). While some academics might question the value of this section, it is strong testimony to Dickens's enduring presence in popular culture. Furthermore, as Gordon Ross Smith has argued, "It is impossible for a bibliographer to know what will be demanded of his work" (paraphrase in *Shakespeare Newsletter*, April 1972).

The Appendix gives the contents of ten collections too large to be entered fully in the register of secondary sources. Even so, restrictions of space have prevented us from describing the complete contents of all of these collections. Our compromise has been to supply more detail about modern essays than about older ones and to cross-reference those that also appear elsewhere in the bibliography.

The Subject Index has been made as detailed as possible, an attempt that grew out of our decision to organize this work the way we have. Of the several ways to arrange bibliographies, one of the most common is the topical. This is appropriate and convenient, especially for books and articles devoted exclusively to, say, a single novel. But a high percentage of the entries in bibliographies usually deal significantly with more than one work, and a topical arrangement requires entering a given book or article under two or more rubrics, or developing a system of cross-referencing, or putting such multi-interest items in a section labeled "General," which requires the user to scan a large number of entries in order to locate the few items wanted. Another way —the one we have chosen—is to arrange entries alphabetically by author and to provide an index. But some bibliographies produced this way are flawed because (to invent an example) the user who wishes to find material on, say, the theme of education in *Hard Times* looks under that title in the index only to find a large block of numbers with no indication of the specific subject(s) covered by any of the items to which they refer. Under "Education," there might be another block of such numbers, with no indication of the novels in which the subject is treated.

In creating the present index, our chief aim has been—within the limits of space and reason—to avoid confronting our user with such large blocks of undifferentiated numbers. To continue the example, this index presents six numbers under "Works—*Hard Times*—Education." The remaining 186 numbers under *Hard Times* are sub-divided under fifty-five subject headings, beginning with "General Criticism" (studies so broad-based as to resist detailed analysis) and ranging from "Adaptation" to "Utilitarianism," with these headings further divided into over forty subheadings. All the numbers under *Hard Times* also appear in reversed form under their respective subjects elsewhere in the index. Thus the numbers under "Works—*Hard Times*—Education" will be found under "Education—*Hard Times*," and so forth.

Any item indexed under "General Criticism" (our only large block of undifferentiated numbers) may include brief discussions of other subjects in the index, but such items have been indexed further only for subjects treated extensively. The Leavises' book, for example, appears under "General Criticism," but since its individual chapters concentrate on specific subjects in separate novels, we thought it useful to index each chapter. It should also be noted that a subject heading subsumes its subheadings. Thus a number under "Words—*Hard Times*—Society" may refer to an item that discusses (not centrally, but perhaps significantly) any or all of that subject heading's six subheadings. Similarly, a number under "Society" may refer to an item that discusses any or all of that subject heading's twenty-two subheadings.

Perhaps this last point can be more easily illustrated by going outside the confines of our index. A patron wanting a book on a species of tree—say the Loblolly pine—would look in a library catalog under that heading directly. On the other hand, books dealing with the order to which this species belongs would also yield pertinent information, and so the broader subject heading "Coniferae" might be checked. Of course books listed under "Trees" would have relevant sections as well. There would not be entries in the catalog, however, for all the trees dealt with in the last two instances; such a catalog would have to be immense in the extreme. Similarly, we have tried to construct this index so that a user can move from the specific to the more general subject entries in search of materials.

We have used one other curb to control the size of the index. In general, entries that treat three or fewer of Dickens's works are indexed under those specific titles, while entries that treat four or more works are not. A study of education in more than three novels, therefore, would not be found under any titles but only under "Education," even though the author might discuss *Hard Times*. Thus our user would want to look up not only the six entries referred to under "Works—*Hard Times*—Education" but also the eleven under "Education." The annotations to those eleven entries will tell which ones cover *Hard Times*. Again, restrictions of space have led us to introduce one variation of this scheme: dissertations must treat only one of Dickens's works to be indexed under a specific title.

The Foreign Language Index directs users to several hundred entries in nineteen different languages.

The Name Index brings together all names in the bibliography not in first position, excepting those of editors (say of festschriften) who do not discuss Dickens. This index includes, to give a few examples: reviewers; editors of Dickens's works; illustrators; writers of introductions and letters to editors; contributors to the large collections found in the Appendix; speakers at conferences; co-authors; translators; directors; screenwriters; narrators of phonorecordings; and the medium who completed *The Mystery of Edwin Drood*. The Name Index thus helps provide the user with a complete record of individual contributions to Dickensian activities in the 70s. For instance, a user who wishes to find out about Edgar Johnson's work on Dickens during this period will need to check this bibliography at a number of points. The register of secondary sources includes Johnson's revised abridgment of his Dickens biography (#1011) and an essay by him in a festschrift (#1012); the Subject Index refers to an article on his biography in relation to Forster research (#520) and to Lionel Trilling's reprinted review of his biography (#2015); but the Name Index leads to further material: Johnson's review of three works in this bibliography (#9, #15, #1559), his reprinted edition of Dickens's letters to Angela Burdett Coutts (#2263), an essay by him in a reprinted collection (#2331), and his comments on the inaccuracies of Wolf Mankowitz's television serial on Dickens's life (#2906).

Finally, we have been rather stringent in assigning subjects, and some—like "Feminist Criticism" and "Structuralist Criticism"—we have handled gingerly, using them only if the author's orientation is obvious. When we began this cumulation, we set out personally to examine all the items in it. We have done that with but few exceptions: some foreign (especially Far Eastern) criticism and dissertations remained inaccessible and had to be indexed by title or abstract, and we have used abstracts for most domestic dissertations as well. Despite our efforts, many of the index categories are closely related, some overlap, and some, like "Society" and "Morality," veer on the edge of control; many entries could have been indexed almost as well under one set of terms as another; and a few items have subjects we still do not quite know how to name. In compensation, we have cross-referenced the index terms lavishly and have decided, after that, to trust to our user's judgment and patience.

Abbreviations of Dickens's Works

AllYR	*All the Year Round*
AmerN	*American Notes*
BarnR	*Barnaby Rudge*
BattL	*The Battle of Life*
BleakH	*Bleak House*
CHistEng	*A Child's History of England*
Chimes	*The Chimes*
CBooks	*Christmas Books*
CCarol	*A Christmas Carol*
CStories	*Christmas Stories*
CrickH	*The Cricket on the Hearth*
DavidC	*David Copperfield*
DSon	*Dombey and Son*
FDeep	*The Frozen Deep*
"GS'sExpl"	"George Silverman's Explanation"
GreatEx	*Great Expectations*
HardT	*Hard Times*
"HDown"	"Hunted Down"
"HHouse"	"The Haunted House"
HMan	*The Haunted Man*
"HRom"	"A Holiday Romance"
"HTree"	"The Holly Tree"
HsldWds	*Household Words*
IsShe	*Is She His Wife?*
LampLtr	*The Lamplighter*
LazyT	*A Lazy Tour of Two Idle Apprentices*
LifeL	*Life of Our Lord*
LittleDor	*Little Dorrit*
MChuz	*Martin Chuzzlewit*
MH'sClock	*Master Humphrey's Clock*
MemGrim	*Memoirs of Grimaldi*
"MSea"	"A Message from the Sea"
N'sDiary	*Mr. Nightingale's Diary*
"MudP"	"The Mudfog Papers"
"MugJ"	"Mugby Junction"

MEDrood	*The Mystery of Edwin Drood*
NichN	*Nicholas Nickleby*
"NoTho"	"No Thoroughfare"
OCShop	*The Old Curiosity Shop*
OliverTw	*Oliver Twist*
OurMF	*Our Mutual Friend*
"Perils"	"The Perils of Certain English Prisoners"
PickP	*The Pickwick Papers*
PictIt	*Pictures from Italy*
SBoz	*Sketches by Boz*
"SomeLug"	"Somebody's Luggage"
SGent	*The Strange Gentleman*
TaleTwoC	*A Tale of Two Cities*
UncomTr	*The Uncommercial Traveller*
VCoq	*The Village Coquettes*

Abbreviations of Newspapers, Periodicals, and Serials
(Based Mainly upon the Master List of the *MLA International Bibliography*)

ABC	*American Book Collector*
ACer	*Anales cervantinos*
AEB	*Analytical & Enumerative Bibliography*
AF	Anglistische Forschungen
AH	*American Heritage*
AI	*American Imago*
AION-SG	*Annali istituto universitario orientale, Napoli, sezione germanica*
AL	*American Literature*
ALS	*Australian Literary Studies*
AN&Q	*American Notes & Queries*
APh	*Acta Philologica*
ARBA	*American Reference Books Annual*
ArielE	*Ariel: A Review of International English Literature*
ArmD	*Armchair Detective*
ArQ	*Arizona Quarterly*
ASch	*American Scholar*

ASUI	*Analele stiintifice ale universitatii Iasi*
AUB-LG	*Analele universitatii, Bucuresti, limbi germanice*
AUJR-L	*Agra University Journal of Research (Letters)*
AUMLA:	*Journal of the Australasian Universities Language &*
	Literature Association
AWR	*Anglo-Welsh Review*
B&B	*Books & Bookmen*
BBkN	*British Book News*
BC	*Book Collector*
BCCB	*Bulletin of the Center for Children's Books*
BIS	*Browning Institute Studies*
BJA	*British Journal of Aesthetics*
BJRL	*Bulletin of the John Rylands University Library*
BNYPL	*Bulletin of the New York Public Library*
BRMMLA	*Rocky Mountain Review of Language and Litera-*
	ture
BSE	Brno Studies in English
BSLP	*Bulletin de la Société de Linguistique de Paris*
BSNotes	*Browning Society Notes*
BSUF	*Ball State University Forum*
BWVACET	*Bulletin of the West Virginia Association of Col-*
	lege English Teachers
CA	*Cuadernos americanos*
CalR	*Calcutta Review*
C&L	*Christianity & Literature*
CanL	*Canadian Literature*
CCrit	*Comparative Criticism*
CE	*College English*
CEA	*CEA Critic*
CentR	*Centennial Review*
CeS	*Cultura e scuola*
Ch	*Choice*
ChildL	*Children's Literature*
ChLB	*Charles Lamb Bulletin*
CL	*Comparative Literature*
CLAJ	*College Language Association Journal*
ClioI	*CLIO: An Interdisciplinary Journal of Literature,*
	History, and the Philosophy of History
CLS	*Comparative Literature Studies*
CnL	*Country Life*
ConLit	*Convorbiri literare*
ContempR	*Contemporary Review*
CQ	*Cambridge Quarterly*

CR	*Critical Review*
CRev	*Chesterton Review*
CRevAS	*Canadian Review of American Studies*
CritI	*Critical Inquiry*
CritQ	*Critical Quarterly*
CSM	*Christian Science Monitor*
CUBDE	*Calcutta University Bulletin of the Department of English*
DAI	*Dissertation Abstracts International*
DiS	*Dickens Studies*
Dkn	*Dickensian*
DQR	*Dutch Quarterly Review of Anglo-American Letters*
DR	*Dalhousie Review*
DSN	*Dickens Studies Newsletter*
DUJ	*Durham University Journal*
DVLG	*Deutsche Vierteljahrsschrift für Literaturwissenschaft und Geistesgeschichte*
EA	*Études anglaises*
EAA	*Estudos anglo-americanos*
E&S	*Essays & Studies*
EASG	*English and American Studies in German*
Ecn	*Economist*
EIC	*Essays in Criticism*
EigoS	*Eigo seinen*
EJ	*English Journal*
ELH:	*English Literary History*
ELLS	*English Literature and Language*
ELN	*English Language Notes*
ELT	*English Literature in Transition*
ELWIU	*Essays in Literature*
EM	*English Miscellany*
Enc	*Encounter*
EngR	*English Record*
ES	*English Studies*
ESA	*English Studies in Africa*
ESC	*English Studies in Canada*
ETJ	*Educational Theatre Journal*
EWN	*Evelyn Waugh Newsletter*
Expl	*Explicator*
FK	*Filológiai közlöny*
FL	*Figaro littéraire*

FMonde	*Français dans le monde*
FN	*Filologiceskie nauki*
FP	*Filoloski pregled*
FT	*Finsk tidskrift*
GaR	*Georgia Review*
GEP	*Graduate English Papers*
GothSE	Gothenburg Studies in English
GRLH	Garland Reference Library of the Humanities
GRM	*Germanisch-Romanische Monatsschrift*
HAB	*Humanities Association Review*
HES	Harvard English Studies
HLB	*Harvard Library Bulletin*
HLQ	*Huntington Library Quarterly*
HSCL	Harvard Studies in Comparative Literature
HSELL	*Hiroshima Studies in English Language and Literature*
HSL	*University of Hartford Studies in Literature*
HSN	*Hawthorne Society Newsletter*
HudR	*Hudson Review*
HUSL	*Hebrew University Studies in Literature*
IFR	*International Fiction Review*
IJES	*Indian Journal of English Studies*
ILN	*Illustrated London News*
IowaR	*Iowa Review*
ISLL	Illinois Studies in Language and Literature
JAAC	*Journal of Aesthetics and Art Criticism*
JAMA	*Journal of the American Medical Association*
JAmS	*Journal of American Studies*
JEGP	*Journal of English and Germanic Philology*
JES	*Journal of European Studies*
JFI	*Journal of the Folklore Institute*
JFNL	*John Forster Newsletter*
JHI	*Journal of the History of Ideas*
JJQ	*James Joyce Quarterly*
JML	*Journal of Modern Literature*
JNT	*Journal of Narrative Technique*
JPC	*Journal of Popular Culture*
JWSL	*Journal of Women's Studies in Literature*
KanQ	*Kansas Quarterly*
KBDF	*Kleine Beiträge zur Droste-Forschung*
KN	*Kwartalnik neofilologiczny*
KR	*Kenyon Review*

L&H	*Literature & History*
L&P	*Literature & Psychology*
Lang&S	*Language and Style*
LanM	*Langues modernes*
LCUT	*Library Chronicle of the University of Texas*
LFQ	*Literature/Film Quarterly*
LJ	*Library Journal*
Lstr	*Listener*
LuL	*Literatur und Leben*
LWU	*Literatur in Wissenschaft und Unterricht*
MAPS	Memoirs of the American Philosophical Society
MDAC	*Mystery and Detection Annual*
MFS	*Modern Fiction Studies*
MHRev	*Malahat Review*
MissQ	*Mississippi Quarterly*
MLQ	*Modern Language Quarterly*
MLR	*Modern Language Review*
MLS	*Modern Language Studies*
MMLA	*Midwest Modern Language Association*
MP	*Modern Philology*
MQ	*Midwest Quarterly*
MQR	*Michigan Quarterly Review*
MSE	*Massachusetts Studies in English*
MSpr	*Moderna Språk*
NA	*Nuova antologia*
N&Q	*Notes & Queries*
NCF	*Nineteenth-Century Fiction*
NConL	*Notes on Contemporary Literature*
NDEJ	*Notre Dame English Journal*
NDQ	*North Dakota Quarterly*
Neophil	*Neophilologus*
NEQ	*New England Quarterly*
NewSt	*New Statesman*
NL	*Nouvelles littéraires*
NLH	*New Literary History*
NM	*Neuphilologische Mitteilungen*
NMAL	*Notes on Modern American Literature*
NMW	*Notes on Mississippi Writers*
NRF	*Nouvelle revue française*
NS	*Neueren Sprachen*
NSAA	Neue Studien zur Anglistik und Amerikanistik
NSE	Norwegian Studies in English

NY	*New Yorker*
NYRB	*New York Review of Books*
NYSJM	*New York State Journal of Medicine*
NYT	*New York Times*
NYTBR	*New York Times Book Review*
NZSJ	*New Zealand Slavonic Journal*
Obs	*Observer*
PAPA	*Publications of the Arkansas Philological Association*

PBSA: Papers of the Bibliographical Society of America

PCP	*Pacific Coast Philology*
Phil&Lit	*Philosophy & Literature*
PHum	*Przeglad humanistyczny*
PLL	*Papers on Language and Literature*
PMHB	*Pennsylvania Magazine of History and Biography*

PMLA: Publications of the Modern Language Association of America

PoeS	*Poe Studies*
PP	*Philologica pragensia*
PQ	*Philological Quarterly*
Prvs	*Previews*
PsyculR	*Psychocultural Review*
QJS	*Quarterly Journal of Speech*
QL	*Quinzaine littéraire*
QQ	*Queen's Quarterly*
RALS	*Resources for American Literary Study*
RDM	*Nouvelle revue des deux mondes*
RecL	*Recovering Literature*
REL	*Review of English Literature*
RES	*Review of English Studies*
RevBib	*Revista bibliotecilor*
RITL	*Revista de istorie si teorie literara*
RLC	*Revue de littérature comparée*
RLMC	*Rivista di letterature moderne e comparate*
RLV	*Revue des langues vivantes*
RMS	*Renaissance & Modern Studies*
RO	*Revista de occidente*
RoLit	*România literara*
RomN	*Romance Notes*
RS	*Research Studies*
RUS	*Rice University Studies*
SAB	*South Atlantic Bulletin*

SAF	*Studies in American Fiction*
SAJL	*Studies in American Jewish Literature*
SAP	*Studia anglica posnaniensia*
SAQ	*South Atlantic Quarterly*
SatR	*Saturday Review*
SCB	*South Central Bulletin*
SCR	*South Carolina Review*
SEEJ	*Slavic and East European Journal*
SEER	*Slavonic and East European Review*
SEL:	*Studies in English Literature, 1500-1900*
SELit	*Studies in English Literature* (Tokyo)
ShawR	*Shaw Review*
SHR	*Southern Humanities Review*
SinN	*Sin nombre*
SJ	*Silliman Journal*
SJS	*San Jose Studies*
SlavR	*Slavic Review*
SN	*Studia neophilologica*
SNNTS	*Studies in the Novel*
SoR	*Southern Review* (Baton Rouge)
SoRA	*Southern Review* (Adelaide)
SovL	*Soviet Literature*
Spec	*Spectator*
SR	*Sewanee Review*
SRAZ	*Studia romanica et anglica zagrabiensia*
SSF	*Studies in Short Fiction*
SSl	*Scando-slavica*
SSL	*Studies in Scottish Literature*
STimes	*Sunday Times* (London)
StHum	*Studies in the Humanities*
SXX	*Secolul XX*
SzDL	Studien zur deutschen Literatur
SzEP	Studien zur englischen Philologie
TEAS	Twayne's English Authors Series
TES	*Times Educational Supplement*
THES	*Times Higher Education Supplement*
TJ	*Theatre Journal*
TkR	*Tamkang Review*
TLS:	*Times Literary Supplement*
TM	*Temps modernes*
TPB	*Tennessee Philological Bulletin*
TSLL	*Texas Studies in Literature and Language*
TUSAS	Twayne's United States Authors Series

TWAS	Twayne's World Authors Series
UCTSE	*University of Cape Town Studies in English*
UDR	*University of Dayton Review*
UES	*Unisa English Studies*
UKPHS	University of Kansas Humanistic Studies
UTQ	*University of Toronto Quarterly*
VC	*Virginia Cavalcade*
VF	*Voprosy filologii*
VIJ	*Victorians Institute Journal*
ViR	*Viata româneasca*
VLit	*Voprosy literatury*
VLU	*Vestnik Leningradskogo Universiteta. Serija istorii, jazyka i literatury*
VN	*Victorian Newsletter*
VPN	*Victorian Periodicals Newsletter*
VPR	*Victorian Periodicals Review*
VQR	*Virginia Quarterly Review*
VS	*Victorian Studies*
WCR	*West Coast Review*
WHR	*Western Humanities Review*
WLT	*World Literature Today*
WN	*Wake Newslitter*
WZUR	*Wissenschaftliche Zeitschrift der Wilhelm-Pieck-Universität Rostock. Gesellschafts- und Sprachwissenschaftliche Reihe*
YES `	*Yearbook of English Studies*
YR	*Yale Review*
YSE	Yale Studies in English
YULG	*Yale University Library Gazette*
ZAA	*Zeitschrift für Anglistik und Amerikanistik*
ZLit	*Zycie literackie*

Some Other Abbreviations

abrg.	abridged, abridgment
abst.	abstract
adap.	adaptation, adapted
afwd.	afterword

annot.	annotated, annotation
art.	article
bibliog.	bibliographer, bibliographical, bibliography
CBEL	*Cambridge Bibliography of English Literature*
col.	column
coll.	collection, college
comp.	compiled, composition
cond.	conducted, conductor
corr.	correspondence
D	Dickens
diff.	different
dir.	directed, direction
diss.	dissertation
doc.	document
ed.	edited, edition (and foreign equivalents), educational
enl.	enlarged
facs.	facsimile
foll.	followed by, following
fr	frames
fwd.	foreward
gr.	grade
illus.	illustrated, illustration, illustrator
incl.	includes, including
infl.	influence(d)
intro.	introduction, introductory
J	*Journal*
ltr.	letter
ms	manuscript
narr.	narrated by, narration
NL	*Newsletter*
NS	New Series
OHEL	*Oxford History of English Literature*
pbk.	paperback
phil.	philosophical, philosophy
pref.	preface
proc.	proceedings
pt.	part
pub.	public, publication, published, publisher
Q	*Quarterly*
rev.	review(ed), revised
rpt.	reprint(ed)

sa	see also
sau	see also under
sel.	selected, selection
ser.	series
st.	study (and foreign equivalents)
su	see under
supp.	supplement(ary)
trans.	translation, translated
unpub.	unpublished
UP	University Press
vol.	volume

DICKENS'S WORKS

Anthologies, Collections, etc.

1 (*The Bedside Dickens: An Anthology for Pleasure*, comp. J. W. Garrod. 1969.) [Rev.: John Greaves, *Dkn* 66 (Jan. 1970): 61-62.]

2 A *Charles Dickens Christmas*, illus. Warren Chappell. New York: Oxford UP, 1976. 308 pp. [Children's ed.—Incl. *CCarol, Chimes, CrickH.*—Note also exhib. cat. of same title (Charlottesville: Univ. of Virginia Art Museum, 1976), 19 pp.—Rev. Brigitte Weeks, *Washington Post* 25 Dec. 1976: C1, C6.]

3 *Charles Dickens, 1812-1870: An Anthology*, ed. Lola L. Szladits. New York: New York Pub. Lib. and Arno Press, 1970. 165 pp. [Materials in the Berg Coll.—Rev.: Thomas J. Galvin, *LJ* 95 (15 Oct. 1970): 3462; Richard A. Vogler, *DSN* 1 (Dec. 1970): 17; *Ch* 7 (Dec. 1970): 1372; *DSN* 1 (Sept. 1970): 10; *TLS* 14 Aug. 1970: 906; also rev. in 1181.]

4 (*Charles Dickens's Uncollected Writings from Household Words 1850-1859*, ed. Harry Stone. 1968.) [Rev.: Richard C. Carpenter, *JPC* 4 (Fall 1970): 540-549; John Archer Carter, *DSN* 2 (June 1971): 45-47; Philip Collins, *Dkn* 66 (Jan. 1970): 42-50; Sylvère Monod, *EA* 33 (Apr.-June 1970): 219-222; James Stone, *VN* 7 (Jan. 1970): 8; also rev. in 198, 948, 2138, 2204.]

5 *The Christmas Books*, ed., intro., notes Michael Slater, illus. John Leech et al. Harmondsworth and Baltimore: Penguin, 1971. 2 vols. [Rev.: Angus Easson, *DSN* 4 (Sept. 1973): 68-71; Sylvère Monod, *Dkn* 68 (May 1972): 122-124; also rev. in 981.]

6 *Complete Plays and Selected Poems*. London: Vision, 1970. 245 pp. [Rev. in 314, 2237.]

7 A *Dickens Anthology*, ed. H. Pluckrose and F. Peacock. London: Mills and Boon, 1970; rpt. Norwood, Pa.: Norwood Eds., 1973. 96 pp.

8 *Dickens in Europe: Essays*, ed. Rosalind Vallance. London: Folio

Soc., 1975. 212 pp. [Incl. extracts from ltrs., arts., *PictIt.*—Rev. in 967 (Jan. 1976).]

9 *Dickens on America and the Americans,* ed. Michael Slater. Austin and London: Univ. of Texas Press; Hassocks: Harvester Press, 1978. 245 pp. [Extracts chiefly from ltrs., *AmerN, MChuz.*— Intro. with minor changes also in *Dutch Dkn* 7, xvi (Dec. 1978): 10-45.—Rev.: *Helen Ashmore, *Kansas City Star* 14 Jan. 1979; Edgar Johnson, *NYRB* 22 Mar. 1979: 24-25, 28; John Jordan, *Hibernia* 2 Aug. 1979; 14, 16; Edgar Rosenberg, *Dkn* 76 (Summer 1980): 104-106; Harry Stone, *NCF* 34 (Mar. 1980): 443-444; Angus Wilson, *Obs* 15 July 1979: 36; *Ch* 16 (Mar. 1979): 77; also rev. in 1123.]

10 *Manuscripts of the Works of Charles Dickens: From the Forster Collection in the Victoria and Albert Museum, London.* Wakefield: Micro Methods, 1970. 10 reels. [*BarnR, BleakH* (incl. marked proofs), *Chimes, DavidC* (incl. marked proofs), *DSon, HardT, LittleDor, MChuz, MEDrood, OCShop, TaleTwoC.*]

11 *The Public Readings,* ed. Philip Collins. Oxford: Clarendon Press, 1975. lxix, 486 pp. [Rev.: Malcolm Y. Andrews, *DSN* 10 (June-Sept. 1979): 75-77; C. C. Barfoot, *ES* 57 (Oct. 1976): 442; John Carey, *Lstr* 94 (20 Nov. 1975): 677-678; Pierre Coustillas, *EA* 30 (July-Sept. 1977): 370-371; Angus Easson, *N&Q* NS 26 (Aug. 1979): 353-354; K. J. Fielding, *Dkn* 72 (May 1976): 104-105; George Ford, *TLS* 20 Feb. 1976: 185; Mollie Hardwick, *B&B* 21 (Mar. 1976): 42-43; Sylvère Monod, *MLR* 72 (Oct. 1977): 923-924; Robert L. Patten, *NCF* 31 (Dec. 1976): 344-351; I. Stewart, *CnL* 159 (1976): 259; Helmut Viebrock, *Archiv* 214, i (1977): 167-169 and (a slightly diff. version in Eng.) *DQR* 7, ii (1977): 150-154; *BBkN* Feb. 1976: 138-139; *Ch* 13 (Apr. 1976): 222; *Ecn* 257 (1 Nov. 1975): 105-106; also rev. in 1062.]

12 *Selected Short Fiction,* ed. Deborah A. Thomas. Harmondsworth and Baltimore: Penguin, 1976. 431 pp. [Chiefly from *AllYR, HsldWds, SBoz.*—Rev.: Malcolm Andrews, *BBkN* July 1976: 534; Duane DeVries, *DSN* 9 (June 1978): 54-55; Suzanne Ferguson, *Dkn* 73 (Jan. 1977): 43-46; also rev. in 981.]

13 *The Short Stories,* intro. Walter Allen, illus. Edward Ardizzone. New York: Ltd. Eds. Club, 1971. xx, 423 pp.

14 *The Strange Gentleman and Other Plays,* intro. Jeffery Tillett. London: Heinemann Ed., 1972. xiv, 119 pp. [Also incl. *IsShe, Lampltr, N'sDiary.*—Rev.: Celia Boyd, *Young Drama* 1 (Feb. 1973):49-

50; David Isenberg, *Speech and Drama* 22 (Spring 1973): 32; R. P., *UES* 14 (Sept. 1976): 110-111; Jeremy Treglown, *TES* 9 Mar. 1973: 27; *Dkn* 69 (Sept. 1973): 192; *TLS* 2 Mar. 1973: 235.]

15 *The Supernatural Short Stories,* ed., intro. Michael Hayes. London: J. Calder; Dallas: Riverrun Press, 1978. 159 pp. [Rev.: Edgar Johnson, *NYRB* 22 Mar. 1979: 24-25, 28.]

16 *Three Novels.* London: Spring, 1977. 1088 pp. [*GreatEx, OliverTw, TaleTwoC.*]

17 *Works,* intro. Harriet Weitzner, illus. George Cruikshank et al. New York: Avenel Books, 1978. xiii, 1113 pp. [*CCarol, DavidC, GreatEx, HardT, OliverTw, PickP, TaleTwoC.*]

Individual Titles

Virtually every title is also available in Everyman's Library, Oxford Illustrated Dickens, and Heron (from Oxford Illustrated) reissue.

American Notes

18 *American Notes, 1842,* illus. William Henry Bartlett. [New York]: Westvaco, 1970. 274 pp.

19 *American Notes for General Circulation,* ed. John S. Whitley and Arnold Goldman. Harmondsworth and Baltimore: Penguin, 1972. 361 pp. [Rev.: K. J. Fielding, *Dkn* 68 (Sept. 1972): 193-194; also rev. in 2223.]

20 *American Notes for General Circulation,* [notes John S. Whitley and Arnold Goldman], intro. Angus Wilson, illus. Raymond F. Houlihan. Avon, Conn.: Ltd. Eds. Club, 1975. xv, 272 pp.

Barnaby Rudge

21 *Barnaby Rudge,* ed., intro., notes Gordon Spence, illus. George Cattermole and Hablot K. Browne. Harmondsworth: Penguin, 1973. 765 pp. [Based on 1868 ed.—Incl. historical sources.—Rev.: J. C. Maxwell, *N&Q* NS 23 (Feb. 1976): 86-89; C. H. M[uller], *UES* 13 (Mar. 1975): 71-72; Barry Westburg, *Dkn* 70 (May 1974): 133-134; *BBkN* Feb. 1974: 131; *ContempR* 224 (Jan. 1974): 56; *TLS* 11 Jan. 1974: 22 and James Cochrane's ltr. to ed., 1 Feb., p. 109.]

Bleak House

22   *Bleak House,* intro., notes Arthur Calder-Marshall. London: Pan,
      1976. 891 pp. [Rev.: M. H., *UES* 18 (Apr. 1980); 72; Peter
      Preston, *N&Q* NS 25 (June 1978): 262-263.]

23   *Bleak House,* ed. Duane DeVries. New York: Crowell, 1971. xix,
      1080 pp. [For contents see this number in Appendix.—Rev. in
      236.]

24   *Bleak House,* ed. George Ford and Sylvère Monod. New York: Nor-
      ton; Toronto: McLeod, 1977. xx, 986 pp. [For contents see this
      number in Appendix.—Rev.: Pierre Coustillas, *EA* 33 (Jan.-Mar.
      1980): 88-90; Michael Slater, *TLS* 20 June 1980: 716; Harvey
      Peter Sucksmith, *Dkn* 75 (Summer 1979): 107-108; Kathleen
      Tillotson, *NCF* 34 (Sept. 1979): 220-224; *Ch* 15 (Nov. 1978):
      1214; also rev. in 531.]

25   *Bleak House,* intro., notes Albert J. Guerard. New York and London:
      Holt, Rinehart and Winston, 1970. xxxvi, 857 pp. [Rev.: Lauriat
      Lane, Jr., *HAB* 21 (Summer 1970): 66-68; also rev. in 236.]

26   *Bleak House,* ed. Norman Page, intro. J. Hillis Miller, illus. Hablòt K.
      Browne. Harmondsworth and Baltimore: Penguin, 1971. 965 pp.
      [Rev. in 236, 981.]

A Christmas Carol

27   *The Annotated Christmas Carol,* intro., notes., bibliog. Michael
      Patrick Hearn, illus. John Leech et al. New York: Potter, 1976.
      182 pp. [Text facs. of 1st ed.—Note also pbk. rpt. New York:
      Avon, 1977.—Rev.: Edith Herman, *Chicago Tribune* 23 Dec. 1976:
      B1, B3; Robert Kirsch, *Los Angeles Times* 5 Dec. 1976: 1 (Book
      Section); Justin G. Schiller, *AB Bookman's Weekly* 58 (8 Nov.
      1976): 2537-2538; Brigitte Weeks, *Washington Post* 25 Dec. 1976:
      C1, C6; George J. Worth, *NCF* 32 (Dec. 1977): 348-351; *Ch* 13
      (Feb. 1977): 1594.]

28   *A Christmas Carol.* Louisville: American Printing House for the
      Blind, 1977. [Braille.]

29   *A Christmas Carol.* Bath: Chivers, 1979. xi, 159 pp. [Large type.]

30   *A Christmas Carol,* illus. John Ahee. Norcross, Ga.: Harrison, 1978.
      [Ca. 130 pp.]

31   A *Christmas Carol,* illus. Peter Fluck and Roger Law, photos. John
     Lawrence Jones. New York: St. Martin's Press, 1979. 78 pp.

32   A *Christmas Carol,* illus. Lynette Hemmant. Kingswood: World's
     Work, 1978. 95 pp. [Rev.: Virginia Makins, *TES* 17 Nov. 1978:
     26.]

33   A *Christmas Carol: The Public Reading Version: A Facsimile of the
     Author's Prompt-Copy,* intro., notes Philip Collins. New York:
     New York Pub. Lib., 1971. xxvi, 206 pp. [See also *BNYPL* 75
     (Oct. 1971): 336-337.—Rev.: Sylvère Monod, *EA* 26 (July-Sept.
     1973): 373; L[eslie] C. S[taples], *Dkn* 68 (May 1972): 127-128;
     Cb 9 (May 1972): 367; *TLS* 3 Mar. 1972: 256.]

David Copperfield

34   *David Copperfield,* abrg. Maidenhead: Purnell, 1976. 208 pp.

35   *David Copperfield,* illus. H. K. Browne. London: Fraser, 1970. 795
     pp. [Ltd. ed.]

36   *David Copperfield,* illus. Hablot K. Browne. Franklin Center, Pa.:
     Franklin Lib., 1976. 816 pp. [Ltd. "collector's" ed.]

37   *David Copperfield,* intro., notes Arthur Calder-Marshall. London:
     Pan, 1975. xxii, 873 pp. [This ed. 1st pub. 1967.—Rev.: C. H.
     M[uller], *UES* 13 (Sept. 1975): 77-78.]

38   *David Copperfield,* abrg. Olive Jones, illus. Faith Jacques. London:
     Collins, 1971. 234 pp.

39   *David Copperfield,* intro. Angus Wilson. London: Franklin Watts,
     1971. 2 vols. [Large type.]

40   *The Story of David Copperfield,* abrg. W. Jewesbury. London: Pan,
     1970. 128 pp.

Dombey and Son

41   *Dombey and Son,* ed. Peter Fairclough, intro. Raymond Williams,
     illus. Hablot K. Browne. Harmondsworth: Penguin, 1970. 992 pp.
     [Rev.: Philip Collins, *Dkn* 67 (Jan. 1971): 47-49 (chiefly on
     intro.); also rev. in 1171.]

42 *Dombey and Son,* ed. Alan Horsman. Oxford: Clarendon Press, 1974. xlix, 871 pp. [Rev.: Richard J. Dunn, *Dkn* 71 (Jan. 1975): 47-49; K. J. Fielding, *DUJ* 67 (June 1975): 249-251; Mollie Hardwick, *B&B* 20 (August 1974): 30-32; J. C. Maxwell, *N&Q* NS 23 (Feb. 1976): 86-89; Sylvère Monod, *EA* 28 (Jan.-Mar. 1975): 101-103; Norman Page, *DSN* 6 (Mar. 1975): 19-23; Michael Slater, *TLS* 20 Sept. 1974: 1020; *BBkN* Oct. 1974: 695-696; *Cb* 11 (Jan. 1975): 1628; also rev. in 981.]

Great Expectations

43 *Great Expectations.* New York: Amsco, 1970. [Rev. in 544.]

44 *Great Expectations.* [London: Scolar Press, 1978]. [Color microfilm of the ms and related papers in Wisbech and Fenland Museum; see notices, *Scolar NL* no. 9 (8 May 1975): 6; no. 10 (23 Apr. 1976): 4; *TLS* 25 June 1976: 803.—Rev.: Philip Collins, *TLS* 22 Sept. 1978: 1063.]

45 *Great Expectations,* abrg. Maidenhead: Purnell, 1976. 208 pp.

46 *Great Expectations,* illus. Edward Ardizzone. Norwalk, Conn.: Easton Press, 1979. iii, 457 pp.

47 *Great Expectations,* ed. N. L. Clay. London: Heinemann Ed., 1971. 446 pp. [Rev.: C. H. M[uller], *UES* 10 (Sept. 1972): 96.]

48 *Great Expectations,* ed., intro. Earle Davis, 2nd ed. New York: Holt, Rinehart and Winston, 1972. xvi, 470 pp. [Rev. in 544.]

49 *Great Expectations,* illus. F. A. Fraser. New York: Hart, 1977. 558 pp.

50 *Great Expectations,* intro. Kenneth Hayens. London and New York: Collins, 1973. 444 pp.

51 *Great Expectations,* illus. John McLenan. Franklin Center, Pa.: Franklin Lib., 1977. 553 pp. [Ltd. "collector's" ed.]

52 *Great Expectations,* abrg. Rosemary Manning, illus. Gareth Floyd. London: Collins; Middletown, Conn.: American Ed. Pubs., 1970. 217 pp.

53 *Great Expectations,* intro., annot. Julian Symons. London, etc.: Pan, 1974; rpt. 1979. 476 pp. [Rev.: M. J. F. C[hapman], *UES* 18

(Apr. 1980): 72; S. C., *UES* 15 (Sept. 1977): 105-106.]

54   *Great Expectations*, intro. Warrington W. Winters. New York: Pocket Books, 1973. 466 pp. [Incl. 48-page reader's supp.—Rev. in 544.]

Hard Times

55   *Hard Times*, ed. N. L. Clay. London: Heinemann Ed., 1971. 204 pp. [Rev.: C. H. M[uller], *UES* 10 (Sept. 1972): 96.]

56   *Hard Times*, intro. Philip Collins. London: J. M. Dent; New York: E. P. Dutton, 1978. xxiv, 268 pp.

57   *Hard Times*, commentary, notes D. R. Elloway. Harlow: Longmans, 1970. 389 pp.

58   *Hard Times*, intro., annot. George Levine. London: Pan, 1977. 297 pp.

59   *Hard Times for These Times*, fwd. Asa Briggs. St. Albans: Panther, 1977. xiv, 303 pp.

60   *Hard Times for These Times*, intro. Monica Dickens, illus. Richard Scollins. Barre, Mass.: Imprint Soc., 1972. xviii, 218 pp. [Ltd. ed.—Rev.: *Reprint Bull* 19 (Spring 1974): 47-48.]

"A Holiday Romance"

61   *The Magic Fishbone*, illus. Dagmar Berková. Feltham: Hamlyn, 1970. 55 pp.

The Life of Our Lord

62   *The Life of Our Lord*. London: Collins; New York: Crescent, 1970. 128 pp.

Little Dorrit

63   *Little Dorrit*, afwd. Richard D. Altick. New York: New American Lib., 1980. viii, 820 pp.

64   *Little Dorrit*, ed. Harvey Peter Sucksmith, illus. Hablot K. Browne.

Oxford: Clarendon Press, 1979. lxv, 835 pp. [Rev.: Sylvère Monod, *Dkn* 76 (Summer 1980): 106-107; Alan Shelston, *CritQ* 22 (Summer 1980): 87-88; Michael Slater, *BBkN* Apr. 1980: 246, 248 and (a diff. rev.) *TLS* 20 June 1980: 716; *Ch* 17 (Apr. 1980): 219.]

The Mystery of Edwin Drood

65 *The Mystery of Edwin Drood*, ed. Margaret Cardwell. Oxford: Clarendon Press, 1972. lvii, 269 pp. [Note also diss., *"Edwin Drood:* A Critical and Textual Study" (London, 1968-1969).—Rev.: J. F. Burrows, *AUMLA* no. 44 (Nov. 1975): 275-277; Arthur J. Cox, *MDAC* 1973: 307-312; Benjamin Franklin Fisher IV, *NCF* 28 (Sept. 1973): 229-232; J. C. Maxwell, *N&Q* NS 23 (Feb. 1976): 86-89; Dieter Mehl, *Archiv* 210, ii (1973): 419-420; Sylvère Monod, *EA* 25 (Oct.-Dec. 1972): 567-568; Edgar Rosenberg, *DSN* 5 (Sept. 1974): 70-84; T. A. Shippey, *Library* 5th ser., 28 (Sept. 1973): 255-257; Harvey Peter Sucksmith, *YES* 4 (1974):326-328; Angus Wilson, *Dkn* 69 (Jan. 1973): 48-51; *Ch* 10 (Mar. 1973): 92; also rev. in 981, 1026, 2223.]

66 *The Mystery of Edwin Drood*, ed. Arthur J. Cox, intro. Angus Wilson. Harmondsworth: Penguin, 1974. 314 pp. [Rev.: J. C. Maxwell, *N&Q* NS 23 (Feb. 1976): 86-89; W. D. Maxwell-Mahon, *UES* 13 (June 1975): 42; J. I. M. Stewart, *Dkn* 70 (Sept. 1974): 211-212; *BBkN* June 1974: 408.]

Nicholas Nickleby

67 *Nicholas Nickleby*, ed., intro., annot. Michael Slater, illus. Hablot K. Browne. Harmondsworth, etc.: Penguin, 1978. 974 pp. [Rev.: P. A. B[urger], *UES* 16 (Sept. 1978): 78; Philip Collins, *TLS* 21 Apr. 1978: 446; Margaret Ganz, *DSN* 9 (Dec. 1978): 117-119; Sylvère Monod, *EA* 32 (Oct.-Dec. 1979): 485-486; Jan Stephens, *Times* (London) 11 Mar. 1978: 9; Angus Wilson, *Dkn* 74 (May 1978): 110-111.]

The Old Curiosity Shop

68 *Mister Quilp (The Old Curiosity Shop)*, abrg., ed. Doris Dickens. London: Armada, 1975. 126 pp.

69 *The Old Curiosity Shop*, abrg. Maidenhead: Purnell, 1976. 216 pp.

70   *The Old Curiosity Shop*, ed. Angus Easson, intro. Malcolm Andrews, illus. George Cattermole and Hablot K. Browne. Harmondsworth and Baltimore: Penguin, 1972. 719 pp. [Rev.: Robert L. Patten, *Dkn* 69 (Jan. 1973): 54-56; also rev. in 2223.]

71   *The Old Curiosity Shop*, abrg. J. P. Reading. New York: Scholastic Book Services, 1976. 364 pp.

Oliver Twist

72   *Oliver Twist*. London: Macdonald and Jane's, 1975. xvii, 451 pp.

73   *Oliver Twist*. New York: Pocket Books, 1975. 457 pp. [Incl. 48 pp. reader's supp.]

74   *Oliver Twist*, abrg. Maidenhead: Purnell, 1976. 194 pp.

75   *Oliver Twist*, abrg., illus. B. Manson and John F. A. Wood. London: Jupiter, 1973. 128 pp.

Our Mutual Friend

76   *Our Mutual Friend*, ed., intro. Stephen Gill. Harmondsworth: Penguin, 1971. 911 pp. [Rev.: Robin Gilmour, *Dkn* 67 (Sept. 1971): 173-174; also rev. in 667, 2065.]

77   *Our Mutual Friend*, intro. Harriet Weitzner, illus. E. G. Dalziel et al. New York: Bounty, 1978. x, 857 pp.

Pickwick Papers

78   *A Full and Faithful Report of the Memorable Trial of Bardell against Pickwick*, fwd., afwd. John F. Banker, illus. Wolfgang Lederer. [Neveda City, Cal.: Harold Berliner, 1974.] 69 pp. [Ltd. to 750 copies.]

79   *The Pickwick Papers*, abrg. Joshua G. M. Karton, illus. Thomas Nast and Hablot K. Browne. New York: Hart, 1976. xiii, 430 pp.

80   *The Posthumous Papers of the Pickwick Club*, ed., intro. Robert L. Patten, illus. Robert Seymour, Robert W. Buss, Hablot K. Browne. Harmondsworth and Baltimore: Penguin, 1972. 952 pp. [Rev.: Rachel Trickett, *Dkn* 69 (May 1973): 119-121; also rev. in 981,

1758, 2223.]

Pictures from Italy

81   *Pictures from Italy,* intro., notes David Paroissien. London: A. Deutsch, 1973; New York: Coward, McCann and Geoghegan, 1974. 270 pp. [Rev.: Duane DeVries, *DSN* 7 (Sept. 1976): 90-91; E[lizabeth] H[all], *Psychology Today* 8 (Oct. 1974): 24; Alan Horsman, *Dkn* 70 (May 1974): 134-135, Cecil Roberts, *B&B* 19 (Apr. 1974): 32-35; *BBkN* Feb. 1974: 131; *Ch* 11 (July-Aug. 1974): 757; *TLS* 23 Nov. 1973: 1451.]

A Tale of Two Cities

82   *A Tale of Two Cities.* New York: Amsco School Pubs., 1971. vi, 436 pp. [Incl. reader's guide.]

83   *A Tale of Two Cities.* New York: Pocket Books, 1973. 470 pp. [Incl. 48 pp. reader's guide.]

84   *A Tale of Two Cities.* New York and London: Peebles Press, 1975. 320 pp.

85   *A Tale of Two Cities.* Westport, Conn.: Easton Press, 1975. xiii, 372 pp. [Ltd. ed.]

86   *A Tale of Two Cities.* Boston: G. K. Hall, 1980. 630 pp. [Large type.]

87   *A Tale of Two Cities,* abrg. Maidenhead: Purnell, 1976. 210 pp.

88   *A Tale of Two Cities,* illus. Hablot K. Browne. London: Macdonald, 1975. xi, 392 pp.

89   *A Tale of Two Cities,* [ed., abrg., annot. Joanna Jellinek, illus. Harold King and Penelope Anstee]. London: Studio Vista, 1973; New York: D. McKay, 1976. 112 pp. [Rev.: Michael Ann Moskowitz, *School Lib J* 23 (Mar. 1977): 150-151.]

90   *A Tale of Two Cities,* abrg. Josephine Kamm, illus. Barry Wilkinson. London: Collins, 1973. 230 pp.

91   *A Tale of Two Cities,* illus. Richard Sharp. London: Folio Press, 1973. 329 pp.

92 *A Tale of Two Cities,* ed., intro. George Woodcock, illus. Hablot K. Browne. Harmondsworth: Penguin, 1970. 410 pp. [Rev.: Sylvère Monod, *Dkn* 67 (May 1971): 114-115; also rev. in 1229.]

Miscellanea

93 "Boz in the Black Country?," intro. David W. Reeves. *Blackcountry-man* 10 (Spring 1977): 68. [Brief excerpt purportedly from "a collection of sketches and essays supposedly from the pen of Charles Dickens."]

94 "The Ivy Green." *LCUT* NS no. 6 (Dec. 1973): 80-81. [Facs. of ms with descriptive notes.]

95 "Some Unpublished Comic Duologues of Dickens," ed., intro. Philip Collins. *NCF* 31 (Mar. 1977): 440-449.

96 "An Unpublished Satirical Sketch by Dickens," ed., intro. Graham Storey. *Dkn* 74 (Jan. 1978): 6-7.

Letters

For critical articles including unpublished letters, see Letters in Index.

97 "Charles Dickens to Thomas Mitton, 31 Jan. 1842," in *Letters in Manuscript,* sel., intro. James Thorpe (San Marino: Huntington Lib., 1971), 28-29. [Facs.]

98 "Charles Dickens to Viscount Palmerston, 30 Aug. 1862," in *Men of Letters,* intro. Ann Morton. Pub. Record Office Museum Pamphlets, 6 (London: HMSO, 1974), pl. viii. [Facs.]

99 "Eight Letters to Comte D'Orsay (1847-1851)," ed. Claire-Eliane Engel. In 846, pp. 23-28.

100 "Five New Dickens Letters," commentary Bert G. Hornback. *MQR* 10 (Fall 1971): 255-260. [Note also rpt. of two ltrs., "Very Truly Yours, Charles Dickens," *Intellectual Digest* 2 (Feb. 1972): 96-97.]

101 (*The Letters of Charles Dickens: 1820-1839,* ed. Madeline House and Graham Storey. Vol. 1. 1965.) [Rev.: Richard D. Altick, *DSN* 2

(June 1971): 34-37; Alexander Welsh, *YR* 65 (Autumn 1975): 115-121.]

102 (*The Letters of Charles Dickens: 1840-1841*, ed. Madeline House and Graham Storey. Vol. 2. 1969.) [Rev.: Richard D. Altick, *DSN* 2 (June 1971): 34-37; T. J. Cribb, *RES* NS 22 (Aug. 1971): 388-389; Sylvère Monod, *EA* 33 (Apr.-June 1970): 210-212; Heinz Reinhold, *Anglia* 90, i-ii (1972): 258-259; Michael Slater *Dkn* 66 (Sept. 1970): 242-244; Alfred Starkman, *Die Welt der Literatur* 28 May 1970: 4; Harry Stone, *NCF* 30 (Sept. 1975): 230-236; Alexander Welsh, *YR* 65 (Autumn 1975): 115-121; *VQR* 46 (Spring 1970): lxvii; also rev. in 948, 2065, 2138.—Note also Philip Wright's rev. of James Thornton's index, *Indexer* 7 (Spring 1970): 16-17.]

103 *The Letters of Charles Dickens: 1842-1843*, ed. Madeline House, Graham Storey, and Kathleen Tillotson. Vol. 3. Oxford: Clarendon Press, 1974. xxv, 692 pp. [Rev.: Richard D. Altick, *DSN* 6 (Mar. 1975): 17-19; C. C. Barfoot, *ES* 51 (Aug. 1970): 386; John Carey, *Lstr* 92 (22 Aug. 1974): 249; R. C. Churchill, *ContempR* 225 (Sept. 1974): 161-162; Philip Collins, *MLR* 71 (Jan. 1976): 146-148; Timothy Cribb, *RES* NS 27 (Feb. 1976): 93-96; Angus Easson, *THES* 18 Oct. 1974: 16; George H. Ford, *Dkn* 71 (May 1975): 106-109; Jean Gattégno, *EA* 28 (Oct.-Dec. 1975): 479-483; Mollie Hardwick, *B&B* 21 (Oct., Nov. 1974): 24-25, 25-26; Ian Jack, *Cambridge Rev* 98 (31 Jan. 1975): 85-88; Francis King, *Spec* 233 (7 Sept. 1974): 306; Sylvère Monod, *TLS* 6 Dec. 1974: 1359; Pansy Pakenham, *Irish Times* 7 Sept. 1974: 12; V. S. Pritchett, *NewSt* 88 (23 Aug. 1974): 255-256; Michael Ratcliffe, *Times* (London) 29 Aug. 1974: 11; Christopher Ricks, *STimes* 8 Sept. 1974: 38; Harry Stone, *NCF* 30 (Sept. 1975): 230-236; Angus Wilson, *Obs* 25 Aug. 1974: 23; Alexander Welsh, *YR* 65 (Autumn 1975): 115-121; *BBkN* Dec. 1974: 838-839; *Econ* 252 (Sept. 1974): 114; also rev. in 981, 1022.]

104 *The Letters of Charles Dickens: 1844-1846*, ed. Kathleen Tillotson and Nina Burgis. Vol. 4. Oxford: Clarendon Press, 1977. xxiv, 771 pp. [Rev.: Richard D. Altick, *DSN* 9 (Sept. 1978): 84-86; Trevor Blount, *N&Q* NS 27 (June 1980): 253-254; John Carey, *STimes* (London) 9 Apr. 1978: 41; A. O. J. Cockshut, *THES* 26 May 1978: 13; Martin Dodsworth, *English* 27 (Summer-Autumn 1978): 298-299; Benny Green, *Spec* 240 (6 May 1978): 20-21; William Haley, *Times* (London) 13 Apr. 1978: 16; Mollie Hardwick, *B&B* 23 (July 1978): 48-50; Ian Jack, *Cambridge Rev* 100 (9 Feb. 1979): 76-77; Rosemary Jackson, *Enc* 51 (July 1978): 77-78; Dan Jacobson, *Guardian* 9 Apr. 1978: 23; Rosalind

Mitchison, *Lstr* 99 (25 May 1978): 682-683; Sylvère Monod, *EA* 32 (July-Sept. 1979): 343-345; John Romano, *NewSt* 96 (8 Sept. 1978): 300-301; Andrew Sanders, *Dkn* 74 (Sept. 1978): 172-173; Michael Slater, *TLS* 23 June 1978: 715 and (a diff. rev.) *BBkN* July 1978: 578-579; Stephen Wall, *New Rev* 4 (Mar. 1978): 49-51; Angus Wilson, *Obs* 2 Apr. 1978: 24; *Ch* 15 (Sept. 1978): 864; *ContempR* 232 (June 1978): 334-335; *Ecn* 267 (8 Apr. 1978): 116; also rev. in 182 (Dec. 1979), 531, 981, 2094.]

105 "Newly Discovered Dickens Letters," ed. E. W. F. Tomlin. *TLS* 22 Feb. 1974: 183-186. [To Ernest Legouvé.—Note also ltrs. to ed. from Christopher Starr, 1 Mar. 1974: 213, Ernest Mehew, 15 Mar. 1974: 265; E. W. F. Tomlin, 5 Apr. 1974: 369.]

106 "Two Unpublished Letters of Charles Dickens," ed. Conny Nelson, *RS* 38 (June 1970): 154-156.

SECONDARY SOURCES

Signed

107 Abrahams, Beth-Zion. "The Atonement of Charles Dickens." *Common Ground* 24 (Autumn 1970): 18-23. [Eliza Davis's 1863-1867 corr. with D on Fagin and Riah.—Orig. pub. *Jewish Herald* (Johannesburg), 1970.]

108 Abromson, Herman. "Who Killed Edwin Drood?" *J of the Long Island Book Collectors* 3 (1975): 35-40. [Endings with checklist.]

109 Adamowski, Thomas H. "Dombey and Son and Sutpen and Son." *SNNTS* 4 (Fall 1972): 378-389. [Individualism in *DSon* and Faulkner's *Absolom, Absolom!*]

110 Adell, Alberto. "El Shakespeare de la novela." *Insula* 27 (Jan. 1972): 13.

111 Adorno, Theodor W. "Rede über den *Raritätenladen* von Charles Dickens." *Noten zur Literatur*, [ed. Rolf Tiedemann]. His *Gesammelte Schriften*, 11 (Frankfurt: Suhrkamp, 1974), 515-522. [Characterization, symbolism, realism in *OCShop*.—Rpt. from *Frankfurter Zeitung*, 18 Apr. 1931.]

112 Adrian, Arthur A. "Dickens and Inverted Parenthood." *Dkn* 67 (Jan. 1971): 3-11. [*BleakH, LittleDor, OCShop, OurMF.*]

113 — and Vonna. "Charles Dickens: A Twentieth-Century Postmortem." In 651, pp. 3-14.

114 Ainette, Jacques-Pierre. "Un roman de Dickens." *NRF* NS 36 (Nov. 1970): 72-75. [Social class in *LittleDor.*]

115 Aisenberg, Nadya. "Dickens and the Crime Novel." *A Common Spring: Crime Novel and Classic* (Bowling Green, Ohio: Bowling Green Univ. Popular Press, 1979), 68-110; et passim. [Esp. *BarnR, BleakH, MEDrood, OCShop, OurMF.*—Note also "The Crime Novel: The Poetry of Justice," *DAI* 39 (Sept. 1978): 1541A (Wisconsin).]

34 *Secondary Sources*

116 Aiyyar, Poppy. "Dickens and His Modern Readers." In 262, pp. 14-17. [*BleakH, DavidC, DSon, HardT.*]

117 Alderman, Ian. "Dickens's 'Pianoforte Van' in *The Uncommercial Traveller.*" *Dkn* 73 (Jan. 1977): 36-37.

118 Allen, Michael and David Parker. "Inside Devonshire Terrace." *Dkn* 75 (Autumn 1979): 145-155.

119 Allen, Walter. "The Comedy of Dickens." In 1786, pp. 3-27. [*BleakH, GreatEx, HardT, MChuz, OliverTw, OurMF, PickP.*]

120 Allombert, Guy. "Dickens au cinéma." In 743, pp. 42-50.

121 —. "Essai de filmographie de Dickens." In 743, pp. 51-54.

122 Alter, Robert. "The Demons of History in Dickens's *Tale.*" *Novel* 2 (Winter 1969): 135-142.

123 —. *Partial Magic: The Novel as a Self-Conscious Genre* (Berkeley: Univ. of California Press, 1975), passim. [Incl. fictitiousness, language, realism of *LittleDor.*—Incorporates parts of "History and Imagination in the Nineteenth-Century Novel," *GaR* 29 (Spring 1975): 42-60.]

124 Altick, Richard D. "Borrioboola-Gha, Bushmen, and Brickmakers." *Dkn* 74 (Sept. 1978): 157-159.

125 —. "Education, Print, and Paper in *Our Mutual Friend.*" In 1683, pp. 237-254.

126 —. "Varieties of Readers' Response: The Case of *Dombey and Son.*" *YES* 10 (1980): 70-94. [Postulates first readers' responses.]

127 —. *Victorian People and Ideas* (New York: Norton, 1973), passim. [Rev.: James W. Christie, *DSN* 7 (Mar. 1976): 23-25; Sheila M. Smith, *Dkn* 71 (Jan. 1975): 52-54.]

128 —. *Victorian Studies in Scarlet* (New York: Norton, 1970), passim. [Rev.: Philip Collins, *Dkn* 67 (Sept. 1971): 174 175.]

129 Amalric, Jean-Claude. "Dickens." *Bernard Shaw: Du réformateur victorien au prophète édouardien.* EA, 67 (Paris: Didier, 1977), 122-126; et passim.

130 —. "Some Reflections on *Great Expectations* as an Allegory." In 131,

pp. 127-133.

131 —, ed. *Studies in the Later Dickens*. Montpellier: Univ. Paul Valéry, Centre d'Études et de Recherches Victoriennes et Édouardiennes, 1973. [Ed., "Foreword," 9-10.—Incl. 130, 170, 445, 672, 1361, 1692, 2042.—Rev.: George H. Ford, *DSN* 6 (June 1975): 61-64; James R. Kincaid, *NCF* 30 (Mar. 1976): 535-538; L. Pothet, *EA* 28 (Apr.-June 1975): 230-231; Edgar Rosenberg, *Dkn* 70 (May 1974): 130-132.]

132 Ambrosino, Salvatore V. "Analysis of Scrooge, Child of the Earth." *NYSJM* 71 (15 Dec. 1971): 2884-2885.

133 Amis, Kingsley. "The Cockney's Homer." *What Became of Jane Austen? And Other Questions* (London: Jonathan Cape, 1970; New York: Harcourt Brace Jovanovich, 1971), 29-33. [Rpt. of rev. of 2330.]

134 A[mis], M[artin]. "Charles Dickens: *Bleak House:* How Awful Goodness Is." *TES* 21 Sept. 1973: 61. [Esther Summerson.]

135 Anastaplo, George. "Notes from Charles Dickens's *Christmas Carol*." *Interpretation* 7 (Jan. 1978): 52-73.

136 Andersen, Sally S. "The De-Spiritualization of the Elements in *Our Mutual Friend*." *Discourse* 12 (Autumn 1969): 423-433.

137 Ando, Sadao. [The structure and system of a theory of expression with reference to *GreatEx*.] In 1287, pp. 189-205. [In Jap.—Eng. abst., pp. 274-275 and in 1285, pp. 61-62.]

138 Andrews, Malcolm Y. "Charles Dickens: British Publications in the 1960s." *BBkN* June 1970: 427-429.

139 —. *Dickens on England and the English*. Hassocks: Harvester Press; New York: Barnes and Noble, 1979. xx, 201 pp. [Rev.: Thom Braun, *Dkn* 76 (Spring 1980): 48-49; John Jordan, *Hibernia* 2 Aug. 1979: 14, 16; Angus Wilson, *Obs* 15 July 1979: 36; *Ch* 16 (Oct. 1979): 1013; also rev. in 1751.]

140 —. "Dickens, Samuel Rogers and *The Old Curiosity Shop*." *N&Q* NS 18 (Nov. 1971): 410-411. [Infl. of Rogers's *Pleasures of Memory*.]

141 —. "Introducing Master Humphrey." *Dkn* 67 (May 1971): 70-86. [Esp. alienation.]

142 —. "A Note on Serialisation." In 1458, pp. 243-247. [Incl. *BleakH, HardT.*]

143 —. "[Survey of periodical literature in] The Year's Work in Dickens Studies." [See 618, 2239.]

144 Anikst, Alexander. "Dickens in Russia." *TLS* 4 June 1970: 617. [Infl. and reception 1832-1960.]

145 Anjum, A. R. "Social Problems as Themes for Fiction." *Explorations* 2, ii (1975): 13-21. [Incl. *BleakH.*]

146 Arac, Jonathan. *Commissioned Spirits: The Shaping of Social Motion in Dickens, Carlyle, Melville and Hawthorne.* New Brunswick: Rutgers UP, 1979. xiii, 200 pp. [Esp. *BleakH, DSon, LittleDor, MChuz, OurMF.*—Incorporates "The House and the Railroad: *Dombey and Son* and *The House of the Seven Gables*," *NEQ* 51 (Mar. 1978): 3-22 and "Narrative Form and Social Sense in *Bleak House* and *The French Revolution*," *NCF* 32 (June 1977): 54-72.— Note also diss., "The Sense of Society in Dickens, Carlyle, and Melville" (Harvard, 1974).—Rev.: Richard J. Dunn, *SNNTS* 12 (Spring 1980): 84-86; Walter L. Reed, *NCF* 35 (Sept. 1980): 236-240; Eric J. Sundquist, *SCR* 13 (Fall 1980): 104-106; Michael Wheeler, *Dkn* 76 (Spring 1980): 50-51; *Ch* 16 (Dec. 1979): 1302.]

147 Argento, Dominick interviewed by Allan Kozinn. "Argento at Ease." *World of Opera* 1, vi (1979): 1-10. [Note also 2932.]

148 Cancelled.

149 Arkin, Marcus. *Notes on Charles Dickens's Nicholas Nickleby.* Study-Aid Ser. London: Methuen, 1976. 67 pp.

150 Arneson, Richard J. "Benthamite Utilitarianism and *Hard Times.*" *Phil&Lit* 2 (Spring 1978): 60-75.

151 Arnoldi, Richard. "Parallels Between *Our Mutual Friend* and the Alice Books." *ChildL* 1 (1972): 54-57.

152 Aryan, Subhashini. "Charles [sic] and the Continental Novelists." *Thought* (Delhi) 26 (26 Oct. 1974): 17-18.

153 Ashby, Ruth. "David Copperfield's Story—Telling in the Dark." *DSN* 9 (Sept. 1978): 80-83.

154 Asselineau, R. et al., eds. *EA* 23 (Apr.-June 1970). [Incl. 254, 417, 767, 1230, 1350, 1565, 1681, 1774, 2008.—Rev.: Sheila M. Smith, *Dkn* 67 (Jan. 1971): 51-52; Lionel Stevenson, *DSN* 2 (June 1971): 42-45; also rev. in 1961.]

155 Atherton, J. S. "Shem as 'Artful Dodger?' " *WN* NS 9 (Oct. 1972): 99. [Possible source for Joyce's *Finnegans Wake*.]

156 Auerbach, Nina. "Dickens and Dombey: A Daughter After All." In 1493, pp. 95-114.

157 —. "Incarnations of the Orphan." *ELH* 42 (Fall 1975): 395-419. [Incl. *GreatEx.*]

158 Austen, Zelda. *"Oliver Twist:* A Divided View." *DSN* 7 (Mar. 1976): 8-12. [Crime.]

159 Avery, Gillian. *Victorian People in Life and Literature* (London: Collins; New York: Holt, Rinehart and Winston, 1970), passim. [Touches on *BleakH, DavidC, DSon, GreatEx, HardT, LittleDor, OCShop, OliverTw.*]

160 (Axton, William F. *Circle of Fire: Dickens's Vision and Style and the Popular Victorian Theatre.* 1966.) [Excerpt rpt. in 23, pp. 1041-1051.—Rev.: J. O. Bailey, *Style* 4 (Winter 1970): 81-83; Richard C. Carpenter, *JPC* 4 (Fall 1970): 540-549.]

161 —. "Dickens Now," in *The Victorian Experience: The Novelists,* ed. Richard A. Levine (Athens: Ohio UP, 1976), 19-48. [Esp. *BleakH.* —Rev. in 1488.]

162 —. "From the Editors." *DSN* 2 (Sept. 1971): 68-72. [Pbk. eds. of D's novels in print.]

163 —. *"Great Expectations* Yet Again." In 1490, pp. 278-293.

164 — and Robert L. Patten. "Opportunities for Research." *DSN* 2 (Dec. 1971): 106-111. [Note also 1497.]

165 Ayoub, Mireille T. "European Travelers: 19th Century Visitors to America Comment on Its Emerging Architecture." *Architectural Forum* 139 (Sept. 1973): 60-65.

166 Bachman, Maria. "Dickens i Kafka: Dwic powiesci o dorastaniu." *APh* (Warsaw) 4 (1972): 47-57. [Adolescent and society in *DavidC, Amerika.*—Eng. abst., pp. 56-57.]

167 —. "Dickens Plagiarisms in Poland." *KN* 21, ii (1974): 227-230. [Polish abst., p. 231.]

168 —. "Some Recent Tendencies in Contemporary Dickens Criticism." *SAP* 4, i-ii (1972): 173-182.

169 Baird, John D. " 'Divorce and Matrimonial Causes': An Aspect of *Hard Times.*" *VS* 20 (Summer 1977): 401-412.

170 Baïssus, Jean-Marie. "L'adjectif dickensien: Essaie d'analyse semantique de procédés stylistiques dans le chapitre I de *Our Mutual Friend.*" In 131, pp. 135-144.

171 Baker, Charles, ed. *Bibliography of British Book Illustrators, 1860-1900* (Birmingham: Birmingham Bookshop, 1978), I, passim. [Charles E. Brock, Henry M. Brock, W. Cubitt, William Cooke, Frederick George Kitton, Henry Marriott Paget, Fred Pegram.]

172 Baker, Michael. *The Rise of the Victorian Actor* (London: Croom Helm; New York: Rowman and Littlefield, 1978), passim. [Rev.: Jean M. Elliott, *Dkn* 74 (Sept. 1978): 175-176.]

173 Baker, Robert S. "Imagination and Literacy in Dickens's *Our Mutual Friend.*" *Criticism* 18 (Winter 1976): 57-72.

174 Baker, William. "*Hard Times* and Orr's *Circle of the Sciences.*" *DSN* 8 (Sept. 1977): 78.

175 —. "Wilkie Collins, Dickens and *No Name.*" *DSN* 11 (June 1980): 49-52. [D's ltd. infl.]

176 Baldi, Sergio. "Dickens: Lettura adulta." *Approdo* 52 (1970): 3-13. [Gen. crit. of late novels.]

177 Balota, Nicolae. "Dickens si ceata." *Umanitati: Eseuri* (Bucharest: Eminescu, 1973), 197-199. [Beginning of *BleakH.*—Rpt. from *RoLit* 10 (Feb. 1972): 13.]

178 Bandelin, Carl. "David Copperfield: A Third Interesting Penitent." *SEL* 16 (Autumn 1976): 601-611.

179 Banerjee, N. K. "*Hard Times:* A Note on the Descriptive Titles of Its

Books." *IJES* 13 (1972): 22-28.

180 Barclay, Glen St. John. *Anatomy of Horror: The Masters of Occult Fiction* (London: Weidenfeld and Nicolson, 1978), 15-18. [Ending of *MEDrood*.]

181 Bardavío, José Ma. "Los 'núcleos de coherencia': Aproximación al problema de las unidades mínimas del relato," in *Teoría de la novela,* ed. Santos Sanz Villanueva and Carlos J. Barbachano. Col. Temas, 6 (Madrid: Sociedad General Española de Librería, 1976), 291-304. [Incl. *DavidC.*]

182 Barfoot, C. C. "Current Literature. . . ." *ES* 52 (Aug. 1971): 389-390; 53 (Aug. 1972): 385-387; 60 (Dec. 1979): 780-781. [Aug. 1971 rev.-art. incl. 592, 1150, 1786, 1917, 2064.—Aug. 1972 rev.-art. incl. 294, 438, 1253, 2093.—Dec. 1979 rev.-art. incl. 104, 1504, 1733, 2101.]

183 —. "*Great Expectations:* The Perception of Fate." *DQR* 6, i (1976): 2-33.

184 Barickman, Richard. "The Comedy of Survival in Dickens's Novels." *Novel* 11 (Winter 1978): 128-143. [Esp. *BleakH, GreatEx, MChuz, PickP.*]

185 —. "The Spiritual Journey of Amy and Arthur Clennam: 'A Way Wherein There Is No Ecstasy'." In 1495, pp. 163-189.

186 Barker, Dudley. "Essays and Dickens." *G. K. Chesterton: A Biography* (New York: Stein and Day, 1973), 160-174.

187 Barnard, Robert. *Imagery and Theme in the Novels of Dickens.* NSE, 17. Bergen, Oslo, and Tromsö: Universitetsforlaget; New York: Humanities Press, 1974. 163 pp. [Chaps. on *BleakH, DSon, GreatEx, HardT, LittleDor, MChuz, MEDrood, NichN, OurMF.*— Incorporates "Imagery and Theme in *Great Expectations,*" in 1489, pp. 238-251 and "The Imagery of *Little Dorrit,*" *ES* 52 (Dec. 1971): 520-532.—Rev.: Erik Frykman, *Samlaren* 95 (1974): 168-169; J. C. Maxwell, *N&Q* NS 23 (Feb. 1976): 83-86; Margaret Myers, *VS* 19 (June 1976): 541-543; Alan Wilde, *DSN* 7 (Mar. 1976): 25-28; *Ch* 11 (Feb. 1975): 1774; also rev. in 967 (May 1975), 981, 1022.]

188 Barnes, James J. "Efforts to Influence Parliament, 1838-44"; "Bribery, or the Necessary Expenses of Congressional Action: Nov. 1851-Feb. 1853." *Authors, Publishers and Politicians: The Quest*

for an Anglo-American Copyright Agreement, 1815-1854 (London: Routledge and Kegan Paul; Columbus: Ohio State UP, 1974), 116-137; 216-240; et passim. [Rev.: Donald Hawes, *DSN* 7 (June 1976): 48-51; also rev. in 967 (May 1975).]

189 Barnes, Samuel G. "Dickens and Copperfield: The Hero as Man of Letters," in *The Classic British Novel,* ed. Howard M. Harper, Jr. and Charles Edge (Athens: Univ. of Georgia Press, 1972), 85-102. [Infl. of Carlyle.—Rev.: Benjamin Franklin Fisher IV, *DSN* 4 (Mar. 1973): 23-24.]

190 Barrett, Barbara. "Charles Dickens, the Children's Champion." *Instructor* 84 (Feb. 1975): 105-106, 108. [Juvenile biog.]

191 Barrett, Edwin B. "*Little Dorrit* and the Disease of Modern Life." *NCF* 25 (Sept. 1970): 199-215. [Social reform, sanitation, images of disease.]

192 Barstow, Jane. "Charles Dickens, Marcel Proust, and Günter Grass on Childhood." *ChildL* 7 (1978): 147-168. [*DavidC, À la recherche du temps perdu, Blechtrommel.*]

193 Barthold, Bonnie Jo. "*Bleak House,* Little Red Riding Hood, and Sleeping Beauty." *GEP* (Univ. of Arizona) 6, i (1974): 16-26.

194 Bartrip, Peter W. J. "*Household Words* and the Factory Accident Controversy." *Dkn* 75 (Spring 1979): 17-29. [Note also Anne Lohrli's ltr. to ed., 76 (Spring 1980): 19-20.]

195 Basch, Françoise. "Charles Dickens's Anti-Woman"; "Dickens's Sinners." *Relative Creatures: Victorian Women in Society and the Novel,* trans. Anthony Rudolf (London: Allen Lane; New York: Schocken, 1974), 141-151; 210-228; et passim. [Esp. *BleakH, DavidC, DSon, HardT, OliverTw.*—Note also "Le myth de l'épouse mère dans le roman: Dickens, Thackeray"; "Anti-femmes: Dickens"; "Pécheresses de mélodrame: Dickens," *Les femmes victoriennes: Roman et société (1837-1867),* [rev. and enl. ed.] (Paris: Payot, 1979), 76-94; 164-175; 241-258; et passim.—1st chap. in part from *Romantisme* no. 13-14 (1976): 198-214, a special no. issued separately as *Mythes et représentations de la femme au dix-neuvième siècle* (Paris: Champion, 1977).—Rev.: Frederica Wolf Brind, *DSN* 7 (Dec. 1976): 122-125.]

196 Batterson, Richard F. "The Manuscript and Text of Dickens's 'George Silverman's Explanation'." *PBSA* 73, iv (1979): 473-476.

197 Bayley, John. "Dickens and His Critics." *The Uses of Division: Unity and Disharmony in Literature* (London: Chatto and Windus; New York: Viking Press; Toronto: Clarke, Irwin, 1976), 90-103. [Rev.-art. on 1150.—Rev.: Charles Kostelnick, *DSN* 10 (Dec. 1979): 119-121.]

198 —. "Irresistible Dickens." *NYRB* 8 Oct. 1970: 8-14. [Rev.-art. on 4, 592, 884, 1496, 1786, 2118, 2128.]

199 Beadle, George. "George Orwell and Charles Dickens: Moral Critics of Society." *J of Hist St* 2, iv (1969-1970): 245-255. [Esp. Orwell.]

200 Beasley, Jerry C. "The Role of Tom Pinch in *Martin Chuzzlewit.*" *ArielE* 5 (Apr. 1974): 77-89. [Moral vision.]

201 Beatty, M. T. "Dickens and the Good-Natured Man: Eating and Drinking in *Martin Chuzzlewit.*" *UCTSE* no. 6 (Oct. 1976): 24-32.

202 Beaty, Jerome. "The 'Soothing Songs' of *Little Dorrit:* New Light on Dickens's Darkness." In 1683, pp. 219-236.

203 Bebenek, Stanislaw, gen. ed. [Dickens.] *Bibliografia literatury tlumaczonej na jezyk polski wydanej w latach, 1945-1976* (Warsaw: Czytelnik, 1977), I, 308-311. [49 entries of trans. of D's works.]

204 Becherand, André. "*Oliver Twist* et les lois sur les pauvres." *LanM* 70, iv-v (1976): 369-381.

205 Beckwith, Charles E., ed. *Twentieth Century Interpretations of A Tale of Two Cities.* Englewood Cliffs, N. J.: Prentice-Hall, 1972. [For contents see this number in Appendix.—Rev.: Sylvère Monod, *DSN* 4 (Dec. 1973): 100-102; George Woodcock, *Dkn* 69 (Jan. 1973): 53-54.]

206 Beer, Gillian. " 'Coming Wonders': Uses of the Theatre in the Victorian Novel," in *English Drama: Forms and Development: Essays in Honour of Muriel Clara Bradbrook,* ed. Marie Axton and Raymond Williams (Cambridge, etc.: Cambridge UP, 1977), 164-185. [Esp. *HardT, NichN, OCShop.*]

207 Beja, Morris. "*Great Expectations.*" *Film and Literature: An Introduction* (New York and London: Longman, 1979), 146-155. [David Lean's 1946 version.]

208 Belden, Daniel. "Dickens's *Great Expectations*, XXXI." *Expl* 35 (Summer 1977): 6-7. [Wopsle.]

209 Bell, Vereen M. "Accents and Persuasion." *SoR* 6 (Spring 1970): 529-538. [Rev.-art. incl. 755, 1890, 2058, 2059.]

210 Bengis, Nathan L. "John Jasper's Devotion." *ArmD* 8 (May, Aug. 1975): 167-178, 257-270; 9 (Nov. 1975): 25-40.

211 Benn, J. Miriam. "The Dickens Centenary Year in Australia." *DSN* 2 (Mar. 1971): 8-10.

212 —. "A Landscape with Figures: Characterization and Expression in *Hard Times*." In 1489, pp. 168-182.

213 Bennett, Arnold. *The Evening Standard Years: 'Books and Persons' 1926-1931,* ed. Andrew Mylett (London: Chatto and Windus; Hamden, Conn.: Archon, 1974), passim. [Generally negative.]

214 Bennett, Joseph T. "A Note on Lord Acton's View of Charles Dickens." *ELN* 7 (June 1970): 282-285. [Morals, crime.]

215 Bennett, Rachel. "Punch versus Christian in *The Old Curiosity Shop*." *RES* NS 22 (Nov. 1971): 423-434. [Novel's self-division.]

216 Bergmann, Helena. "*Hard Times* (1854)." *Between Obedience and Freedom: Woman's Role in the Mid-Nineteenth Century Industrial Novel.* GothSE, 45 (Götheborg: Acta Universitatis Gothoburgensis, 1979), 40-44; et passim.

217 Bergonzi, Bernard. "Streets Ahead: Dickens and Victorian Literature." *Enc* 53 (July 1979): 67-72. [Rev.-art. on 1223, 1728, 1733.]

218 Berrone, Louis. "A Dickensian Echo in Faulkner." *Dkn* 71 (May 1975): 100-101.

219 —. "Sing Us an Irish Song and the Mortadarthella Taradition: Some Thoughts on Dickensian Correspondences in the First Chapter of Joyce's *Ulysses*." *Trinity Reporter* 7 (Nov. 1978): 1-8. [*DavidC.*]

220 Berry-Rogghe, Godelieve L. M. "The Computation of Collocations and Their Relevance in Lexical Studies," in *The Computer and Literary Studies,* ed. A. J. Aitken et al. (Edinburgh: Edinburgh UP, 1973), 103-112. [Incl. *CCarol.*]

221 Beyers, Brian. "Novels of Social Conscience." *Standpunte* 26 (Aug. 1973): 30-35. [Incl. *BleakH.*]

222 Bianciotti, Hector. "Dickens, dieu et diable à la fois." *Nouvel observateur* 2 Aug. 1980: 48-49. [Gen. crit. based on recent trans. and reissues.]

223 Bićanić, Sonia. "Cats, Birds and Freedom." *SRAZ* no. 29-32 (1970-1971): 515-522. [Amis's *Anti-Death League, BleakH.*]

224 —. "The Function of Language in our Experience of Oliver Twist and Nancy." *SRAZ* 37 (July 1974): 277-286.

225 Biddison, Larry T. "*The Pickwick Papers:* Nostalgia and Social Satire." *MLS* 3 (Spring 1973): xxx. [Abst.]

226 Bilan, R. P. *The Literary Criticism of F. R. Leavis* (Cambridge, etc.: Cambridge UP, 1979), passim.

227 Billington, Michael. "Dickens on the Screen." *ILN* 257 (28 Nov. 1970): 19-21. [Survey.]

228 Bizaḿ, Lenke. "A dickensi karácsonyutópia." *Világosság* 12, ii (1971): 91-98.

229 —. *Kritikai allegóriák dickensról és kafkaról.* Budapest: Akadémiai Kiadó, 1970. 311 pp. [On recent criticism.—Note also diss., "Dickens és Kafka egynemüsitése a modern kritikában" (Hungarian Acad. of Sciences, 1969).—Rev.: Péter Egri, *FK* 18 (1972): 276-278; Anna Katona, *DSN* 4 (Dec. 1973): 97-98.]

230 Black, Michael. "David Copperfield: Self, Childhood and Growth." *The Literature of Fidelity* (London: Chatto and Windus; New York: Barnes and Noble; Toronto: Clarke, Irwin, 1975), 82-102.

231 Blackall, Jean Frantz. "Cruikshank's *Oliver* and 'The Turn of the Screw'." *AL* 51 (May 1979): 161-178. [Infl. of gothic illus.]

232 —. "A Suggestive Book for Charlotte Brontë?" *JEGP* 76 (July 1977): 363-383. [Infl. of *BleakH* on *Villette.*]

233 Bledsoe, Robert. "Dickens and Chorley." *Dkn* 75 (Autumn 1979): 157-166.

234 Bloch, Harry. "Defenders of Human Welfare: William Blake (1757-

1827), Poet, and Charles Dickens (1812-1870), Novelist." *NYSJM* 79 (Jan. 1979): 112-113.

235 Blom, J. M. "*Dickens the Novelist* and the History of Dickens Criticism." *DQR* 4, i (1974): 11-27. [On 1150.]

236 Blount, Trevor. "Bleak, Bleaker, Bleakest. . . ." *Dkn* 67 (Sept. 1971): 168-172. [Rev. of recent study and eds. of *BleakH*, incl. 23, 25, 26, 424.]

237 —. "Dickens and Mr. Krook's Spontaneous Combustion." In 1489, pp. 183-211. [Note also R. T. Schrock's response, *DSN* 2 (Dec. 1971): 121-122, and Blount's reply, pp. 122-123.]

238 (—. *Dickens: The Early Novels.* 1968.) [Rev. in 2138.]

239 —. "Dickens's Ironmaster Again." *EIC* 21 (Oct. 1971): 429-436. [Rouncewell of *BleakH.*—Note also 1801.]

240 —. " 'Inimitable' Exhibitions." *Dkn* 66 (Sept. 1970): 231-236.

241 —. "Literature and Medicine: Disease and Graveyards in Dickens's *Bleak House.*" *Soc of Social Hist Med Bull* 8 (Sept. 1972): 11. [Abst.]

242 Bodeen, DeWitt. "*Oliver Twist*"; "*A Tale of Two Cities.*" In 1238, III, 1256-1258; IV, 1667-1670. [David Lean's 1951 film; Jack Conway's 1935 film.]

243 Bodenheimer, Rosemarie. "Dickens and the Art of Pastoral." *CentR* 23 (Fall 1979): 452-467. [Relation between landscape and characterization in *DavidC, GreatEx, OliverTw.*]

244 Bogel, Fredric V. "Fables of Knowing: Melodrama and Related Forms." *Genre* 11 (Spring 1978): 83-108. [Incl. *BleakH, GreatEx, TaleTwoC.*]

245 Bogolepova, T. G. "Izobrazhenie gorodskoi zhizni v 'Ocherkakh Boza'." *VLU* 24, iv (1969): 100-109. [City in *SBoz.*]

246 Bogusch, George E. "Clarkson Stanfield, R. A.: Scene Painter, Artist, Gentleman, and Friend." *QJS* 56 (Oct. 1970): 245-255. [Contributor to D's amateur theatrical prods.]

247 Boime, Albert. "Sources for Sir John Everett Millais's *Christ in the House of His Parents.*" *Gazette des beaux-arts* ser. 6, 86 (Sept.

1975): 71-84. [D's distaste for picture.]

248 Bollenbacher, Bernice, ed. *Open Shelf* (Cleveland Pub. Lib.) 10-12 (Oct.-Dec. 1970): 33-48. [D issue.—Brief survey of books about D.]

249 Bomans, Godfried. "Charles Dickens: Causerie voor 'De Gong' op 19 mei 1942." *Dutch Dkn* 7, xvi (Dec. 1978): 46-48.

250 —. "Dagboeknotities van een reis naar Engeland." *Dutch Dkn* 6, xv (Dec. 1976): 24-30.

251 —. *Dickens, waar zijn uw spoken?*, intro. Michel van der Plas. Amsterdam: Elsevier, 1972. 159 pp. [Rev.: M[ichael] S[later], *Dkn* 69 (Sept. 1973): 183-184.—Note also obit. by J[ohn] G[reaves], *Dkn* 68 (May 1972): 145-147.—Note also 2nd rev. ed. (Amsterdam: Elsevier, 1979), 137 pp.]

252 Bonham-Carter, Victor. "Journalism and Authorship in the Mid-19th Century; Carlyle, Macaulay, Thackeray, Dickens"; "Copyright, Domestic and International, 1830s-1860s; Dickens's Visit to the USA in 1842; The First Society of British Authors, 1843." *Authors by Profession* (London: Soc. of Authors; Los Altos, Cal.: William Kaufmann, 1978), I, 51-70; 71-89.

253 Bonnefoy, Claude. "Dickens: L'enfant de Londres." *Écrivains illustres* (Paris: Hachette, 1972), 116-125. [Gen. crit.]

254 Bony, Alain. "Réalité et imaginaire dans *Hard Times*." In 154, pp. 168-182.

255 Borgen, Johan. "*Pickwick-klubben:* Verdens morsomste bok." *Borgen om bøker: Fremmed*, ed. Lone Klem (Oslo: Gyldendal, 1977), 221-223. [Comedy.—Rpt. from *Dagbladet* (Oslo) 12 May 1932.]

256 Borgmeier, Raimund. "Soziale Probleme zum Zeitvertreib?—Unterhaltung des Lesers und Gesellschaftskritik im viktorianischen Industrieroman," in *Text—Leser—Bedeutung: Untersuchungen zur Interaktion von Text und Leser*, ed. Herbert Grabes (Grossen-Linden: Hoffmann, 1977), 19-41. [Incl. *HardT*.]

257 Borinski, Ludwig. "Dickens als Politiker." *NS* 72 (Nov. 1973): 585-595. [Touches on *BarnR, BleakH, ChildH, HsldWds, MChuz, PictIt*.]

258 Bornstein, George. "Miscultivated Field and Corrupted Garden:

Imagery in *Hard Times.*" *NCF* 26 (Sept. 1971): 158-170.

259 Borowitz, Albert I. *"The Mystery of Edwin Drood."* *Innocence and Arsenic: Studies in Crime and Literature* (New York, London, etc.: Harper and Row, 1977), 53-62. [Ending.—Rpt. from *ArmD* 10 (Jan. 1977): 14-16, 82.]

260 —. "The Unpleasantness at the Garrick Club." *VN* no. 53 (Spring 1978): 16-23. [D, Thackeray, and the 1858 Edmund Yates affair.]

261 Borowitz, David. "George Cruikshank: Mirror of an Age," in *Charles Dickens and George Cruikshank: Papers Read at a Clark Library Seminar on May 9, 1970 by J. Hillis Miller and David Borowitz*, intro. Ada B. Nisbet ([Los Angeles]: William Andrew Clark Memorial Lib., 1971), 73-95. [Also incl. 1332.—Rev.: Jane Rabb Cohen, *Dkn* 68 (Jan. 1972): 58-60; Sylvère Monod, *EA* 25 (July-Sept. 1972): 436-437; Michael Steig, *DSN* 3 (Dec. 1972): 112-114; Harvey Peter Sucksmith, *YES* 3 (1973): 316-317; Lawrence S. Thompson, *PBSA* 65, iv (1971): 435; *TLS* 29 Oct. 1971: 1361; also rev. in 981.]

262 Bose, Amalendu, ed. *Calcutta University: Bulletin of the Department of English* NS 6, ii (1970-1971). [Incl. 116, 784, 1108, 1118, 1241, 1696, 1738, 1768.]

263 Botez, Monica. "An Undercurrent in Dickens's Late Novels." *AUB-LG* 20 (1971): 129-134.

264 Boulton, Marjorie. *The Anatomy of the Novel* (London: Routledge and Kegan Paul, 1975), passim. [Esp. *HardT.*]

265 Bouvier-Ajam, Maurice. "L'Angleterre au temps de Dickens." In 743, pp. 3-12.

266 Bowen, Elizabeth. "A Novelist at Bleak House." *Dkn* 71 (Sept. 1975): 159-163. [From *Eva Trout.*]

267 Bracher, Peter S. "The Early American Editions of *American Notes:* Their Priority and Circulation." *PBSA* 69, iii (1975): 365-376.

268 —. "Harper & Brothers: Publishers of Dickens." *BNYPL* 79 (Spring 1976): 315-335.

269 —. "The Lea & Blanchard Edition of Dickens's *American Notes,* 1842." *PBSA* 63, iv (1969): 296-300.

270 —. "Muddle and Wonderful No-Meaning: Verbal Irresponsibility and Verbal Failures in *Hard Times.*" *SNNTS* 10 (Fall 1978): 305-319.

271 —. "The New York *Herald* and *American Notes.*" *DiS* 5 (May 1969): 81-85.

272 —. "Poe as a Critic of Dickens." *DSN* 9 (Dec. 1978): 109-111.

273 —. "Thwarting the Pirates: Timing the Publication of *American Notes.*" *DSN* 7 (June 1976): 33-34.

274 Bradbury, Malcolm. "Dangerous Pilgrimages." *Enc* 48 (Feb. 1977): 50-65. [Incl. *MChuz.*]

275 Bradley, Ian. *The Call to Seriousness: The Evangelical Impact on the Victorians* (London: Jonathan Cape; New York: Macmillan, 1976), passim. [Esp. *BleakH, LittleDor.*—Rev.: Donald Hawes, *DSN* 9 (Dec. 1978): 121-123.]

276 Brady, John. "The Coincidental Mr. Dickens." *Indiana Eng J* 6, iii-iv (1972): 32-33. [Esp. *DavidC.*]

277 Brantlinger, Patrick. "Benthamite and Anti-Benthamite Fiction"; "Two Responses to Chartism: Dickens and Disraeli." *The Spirit of Reform: British Literature and Politics, 1832-1867* (Cambridge, Mass., and London: Harvard UP, 1977), 35-59; 81-107; et passim. [Esp. *BarnR, OliverTw.*—Incorporates "Bluebooks, The Social Organism, and the Victorian Novel," *Criticism* 14 (Fall 1972): 328-344 and "Dickens and the Factories," *NCF* 26 (Dec. 1971): 270-285.]

278 Braymer, John W. " 'The Role of John Forster in Victorian Letters': Forster at the MLA." *JFNL* 1 (Oct. 1979): 42-48.

279 Bredsdorff, Elias. "Two Visits to Britain, 1847 and 1857." *Hans Christian Andersen: The Story of His Life and Work, 1805-75* (London: Phaidon; New York: Scribners, 1975), 183-218.

280 Breslow, Julian W. "The Narrator in *Sketches by Boz.*" *ELH* 44 (Spring 1977): 127-149. [Language and communication.]

281 Breuninger, Margarete. *Funktion und Wertung des Romans im früh-viktorianischen Roman.* SzEP, NS 14 (Tübingen: Max Niemeyer, 1970), passim. [Theme of novel-reading.—All novels except *BarnR, MEDrood, OurMF, TaleTwoC.*]

282 Brice, Alec W. "The Compilation of the Critical Commentary in Forster's *Life of Charles Dickens*." *Dkn* 70 (Sept. 1974): 185-190.

283 —. "Reviews of Dickens in the *Examiner:* Fonblanque, Forster, Hunt, and Morley." *DSN* 3 (Sept. 1972): 68-80. [1836-1865.]

284 —. " 'A Truly British Judge': Another Article by Dickens." *Dkn* 56 (Jan. 1970): 30-35. [19 Aug. 1848 *Examiner* art. on Sir Thomas Platt.]

285 — and K. J. Fielding. "On Murder and Detection: New Articles by Dickens." *DiS* 5 (May 1969): 45-61.

286 Brier, Peter A. "Lamb, Dickens, and the Theatrical Vision." *ChLB* NS no. 10-11 (Apr.-July 1975): 65-70. [*DavidC, DSon, OliverTw*.]

287 Briggs, Julia. *Night Visitors: The Rise and Fall of the English Ghost Story* (London: Faber and Faber, 1977), passim.

288 Briggs, Katharine M. "The Folklore of Charles Dickens." *JFI* 7 (June 1970): 3-20. [Incl. *BarnR, DSon, LittleDor, MChuz, NichN, OCShop, OliverTw, TaleTwoC, UncomTr*.]

289 Brogan, Denis. "Making Amends to Boz." *Spec* 225 (8 Aug. 1970): 128. [Appreciation.]

290 Brojde, A. M. "Belinsky, Dikkens i natural'naia shkola." *SSl* 18 (1972): 45-68.

291 Bronzwaer, W. "Implied Author, Extradiegetic Narrator and Public Reader: Gérard Genette's Narratological Mode and the Reading Version of *Great Expectations*." *Neophil* 62 (Jan. 1978): 1-18.

292 Brook, G. L. *The Language of Dickens*. London: Deutsch, 1970. 269 pp. [Rev.: Richard P. Badessa, *DSN* 2 (Sept. 1971): 76-78; James R. Bennett, *Style* 10 (Winter 1976): 100-101; John Carey, *Lstr* 83 (28 May 1970): 724-725; S. Robert Greenberg, *NCF* 27 (Dec. 1972): 357-361; D. A. Low, *JES* 1 (Sept. 1971): 270; Norman Page, *Dkn* 66 (Sept. 1970): 250-251; Angela Smith, *YES* 1 (1971): 305-306; A. R. Tellier, *EA* 33 (Apr.-June 1970): 222-223; Nicholas Vinnicombe, *Haltwhistle Q* no. 6 (Winter 1977): 50-52; also rev. in 948, 981, 1961, 2065, 2138.]

293 Brooks, Peter. "Repetition, Repression, and Return: *Great Expectations* and the Study of Plot." *NLH* 11 (Spring 1980): 503-526.

[Method partly derived from Freud.]

294 Brown, Arthur Washburn. *Sexual Analysis of Dickens's Props.* New York: Emerson Books, 1971. 255 pp. [Rev.: Martin Dodsworth, *Dkn* 68 (Sept. 1972): 191-193; Susan Horton, *VS* 16 (Dec. 1972): 251-252; Laurence Senelick, *DSN* 4 (June 1973): 50-52; Deborah A. Thomas, *L&P* 23, iii (1973): 129-131; *TLS* 8 Oct. 1971: 1214; also rev. in 182 (Aug. 1972), 981, 1956.]

295 Brown, Ivor, comp. *Charles Dickens, 1812-1870.* London: Jackdaw, 1970. [An explanatory 8 p. pamphlet, 14 reprods. of contemporary docs., 6 explanatory broadsheets, in a portfolio.—Rev.: William Kean Seymour, *ContempR* 217 (Sept. 1970): 161-162.]

296 —. *Dickens and His World.* New York: Walck; London: Lutterworth, 1970. 48 pp. [For young adults.—Rev.: [Lavinia Russ], *Publishers' Weekly* 198 (31 Aug. 1970): 279; *Best Sellers* 30 (15 Oct. 1970): 297; *Bull of the Center for Children's Books* 24 (Jan. 1971): 71; *Horn Book* 46 (Oct. 1970): 492; *Kirkus Revs* 38 (1 Aug. 1970): 808.]

297 —. "Dickens as Dramatist." *Drama* 98 (Autumn 1970): 43-46.

298 —. "A Medical History of Charles Dickens." *Hist of Med* 2, ii (1970): 2-5.

299 Brown, James Wesley. "Charles Dickens and Norwegian Belles-Lettres in the Nineteenth Century." *Edda* 70, ii (1970): 65-84.

300 Brown, Janet H. "The Narrator's Role in *David Copperfield*." In 1490, pp. 197-207.

301 Bruce, M. "[Toast at] 66th Annual Conference." *Dkn* 68 (Sept. 1972): 204-205.

302 Bryant, Arthur. "Charles Dickens: He Changed Men's Hearts and Minds." *ILN* 256 (30 May 1970): 30-31.

303 Buchanan-Brown, John. *Phiz! The Book Illustrations of Hablot Knight Brown* (Newton Abbot, etc.: David and Charles; New York: Scribners, 1978), passim. [Note U.S. subtitle: *Illustrator of Dickens's World.*—Rev.: Joseph H. Gardner, *DSN* 11 (June 1980): 58-61; John Harvey, *Dkn* 75 (Autumn 1979): 175.]

304 B[uchloh], P[aul] G. "Der viktorianische Detektivroman: Dickens und Collins," in *Der Detektivroman: Studien zur Geschichte und Form der englischen und amerikanischen Detektivliteratur*, by Paul

G. Buchloh and Jens P. Becker (Darmstadt: Wissenschaftliche Buchgesellschaft, 1973), 47-56. [Incl. *BarnR, BleakH, MEDrood.*—Note also 2nd rev. enl. ed., which leaves this essay unchanged except for brief update to the "Literaturbericht."]

305 Buckley, Jerome Hamilton. "Dickens, David and Pip." *Season of Youth: The Bildungsroman from Dickens to Golding* (Cambridge: Harvard UP, 1974), 28-62. [Rev.: George Goodin, *DSN* 6 (Sept. 1975): 95-96; B[ryan] H[ulse], *Dkn* 71 (Jan. 1975): 54-55.]

306 —, ed. *The Worlds of Victorian Fiction.* HES, 6. Cambridge and London: Harvard UP, 1975. [Incl. 771, 856, 1170.—Rev. in 967 (Jan. 1977), 1312.]

307 Burgan, William. "Little Dorrit in Italy." *NCF* 29 (Mar. 1975): 393-411. [Also *PictIt.*]

308 —. "People in the Setting of *Little Dorrit.*" *TSLL* 15 (Spring 1973): 111-128.

309 —. "The Refinement of Contrast: Manuscript Revision in *Edwin Drood.*" In 1494, pp. 167-182.

310 —. "Reviews—Paperback Editions: *Little Dorrit.*" *DSN* 3 (Mar. 1972): 22-24. [All eds. prior to 1970.]

311 —. "Tokens of Winter in Dickens's Pastoral Settings." *MLQ* 36 (Sept. 1975): 293-315. [*BleakH, LittleDor, MEDrood, OCShop, OurMF.*]

312 Burke, Alan R. "The House of Chuzzlewit and the Architectural City." In 1491, pp. 14-40.

313 —. "The Strategy and Theme of Urban Observation in *Bleak House.*" *SEL* 9 (Autumn 1969): 659-676.

314 B[urton], A[nthony]. *Dkn* 66 (Sept. 1970): 244-247. [Rev.-art. on 6, 592, 653, 690, 831, 857, 876, 879, 974, 1662, 2135.]

315 Burton, Anthony. "Cruikshank as an Illustrator of Fiction." In 1510, pp. 93-128.

316 —. "The Forster Library as a Dickens Collection." *DSN* 9 (June 1978): 33-37.

317 —. "Forster on the Stage." *Dkn* 70 (Sept. 1974): 171-184.

318 [Burton, Anthony?]. "Introduction." *Dkn* 70 (Sept. 1974): 142-144. [Special no. in commemoration of John Forster.]

319 Burton, Anthony. "Literary Shrines: The Dickens House and Other Writers' House Museums." *Dkn* 73 (Sept. 1977): 138-146.

320 Burton, H. M. *Dickens and His Works.* Methuen's Outlines. London, etc.: Methuen Ed.; New York: Roy, 1968. 91 pp. [Rev. in 2138.]

321 Busch, Frederick. "Dickens: The Smile on the Face of the Dead." In 461, pp. 149-156. [Esp. *DavidC, OliverTw, OurMF.*]

322 Buscombe, Edward. "Dickens and Hitchcock." *Screen* 11 (July-Oct. 1970): 97-114. [Incl. *GreatEx, North by Northwest.*]

323 Butalia, Subhadra. "The World of Dickens and Prem Chand." *Times of India* 17 Jan. 1971: 7.

324 Butler, Amy. "Dickens's Swiss Chalet." *Dkn* 73 (Sept. 1977): 147-148.

325 Butler, Ivan. "Dickens on the Screen (with a Glance at Other Victorian Novelists)." *Film Rev* 1972-1973: 18-25. [Adaps. listed work-by-work, pp. 18-21.]

326 Butt, John. "Editing a Nineteenth-Century Novelist," in *Art and Error: Modern Textual Editing,* ed. Ronald Gottesman and Scott Bennett (Bloomington: Indiana UP, 1970), 155-167. [Rpt. from *Eng St Today,* 2nd ser., 1961.]

327 Butwin, Joseph. *"Hard Times:* The News and the Novel." *NCF* 32 (Sept. 1977): 166-187. [Novel in context.]

328 —. "The Paradox of the Clown in Dickens." In 1493, pp. 115-132. [*GreatEx, HardT, OCShop, PickP, SBoz.*]

329 Byrd, Max. " 'Reading' in *Great Expectations.*" *PMLA* 91 (Mar. 1976): 259-265. [Moral implications of (mis)interpretation.—Note also Elizabeth Bergen Brophy's response and Byrd's reply, Oct. 1976, p. 915.]

330 Cain, Tom. "Tolstoy's Use of *David Copperfield.*" *CritQ* 15 (Autumn 1973): 237-246. [*War and Peace.*]

331 Calder, Jenni. "The Doll in the Doll's House"; "Passionate Women

and Predatory Men." *Women and Marriage in Victorian Fiction*
(London: Thames and Hudson; New York: Oxford UP, 1976),
96-106; 107-119; et passim. [Esp. *BleakH, DavidC, DSon,
LittleDor, OurMF.*]

332 Calin, Vera. "Charles Dickens: 100 de ani de la moartea sa." *RevBib*
23 (June 1970): 377-378.

333 Camerer, Rudi. *Die Schuldproblematik im Spätwerk von Charles
Dickens.* NSAA, 14. Frankfurt a.M., Bern, Las Vegas: Lang, 1978.
243 pp. [Freiburg diss.—Eng. abst., pp. 242-243 and *EASG* 1979:
74-75.]

334 Cannon, Susan Faye. *Science in Culture: The Early Victorian Period*
(New York: Science Hist. Pubs.; Folkestone: Dawson and Sons,
1978), 20-23. [Incl. *Chimes, HardT.*]

335 Cappel, William. "Repetition in the Language of Fiction." *Style* 4
(Fall 1970): 239-244. [*GreatEx.*—Method derived from Lodge.]

336 Carabine, Keith. "Reading *David Copperfield.*" In 1458, pp. 150-
167. [Reader's response.]

337 Cardwell, Margaret. "Dickens's Correspondence with the Illustrator
of *Edwin Drood.*" *Dkn* 69 (Jan. 1973): 42-43.

338 —. "A Newly-Discovered Version of a Collins Sketch for *Edwin
Drood.*" *Dkn* 70 (Jan. 1974): 31-34. [Note also postscript, 71
(Jan. 1975): 45-46.]

339 Cardy, Jean. "Letter to the Editor." *Dkn* 72 (May 1976): 113-
114. [Incl. photograph of orig. of serious stationer in "LazyT."]

340 Carey, John. *The Violent Effigy: A Study of Dickens's Imgination.*
London: Faber and Faber, 1973; rpt. 1979. 183 pp. [Violence,
order, humor, death, symbols, children, sex.—Note also *Here
Comes Dickens: The Imagination of a Novelist* (New York:
Schocken, 1974).—Rev.: Martin Amis, *NewSt* 86 (23 Nov. 1973):
776-777; Cary Archard, *Use of Eng* 31 (Summer 1980): 86-87;
W. F. Axton, *JEGP* 74 (Apr. 1975): 251-254; Paul Bailey, *Obs*
(London) 16 Dec. 1973: 32; C. C. Barfoot, *ES* 55 (Aug. 1974):
373; John Bayley, *Lstr* 90 (22 Nov. 1973): 714-715; W. Bronz-
waer, *DQR* 4, iii (1974): 139-140; C. Clarke, *JES* 4 (Dec. 1974):
393-394; Terry Eagleton, *Tablet* 228 (9 March 1974): 226-227;
K. J. Fielding, *RES* NS 26 (May 1975): 235-237; T. J. Galvin,
LJ 99 (15 May 1974): 1390; Robert Giddings, *DSN* 6 (Dec. 1975):

115-119; Michael Goldberg, *NCF* 29 (Dec. 1974): 354-357; Kenneth Grose, *English* 23 (Autumn 1974): 116, E[lizabeth] H[all], *Psychology Today* 8 (Nov. 1974): 154; Mollie Hardwick, *B&B* 24 (Aug. 1979): 65-66; Barbara Hardy, *Dkn* 71 (Jan. 1975): 49-51; Lauriat Lane, Jr., *IFR* 3 (Jan. 1976): 62-64; Laurence Lerner, *Enc* 44 (Feb. 1975): 77-80; J. C. Maxwell, *N&Q* NS 23 (Feb. 1976): 83-86; S. Monod, *EA* 27 (Apr.-June 1974): 236-237 and 33 (Apr.-June 1980): 238; Margaret Myers, *VS* 19 (June 1976): 541-543; Sam Pickering, Jr., *MP* 73 (Nov. 1975): 205-207; Craig Raine, *TES* 14 Dec. 1973: 23; P. L. Stephen, *Thought* (Delhi) 27 (4 Jan. 1975): 20; Harvey Peter Sucksmith, *YES* 6 (1976): 306-308; Conny Svensson, *Samlaren* 95 (1974): 231-232; David Williams, *Punch* 276 (23 May 1979): 912; *Ch* 11 (Dec. 1974): 1474; *TLS* 11 Jan. 1974: 21-22; also rev. in 504, 584, 981.]

341 Carlisle, Janice. *"Dombey and Son:* The Reader and the Present Tense." *JNT* 1 (Sept. 1971): 146-158.

342 —. *"Little Dorrit:* Necessary Fictions." *SNNTS* 7 (Summer 1975): 195-214.

343 Carlton, W. J. "A Friend of Dickens's Boyhood." *Dkn* 66 (Jan. 1970): 8-16. [Louis D'Elboux.]

344 —. "Janet Barrow's Portrait Miniatures: An Australian Epilogue." *Dkn* 68 (May 1972): 100-103.

345 Carlyle, Jane Welsh. *I Too Am Here: Selections from the Letters,* ed. Alan and Mary McQueen Simpson (Cambridge, etc.: Cambridge UP, 1977), passim. [Incl. meetings with D.]

346 Carney, T. J. *Great Expectations.* Folens's Student Aids. Dublin: Folens, 1977. 68 pp.

347 Carolan, Katherine. *"The Battle of Life:* A Love Story." *Dkn* 69 (May 1973): 105-110.

348 —. "Dickensian Echoes in a Thackeray Christmas Book." *SSF* 11 (Spring 1974): 196-199. [*DSon,* "Dr. Birch."]

349 —. "Dickens's American Secretary and *Martin Chuzzlewit.*" *DSN* 7 (Dec. 1976): 109.

350 —. "Dickens's Last Christmases." *DR* 52 (Autumn 1972): 373-383.

351 —. "The Dingley Dell Christmas." *DSN* 4 (June 1973): 41-48. [Infl.

of Irving's *Sketch Book*.]

352 —. "The Dingley Dell Christmas Continued: 'Rip Van Winkle' and the Tale of Gabriel Grub." *DSN* 5 (Dec. 1974): 104-106.

353 —. *"Great Expectations* and a *Household Words* Sketch." *DSN* 3 (Mar. 1972): 27-28.

354 (Carr, Lucile. *A Catalogue of the VanderPoel Dickens Collection at the University of Texas*. 1968.) [Rev.: Janet Fletcher, *LJ* 95 (June 1970): 2157; Simon Nowell-Smith, *Library* ser. 5, 25 (June 1970): 170; Timothy d'Arch Smith, *Dkn* 66 (Sept. 1970): 251-253; Richard A. Vogler, *DSN* 1 (Dec. 1970): 17-18; *Ch* 7 (Mar. 1970): 49; *TLS* 26 Feb. 1970: 232; also rev. in 2138.]

355 Carré, Jacques. "Personnage, sens et idéologie dans 'The Signalman' de Dickens." *LanM* 70, iv-v (1976): 359-368.

356 —. "Le prolétariat industriel dans *Hard Times* de Dickens," in *Hommage à Georges Fourrier*. Centre de Recherches d'Histoire et Littérature aux XVIIIe et XIXe Siècles, 4; Annales littéraires de l'Univ. de Besançon, 142 (Paris: Belles Lettres, 1973), 71-85. [Paper discussed by R. Barny, Jacques Carré, A. Dérozier, Jaime Díaz-Rozzotto, P. Lehmann, André Rault, pp. 81-85.]

357 Carter, Duncan A. and Laurence W. Mazzeno. "Dickens's Account of the Shakers and West Point: Rhetoric or Reality?" *Dkn* 72 (Sept. 1976): 131-139.

358 Carter, John. "The Suzannet Sale at Sotheby's." *Dkn* 68 (Jan. 1972): 43-47.

359 Carter, W. R. "Do Creatures of Fiction Exist?" *Philosophical St* 30 (Aug. 1980): 205-215. [Incl. Sarah Gamp and Pickwick.—Reply to 2036.]

360 Cartianu, Ana. "Charles Dickens: Autobiografie si fantezie"; "Romanul de maturitate la Dickens (Aspecte de structura)"; "Un roman neterminat: *Misterul lui Edwin Drood.*" *Eseuri de literatura engleza si americana* (Cluj: Dacia, 1973), 80-92; 93-98; 99-109. [Third title rpt. from 588, pp. 21-31.—Note also "The Late Novels of Charles Dickens: Remarks on Structure," *AUB-LG* 20 (1971): 123-128.]

360a —. "Charles Dickens on the 100th Anniversary of His Death." *AUB-LG* 19 (1970): 109-113.

361 Cary, Joyce. "Including Mr. Micawber." *Selected Essays,* ed. A. G. Bishop (London: Michael Joseph; New York: St. Martin's Press, 1976), 172-175. [Rpt. from *NYTBR,* 1951.]

362 Caserio, Robert L. "Plot and the Point of Reversal: Dickens and Poe"; "The Featuring of Act as 'The Rescue': Story in Dickens and George Eliot." *Plot, Story and the Novel: From Dickens and Poe to the Modern Period* (Princeton and Guildford: Princeton UP, 1979), 57-90; 91-132. [Esp. infl. of Scott on and reversal in *BarnR, NichN;* plot and realism in *BleakH, Felix Holt.*—Note also "Plot, Story and the Novel: Problematic Aspects of English and American Narrative, from Dickens to Gertrude Stein," *DAI* 34 (Nov. 1973): 2613A (Yale).]

363 Casotti, Francesco. "Dickens e Rousseau." *RLMC* 22 (Dec. 1969): 279-293.

364 —. "Lo sviluppo delle tematiche dickensiane in *Nicholas Nickleby.*" *Miscellanea* (Trieste) 1 (1971): 83-112.

365 Casparis, Christian Paul. *Tense without Time: The Present Tense in Narration.* Schweizer anglistische Arbeiten, 84 (Bern: Francke, 1975), passim. [Incl. *BleakH, DavidC, DSon, GreatEx, MEDrood, OurMF, TaleTwoC.*]

366 Cassid, Donna. "Dickens: A Feminist View." *Women* 2 (Fall 1970): 21-22. [Charlotte Claypole, Nancy, Louisa Gradgrind.]

367 Castroviejo, Concha. "Los niños de Dickens." *Urogallo* no. 3 (June-July 1970): 77-83. [*DavidC, NichN, OliverTw.*]

368 Cavalcanti, Alberto interviewed by John Harrington and David Paroissien. "Alberto Cavalcanti on *Nicholas Nickleby.*" *LFQ* 6 (Winter 1978): 48-56. [Note also 1485.]

369 Cawelti, John G. "The Best-Selling Social Meoldrama." *Adventure, Mystery, and Romance: Formula Stories as Art and Popular Culture* (Chicago and London: Univ. of Chicago Press, 1976), 260-295 passim. [*BleakH, MEDrood, NichN, OliverTw.*]

370 Cazamian, Louis. "Dickens: The Philosophy of Christmas"; "Implicit Social Comment in Dickens's Novels." *The Social Novel in England 1830-1850: Dickens, Disraeli, Mrs. Gaskell, Kingsley,* trans. and fwd. Martin Fido (London and Boston: Routledge and Kegan Paul, 1973), 117-147; 148-174. [Social conscience in early novels.—Trans. of *Le Roman social en Angleterre,* 1903; part of

1st chap. in diff. trans. in 2064, pp. 240-243.—Rev.: P. J. Keating, *DSN* 5 (Mar. 1974): 21-24; Sylvère Monod, *Dkn* 69 (Sept. 1973): 184-186.]

371 Cerny, Lothar. *Erinnerung bei Dickens.* Bochumer anglistische St., 3. Amsterdam: B. R. Grüner, 1975. 283 pp. [*BleakH, DavidC, GreatEx, HMan, TaleTwoC,* "MugJ."—Eng. abst. in *EASG* 1975: 107-109 (Münster diss., 1974).—Rev.: Hans-Dieter Gelfert, *GRM* NS 28, i (1978): 120-121; Dieter Mehl, *Archiv* 215, i (1978): 181-183; Sylvère Monod, *EA* 31 (Jan.-Mar. 1978): 90-91; Heinz Reinhold, *Dkn* 72 (Sept. 1976): 175-176; F. K. Stanzel, *MLR* 73 (Apr. 1978): 417-418; also rev. in 981.]

372 —. " 'A General Number One': Utilitarismuskritik in Dickens *Oliver Twist*," in *Studien zur englischen und amerikanischen Sprache und Literatur: Festschrift für Helmut Papajewski,* ed. Paul G. Buchloh, Inge Leimberg, and Herbert Rauter. Kieler Beiträge zur Anglistik und Amerikanistik, 10 (Neumünster: Karl Wachholtz, 1974), 119-156.

372a Chajecka, Maria. "Lew Tolstoj, Stefan Zeromski i Charles Dickens: Z badań porównawczych nad powieścia autobiograficzna—*Dzieciństwo, Lata chlopiece, Mlodość, Syzyfowe prace, Dawid Copperfield.*" *Studia polono-slavica-orientalia* 5 (1979): 7-42.

373 Chakravarty, Sudeshna. "The City in the Novels of Dickens and Dostoevsky." *Bull of the Dept of Eng Calcutta Univ* 12, i (1976-1977): 65-84. [Esp. *BleakH, DSon, LittleDor, OliverTw, OurMF.*]

374 Charles, Don C. and Linda A. "Charles Dickens's Old People." *International J of Aging and Human Development* 10, iii (1979-1980): 231-237. [Various, not age-stereotyped.]

375 Chatman, Seymour. *Story and Discourse: Narrative Structure in Fiction and Film* (Ithaca and London: Cornell UP, 1978), passim. [*BleakH, DavidC, GreatEx.*]

376 Chatterton, Wayne. *"Mr. Dickens Goes to the Play."* *Alexander Woollcott.* TUSAS, 305 (Boston: Twayne, 1978), 121-124.

377 Chaudhry, G. A. "The Mudfog Papers." *Dkn* 70 (May 1974): 104-112.

378 Chaudhuri, B. P. *Charles Dickens.* New Delhi: Aarti, 1970. vi, 128 pp. [Esp. *MChuz.*]

379 Chaudhuri, Brahma. "Leonard Skimpole in *Bleak House.*" *DSN* 6 (Sept. 1975): 75-78.

380 Chavkin, Allan and Fritz Oehlschlaeger. "An American Publisher in Europe with Dickens, Lamartine, Landor, and Thackeray: Six Letters of James T. Fields to Edwin P. Whipple." *RALS* 8 (Spring 1979): 61-72.

381 Cheek, Edwin R. "Dickens and Women's Lib: Pro and Con." In 651, pp. 39-48. [*AllYR, BleakH, DSon, HardT, HsldWds, LittleDor, MChuz, MEDrood, NichN, OurMF.*]

382 Cheeseman, J. L. *Notes on Charles Dickens's Pickwick Papers.* Study-Aid Ser. London: Methuen, 1978. 70 pp.

383 Cheney, David R. "Correction of the Misattribution of a Poem in *Household Words.*" *N&Q* NS 24 (Feb. 1977): 15-16. [Edmund Ollier.—Corrects an entry in 1186.]

384 Chesterton, G. K. "The Boyhood of Dickens"; "Dickens the Myth-Maker"; "Dickens and Scott"; "The Optimism of Dickens." *G. K. Chesterton: A Selection from His Non-Fictional Prose,* ed. W. H. Auden (London: Faber and Faber, 1970), 41-49; 50-55; 56-58; 59-67. [Rpt. from 2283.]

385 —. *Charles Dickens,* trans. Teodora Sadoveanu, intro. Dan Grigorescu. Buchaest: Univers, 1970. 232 pp. [Trans. of 2283.]

386 —. "Dickens and Little Bethel." *CRev* 2 (Spring-Summer 1976): 291-293. [Undated (ca. 1910?) ltr. to ed. of *Nation* (London).—Not in Sullivan; here 1st pub.?]

387 Chialant, Maria Teresa. "Dickens, Gissing e Orwell." *AION-SG* 12 (1969): 373-394. [Their views of D and society.]

388 Choudhury, M. K. "The Influence of Dickens on George Gissing." *IJES* 14 (1973): 13-19.

389 Christensen, Allan Conrad. "A Dickensian Hero Retailored: The Carlylean Apprenticeship of Martin Chuzzlewit." *SNNTS* 3 (Spring 1971): 18-25.

390 —. "The Influence of Bulwer-Lytton in His Own Times." *Edward Bulwer-Lytton: The Fiction of New Regions* (Athens: Univ. of

Georgia Press, 1976), 222-234; et passim. [Rev.: Andrew Sanders, *Dkn* 73 (Sept. 1977): 172-174; F. S. Schwarzbach, *DSN* 9 (June 1978): 59-60.]

391 Christmas, Peter. "*Little Dorrit:* The End of Good and Evil." In 1494, pp. 134-153.

392 Church, Randolph W. "Charles Dickens Sends His Sympathy: An Epitaph for a Virginia Child." *VC* 21 (Summer 1971): 42-47. [Charles Irving Thornton's 1842 death.]

393 Churchill, R. C. *A Bibliography of Dickensian Criticism, 1836-1975.* GRLH, 12. New York: Garland; London: Macmillan, 1975. xiv, 314 pp. [Rev.: Alan M. Cohn, *DSN* 7 (Dec. 1976): 120-122; Philip Collins, *Dkn* 72 (May 1976): 108-110 and Churchill's response, 73 (May 1977): 113; Angus Easson, *L&H* no. 7 (Spring 1978): 121-122; K. J. Fielding, *MLR* 72 (Oct. 1977): 924-925; Paul Koda, *Book Collector's Market* 3 (Mar.-June 1977): 34-35; Charles Mann, *ARBA* 7 (1976): 613-614; Allen Samuels, *Library* ser. 5, 32 (Mar. 1977): 82-84; Marianne Seydoux, *Bull de documentation bibliographique* (pt. 2 of *Bull des bibliothèques de France*) 22 (Jan. 1977): 70; Marsha H. Zack, *LJ* 100 (1 Oct. 1975): 1810; *BBkN* Apr. 1976: 297-298; *Ch* 12 (Feb. 1976): 1550; also rev. in 1062.]

394 —. "Chesterton on Dickens: The Legend and the Reality." *DSN* 5 (June 1974): 34-38. [Note also K. J. Fielding's and Trevor Blount's responses, 6 (Mar. 1975): 14-16 and Churchill's reply, 7 (Mar. 1976): 15-16.]

395 —. "Growing Up with Dickens: 1923-1937." *DSN* 9 (Dec. 1978): 97-100.

396 —. "The Monthly Dickens and the Weekly Dickens." *ContempR* 234 (Feb. 1979): 97-101.

397 Cirillo, Vincent J. "Ghosts and Witches." *Dkn* 73 (Jan. 1977): 38. [Infl. of *Macbeth* on *CCarol.*]

398 Clades, Urio. "Charles Dickens, *Visioni d'Italia.*" *NA* 513 (Nov. 1971): 449-450. [Rev.-art. on Pasquale Maffeo trans of *PictIt.*]

399 Clark, John W. "Dickens." *The Language and Style of Anthony Trollope* (London: Deutsch, 1975), 148-153.

400 Clarke, Graham. " 'Bound in Moss and Cloth': Reading a Long Vic-

torian Novel." In 1458, pp. 54-71. [Esp. *BleakH.*]

401 Clarke, Marcus. "Charles Dickens." *A Colonial City: High and Low Life: Selected Journalism of Marcus Clarke,* ed. L. T. Hergehan (St. Lucia: Univ. of Queensland Press, 1972), 228 235. [Obit. from *Argus* (Melbourne) 18 July 1870.]

402 Claverton, Douglas. "Big Money in First Editions of Dickens." *Collector's Weekly* 26 Sept. 1970: 8.

403 Clej, Alina. "Dickens." *SXX* no. 166-167 (Nov.-Dec. 1974): 167-169.

404 Clément, Marilène. "Le grillon du foyer." In 743, pp. 83-87.

405 Clift, Jean Dalby. "Dickens's Little Nell and the Lost Feminine: An Archetypal Analysis of Projections in Victorian Culture." *Albion* 8 (Summer 1976): 180. [Abst.]

406 Cohan, Steven. " 'They Are All Secret': The Fantasy Content of *Bleak House.*" *L&P* 26, ii (1976): 79-91.

407 Cohen, Jane R. " 'A Melancholy Clown': The Relationship of Robert Seymour and Charles Dickens." *HLB* 19 (July 1971): 250-279. [Illus. for *PickP.*]

408 —. "The Portrayal of Sir John Chester by Browne and Cattermole." *Dkn* 72 (May 1976): 93-97.

409 —. "Strained Relations: Charles Dickens and George Cattermole." In 1489, pp. 81-92.

410 Cohn, Alan M. "The Dickens Checklist." *DSN* each no. from Sept. 1970. [Successively with the following collaborators: Kenneth Denning, William D. Faulhaber, J. E. Kasel, George V. Griffith, James T. Jones, K. K. Collins.]

411 Colby, Robert A. *Thackeray's Canvass of Humanity: An Author and His Public* (Columbus: Ohio State UP, 1979), passim.

412 Colby, Vineta. *Yesterday's Woman: Domestic Realism in the English Novel* (Princeton: Princeton UP, 1974), passim. [Touches on all novels except *BarnR, MChuz, OCShop, PickP.*]

412a Colegrove, C. L. "My Love for Dickens." *Eigo Kenkyu: The Study of English* supp. issue (June 1970): 37-39. [Also incl. "Dickens Bibliography," pp. 103-104 and 422 (Jap. trans.), 698, 729a, 904a, 924a, 980a, 1094a, 1096a, 1290a, 1343a, 1346a, 1701a, 1756, 1933, 1934a, 1941a, 2162a, 2168a.—All arts. in Jap. except 698.— Note also 1292.]

413　Collin, Dorothy W. "The Composition of Mrs. Gaskell's *North and South*." *BJRL* 54 (Autumn 1971): 67-93. [Also *HardT*.]

414　Collins, Norman. "[Toast at] The London Birthday Dinner." *Dkn* 68 (May 1972): 139-140.

415　Collins, Philip. "The *All the Year Round* Letter Book." *VPN* 10 (Nov. 1970): 23-29.

416　—. "Arthur Clennam Arrives in London: A Note on *Little Dorrit*, Chapter III." *L&H* no. 8 (Autumn 1978): 214-222.

417　—. " '*Carol* Philosophy, Cheerful Views'." In 154, pp. 158-167.

418　—. "Charles Dickens," in *Victorian Fiction: A Second Guide to Research*, ed. George H. Ford (New York: MLA, 1978), 34-113; et passim. [1963-1974.]

419　—. "Charles Dickens and Rockingham Castle." *Northamptonshire Past and Present* 6 (1980): 133-140. [Friendship 1848-1852 with Lavinia and Richard Watson, owners of orig. of Chesney Wold.]

420　—. *Charles Dickens: David Copperfield*. St. in Eng. Lit., 67. London: Arnold, 1977. 64 pp. [Rev.: Edwin M. Eigner, *MLR* 74 (Oct. 1979): 920-921; Sylvère Monod, *EA* 31 (July-Dec. 1978): 403; Peter Preston, *N&Q* NS 25 (June 1978): 262-263; Andrew Sanders, *THES* 6 May 1977: 21; *Cb* 15 (Apr. 1978): 225.]

421　—. "Charles Dickens, 1812-1870," in *Abroad in America: Visitors to the New Nation, 1776-1914*, ed. Marc Pachter and Frances Wein. (Reading, Mass.: Addison-Wesley in assoc. with National Portrait Gallery, Smithsonian Inst., 1976), 82-91. [Note also pp. 319-320 of the "Checklist of the Exhibition" at the Gallery.]

422　—. "Christmas All Year Round: Dickens's Public Readings." *Lstr* 82 (25 Dec. 1969): 881-883. [From BBC 3rd Programme.—Jap. trans. Akira Takeuchi in 412a, pp. 98-100.]

423　—. "Christmas and Christianity in Charles Dickens." *Times* (London) 22 Dec. 1979: 14.

424　—. *A Critical Commentary on Dickens's Bleak House*. London: Macmillan, 1971. 80 pp. [Rev.: Norman Friedman, *DSN* 4 (Dec. 1973): 109-113; also rev. in 236.]

425　—. "*David Copperfield*: 'A Very Complicated Interweaving of Truth and Fiction'." *E&S* 23 (1970): 71-86.

426 —. "Dickens and Carlyle." *TLS* 19 Mar. 1971: 325. [Ltr. to ed.; note also Margaret Clarke, 16 Apr. 1971: 449.]

427 (—. *Dickens and Crime.* 1962; rpt. 1968.) [Excerpt rpt. in 2064, pp. 468-472.—Rev.: Sylvère Monod, *EA* 23 (Apr.-June 1970): 219.]

428 —. "Dickens and Industrialism." *SEL* 20 (Autumn 1980): 651-673. [*BleakH, DavidC, DSon, HardT,* "MugJ."]

429 —. "Dickens and London," in *The Victorian City: Images and Realities,* ed. H. J. Dyos and Michael Wolff (London and Boston: Routledge and Kegan Paul, 1973), II, 537-557. [Rev. of book: Anthony Burton, *Dkn* 70 (May 1974): 127-130.]

430 —. *A Dickens Bibliography.* [London] : Dickens Fellowship by arr. with Cambridge UP, 1970. [72 cols.] [1836-1967.—Extract from *New CBEL,* III.]

431 C[ollins], Ph[ilip]. "Dickens, Charles," in *New Encyclopaedia Britannica: Macropaedia,* 15th ed. (Chicago: Encyclopaedia Britannica, 1974), V, 706-712. [Note also *Micropaedia,* III, 530-531.]

432 Collins, Philip. "Dickens Editions." *TLS* 16 Apr. 1970: 340. [Ltr. to ed. on coll. of D in parts.—Note also J. G. Phillip, A. H. Chaplin, A. G. S. Enser, 30 Apr. 1970: 480; Joan M. Gladstone, 14 May 1970: 539.]

433 —. "Dickens in America, 1867-68." *DSN* 4 (June 1973): 48-50.

434 —. "Dickens in 1870." *TLS* 4 June 1970: 605-606.

435 —. "The Dickens Reading-Copies in Dickens House." *Dkn* 68 (Sept. 1972): 173-179.

436 —. "Dickens Reading-Copies in the Beinecke Library." *YULG* 46 (Jan. 1972): 153-158.

437 —. "Dickens the Citizen," in *Politics in Literature in the Nineteenth Century* (Lille: Univ. de Lille III; Paris: Éds. Univ. 1974), 61-81. [*AllYR, DSon, HardT, HsldWds, LittleDor, MH'sClock, OliverTw, TaleTwoC.*]

438 —, ed. *Dickens: The Critical Heritage.* London: Routledge and Kegan Paul; New York: Barnes and Noble, 1971. xxi, 641 pp. [For contents see this number in Appendix.—Rev.: Donald Hawes, *DSN* 5

(Dec. 1974): 115-117; John Lucas, *Spec* 226 (30 Jan. 1971): 162;
J. C. Mays, *Hibernia* 30 Apr. 1971: 17; Irma Rantavaara, *Dkn* 67
(May 1971): 109-111; A. P. Robson, *VS* 15 (June 1972): 475-480;
Booklist 67 (15 July 1971): 924; *Ch* 8 (June 1971): 549; *Ecn* 238
(23 Jan. 1971): 53; *TLS* 5 Mar. 1971: 269-270; also rev. in 182
(Aug. 1971), 2065.]

439 Cancelled.

440 —. "Dickens's Public Readings: Texts and Performances." In 1491,
pp. 182-197. [Paper from 2180.]

441 —. "Dickens's Public Readings: The Kit and the Team." *Dkn* 74 (Jan.
1978): 8-16.

442 —. "Dickens's Self-Estimate: Some New Evidence." In 1496, pp. 21-
43.

443 —. "Dorothea's Husbands." *TLS* 18 May 1973: 556-557. [George
Eliot's *Middlemarch* and *DavidC*.]

444 —. *From Manly Tear to Stiff Upper Lip: The Victorians and Pathos.*
[Wellington, N.Z.: Victoria UP, n.d.] 24 pp. [Incl. *BleakH,
Chimes, DavidC, DSon, NichN, OCShop*.]

445 —. "How Many Men Was Dickens the Novelist?" In 131, pp. 145-168.

446 —. "Letter to the Editor." *Dkn* 70 (Jan. 1974): 29. [Actual bargee
compared to Gaffer Hexam.]

447 —. "*Little Dorrit:* The Prison and the Critics." *TLS* 18 Apr. 1980:
445-446. [Note also H. M. Page's ltr. to ed., 16 May 1980: 556.]

448 —. "1940-1960: Enter the Professionals." *Dkn* 66 (May 1970): 143-
161. [Special no. on D's reputation 1870-1970.—Also incl. 656,
700, 1129, 1363, 1566, 1793.—Rev.: Jerome Meckier, *DSN* 1
(Dec. 1970): 9-11; also rev. in 981, 1181, 1228, 1808, 1961, 2200,
2227.]

449 —. "Pip the Obscure: *Great Expectations* and Hardy's *Jude*." *CritQ*
19 (Winter 1977): 23-35.

450 —. "The Popularity of Dickens." *Dkn* 70 (Jan. 1974): 5-20.

451 —. "Presidential Message to the Dickens Society [27 Dec. 1975]."

DSN 7 (Mar. 1976): 3-8. [Note also Coral Lansbury's ltr. to ed., Sept., p. 93.]

452 —. *Reading Aloud: A Victorian Métier.* Tennyson Soc. Monographs, 5 (Lincoln: Tennyson Research Centre, 1972), passim. [*BleakH, DavidC, DSon, OCShop, PickP.*]

453 —. " 'Sikes and Nancy': Dickens's Last Reading." *TLS* 11 June 1971: 681-682.

454 —. "Some Uncollected Speeches by Dickens." *Dkn* 73 (May 1977): 89-99.

455 —. "A Tale of Two Novels: *A Tale of Two Cities* and *Great Expectations* in Dickens's Career." In 1416, pp. 40-57 and in 1490, pp. 336-351.

456 —. "The Texts of Dickens's Readings." *BNYPL* 74 (June 1970): 360-381. [Note also his "Postscript," 75 (Feb. 1971): 63.]

457 —. "[Toast at] 68th Annual Conference." *Dkn* 70 (Sept. 1974): 215-216.

458 —. "[Toast at] The London Birthday Dinner." *Dkn* 75 (Summer 1979): 120-126.

459 —. "W. H. Wills' Plans for *Household Words.*" *VPN* 8 (Apr. 1970): 33-46.

460 Collins, R. G. "Dickens and Grimaldi." *Thalia* 1 (Autumn 1978): 55-56. [Followed by facs. rpt. of D's intro. to *MemGrim* plus Cruikshank's illus., pp. 57-73.]

461 —, ed. *Mosaic* 9 (Summer 1976). [Special no. on literary humor of the nineteenth century.—Incl. 321, 747, 853 (chap. on *MChuz*).]

462 —, ed. *The Novel and Its Changing Form.* Winnipeg: Univ. of Manitoba Press, 1972. [Incl. 890, 1309, 1879.]

463 Colmer, John. *Coleridge to Catch-22: Images of Society* (London: Macmillan; New York: St. Martin's, 1978), passim. [Esp. *HardT.*]

464 Colwell, C. Carter. "*Great Expectations.*" *The Tradition of British Literature* (New York: G. P. Putnam's Sons, 1971), 311-318.

465 Comyn, Veronica. "John Jasper, Schizophrenic." *UES* 13 (June

1975): 1-5.

466　Conger, Lesley. "Joy, Joy!—and Pull Out All the Stops!" *Writer* 85 (Dec. 1972): 8, 43. [*CCarol.*]

467　Conlon, D. J., ed. "*Charles Dickens* (30 Aug. 1906)"; "*Appreciations and Criticisms of Charles Dickens* (24 Feb. 1911)." *G. K. Chesterton: The Critical Judgments, Part I, 1900-1937* (Antwerp: Antwerp St. in Eng. Lit., 1976), 112-131; 259-262. [Rpts. 9 contemporary revs. of 1st title and 1 of 2nd.—Note also 2282, 2283.]

468　Conrad, Peter. "The City and the Picturesque." *The Victorian Treasure-House* (London: Collins, 1973), 65-105; et passim. [*SBoz, UncomTr,* all novels except *MEDrood, NichN, PickP.*—Rev.: John R. Reed, *DSN* 5 (Dec. 1974): 121-123.]

469　—. "Institutional America: Frances Trollope, Anthony Trollope, Charles Dickens." *Imagining America* (New York: Oxford UP; London: Routledge and Kegan Paul, 1980), 36-60.

470　Cooper, David W. *The Lesson of the Scaffold: The Public Execution Controversy in Victorian England* (Athens: Ohio UP; London: Allen Lane, 1974), 77-88; et passim. [Esp. *AllYR.*—Rev.: Ian Ousby, *DSN* 8 (Mar. 1977): 25-26.]

471　Cooper, Lettice. *A Hand Upon the Time: A Life of Charles Dickens.* London: Gollancz, 1971. 144 pp. [Juvenile.—Orig. pub. 1968.]

472　Copley, I. A. "Two Dickensian Chamber Operas." *Dkn* 69 (May 1973): 102-104. [By Charles Wood (1866-1926) based upon *MChuz, PickP.*—Note also 815, pp. 215, 229.]

473　Coppock, Barbara M. "Dickens's Attitude to Jews." *Common Ground* 24 (Autumn 1970): 23-26. [Riah.]

474　Cordery, Gareth. "The Cathedral as Setting and Symbol in *The Mystery of Edwin Drood.*" *DSN* 10 (Dec. 1979): 97-103.

475　Corr, Patricia. *Charles Dickens: Great Expectations.* Study-Guide Notes. Dublin: Gill and Macmillan, 1978. 27 pp.

476　Costigan, Edward. "Drama and Everyday Life in *Sketches by Boz.*" *RES* NS 27 (Nov. 1976): 403-421.

477　Coudert, Marie-Louise. "Le brouillard et le réel." In 743, pp. 37-42. [Esp. *GreatEx.*]

478 Coustillas, Pierre. *Gissing's Writings on Dickens: A Biobibliographical Survey.* London: Enitharmon Press, 1969. 25 pp. [1st pub. *Dkn,* 1969.—Rev.: Anthony Curtis, *DSN* 4 (Mar. 1973): 26-28; Michael Slater, *Dkn* 66 (Sept. 1970): 253.]

479 — and Colin Partridge, eds. *"Charles Dickens: A Critical Study"*; "Forster's *Life of Dickens,*" in *Gissing: The Critical Heritage* (London: Routledge and Kegan Paul, 1972), 320-337; 403-408. [Rpts. contemporary revs. of Gissing's *Dickens* by William Archer, W. E. Henley, and three anon. reviewers; and three anon. revs. of Gissing's abrg. ed. of Forster's *Life.*—Rev.: B[ryan] H[ulse], *Dkn* 69 (Sept. 1973): 191.]

480 Cowden, Roy W. "Dickens at Work." *MQR* 9 (Spring 1970): 125-132. [*DavidC.*]

481 Cowley, Malcolm and Howard E. Hugo. *"Bleak House* (1853)." *The Lesson of the Masters: An Anthology of the Novel from Cervantes to Hemingway: Texts with Commentaries* (New York: Scribners, 1971), 221-232. [With chap. 1 of the novel.]

482 Cox, Arthur J. "The Haggard Woman." *MDAC* 1972: 65-77. [*MEDrood.*]

483 Cox, C. B. "Realism and Fantasy in *David Copperfield.*" *BJRL* 52 (Spring 1970): 267-283.

484 Cox, Don Richard. "The Birds of *Bleak House.*" *DSN* 11 (Mar. 1980): 6-11.

485 Cox, Helen. *Mr. and Mrs. Charles Dickens Entertain at Home.* London: Pergamon, 1971. ix, 214 pp. [Incl. "Dickens on Food," sel. Stuart McHugh.—Rev.: M. F. K. Fisher, *DSN* 3 (June 1972): 50-53; *Ecn* 238 (9 Jan. 1971): 53-54; *TLS* 5 Mar. 1971: 270; also rev. in 1956.]

486 Crabbe, Katharyn. "Lean's *Oliver Twist:* Novel to Film." *Film Criticism* 2 (Fall 1977): 46-51.

487 Crago, H. "Charles Dickens and George MacDonald: A Note." *DiS* 5 (May 1969): 86-90. [Infl. of *GreatEx* on "Day Boy and Night Girl."]

488 Craig, Clifford. *The Van Diemen's Land Edition of the Pickwick Papers: A General and Bibliographical Study with Some Notes on Henry Dowling.* Hobart, Tasmania: Cat and Fiddle Press, 1973.

xiii, 65 pp.

489 Craig, David. *"Hard Times* and the Condition of England." *The Real Foundations: Literature and Social Change* (London: Chatto and Windus, 1973; New York: Oxford UP, 1974), 109-131.

490 Craig, David M. "Origins, Ends, and Pip's Two Selves." *RS* 47 (Mar. 1979): 17-26.

491 Crawford, John W. "The Garden Imagery in *Great Expectations.*" *Discourse: Essay* [sic] *on English and American Literature.* Costerus, NS 14 (Amsterdam: Rodopi, 1978), 109-115. [Rpt. from *RS* 39 (Mar. 1971): 63-67.]

492 Creidy, Olga. "The Dickens Country: Traveller's Notes." *EAA* no. 1 (1977): 71-75. [Kent.]

493 Crew, Louie. "Charles Dickens as a Critic of the United States." *MQ* 16 (Oct. 1974): 42-50.

494 —. "Dickens with a Voice like Burke's?" *VN* no. 54 (Fall 1978): 22. [*DavidC.*—Rebuts Richard Ohmann, *VN,* 1965.]

495 Critchley, Macdonald. "The Miss Havisham Syndrome." *Hist of Med* 1 (Summer 1969): 2-6.

496 Crowder, Ashby Bland. "A Source for Dickens's Sir Mulberry." *PLL* 12 (Winter 1976): 105-109.

497 Crowther, Bosley. *"Great Expectations." Vintage Films* (New York: G. P. Putnam's Sons, 1977), 89-92. [Lean's 1946 prod.]

498 Cruikshank, George. *Graphic Works of George Cruikshank,* ed., intro., notes Richard A. Vogler (New York: Dover, 1979), 59-67.

499 Crum, Margaret. *English and American Autographs in the Bodmeriana.* Bibliotheca Bodmeriana, Catalogues, 4 (Cologny-Genève: Fondation Martin Bodmer, 1977), 31. [Describes ms.]

500 Cuadrado, Beatriz P. de. "La última novela de Charles Dickens: *Nuestro común amigo." Revista de lenguas extranjeras* no. 1 (1970): 17-28.

501 Cudworth, Charles. "Dickens and Music." *Musical Times* 111 (June 1970): 588-590.

502 Culmer, W. Harrison. *Billy the Cartwheeler: "The Last of the Dickens Boys."* Metuchen, N.J.: Scarecrow Press; Folkestone: Bailey Bros. and Swinfen, 1970. xv, 274 pp. [Purports to have known D in 1860s.—Rev.: Mary L. Garvey, *LJ* 96 (1 May 1971): 1603; Leslie C. Staples, *Dkn* 67 (Jan. 1971): 55-56; also rev. in 981, 1171.]

503 Cunningham, Valentine. "Charles Dickens." *Everywhere Spoken Against: Dissent in the Victorian Novel* (Oxford: Clarendon Press, 1975), 190-230; et passim. [Esp. *HardT*.—Rev.: James R. Kincaid, *DSN* 8 (June 1977): 60-62; also rev. in 967 (Jan. 1976).]

504 Curran, Stuart. *SEL* 14 (Autumn 1974): 655-658. [Rev.-art. on 340, 830, 845, 1186, 1457, 1491.]

505 —. "The Lost Paradises of *Martin Chuzzlewit*." *NCF* 25 (June 1970): 51-68. [Rev. in 1961.]

506 Curreli, Mario. "Conrad and Dickens: A Minor Source." *KN* 23, iv (1976): 449-453. [*NichN, Nostromo*.]

507 Curry, George. *Copperfield '70: The Story of the Making of the Omnibus 20th Century Fox Films David Copperfield*. London: Pan; New York: Ballantine, 1970. vii, 210 pp. [Incl. Frederick Brogger and Jack Pulman's screenplay, pp. 107-210.—Note also 2927.]

508 Daiches, David and John Flower. "Charles Dickens's London." *Literary Landscapes of the British Isles: A Narrative Atlas* (New York and London: Paddington Press, 1979), 56-68; et passim. [Note also "Atlas and Gazetteer," passim.]

509 Daleski, H. M. *Dickens and the Art of Analogy*. London: Faber and Faber; New York: Schocken, 1970. 249 pp. [Chaps. on unifying analogies, esp. to money and love, in *BleakH, DSon, GreatEx, LittleDor, MChuz, OliverTw, OurMF, PickP*.—Excerpt rpt. in 24, pp. 970-974.—Incorporates "The Analogical Structure of *Great Expectations*," in *Univ Teachers of Eng: Proc of the Conf Held at Bar Ilan Univ, April 1970*, ed. Ruth Nevo (Ramat Gan, Israel: Bar Ilan UP, 1970), 35-51 (note also discussion by Daleski, Nevo, et al., pp. 51-55).—Rev.: W. F. Axton, *MLQ* 33 (June 1972): 203-205; Peter Bryant, *UES* 9 (June 1971): 34-35; Keith Cushman, *LJ* 96 (1 Jan. 1971): 79; Margaret Ganz, *VS* 15 (Dec. 1971): 234-236; Stephen Gill, *N&Q* NS 18 (Nov. 1971): 425-427; Michael S. Helfand, *Novel* 5 (Winter 1972): 186-189; John Lucas, *Spec* 226 (30 Jan. 1971): 162; Grahame Smith, *Dkn* 67 (Jan. 1971): 49-51; Harvey Peter Sucksmith, *NCF* 26 (Dec. 1971): 352-357; Patricia Thomson, *RES* NS 22 (Nov. 1971): 509-512; George Wing, *DSN* 1 (Dec. 1970):

13-15; *Ch* 8 (Apr. 1971): 222; also rev. in 981, 1126, 1578, 1961, 1972, 2065, 2205, 2216.]

510 —. [*OliverTw:* Home, street, and virtue.] *Hasifrut* 2 (Jan. 1970): 333-346. [In Heb.—Eng. abst., pp. 442-440 (sic).]

511 Daniels, Steven V. "Pickwick and Dickens: Stages of Development." In 1492, pp. 56-77.

512 Das, Manoj. "Dickens: 'A Hundred Years Hence'." *Thought* (Delhi) 22 (7 Feb. 1970): 19.

513 Davalle, Peter. "What Kind of Demon Drove Dickens to Read Himself to Death?" *Times* (London) 1 Feb. 1975: 14.

514 —. "When Dickens Went to Court to Protect Mr. Scrooge." *Times* (London) 20 Dec. 1975: 12. [1844 copyright problems.]

515 Davids, E. A. "*Great Expectations:* Mrs. Joe and Estella: Reality and Fancy." *Dutch Dkn* 7, xvi (Dec. 1978): 49-62.

516 Davids, Engelina. "Forster: 'Not the Slightest Comprehension': A Letter by Dickens's Secretary." *JFNL* 1 (May 1978): 3-9. [1885 George Washington Putnam ltr.]

517 Davids, Jens-Ulrich and Peter Schmoll. " 'Now, what I want is, Facts': Romanbehandlung unter dem Aspekt der Wertung in der Sekundarstufe II am Beispiel von Dickens's *Hard Times*." *Englisch Amerikanische St* 1 (Dec. 1979): 508-538. [Eng. abst., p. 508.]

518 Davies, H. Neville. "The Tauchnitz Extra Christmas Numbers of *All the Year Round*." *Library* ser. 5, 33 (Sept. 1978): 215-222. [Attributions.]

519 Davies, James A. "Boffin's Secretary." *Dkn* 72 (Sept. 1976): 148-157.

520 —. "Edgar Johnson's Biography of Charles Dickens and Forster Research." *JFNL* 1 (Oct. 1979): 50-53.

521 —. "Forster and Dickens: The Making of Podsnap." *Dkn* 70 (Sept. 1974): 145-158.

522 —. "John Forster at the Mannings' Execution." *Dkn* 67 (Jan. 1971): 12-15.

523 —. "Negative Similarity: The Fat Boy in *The Pickwick Papers.*" *DUJ* NS 39 (Dec. 1977): 29-34.

524 —. "Striving for Honesty: An Approach to Forster's *Life.*" In 1495, pp. 34-48.

525 Davies, Rick A. "Quodlibet and Etanswill: Kennedy's and Dickens's Perceptions of the Democratic Dilemma." *TPB* 17 (July 1980): 65-66. [Infl. of *PickP* on John Pendleton Kennedy.—Abst.]

526 Davis, Dale W. "Charles Dickens and the Human Potential Movement: The Schooling of 'Soft Hearts' in *Hard Times.*" *PAPA* 1 (Fall 1974): 23. [Abst.—Note also similar abst., "The Sentimental Education of 'Soft Hearts' in *Hard Times:* A Transactional Analysis of Charles Dickens's Child-Like Norm." *Proc of the Conf of Coll Teachers of Eng of Texas* 39 (Sept. 1974): 36.]

527 Davis, Earle. "Dickens and Significant Tradition." In 1495, pp. 49-67.

528 —. "The Teaching of Dickens's *Tale of Two Cities* and *Great Expectations.*" In 1416, pp. 76-77.

529 Davis, Jim. " 'Like Comic Actors on a Stage in Heaven': Dickens, John Liston and Low Comedy." *Dkn* 74 (Sept. 1978): 161-166. [*DavidC, MChuz, OliverTw, OCShop, PickP.*]

530 Dawson, Carl. " 'The Lamp of Memory': Wordsworth and Dickens"; "*The Germ:* Aesthetic Manifesto." *Victorian Noon: English Literature in 1850* (Baltimore and London: Johns Hopkins UP, 1979), 123-143; 203-223; et passim. [*DavidC, HsldWds.*]

531 —. "Recent Studies in the Nineteenth Century." *SEL* 18 (Autumn 1978): 749-752. [Rev.-art. incl. 24, 104, 1415, 1494, 2052, 2101.]

532 Dearinger, Lowell A. "Mr. Dickens in Illinois." *Outdoor Illinois* 9 (Nov., Dec. 1970): 7-14, 17-21.

533 DeBruyn, John R. "Charles Dickens Meets the Queen: A New Look." *Dkn* 71 (May 1975): 85-90. [Abst. in *TPB* 11 (July 1974): 25.]

534 Deering, Dorothy. "Dickens's Armory for the Mind: The English Language Studies in *Household Words* and *All the Year Round.*" *DSN* 8 (Mar. 1977): 11-17.

535 DeHaven, Mary Alice. "Pip and the Fortunate Fall." *DSN* 6 (June 1975): 42-46.

535a Dehnel, Tadeusz Jan. "Dickens ciagle zywy." *Literatura na swiecie* no. 4 (Apr. 1971): 156-159. [Appreciation.]

536 Delany, Paul. "*Bleak House* and Doubting Castle." *DSN* 3 (Dec. 1972): 100-106.

537 Dennis, Carl. "Dickens's Moral Vision." *TSLL* 11 (Fall 1969): 1237-1246.

538 DeRose, Peter L. "The Symbolic Sea of *David Copperfield*." *Proc of the Conf of Coll Teachers of Eng of Texas* 41 (Sept. 1976): 45. [Abst.]

539 Dessner, Lawrence Jay. "*Great Expectations:* 'the ghost of a man's own father'." *PMLA* 91 (May 1976): 436-449.

540 —. "*Great Expectations:* The Tragic Comedy of John Wemmick." *ArielE* 6 (Apr. 1975): 65-80.

541 Devienne, Sylvette. "Le syndrome pickwickien." In 743, pp. 80-83. [Obesity and somnolence; note also *Dkn* 68 (Sept. 1972): 201.]

542 [DeVries, Duane, ed.] "The Dickens Forum: Thomas Carlyle." *DSN* 5 (Dec. 1974): 98-102. [Excerpts from Carlyle's corr. on Christmas and New Years.]

543 DeVries, Duane. *Dickens's Apprentice Years: The Making of a Novelist.* Hassocks: Harvester Press; New York: Barnes and Noble, 1976. 195 pp. [Incorporates "Two Glimpses of Dickens's Early Development as a Writer of Fiction," in 1489, pp. 55-64.—Rev.: M. Andrews, *BBkN* Aug. 1976: 609 and (a diff. rev.) *JEGP* 76 (July 1977): 463-464; Edward Costigan, *RES* NS 29 (Nov. 1978): 495-497; Elliot Engel, *MP* 77 (Aug. 1979): 102-105; John Lucas, *L&H* 5 (Spring 1979): 132-133; Jerome Meckier, *SSF* 14 (Fall 1977): 410-412; Robert L. Patten, *DSN* 8 (June 1977): 48-51; Peter Preston, *N&Q* NS 26 (Aug. 1979): 352-353; Andrew Sanders, *THES* 30 July 1976: 16; F. S. Schwarzbach, *Dkn* 72 (May 1976): 106-108; *Ch* 13 (Feb. 1977): 1594; also rev. in 981, 1299.]

544 —. "Reviews—Paperback Editions: *Great Expectations.*" *DSN* 5 (June 1974): 56-61. [Incl. 43, 48, 54.]

545 D[eVries], D[uane]. "Yankee Notes for English Circulation: Or Boz

in A-Merry-Key." *DSN* 7 (Dec. 1976): 97-98. [1842 song.—Note also Ada Nisbet's comments, 8 (Mar. 1977): 27-29, and 815, pp. 203-204.]

546 Dewhurst, Keith. "What the Dickens?" *Guardian Weekly* 6 June 1970: 14. [Appreciation.]

547 D'Hangest, G. "Dickens et les personnages de *Great Expectations*." *EA* 24 (Apr.-June 1971): 126-146.

548 Dias, Earl J. "Charles Dickens: Very Big in Boston." *Yankee* 39 (Dec. 1975): 86-89, 217. [1842 visit.]

549 Dickens, Monica. *An Open Book* (London: Heinemann; New York: Mayflower, 1978), passim.

550 [Dickens, Peter.] "[Remarks at the] Opening of the Suzannet Rooms." *Dkn* 67 (Sept. 1971): 188-191.

551 Diedrick, James. "Dickens's Alter-Ego in *Bleak House:* The Importance of Lawrence Boythorn." *DSN* 9 (June 1978): 37-40.

552 Dilnot, A. F. "The Case of Mr. Jaggers." *EIC* 25 (Oct. 1975): 437-443. [Defense; note also responses by A. L. French, 26 (July 1976): 278-282 and by J. C. Maxwell, Jan. 1976, p. 98.]

553 —. "Dickens to Whitehead: A Newly-Discovered Letter." *Dkn* 73 (Jan. 1977): 33-35.

554 —. "Dickens's Early Fiction and the Idea of Practical Utility." *SoRA* 8 (June 1975): 141-151. [*HardT, OliverTw, NichN, OCShop*.]

555 Dimov, Leonid. "Pickwick si insulele fericite." *RoLit* 5, vii (Feb. 1972): 28. [Humor.]

556 Diskin, Patrick. "The Literary Background of *The Old Curiosity Shop*." *N&Q* NS 21 (June 1974): 210-213.

557 Dobie, Ann B. "Early Stream-of-Consciousness Writing: *Great Expectations*." *NCF* 25 (Mar. 1971): 405-416.

558 Dobrin, David N. "A Dickens Concordance? Why Not a Comsurvance?" *DSN* 11 (June 1980): 53-54. [Comsurvance = computer survey concordance.]

559 —. "A Note on Jenny Wren's Name." *DSN* 9 (June 1978): 48-49.

560 Dobrinsky, Joseph. *La jeuness de Somerset Maugham (1874-1903).* EA, 62 ([Paris] : Didier, [1976]), passim. [D's infl.]

561 Dobrzycka, Irena. *Karol Dickens.* Warsaw: Wiedza Powszechna, 1972. 326 pp. [Survey of life and work with chaps. on *BleakH, DavidC. GreatEx. HardT, OurMF.*—Rev.: Wislawa Szymborska, *ZLit* no. 47 (1972): 11.]

562 Doggart, James. "Dickens and the Doctors: A Centenary Causerie." *Practitioner* 204 (Mar. 1970): 449-453.

563 Donoghue, Denis. "The English Dickens and *Dombey and Son.*" In 1419, pp. 1-21.

564 Dontchev, Nicolaï. "Dickens en Bulgarie." In 743, pp. 130-135.

565 Dorrell, Donald. "The Nineteenth Century Novel in the 1970 Secondary School." In 1416, pp. 70-75.

566 Drabble, Margaret. *A Writer's Britain: Landscape in Literature,* photos. Jorge Lewinski (London: Thames and Hudson; New York: Knopf, 1979), 206-213; et passim.

567 Drake, Dana B. "Charles Dickens." *Don Quijote in World Literature: A Selective, Annotated Bibliography.* GRLH, 187 (New York and London: Garland, 1980), III, 144-149; et passim.

568 Drew, Philip. " 'Childe Roland' and the Urban Wilderness." *BSNotes* 8 (Dec. 1978): 19-22. [Browning and *DavidC, DSon.*]

569 Driver, Clive E., comp. *A Selection from Our Shelves: Books, Manuscripts and Drawings from the Philip H. & A. S. W. Rosenbach Foundation Museum* ([Philadelphia: The Museum, 1973]), items 73-75. [Describes Cruikshank drawing and portions of the *PickP* and *NichN* mss. in the coll.]

570 Duckworth, Alistair M. "*Little Dorrit* and the Question of Closure." *NCF* 33 (June 1978): 110-130. [Rev. of issue: F. S. Schwarzbach, *DSN* 11 (Sept. 1980): 89-92.]

571 Duff, Ian C. "Appalling Rush and Tremble: On the Metaphorical Use of the Railway," in *Critical Dimensions: English German and Comparative Literature Essays in Honour of Aurelio Zanco,* ed. Mario Curreli and Alberto Martino. Critical Dimensions, 3 (Cuneo, Italy: SASTE, 1978), 447-463. [Incl. "MugJ," *DSon.*]

572 Duncan, Robert W. "Madame Defarge's Knitting." *N&Q* NS 24 (July-Aug. 1977): 365.

573 Dunn, Albert A. "The Altered Ending of *Great Expectations:* A Note on Bibliography and First-Person Narration." *DSN* 9 (June 1978): 40-42.

574 —. "Time and Design in *David Copperfield.*" *ES* 59 (June 1978): 225-236.

575 —. "Time, Character, and Narration in the Victorian Novel." *Eng Symp Papers* 4 (1974): 1-40. [Touches on, with comparisons to George Eliot, *BleakH, DavidC, DSon, GreatEx, HardT, LittleDor, OliverTw.*]

576 Dunn, Frank T., comp. *A Cumulative Analytical Index to the Dickensian, 1905-74,* pref. Michael Slater, index to illus. comp. Mary Ford and Michael Slater. Hassocks: Harvester Press, 1976. xi, 199 pp. [Note also reissue in microfiche of *Dkn,* 1905-1974, by Harvester Press.—Rev.: M. D. Anderson, *Indexer* 10 (Apr. 1977): 148-149; Duane DeVries, *Dkn* 72 (Sept. 1976): 173-175; Richard J. Dunn, *DSN* 7 (Sept. 1976): 79-80; K. J. Fielding, *MLR* 72 (Oct. 1977): 926; Mollie Hardwick, *B&B* 21 (Mar. 1976): 42-43; Graham Storey, *TLS* 2 Apr. 1976: 403.]

577 —. "Indexing the *Dickensian* 1905-74." *Dkn* 71 (Sept. 1975): 131-135.

578 Dunn, Richard J., comp. "Charles Dickens." *The English Novel: Twentieth Century Criticism* (Chicago: Swallow Press, 1976), 33-53.

579 —. "David Copperfield's Carlylean Retailoring." In 1496, pp. 95-114.

580 —. "Dickens and Mayhew Once More." *NCF* 25 (Dec. 1970): 348-353. [*BleakH.*]

581 —. "Dickens, Carlyle, and the *Hard Times* Dedication." *DSN* 2 (Sept. 1971): 90-92. [See Rodgers Tarr's response, 3 (Mar. 1972): 25-27, and Dunn's reply, June, pp. 60-61.]

582 —. "Far, Far Better Things: Dickens's Later Endings." In 1495, pp. 221-236.

583 —. " 'Illuminating Distortions' and the Dickens Critics." *Review* 1 (1979): 91-104. [Rev.-art. on 853, 1415, 1493, 1494, 1659, 1984, 2052, 2101.]

584 —. "Imaginative Dickens: A Review Article." _SNNTS_ 8 (Summer 1976): 223-233. [Rev.-art. on 340, 1034, 1881.]

585 —. "In Pursuit of the Dolly Varden." _Dkn_ 74 (Jan. 1978): 22-24. [Note also 708 and 815, pp. 204-205.]

586 Duque, Pedro J. "Dickens en Baroja." _Arbor_ 88 (June 1974): 93-106. [D's infl.]

587 Dutton, A. R. "Jonson and David Copperfield: Dickens and Bartholomew Fair." _ELN_ 16 (Mar. 1979): 227-232.

588 Dutu, Alexandru. "Dickens în România." _St de literatura universala_ 16 (1970): 45-51. [Also incl. 360 (art. on _MEDrood_), 1172, 1957.]

589 Dvorak, Wilfred P. "Noddy Boffin's Dutch Bottle." _DSN_ 9 (Mar. 1978): 19-23.

590 (Dyson, A. E., ed. _Dickens: Modern Judgements._ 1968.) [Rev. in 2138.]

591 (—, ed. _Dickens: Bleak House: A Casebook._ 1969.) [Note also Amer. ed., Nashville: Aurora, 1970.—Rev.: Trevor Blount, _Dkn_ 66 (Jan. 1970): 57-59; Norman Friedman, _DSN_ 4 (Dec. 1973): 109-113; Lauriat Lane, Jr., _HAB_ 21 (Summer 1970): 66-68; W. D. Maxwell-Mahon, _UES_ 8 (Mar. 1970): 47-48; also rev. in 2138, 2204.]

592 —. _The Inimitable Dickens: A Reading of the Novels._ London: Macmillan; New York: St. Martin's Press, 1970. 303 pp. [Chaps. on all the novels except _NichN, OliverTw, PickP._—Incorporates material from 591; _Dkn,_ 1963, 1969; _CritQ,_ 1967 and "The Case for Dombey Senior," _Novel_ 2 (Winter 1969): 123-134 and "_Edwin Drood:_ A Horrible Wonder Apart," _CritQ_ 11 (Winter 1969): 138-157.—Rev.: Elizabeth Bowen, _Spec_ 224 (30 May 1970): 713; John Carey, _Lstr_ 83 (28 May 1970): 724-725; T. J. Cribb, _RES_ NS 22 (Aug. 1971): 388-389; Keith Cushman, _LJ_ 95 (15 Oct. 1970): 3473; M. A. Fido, _VS_ 15 (Sept. 1971): 101-102; Bert G. Hornback, _DSN_ 1 (Dec. 1970): 11-13; V. S. Pritchett, _NewSt_ 79 (5 June 1970): 807-808; Raymond Williams, _Guardian Weekly_ 6 June 1970: 18; _Booklist_ 67 (1 Dec. 1970): 284; _Ch_ 7 (Nov. 1970): 1230; _Ecn_ 235 (20 June 1970): 54; _TLS_ 4 June 1970: 597-598; also rev. in 182 (Aug. 1971), 198, 314, 948, 981, 1126, 1961, 1972, 2065, 2138, 2200.]

593 Eagle, Dorothy and Hilary Carnell, comps. *The Oxford Literary Guide to the British Isles* (Oxford: Clarendon Press, 1977), passim. [Rev.: Edward G. Preston, *Dkn* 74 (Jan. 1978): 52-53.]

594 Eagleton, Mary and David Pierce. "Charles Dickens." *Attitudes to Class in the English Novel from Walter Scott to David Storey* (London: Thames and Hudson, 1979), 41-47; et passim. [Incl. *DSon, HardT.*]

595 Eagleton, Terry. "Charles Dickens." *Criticism and Ideology: A Study in Marxist Literary Theory* (London: NLB; Atlantic Highlands, N.J.: Humanities Press, 1977), 125-130; et passim.

596 Easson, Angus. *Charles Dickens's Hard Times: Critical Commentary and Notes.* London: Univ. of London Press, 1973. 71 pp. [Rev.: P. A. Burger, *UES* 12 (Sept. 1974): 10-11; Ivan Melada, *DSN* 6 (June 1975): 64-66; Anne Smith, *Dkn* 70 (Jan. 1974): 62-63.]

597 —. "Dialect in Dickens's *Hard Times*." *N&Q* NS 23 (Sept. 1976): 412-413. [Source.]

598 —. "Dickens's Marchioness Again." *MLR* 65 (July 1970): 517-519.

599 —. *Elizabeth Gaskell* (London, Boston, Henley: Routledge and Kegan Paul, 1979), passim.

600 —. " 'I, Elizabeth Dickens': Light on John Dickens's Legacy." *Dkn* 67 (Jan. 1971): 35-40. [John Dickens not released from prison by mother's legacy.]

601 —. "John Chivery and the Wounded Strephon: A Pastoral Element in *Little Dorrit*." *DUJ* 67 (June 1975): 165-169.

602 —. "John Dickens and the Navy Pay Office." *Dkn* 70 (Jan. 1974): 35-45.

603 —. "Marshalsea Prisoners: Mr. Dorrit and Mr. Hemens." In 1491, pp. 77-86.

604 —. "The Mythic Sorrows of Charles Dickens." *L&H* no. 1 (Mar. 1975): 49-61. [*DavidC.*]

605 —. "*The Old Curiosity Shop*: From Manuscript to Print." In 1489, pp. 93-128.

606 Eastwood, W. *Brodie's Notes on Charles Dickens's David Copperfield,*

rev. Norman T. Carrington. London, etc.: Pan Books, 1977. vii, 97 pp. [Previous ed. 1967.]

607 Edler, Erich. *Die Anfänge des sozialen Romans und der sozialen Novelle in Deutschland.* St. zur Philosophie und Literatur des neunzehnten Jahrhunderts, 34 (Frankfurt: Klostermann, 1977), passim.

608 Edward, P. D. *Anthony Trollope, His Art and His Scope* (St. Lucia: Univ. of Queensland Press, 1977; New York: St. Martin's Press; Hassocks: Harvester Press, 1978), passim.

609 Edwards, C. Hines, Jr. "Three Literary Parallels to Faulkner's 'A Rose for Emily'." *NMW* 7 (Spring 1974): 20-25. [Incl. *GreatEx.*]

610 Edwards, Jessie K. "The Mode of Address in Victorian Fiction: Dickens, Wilde, and Stevenson." *BSUF* 19 (Winter 1978): 41-47. [Incl. *TaleTwoC.*]

611 Eggert, Paul. "The Real Esther Summerson." *DSN* 11 (Sept. 1980): 74-81.

612 Eigner, Edwin M. "Bulwer-Lytton and the Changed Ending of *Great Expectations*." *NCF* 25 (June 1970): 104-108.

613 —. *The Metaphysical Novel in England and America: Dickens, Bulwer, Melville, and Hawthorne.* Berkeley, Los Angeles, London: Univ. of California Press, 1978. x, 237 pp. [Esp. *BleakH, DavidC, LittleDor, OCSbop, OurMF.*—Rev.: Nina Baym, *JEGP* 77 (Oct. 1978): 601-603; A. M. C. Brown, *Dkn* 75 (Summer 1979): 106-107; Alan Burke, *DSN* 10 (June-Sept. 1979): 71-73; Richard J. Kelly, *LJ* 103 (1 Apr. 1978): 752; Timothy Kidd, *THES* 15 Sept. 1978: 12; Richard A. Levine, *SNNTS* 11 (Spring 1979): 119-120; Ellen Moers, *AL* 50 (Nov. 1978): 522-523; Roger B. Salomon, *NCF* 33 (Dec. 1978): 384-387; Eric J. Sundquist, *SCR* 13 (Fall 1980): 104-106; C. S. B. Swann, *JAmS* 14 (Aug. 1980): 330-331; *Ch* 15 (Oct. 1978): 1048-1049; also rev. in 981.]

614 Eisenstein, Sergei. "Dickens, Griffith, and the Film Today," trans. Jay Leyda, in *Film and/as Literature,* ed. John Harrington (Englewood Cliffs, N.J.: Prentice-Hall, 1977), 122-136. [Rpt. from his *Film Form,* 1949.—Also rpt. in *Film Theory and Criticism: Introductory Readings,* ed. Gerald Mast and Marshall Cohen (New York, London, Toronto: Oxford UP, 1974), 302-313, in *Film and the Liberal Arts,* ed. T. J. Ross (New York: Holt, Rinehart and Winston, 1970), 103-110, and excerpt on *TaleTwoC* rpt. in 205, pp.

100-104.–Note also "Dickens, Griffith et nous," trans. Luda and Jean Schnitzer, *Cahiers du cinéma* no. 231 (Aug.-Sept. 1971): 16-22; no. 232 (Oct. 1971): 24-26, 35-42; no. 233 (Nov. 1971): 11-18; nos. 234-235 (Dec. 1971-Feb. 1972): 27-42.]

615 Elektorowicz, Leszek. "Dickens pesymista?" *Motywy zachodnie* (Cracow: Wydawnictow, 1973), 130-134. [*HardT.*]

616 Eliot, George. *Letters,* ed. Gordon S. Haight (New Haven and London: Yale UP, 1978), VIII-IX, passim.

617 Eliot, T. S. ["Wilkie Collins and Dickens."] *TLS* 5 Aug. 1977: 960. [Excerpt rpt. from 4 Aug. 1927; item partly or wholly rpt. in 2064, pp. 278-280, in 2082, pp. 133-141, and in 2331, pp. 151-152.]

618 Elliott, Jean. "[Survey of periodical literature in] The Year's Work in Dickens Studies 1978." *Dkn* 76 (Spring 1980): 53-57. [Note also 143.]

619 Ellis, Katherine. "Paradise Lost: The Limits of Domesticity in the Nineteenth-Century Novel." *Feminist St* 2, ii-iii (1975): 55-63. [Incl. *GreatEx.*]

620 Elmalih, N. "Valeurs et récit: *Oliver Twist,*" in *Récit et roman: Formes du roman anglais du XVIe au XXe siècle.* Soc. des Anglicistes de l'Enseignment Supérieur, Actes du Congrès de Dijon, 1968; EA, 42 (Paris: Didier, 1972), 53-61.

621 Emerson, Ralph Waldo. "Dickens." *Emerson's Literary Criticism,* ed. Eric W. Carlson (Lincoln and London: Univ. of Nebraska Press, 1979), 210-211. [Journal entries of 1839 (on *OliverTw*) and 1842 (on *AmerN*).–2nd rpt. in 2064, p. 62.]

622 Emmett, V. J., Jr. "The Endings of *Great Expectations.*" *NDQ* 41 (Autumn 1973): 5-11.

623 –. "Major Trends in Dickens Criticism." In 1416, pp. 82-83. [For non-specialist.]

624 Engel, Elliot. "Dickens's Obscure Childhood in Pre-Forster Biography." *Dkn* 73 (Jan. 1976): 2-12.

625 –. "The Wizard of Boz: G. K. Chesterton and Dickensian Humour." *CRev* 3 (Spring-Summer 1977): 211-229.

626 Engel, Monroe. "A Kind of Allegory: *The Old Curiosity Shop*," in *The Interpretation of Narrative: Theory and Practice*, ed. Morton W. Bloomfield. HSE, 1 (Cambridge: Harvard UP, 1970), 135-149.

627 Enzensberger, Christian. "Das Nützliche in Wirklichkeit: Charles Dickens's *Oliver Twist*." *Literatur und Interesse: Eine politische Ästhetic mit zwei Beispielen aus der englischen Literatur* (Munich and Vienna: Hanser, 1977), II, 91-158.

628 Erhart, Virginia. "Dickens: Crónica de un centenario." *Los libros* (Buenos Aires) 2 (Dec. 1970): 14, 16.

629 Ericksen, Donald H. "Demonic Imagery and the Quest for Identity in Dickens's *Great Expectations*." *Illinois Q* 33 (Sept. 1970): 4-11.

630 —. "Harold Skimpole: Dickens and the Early 'Art for Art's Sake' Movement." *JEGP* 72 (Jan. 1973): 48-59.

631 Evans, Edward J. "The Established Self: The American Episodes of *Martin Chuzzlewit*." In 1493, pp. 59-73.

632 Evans, Hilary and Mary. "Cruikshank and Dickens." *The Man Who Drew the Drunkard's Daughter: The Life and Art of George Cruikshank, 1792-1878* (London: Frederick Muller; New York: S. G. Phillips, 1978), 81-85; et passim. [Rev.: Anthony Burton, *Dkn* 74 (Sept. 1978): 174-175.]

633 Everett, Barbara. "A Visit to *Burnt Norton*." *CritQ* 16 (Autumn 1974): 199-224. [Incl. *TaleTwoC.*]

634 Faber, Richard. "Dickens." *Proper Stations: Class in Victorian Fiction* (London: Faber and Faber, 1971), 68-82. [Esp. *BleakH, DSon, GreatEx, LittleDor, OurMF.*—Rev.: B[ryan] H[ulse], *Dkn* 68 (May 1972): 130; P. J. Keating, *DSN* 5 (Mar. 1974): 21-24.]

635 Fadem, Richard. "*Great Expectations* and the Mnemonics of Pain," in *Humanitas: Essays in Honor of Ralph Ross*, [ed. Quincy Howe, Jr.] (Claremont, Cal.: Scripps Coll., 1977), 34-53.

636 Fader, Daniel. *The Periodical Context of English Literature 1708-1907* (Ann Arbor: Univ. Microfilms, 1971), 26-50. [*AllYR, HsldWds*, esp. *BleakH.*—Rev.: Lance Schachterle, *DSN* 4 (Dec. 1973): 98-100.]

637 Fanger, Donald. "Dickens and Gogol: Energies of the Word," in *Veins of Humor*, ed. Harry Levin. HSE, 3 (Cambridge: Harvard

UP, 1972), 131-145. [Incl. *OurMF, BleakH, OliverTw.*]

638 Farrag, Aida. "Zola, Dickens, and Spontaneous Combustion Again." *RomN* 19 (Winter 1978): 190-195. [*BleakH.*]

639 Farrell, J. "On Safari—Charles Dickens in Italy." *J of the Assn of Teachers of Italian* (Bath) 14 (1974): 8-10.

640 Farrell, John P. "Dickens and the Influence of Wordsworth." In 1416, pp. 58-62. [*OurMF.*]

641 Farrow, Anthony P. "The Cosmic Point of View in *Bleak House.*" *Cithara* 13 (May 1974): 34-45.

642 Faulkner, Peter. "The Humanity of Dickens." *Humanist* (England) 85 (July 1970): 198-199. [*BleakH.*]

643 Fawkner, Harald William. *Animation and Reification in Dickens's Vision of the Life-Denying Society.* St.anglistica upsaliensia, 31. Uppsala: [Uppsala Univ.], 1977. 164 pp. [Uppsala diss.—Rev.: Erik Frykman, *Samlaren* 98 (1977): 132; Sven-Johan Spanberg, *SN* 51, ii (1979): 341-343; also rev. in 981.]

644 Feaver, William. " 'At It Again': Aspects of Cruikshank's Later Work." In 1510, pp. 249-258.

645 Feltes, N. N. "Community and the Limits of Liability in Two Mid-Victorian Novels." *VS* 17 (June 1974): 355-369. [George Eliot's *Mill on the Floss, LittleDor.*]

646 —. " 'The Greatest Plague of Life': Dickens, Masters and Servants." *L&H* no. 8 (Autumn 1978): 197-213. [*BleakH, DavidC, DSon, LittleDor, OCShop.*—Note also Bruce Robbins's response, 5 (Autumn 1979): 216-219.]

647 —. "To Saunter, to Hurry: Dickens, Time, and Industrial Capitalism." *VS* 20 (Spring 1977): 245-267. [*DSon, OCShop.*]

648 Fenstermaker, John J. *Charles Dickens, 1940-1975: An Analytical Subject Index to Periodical Criticism of the Novels and Christmas Books.* Boston: G. K. Hall; London: Prior, 1979. xix, 302 pp. [Note also "Dickens Criticism 1940-1970: An Analytical Subject Index," *DAI* 34 (Dec. 1973): 3340A (Ohio State).—Rev.: Richard J. **Dunn**, *AEB* 4, i (1980): 67-73; Nancy Heiser, *LJ* 104 (Aug. 1979): 1551; Dorey Schmidt, *JPC* 13 (Fall 1979): 371-372; *Ch* 16 (Oct. 1979): 992.]

649 Ferns, John. *"Oliver Twist:* Destruction of Love." *QQ* 79 (Spring 1972): 87-92.

650 Ferris, Norren. "Circumlocution in *David Copperfield.*" *DSN* 9 (June 1978): 43-46.

651 Festa, Conrad, ed. *Victorians Institute Journal,* no. 1 (July 1972). [Incl. 113, 381, 886, 1268.—Rev.: Harry Epstein, *DSN* 3 (Dec. 1972): 109-110.]

652 (Fido, Martin. *Charles Dickens.* 1968.) [Rev.: S. C. Gill, *N&Q* NS 18 (Feb. 1971): 80; also rev. in 2138.]

653 —. *Charles Dickens: An Authentic Account of His Life and Times.* [London and New York] : Hamlyn, [1970] ; rpt. 1973. 140 pp. [Rev.: Robert Greacen, *B&B* 18 (July 1973): 88; also rev. in 314, 2237.]

654 Field, J. C. "Fantasy and Flaw in *The Old Curiosity Shop.*" *RLV* 35, vi (1969): 609-622.

655 Fielding, K. J. "Dickens as J. T. Danson Knew Him." *Dkn* 68 (Sept. 1972): 151-161.

656 —. "1870-1900: Forster and Reaction." *Dkn* 66 (May 1970): 85-100. [Special no. on D's reputation 1870-1970.—For revs. see 448.]

657 —. "Forster: Critic of Fiction." *Dkn* 70 (Sept. 1974): 159-170.

658 [Fielding] , K. J. *W. J. Carlton: A Tribute, with a List of His Writings on Dickens.* [N.p.] : Privately Printed, [1973] . 6 pp. [Also as *Dkn* 69 (Sept. 1973): Supp.—Note also obit. by L[eslie] C. S[taples] , pp. 201-203.]

659 Fielding, K. J. and A. W. Brice. "*Bleak House* and the Graveyard." In 1496, pp. 115-139.

660 — and Anne Smith. "*Hard Times* and the Factory Controversy: Dickens vs. Harriet Martineau." In 1419, pp. 22-45.

661 Filmer, Paul. "Dickens, Pickwick and Realism: On the Importance of Language to Socio-Literary Relations," in *The Sociology of Literature: Applied Studies,* ed. Diana Laurenson. Sociological Rev. Monograph, 26 (Keele: Univ. of Keele, 1978), 64-91.

662 Findlater, Richard. *Joe Grimaldi: His Life and Theatre*, 2nd ed. (Cambridge, etc.: Cambridge UP, 1978), 244-248.

663 Fischer, Lois H. "Charles Dickens (1812-1870)." *A Literary Gazetteer of England* (New York, London, etc.: McGraw-Hill, 1980), 432-442; et passim.

664 Fisher, Benjamin Franklin, IV. "Dickens and Poe: *Pickwick* and 'Ligeia'." *PoeS* 6 (June 1973): 14-16.

665 —. "Edwin's Mystery and Its History: Or, Another Look at Datchery." *Mystery Francier* 4 (1980): 6-8. [Datchery is Bazzard.]

666 —. "Paperback Editions of *The Mystery of Edwin Drood*." *DSN* 8 (Mar. 1977): 19-22.

667 —. "Reviews—Paperback Editions: *Our Mutual Friend*." *DSN* 5 (Sept. 1974): 87-90. [Incl. 76.]

668 — and J. Turow. "Dickens and Fire Imagery." *RLV* 40, iv (1974): 359-370. [*BleakH, DSon, GreatEx, HardT, MEDrood, OCShop, OurMF, PickP*.]

669 FitzGerald, Edward. *FitzGerald to His Friends: Selected Letters*, ed. Alethea Hayter (London: Scolar Press, 1979), passim.

670 Fitzsimons, Raymund. *Garish Lights: The Public Reading Tours of Charles Dickens*. Philadelphia: Lippincott, 1970. 192 pp. [Also pub. as *The Charles Dickens Show* (London: Bles, 1970).—Rev.: Philip Collins, *DSN* 2 (Dec. 1971): 102-103; M. S. Cosgrave, *Horn Book* 47 (Feb. 1971): 72; Keith Cushman, *LJ* 96 (1 Mar. 1971): 836; John Greaves, *Dkn* 67 (Jan. 1971): 54-55; John K. Hutchens, *SatR* 53 (19 Dec. 1970): 30; *Ecn* 237 (21 Nov. 1970): xxi; *Times* (London) 5 Nov. 1970: 14; *TLS* 25 Dec. 1970: 1522; also rev. in 1956, 1961, 2205, 2216.]

671 Flamm, Dudley. "The Prosecutor Within: Dickens's Final Explanation." *Dkn* 66 (Jan. 1970): 16-23. ["GS'sExpl."]

672 Fleishman, Avrom. "The City and the River: Dickens's Symbolic Landscape." In 131, pp. 111-126. [*LittleDor, OurMF*.]

673 —. "Dickens," in *McGraw-Hill Encyclopedia of World Biography* (New York: McGraw-Hill, 1973), III, 367-370.

674 —. "Dickens: Vision of Revolution." *The English Historical Novel:*

Walter Scott to Virginia Woolf (Baltimore: Johns Hopkins Press, 1971), 102-126. [*BarnR, TaleTwoC.*—Rev.: H. M. Leicester, Jr., and Murray Baumgarten, *DSN* 3 (Dec. 1972): 114-118.]

675 —. "The Fictions of Autobiographical Fiction." *Genre* 9 (Spring 1976): 73-86. [Incl. *DavidC.*]

676 —. "Master and Servant in *Little Dorrit.*" *Fiction and the Ways of Knowing: Essays on British Novels* (Austin and London: Univ. of Texas Press, 1978), 64-73. [Rpt. with slight revisions from *SEL* 14 (Autumn 1974): 575-586.]

677 Fleissner, Robert F. "Charles Dickens and His China: The Architecture of *Bleak House.*" *TkR* 3 (Oct. 1972): 159-170. [Author's note: "Largely a parody of over-serious criticism."]

678 —. "Charles Dickens and Sinclair Lewis: An Exordium." *Sinclair Lewis NL* 3 (1971): 10-13. [*BleakH, DSon, GreatEx, OCShop, PickP, PictIt.*]

679 —. "Dickens and the Backwoodsman: An Apocryphal Tale." *DSN* 7 (Dec. 1976): 107-108.

680 —. "Dickens on Slavery: *Great Expectations* as a Novel for Black Students." *Negro Hist Bull* 38 (Dec. 1975): 478-479. [Also in *Central State Univ Alumni J* 1 (Sept. 1975): 4-6.]

681 —. "Dickens's *American Notes:* A New Locale." *AN&Q* 13 (Feb. 1975): 84-86. [Xenia, Ohio.]

682 —. "Dickens's *Dombey and Son,* Chapter XXII." *Expl* 32 (Dec. 1973): item 26.

683 —. "A Drood Awakening." *DSN* 11 (Mar. 1980): 17-19. [Question of Drood's death.]

684 —. "*Drood* the Obscure: The Evidence of the Names." *ArmD* 13 (Winter 1980): 12-16.

685 —. "The Germination of 'Rosebud' in *Citizen Kane.*" *Names* 27 (Dec. 1979): 283-284. [The Welles film and *MEDrood.*]

686 —. "Of Dickensian Bondage: A Probe." *RS* 48 (Mar. 1980): 50-56. [Infl. on Maugham.]

687 —. "Salinger's Caulfield: A Refraction fo Copperfield and His Caul."

NConL 3 (May 1973): 5-7.

688 —. " 'Something out of Dickens' in Sinclair Lewis." *BNYPL* 74 (Nov. 1970): 607-616.

689 —. "The Two Lebanons of Dickens." *Dayton Daily News* (*Leisure* supp.) 24 May 1970: 17. [Lebanon, Ohio, and New Lebanon, N.Y., in *AmerN*.]

690 Fletcher, Geoffrey. *The London Dickens Knew.* London: Hutchinson, 1970. 111 pp. [Rev.: Joseph H. Gardner, *DSN* 2 (Sept. 1971): 84-86.—Also rev. in 314, 1961, 2237.]

691 Fletcher, John. "Literature and the Problem of Evil." *Theology* 79 (Sept. 1976): 274-280. [Incl. *BleakH*.]

692 Flibbert, Joseph T. "Dickens and the French Debate over Realism 1838-1856." *CL* 23 (Winter 1971): 18-31.

693 Flower, Sibylla Jane. "Charles Dickens and Edward Bulwer-Lytton." *Dkn* 69 (May 1973): 79-89.

694 Fluchère, Henri. "Lecture et relecture de *Great Expectations*." In 743, pp. 62-77.

695 Flynn, James. "Miss Havisham." *RecL* 1 (Fall 1972): 40-49.

696 Flynn, Thomas Edward. "Dickens and the Pathos of Freedom." *Humanitas* 15 (May 1979): 209-225. [Esp. *OliverTw*.]

697 Ford, George H. "The Brass Bassoon in *Bleak House*." *Dkn* 68 (May 1972): 104.

698 —. "Dickens and One of his Readers." In 412a, pp. 35-36, 39.

699 —. "Dickens and the Voices of Time." In 1419, pp. 46-66. [*BleakH, CCarol, DavidC, GreatEx, LittleDor, PickP*.]

700 —. "Dickens in the 1960s." *Dkn* 66 (May 1970): 163-182. [Special no. on D's reputation 1870-1970.—For revs. see 448.]

701 —. "Stern Hebrews Who Laugh: Further Thoughts on Carlyle and Dickens," in *Carlyle Past and Present: A Collection of New Essays,* ed. K. J. Fielding and Rodger L. Tarr (London: Vision Press; New York: Barnes and Noble, 1976), 112-126. [Mentions *PickP, DavidC, DSon, BleakH, TaleTwoC, HardT, LittleDor, Chimes,*

CStories.—Incl. full text, here 1st pub., of Carlyle's ltr. on D's death.—Rev. of book: Richard J. Dunn, *Dkn* 73 (Jan. 1977): 46-47.]

702 —. "[Toast at] The London Birthday Dinner." *Dkn* 67 (May 1971): 124-126.

703 —. "[Toast at] The London Birthday Dinner." *Dkn* 72 (May 1976): 121-123.

704 — interviewed by John Barbour. "A Happy Obsession for Dickens." *Contemporary* (supp. to *Denver Post*) 6 Feb. 1977: 18. [AP Feature story; see also, e.g., *New Orleans Times-Picayune* 6 Feb. 1977: H3; etc.]

705 Forson, Daniel. "Dickens og ástir bans." *Lesbók Morgunblathsins* 8 Mar. 1970: 1-2, 10-11. [Ellen Ternan.]

706 Forster, Jean-Paul. [*The Real David Copperfield*.] *Robert Graves et la dualité du réel.* Pub. Univ. Européennes, ser. 14: Langue et littérature anglo-saxonnes, 24 (Bern: Herbert Lang; Frankfurt: Peter Lang, 1975), 145-151. [On Graves's 1933 condensation.]

707 Forsyte, Charles (pseud.). *The Decoding of Edwin Drood.* New York: Scribners; London: Gollancz, 1980. 222 pp. [Critical treatment of subject plus new conclusion.—Rev.: Peter Davalle, *Times* (London) 12 June 1980: 20; Peter Dollard, *LJ* 105 (Aug. 1980): 1635; C[onnie] F[letcher], *Booklist* 77 (1 Nov. 1980): 387; Hilary Spurling, *TES* 3 Oct. 1980: 25.]

708 Foster, Vanda. "The Dolly Varden." *Dkn* 73 (Jan. 1977): 19-24. [In Victorian fashion and popular culture.—Note also 585 and 815, pp. 204-205.]

709 Fowler, Roger. *Linguistics and the Novel* (London: Methuen; Totowa, N.J.: Rowman and Littlefield, 1977), passim. [Esp. *HardT*.]

710 Frank, Joseph. "Internal vs. External Combustion: Dickens's *Bleak House* and Shaw's *Major Barbara* and *Heartbreak House*." In 1593, pp. 126-134.

711 Frank, Lawrence. "Dickens's *A Tale of Two Cities:* The Poetics of Impasse." *AI* 36 (Fall 1979): 215-244.

712 —. "The Intelligibility of Madness in *Our Mutual Friend* and *The Mystery of Edwin Drood*." In 1493, pp. 150-195. [Gothic.]

713 —. " 'Through a Glass Darkly': Esther Summerson and *Bleak House*." In 1492, pp. 91-112.

714 Franklin, Stephen L. "Dickens and Time: The Clock Without Hands." In 1492, pp. 1-35. [Esp. *BarnR, BleakH, DavidC, GreatEx, MEDrood, OCShop*.]

715 Franko, Juraj, comp. *Charles Dickens: Výberová bibliografia*. Bratislava: Mest. Kniznica, 1972. 25 pp.

716 Freese, Peter. "Zwei unbekannte Verweise in J. D. Salingers *The Catcher in the Rye:* Charles Dickens und Ring Lardner." *Archiv* 211, i (1974): 68-72. [*DavidC.*]

717 French, A. L. "Beating and Cringing: *Great Expectations*." *EIC* 24 (Apr. 1974): 147-168.

718 —. "Old Pip: The Ending of *Great Expectations*." *EIC* 29 (Oct. 1979): 357-360.

719 French, Warren G. "The Greening of London Town." *KanQ* 7 (Fall 1975): 99-102. [*CCarol.*]

720 Friedberg, Joan B. "Alienation and Integration in *Barnaby Rudge*." *DSN* 11 (Mar. 1980): 11-15.

721 Friedberg, Maurice. *A Decade of Euphoria: Western Literature in Post-Stalin Russia, 1954-64* (Bloomington: Indiana UP, 1977), passim. [D most widely pub. Eng. lang. writer in USSR.]

722 Friedman, Norman. "Pluralism Exemplified: *Great Expectations* and *The Great Gatsby*"; "The Shadow and the Sun: Archetypes in *Bleak House*." *Form and Meaning in Fiction* (Athens: Univ. of Georgia Press, 1975), 21-41; 359-379. [1st rpt. with changes from *BSUF*, 1957, 2nd from *Accent*, 1954.—Rev.: Philip Weinstein, *DSN* 8 (Sept. 1977): 87-89.]

723 Friedman, Stanley. "Another Possible Source for Dickens's Miss Havisham." *VN* no. 39 (Spring 1971): 24-25.

724 —. "Dickens's Mid-Victorian Theodicy: *David Copperfield*." In 1495, pp. 128-150.

725 —. "Kotzebue's *The Stranger* in *David Copperfield*." *DSN* 9 (June 1978): 49-50.

726 —. "A Loose Thread in *Our Mutual Friend.*" *DSN* 1 (Sept. 1970): 18-20. [Murder of George Radfoot.]

727 —. "The Motif of Reading in *Our Mutual Friend.*" *NCF* 28 (June 1973): 38-61.

728 Froude, James Anthony. *Life of Carlyle,* abrg. and ed. John Clubbe (Columbus: Ohio State UP; London: John Murray, 1979), passim. [Rev.: Ian Campbell, *Dkn* 76 (Summer 1980): 112-113.]

729 Frye, Northrop. "Dickens and the Comedy of Humours." *The Stubborn Structure* (Ithaca: Cornell UP; London: Methuen, 1970), 218-240. [Rpt. from *Experience in the Novel,* 1968.—Rpt. in *Literary Criticism: Idea and Act,* ed. W. K. Wimsatt (Berkeley, etc.: Univ. of California Press, 1974), 537-559, and in 2082, pp. 47-69. —Rev.: Alan Bruke, *DSN* 4 (Sept. 1973): 86-89.]

729a Fujikawa, Kazuo. [*BleakH.*] In 412a, pp. 78-80. [In Jap.]

730 Fujimori, Yoshiko. [Illustrations of D's works.] *Oberon* (Tokyo) 12 (Mar. 1970): 41-47. [In Jap.]

731 —. [On *NichN.*] In 980, pp. 36-46. [In Jap.]

732 Fukasawa, Suguru. [An essay on *DavidC.*] In 980, pp. 62-72. [In Jap.]

733 Fukuoy, Masaharu. [The two endings of D: *GreatEx.*] *Bull of the Faculty of Humanities* (Seikei Univ., Tokyo) 6 (1970): 1-18. [In Jap.]

734 Fulkerson, Richard. "*David Copperfield* in the Victorian Theatre." *VIJ* no. 5 (1976): 29-36.

735 —. "Gilbert's *Great Expectations.*" *DSN* 7 (Mar. 1976): 12-15. [W. S. Gilbert's play adap.]

736 —. "*Oliver Twist* in the Victorian Theatre." *Dkn* 70 (May 1974): 83-95.

737 Furness, Edna L. "Portrait of the Dickensian Schoolteacher." *Ed Forum* 33 (Jan. 1969): 153-161. [*DavidC, HardT, NichN, OurMF.*]

738 Gabel, Gernot M. and Gisela R. "Dickens, Charles." *Dissertations in English and American Literature: Theses Accepted by Austrian, French, and Swiss Universities 1875-1970* (Hamburg: Gernot Gabel, 1977), 90-91. [12 entries.—Rev.: Richard Fulkerson, *DSN*

10 (Dec. 1979): 121-122.]

739 Gál, István. "Dickens és folyóirata Kossuthról es Széchenyiről." *FK* 16, i-ii (1970): 199-214. [1848 Hungarian revolution.—*AllYR, HsldWds.*]

740 Gale, Steven H. "Cervantes's Influence on Dickens, with Comparative Emphasis on *Don Quijote* and *Pickwick Papers.*" *ACer* 12 (1973): 135-156.

741 Gall, Peter. *Die moderne Kritik über Charles Dickens: Ein Beitrag zum 100. Todestag.* Winterthur: Hans Schellenberg, 1970. vii, 81 pp. [Reception 1914-1965.]

742 Gallagher, Catherine. "*Hard Times* and *North and South:* The Family and Society in Two Industrial Novels." *ArQ* 36 (Spring 1980): 70-96.

743 Gamarra, Pierre, ed. *Europe* no. 488 (Dec. 1969). [Special D no.— Incl. 120, 121, 265, 404, 477, 541, 564, 694, 820, 1091, 1143, 1235, 1352, 1474, 1544, 1676, 1707, 1872, 1873, 2176.—Rev.: Paul Neier, *Pensée* Apr. 1970: 145-146; Sheila M. Smith, *Dkn* 67 (Jan. 1971): 51-52; also rev. in 2200.]

744 Gamble, William E. "Dickens's View of History as Phoenix." *TPB* 8 (July 1971): 15. [Abst.—*BleakH, CHistEng, TaleTwoC.*]

745 —. "Retribution and Reward in Dickens's *Little Dorrit.*" *TPB* 11 (July 1974): 25-26. [Abst.]

746 Gantz, Jeffrey Michael. "Notes on the Identity of Dick Datchery." *DSN* 8 (Sept. 1977): 72-78.

747 Ganz, Margaret. "*Nicholas Nickleby:* The Victories of Humor." In 461, pp. 131-148.

748 —. "*Pickwick Papers:* Humor and the Refashioning of Reality." In 1492, pp. 36-55.

749 —. "The Vulnerable Ego: Dickens's Humor in Decline." In 1489, pp. 23-40.

750 Gardner, Joseph H. "Bret Harte and the Dickensian Mode in America." *CRevAS* 2 (Fall 1971): 89-101.

751 —. "Dickens, Romance, and *McTeague:* A Study in Mutual Interpre-

tation." *ELWIU* 1 (Spring 1974): 69-82. [*DavidC, NichN, OCShop.*]

752 —. "Howells: The 'Realist' as Dickensian." *MFS* 16 (Autumn 1970): 323-343.

753 —. "Pecksniff's Profession: Boz, Phiz, and Pugin." *Dkn* 72 (May 1976): 75-86.

754 Gardner, Lytt I. "The Endocrinology of Abuse Dwarfism, with a Note on Charles Dickens as Child Advocate." *Amer J of Diseases of Children* 131 (May 1977): 505-507. [Esp. *OliverTw, OCShop.*]

755 (Garis, Robert. *The Dickens Theatre: A Reassessment of the Novels.* 1965.) [Excerpts rpt. in 23, pp. 1032-1041 and in 2064, pp. 492-499.—Rev. in 209.]

756 Garner, Jim. "Look to Harvard Medical School for Answers in the Mystery of Charles Dickens." *Canadian Med Assn J* 115 (4 Sept. 1976): 455, 458-459, 461. [1849 Parkman murder as source of *MEDrood.*]

757 Garrett, Peter K. "Dickens: He Mounts a High Tower in His Mind"; "Dickens: Machinery in Motion." *The Victorian Multiplot Novel: Studies in Dialogical Form* (New Haven and London: Yale UP, 1980), 23-51; 52-94. [Esp. *BleakH, LittleDor, OurMF.*—Method partly derived from Bakhtin.]

758 Garza Larumbe, Elsa. "El mundo infantil de Dickens." In 813, pp. 11-36. [Esp. *DavidC, DSon, GreatEx, LittleDor, OliverTw, OCShop, OurMF.*]

759 Gaskell, E. *Dickens and Medicine: An Exhibition of Books, Manuscripts and Prints to Mark the Centenary of His Death.* Exhib. Cat., 5. London: Wellcome Inst. of the Hist. of Med. Lib., 1970. 32 pp. [Rev.: David Taylor, *Punch* 259 (16 Dec. 1970): 880.]

760 —. "Dickens and Medicosocial Reform." *JAMA* 216 (5 April 1971): 111-116. [*BleakH, NichN, OliverTw, OurMF, PickP.*]

761 —. "More About Spontaneous Combustion." *Dkn* 69 (Jan. 1973): 25-35.

762 Gaskell, Philip. "Dickens, *David Copperfield*, 1850." *From Writer to Reader: Studies in Editorial Method* (Oxford: Clarendon Press,

1978), 142-155.

763 Gasser, Larry W. and Jack Gifford. "The Victorian Tension: Romanticism and Materialism." *BRMMLA* 34 (Summer 1980): 138-139. [J. S. Mill, *DavidC.*—Abst.]

764 Gates, Barbara T. "Suicide, *Bentley's Miscellany*, and Dickens's *Chimes*." *DSN* 8 (Dec. 1977): 98-100.

765 Gattégno, Jean. "Criminels et détectives, ou la préhistoire du roman policier: À propos d'un livre de Ian Ousby." *EA* 31 (Apr.-June 1978): 188-197. [*AllYR, BleakH, GreatEx, HsldWds, OliverTw, OurMF.*—Corrective to 1452.]

766 —. *Dickens*. Paris: Seuil, 1975. 187 pp. [Rev.: R.-M. Albérès, *NL* 17 Nov. 1975: 4; Bertrand Galimard Flavigny, *Mag littéraire* no. 110 (Mar. 1976): 58; Anne Villelaur, *QL* 16 Dec. 1975: 11; *Bull critique du livre français* no. 367 (July 1976): 1179.]

767 —. "D'une procès à l'autre, ou de Pickwick à Alice." In 154, pp. 208-209.

768 —. "Quel statut pour Dickens?" *QL* 1 Jan. 1980: 11-12. [In "Dossier: Charles Dickens," occasioned by reissue of earlier trans., rev. Gattégno and new trans. by Sylvère Monod.—"Bibliographie," p. 14.—Also incl. 998, 1139, 1382, 1540.]

769 Gelber, Mark. "Teaching 'Literary Anti-Semitism': Dickens's *Oliver Twist* and Freytag's *Soll und Haben*." *CLS* 16 (Mar. 1979): 1-11.

770 Gelfert, Hans-Dieter. *Die Symbolik im Romanwerk von Charles Dickens*. St. zur Poetik und Geschichte der Literatur, 25. Stuttgart: Kohlhammer, 1974. 194 pp. [Eng. abst. in *EASG* 1970: 67-69. (Freie Univ. Berlin diss.).—Rev.: Iris Bünsch, *LWU* 9 (Oct. 1976): 211-212; Paul Goetsch, *NS* 78 (Feb. 1979): 79-80; Edgar Rosenberg, *Dkn* 72 (Jan. 1976): 40-42 and (a diff. rev.) *DSN* 9 (Mar. 1978): 24-28; also rev. in 981.]

771 Gelpi, Barbara Charlesworth. "The Innocent I: Dickens's Influence on Victorian Autobiography." In 306, pp. 57-71. [Mill, Pater, Ruskin.]

772 Genet, Malcolm. *Charles Dickens 1812-1870*. [Austin: Humanities Research Center, Univ. of Texas, 1970]. 48 pp. [Exhib. cat. of books and mss from the VanderPoel coll.]

773 Gentili, Vanna. *"Hard Times:* Per questi tempi," in *Arte e letteratura: Scritti in ricordo di Gabriele Baldini* (Rome: Edizioni di Storia e Letteratura, 1972), 61-106.

774 Georges, Marilyn D. "Tulkinghorn, Hell and the Devil in *Bleak House." SCB* 39 (Fall 1979): 90. [Abst.]

775 Geppert, Hans Wilmar. *Der "andere" historische Roman: Theorie und Strukturen einer diskontinuierlichen Gattung.* SzDL, 42 (Tübingen: Niemeyer, 1976), passim. [Incl. *TaleTwoC.*]

776 Gerbi, Antonello. "Dickens: Nature and Society Equally Putrescent." *The Dispute of the New World: The History of a Polemic, 1750-1900,* rev. and enl. ed., trans. Jeremy Moyle (Pittsburgh: Univ. of Pittsburgh Press, 1973), 497-508. [Orig. It. ed. 1955.—*AmerN, MChuz.*]

777 Gérin, Winifred. *Elizabeth Gaskell: A Biography* (Oxford: Clarendon Press, 1976), passim.

778 Gerson, Stanley. "Can Dickens Survive His Centenary?" *Twentieth Century* 177, ii (1969): 40-43. [Appreciation.]

779 —. "A Great Australian Dickensian." *Dkn* 68 (May 1972): 75-89. [Henry Lawson.]

780 —. "Name-creation in Dickens." *MSpr* 69, iv (1975): 299-315.

781 (—. *Sound and Symbol in the Dialogue of the Works of Charles Dickens.* 1967.) [Rev.: G. Bauer, *ES* 52 (June 1971): 284-286; Sven Jacobson, *SN* 41, i (1969): 221-225; Robert F. Mount, *Word* 26 (Aug. 1970): 302-303; A. R. Tellier, *BSLP* 66, ii (1971): 173-174; Alfred Wollmann, *Anglia* 89 (Feb. 1971): 150-154.]

782 Gervais, David. "The Poetry of *Little Dorrit." CQ* 4 (Winter 1969): 38-53. [Style, dark vision.]

783 Gheorghiu, Mihnea. "Lumea fara Dickens." *Tribuna* 14 (18 June 1970): 1.

784 Ghosh, Krishna. "Dickens: Some Recent Approaches." In 262, pp. 18-25. [1939-1968.]

785 Giddings, Robert. "The Dickens Forum: A Cockney in the Court of Uncle Sam." *DSN* 6 (June 1975): 47-55. [Anglo-American re-

ception 1937-1972.]

786 Gilbert, Elliot L. "The Ceremony of Innocence: Charles Dickens's *A Christmas Carol.*" *PMLA* 90 (Jan. 1975): 22-31. [Note also Don Richard Cox's response and Gilbert's reply, Oct., pp. 922-924.]

787 Gilchrist, Andrea. "The Power of the Grotesque in *Great Expectations.*" *Dkn* 75 (Summer 1979): 75-83.

788 Gill, R. F. "How Not to Read a Novel." *Use of Eng* 28 (Summer 1977): 11-15. [On "image-hunting" in *GreatEx, LittleDor.*—Note also Derek Elders's response and Gill's reply, 29 (Spring 1978): 30-32.]

789 Gilman, Sander L. "On the Use and Abuse of the History of Psychiatry for Literary Studies." *DVLG* 52 (Sept. 1978): 381-399. [*DavidC, HsldWds, MEDrood, PickP.*]

790 Gilmour, Robin. "Dickens and the Self-Help Idea," in *The Victorians and Social Protest: A Symposium,* ed. J. Butt and I. F. Clarke (Newton Abbey: David and Charles; Hamden, Conn.: Archon, 1973), 71-101. [*BleakH, DavidC, DSon, GreatEx, HardT, LittleDor, NichN, OliverTw, OurMF.*]

791 —. "Dickens, Tennyson, and the Past." *Dkn* 75 (Autumn 1979): 131-142. [Esp. *DavidC.*]

792 —. "Memory in *David Copperfield.*" *Dkn* 71 (Jan. 1975): 30-42.

793 Gissing, George. *London and the Life of Literature in Late Victorian England: The Diary of George Gissing, Novelist,* ed. Pierre Coustillas (Hassocks: Harvester Press; Lewisburg, Pa.: Bucknell UP, 1978), passim.

794 Glancy, Ruth F. "Dickens and Christmas: His Framed-Tale Themes." *NCF* 35 (June 1980): 53-72.

795 —. "The Significance of the *Nickleby* Stories." *Dkn* 75 (Spring 1979): 12-15.

796 Glaser, Robert S. and Stephen H. Roth. "In the Matter of Heep, Jaggers, Tulkinghorn & Fogg: An Unjarndyced View of the Dickensian Bar." *Rutgers Law Rev* 29 (Winter 1976): 278-297.

797 Goetsch, Paul. "Literatursoziologische Aspekte des viktorianischen

Romanschlusses." *Poetica* 10, ii-iii (1978): 236-261. [Esp. *DSon,*
HardT, LittleDor, TaleTwoC.]

798   Gold, Joseph. *Charles Dickens: Radical Moralist.* Minneapolis: Univ.
of Minnesota Press, 1972; London: Oxford UP, 1973. xi, 279 pp.
[Chap. on each novel except *MEDrood.*—Incorporates " 'Living in
a Wale': *Martin Chuzzlewit,*" in 1490, pp. 150-161.—Rev.: Rachel
Bennett, *RES* NS 25 (Aug. 1974): 371; Alec Brice, *UTQ* 43 (Sum-
mer 1974): 397-399; Earle Davis, *Clio* 4 (Oct. 1974): 114-117;
Angus Easson, *Dkn* 69 (Sept. 1973): 190-191; Avrom Fleishman,
MLQ 34 (June 1973): 191-199; Stephen Gill, *N&Q* NS 22 (Oct.
1975): 471-472; Bert G. Hornback, *DSN* 4 (June 1973): 56-58;
A. Robert Lee, *Studies* 64 (Summer 1975): 200-202; R. D.
McMaster, *HAB* 24 (Winter 1973): 56-58; William Myers, *VS* 17
(Sept. 1973): 108-110; Norman Page, *DR* 52 (Winter 1972-1973):
691, 693, 695; Robert L. Patten, *NCF* 28 (June 1973): 103-107;
Stephen R. Rounds, *LJ* 97 (1 Nov. 1972): 3591; John R. Sorfleet,
CanL no. 63 (Winter 1975): 118-119; Michael Steig, *WCR* 7 (Jan.
1973): 76-78; Lionel Stevenson, *SAQ* 72 (Spring 1973): 332-333;
Harvey Peter Sucksmith, *YES* 5 (1975): 215-217; Gilbert Thomas,
English 23 (Spring 1974): 37; Alexander Welsh, *YR* 62 (Winter
1973): 281-287; Keith Wilson, *QQ* 80 (Spring 1973): 140-141;
Ch 10 (Mar. 1973): 92-93; *TLS* 25 Jan. 1974: 75; also rev. in 981,
1537, 2158.]

799   —. "The Dickens Centenary Year in Canada." *DSN* 2 (Mar. 1971):
10-11.

800   —. "The Dickens Concordance." *DSN* 7 (Sept. 1976): 65-69.

801   —, comp. *The Stature of Dickens: A Centenary Bibliography.* Toron-
to and Buffalo: Univ. of Toronto Press for Univ. of Manitoba
Press, 1971. xxix, 236 pp. [1870-1968.—Rev.: Richard D. Altick,
NCF 27 (June 1972): 107-110; Charles R. Andrews, *LJ* 96 (15
Oct. 1971): 3312; Duane DeVries, *Dkn* 68 (Sept. 1972): 188-191;
R. C. Ellsworth, *QQ* 79 (Spring 1972): 108 and (a diff. rev.)
Canadian Lib J 29 (May-June 1972): 260; K. J. Fielding, *RES* NS
24 (Feb. 1973): 100-102; Howell J. Heaney, *DSN* 3 (Mar. 1972):
7-12; Robert Partlow, *DSN* 2 (Dec. 1971): 103-105; L. Pothet,
EA 28 (Apr.-June 1975): 233; *Ch* 8 (Dec. 1971): 1317-1318.]

802   Goldberg, Michael. *Carlyle and Dickens.* Athens: Univ. of Georgia
Press, 1972. 248 pp. [Esp. *BleakH, Chimes,CCarol, DSon, HardT,*
TaleTwoC.—Rev.: C. C. Barfoot, *ES* 55 (Aug. 1974): 373-374;
John Clubbe, *SAQ* 73 (Autumn 1974): 569-570; J[erry] A.
D[ibble], *ELN* 11 (Sept. 1973): supp. 40-41; Richard J. Dunn,

DSN 4 (Sept. 1973): 72-76; Angus Easson, *N&Q* NS 25 (Apr. 1978): 191-192; K. J. Fielding, *Dkn* 69 (May 1973): 111-118; George H. Ford, *SNNTS* 6 (Spring 1974): 114-117; Nancy E. Gwinn, *LJ* 97 (1 Dec. 1972): 3913; Sylvère Monod, *EA* 26 (July-Sept. 1973): 373-374; Barry V. Qualls, *SSL* 12 (Oct. 1974): 146-153; John Raymond, *NewSt* 84 (1 Dec. 1972): 827; Charles Richard Sanders, *NCF* 27 (Mar. 1973): 490-492; Edward Sharples, *Criticism* 16 (Spring 1974): 180-183; Michael Slater, *VS* 17 (Mar. 1974): 328-330; John R. Sorfleet, *CanL* no. 63 (Winter 1975): 118-119; Michael Steig, *WCR* 7 (Jan. 1973): 76-78; Harvey Peter Sucksmith, *MLR* 69 (Oct. 1974): 848-849; Rodger L. Tarr, *Costerus* NS 3 (1975): 171-176; E. M. Vida, *HAB* 24 (Summer 1973): 227-229; Alexander Welsh, *YR* 62 (Winter 1973): 281-287; *Ch* 10 (May 1973): 456; *TLS* 27 Apr. 1973: 478; *VQR* 49 (Spring 1973): lxix; also rev. in 981, 1026, 1537, 2158.]

803 —. "The Dickens Debate, G.B.S. vs. G.K.C." In 1593, pp. 135-147.

804 —. "From Bentham to Carlyle: Dickens's Political Development." *JHI* 33 (Jan.-Mar. 1972): 61-76. [*AmerN, BleakH, Chimes, DavidC, DSon, GreatEx, HardT, HsldWds, LittleDor, MEDrood, TaleTwoC.*]

805 —. "Lawrence's 'The Rocking Horse Winner': A Dickensian Fable?" *MFS* 15 (Winter 1969-1970): 525-536. [Note also his "Dickens and Lawrence: More on Rocking Horses," 17 (Winter 1971-1972): 574.]

806 —. "Shaw's Dickensian Quintessence." *ShawR* 14 (Jan. 1971): 14-28.

807 —. "Shaw's *Pygmalion:* The Reworking of *Great Expectations.*" *ShawR* 22 (Sept. 1979): 114-122.

808 Goldfarb, Russell M. "Charles Dickens: Orphan, Incest and Sexual Repression." *Sexual Repression and Victorian Literature* (Lewisburg, Pa.: Bucknell UP, 1970), 114-138. [Esp. *DavidC, DSon, HardT, MChuz, OurMF.*—Rev.: Albert D. Hutter, *DSN* 4 (June 1973): 53-55.]

809 —. "John Jarndyce of *Bleak House.*" *SNNTS* 12 (Summer 1980): 144-152.

810 — and Clare R. *Spiritualism and Nineteenth-Century Letters* (Rutherford, N.J.: Farleigh Dickinson UP; London: Associated Univ. Presses, 1978), passim.

811 Goldknopf, David. "The Morality of Hypocrisy: The Structure of *Hard Times*." *The Life of the Novel* (Chicago and London: Univ. of Chicago Press, 1972), 143-158. [Rev.: Jerome Meckier, *DSN* 5 (Mar. 1974): 18-21.]

812 Gomme, A. H. *Dickens*. London: Evans, 1971. 192 pp. [Esp. *DSon, GreatEx, HardT, LittleDor.*—Rev.: Alec W. Brice, *DSN* 4 (Dec. 1973): 113-115; Peter Bryant, *UES* 10 (Sept. 1972): 75-76; K.J. Fielding, *Dkn* 68 (Jan. 1972): 60-61; Stephen Gill, *N&Q* NS 21 (June 1974): 232; Sylvère Monod, *EA* 25 (Oct.-Dec. 1972): 568-569; Isobel Murray, *Aberdeen Univ Rev* 44 (Autumn 1972): 405-406; Ian Stewart, *CnL* 152 (1972): 630; Harvey Peter Sucksmith, *YES* 3 (1973): 316-317; *TLS* 29 Oct. 1971: 1361; also rev. in 981.]

813 [González Padilla, Ma. Enriqueta, ed.(?)] *Charles Dickens 1812-1870: Homenaje en al primer centenario de su muerte.* Mexico City: Univ. Nacional Autónoma de México, Facultad de Filosofía y Letras/Departamento de Letras Inglesas, 1971. [Ma. Enriqueta González Padilla, "Presentación," 7-9; Carlos Villalobos, "Bibliografía de Charles Dickens," 193-204.—Incl. 758, 814, 1107, 1448, 1499, 1541, 2107, 2175.—Rev.: Salvador Cruz, *México en la cultura* (supp. to *Novedades*) 12 Dec. 1971: 5; A[ntonio] M[agaña] E[squivel?], *Hispano Americano* 60 (6 Dec. 1971): 66-67; Mauricio de la Selva, *CA* 31 (May-June 1972): 253-255.]

814 González Padilla, Ma. Enriqueta. "El último Dickens." In 813, pp. 77-108.

815 Gooch, Bryan N. S. and David S. Thatcher. "Dickens, Charles John Huffam." *Musical Settings of Early and Mid-Victorian Literature: A Catalogue.* GRLH, 149 (New York and London: Garland, 1979), 202-235. [*AmerN, Chimes*, all novels except *MEDrood, TaleTwoC.*]

816 Goode, John. "The Empty Chair." *George Gissing: Ideology and Fiction* (London: Vision, 1978; New York: Barnes and Noble, 1979), 13-40; et passim.

817 Gose, Elliott B., Jr. "*Bleak House.*" *Imagination Indulged: The Irrational in the Nineteenth-Century Novel* (Montreal and London: McGill-Queen's UP, 1972), 73-97. [Rev.: Jerome Beaty, *DSN* 6 (Sept. 1975): 93-95.]

818 Gottschalk, Paul. "Time in *Edwin Drood.*" In 1489, pp. 265-272.

819 Gouirand, Jacqueline. "Charles Dickens et l'Amérique." In 743, pp. 136-146.

820 Gould, W. B. "Dickens and the Law." *Auckland Univ Law Rev* 1, iii (1970): 78-88.

821 Graf-Brawand, Susanna. *Das ausserebeliche Kind und die Problematik der Illegitimität in englischen Romane von Tom Jones bis Lady Chatterley's Lover* (Zurich: Juris, 1971), passim. [Incl. *BleakH.*— Bern diss.]

822 Graff, Gerald. "How Not to Talk about Fictions." *Literature Against Itself: Literary Ideas in Modern Society* (Chicago and London: Univ. of Chicago Press, 1979), 151-180. [Incl. referentiality of *SBoz.*]

823 Grant, Judith Skelton. "Italians with White Mice in *Middlemarch* and *Little Dorrit.*" *ELN* 16 (Mar. 1979): 232-234.

824 (Gray, Paul E., ed. *Twentieth-Century Interpretations of Hard Times.* 1969.) [Rev.: William J. Palmer, *DSN* 4 (Sept. 1973): 81-84.]

825 Greaves, John. *Dickens at Doughty Street,* fwd. Monica Dickens. London: Elm Tree, 1975. 197 pp. [Rev.: Angus Easson, *DSN* 7 (Sept. 1976): 91-93; Margaret Lane, *Dkn* 71 (Sept. 1975): 173-174; W. D. Maxwell-Mahon, *UES* 14 (Apr. 1976): 59-60; Philip Venning, *TES* 20 June 1975: 22 and Greaves's reply, 18 July 1975: 14; George J. Worth, *NCF* 32 (Dec. 1977): 348-351; *BBkN* Sept. 1975: 663-664; *Times* (London) 29 May 1975: 12.]

826 —. "The Dickens Fellowship to Kornei Chukovsky." *SovL* no. 356 (Nov. 1977): 42-43. [Letter of 24 Jan. 1967 to the Russian novelist and critic.]

827 —. "The Dickens House, London." *DSN* 6 (June 1975): 38-42.

828 G[reaves], J[ohn]. "15th Anniversary of the Haarlem Branch." *Dkn* 68 (May 1972): 140-141.

829 Greaves, John. "Going Astray." In 1491, pp. 144-161. [London of *HsldWds.*]

830 —. *Who's Who in Dickens,* fwd. Margaret Lane. London: Hamilton, 1972; New York: Taplinger, 1973. viii, 231 pp. [Rev.: Charles A. Bunge, *Wilson Lib Bull* 48 (Jan. 1974): 418; Gordon Cheese-

wright, *DSN* 5 (June 1974): 40-44; G. B. Cotton, *Lib Rev* 23 (Winter 1972-1973): 359; Charles Mann, *ARBA* 5 (1974): 518-519; P. P. Olevnik, *LJ* 98 (July 1973): 2068; Louise Overbeck, *Dkn* 69 (Jan. 1973): 57-58; Marie Peel, *B&B* 18 (Jan. 1973): 101-102; *Booklist* 70 (1 July 1974): 1215; *TLS* 2 Mar. 1973: 235; also rev. in 504, 981, 2158.]

831 [Greaves, John and Gwen Major.] *The London of Charles Dickens,* fwd. Monica Dickens, illus. Peter Roberson. London: London Transport Executive, 1970; rpt. Speldhurst: Midas, 1979. viii, 166 pp. [Prod. in collaboration with D Fellowship.—Rev.: Elizabeth Bowen, *Spec* 224 (30 May 1970): 713; also rev. in 314, 1961, 2094.]

832 Grech, Anthony P., comp. "Law and Society in the Life and Works of Charles Dickens." *Record of the Assn of the Bar of the City of New York* 27 (Apr. 1972): 275-286. [A bibliog. checklist.]

833 Green, Benny. "In the Pit." *Spec* 230 (3 Mar. 1973): 275. [Frederick Dorrit as musician.]

834 Green, Michael. "Notes on Fathers and Sons from *Dombey and Son*," in *1848: The Sociology of Literature,* ed. Francis Barker et al. Proc. of Essex Conf. on the Sociology of Lit., July 1977. ([Colchester] : Univ. of Essex, 1978), 256-264.

835 Green, Muriel M. "The Variety of Dickens's *Bleak House*." *Lib Rev* (Glasgow) 22 (Autumn 1970): 363-367.

836 Green, Robert. "*Hard Times:* The Style of a Sermon." *TSLL* 11 (Winter 1970): 1375-1397.

837 Greenberg, Robert A. "On Ending *Great Expectations*." *PLL* 6 (Spring 1970): 152-163. [Note also Robert F. Fleissner's ltr. to ed., *DSN* 2 (June 1972): 58-59.]

838 Greenfield, Bob. "Elemental Esthetics and Charles Dickens." *Bachy* no. 5 (Summer 1975): 94-97.

839 Gregor, Ian, ed. *Reading the Victorian Novel: Detail into Form.* London: Vision Press; New York: Barnes and Noble, 1980. [Incl. 142, 336, 400, 987, 997, 1081, 1206.]

840 Gregory, Marshall W. "Values and Meanings in *Great Expectations:* The Two Endings Revisited." *EIC* 19 (Oct. 1969): 402-409.

841 Gribben, Alan. "Dickens, Charles. . . ." *Mark Twain's Library: A Reconstruction* (Boston: G. K. Hall, 1980), I, 186-192. [Annotated.]

842 Gribble, Jennifer. "Depth and Surface in *Our Mutual Friend*." *EIC* 25 (Apr. 1975): 197-214.

843 —. "Pip and Estella: Expectations of Love." *Sydney St in Eng* 2 (1976-1977): 126-138.

844 Griest, Guinevere L. *Mudie's Circulating Library and the Victorian Novel* (Bloomington and London: Indiana UP, 1970), passim. [*AllYR, DavidC, GreatEx.*]

845 Grillo, Virgil. *Charles Dickens's Sketches by Boz: End in the Beginning.* Boulder: Colorado Assn. UP, 1974. xiii, 240 pp. [Also esp. *MChuz, NichN, OCShop, PickP.*—Note also diss., "End in the Beginning: Dickens's *Sketches by Boz*" (California, 1971).—Rev.: Edward Costigan, *VPN* 9 (Sept. 1976): 94-97; David Dillon, *LJ* 99 (1 Oct. 1974): 2480; K. J. Fielding, *YES* 7 (1977): 295-296; Margaret Ganz, *DSN* 7 (June 1976): 53-57; Jerome Meckier, *Criticism* 18 (Spring 1976): 198-202; F. S. Schwarzbach, *Dkn* 72 (May 1976): 106-108; *Ch* 11 (Nov. 1974): 1307; *TLS* 23 Aug. 1974: 902; also rev. in 504, 981.]

846 Grindea, Miron, ed. *Adam*, no. 346-348 (1971). [Ed., "Footnotes to Centenaries," 2-8.—Incl. 99, 1367, 2121.—Rev.: Harry Epstein, *DSN* 3 (Dec. 1972): 109-110; M[ichael] S[later], *Dkn* 67 (May 1971): 116-117.]

847 Gross, John. "Dickens the Great Entertainer." *Obs Mag* (supp. to the weekly) 17 May 1970: 14-20, 22-23. [Infl. on popular culture.—Chiefly pictures.]

848 Gross, Konrad, ed. "Dickens." *Der englische soziale Roman im 19. Jahrhundert.* Wege der Forschung, 466 (Darmstadt: Wissenschaftliche Buchgesellschaft, 1977), 219-308. [For items on D see this number in Appendix.—Rev.: Heinz Reinhold, *Dkn* 76 (Summer 1980): 110-112.]

849 Grove, T. N. "The Psychological Prison of Arthur Clennam in Dickens's *Little Dorrit*." *MLR* 68 (Oct. 1973): 750-755.

850 Grundy, Dominick E. "Growing Up Dickensian." *L&P* 22, ii (1972): 99-106. [*BleakH, DavidC, GreatEx.*]

851 Grylls, David. "Jane Austen and Dickens." *Guardians and Angels:*

Parents and Children in Nineteenth-Century Literature (London and Boston: Faber and Faber, 1978), 111-152; et passim. [Rev.: Arthur M. Adrian, *Dkn* 74 (Sept. 1978): 176-177; Robert Simpson McLean, *DSN* 11 (Mar. 1980): 25-26.]

852 Guerard, Albert J. *"Bleak House:* Structure and Style." *SoR* NS 5 (Apr. 1969): 332-349.

853 —. *The Triumph of the Novel: Dickens, Dostoevsky, Faulkner.* New York: Oxford UP, 1976. 365 pp. [Esp. *BleakH, DavidC, LittleDor, MChuz, OCShop, OliverTw.*—Chap. on *MChuz* rpt. in 461, pp. 107-129.—Rev.: C. C. Barfoot, *ES* 59 (Dec. 1978): 566-567; Jack Beatty, *Washington Post* 30 Dec. 1976: C4; Calvin S. Brown, *MFS* 23 (Summer 1977): 301-304; Keith Cushman, *LJ* 101 (15 Sept. 1976): 1857; Denis Donoghue, *NYTBR* 26 Sept. 1976: 27; Alan Warren Friedman, *SNNTS* 9 (Summer 1977): 232-233; Joseph H. Gardner, *DSN* 9 (June 1978): 55-58; Andrew Gibson, *English* 27 (Summer-Autumn 1978): 268-274; *Harry Goldgar, *New Orleans Times-Picayune* 6 Feb. 1977; Barbara Hardy, *Novel* 11 (Fall 1977): 77-79; Douglas Hewitt, *N&Q* NS 27 (June 1980): 277-278; James M. Holquist, *CL* 31 (Spring 1979): 185-187; Lauriat Lane, Jr., *IFR* 6 (Winter 1979): 67-71; Michael Millgate, *NCF* 32 (Sept. 1977): 255-258; Robert L. Patten, *Dkn* 75 (Spring 1979): 39-41; Branwen Bailey Pratt, *HSL* 9, ii-iii (1977): 223-231; Susan Skelton, *SHR* 12 (Fall 1978): 384; Robert D. Spector, *WLT* 51 (Winter 1977): 167; Tony Tanner, *New Lugano Rev* no. 1 (1979): 63-74; Linda W. Wagner, *Faulkner St* 1 (1980): 185-186; Edward Wasiolek, *SlavR* 37 (Mar. 1978): 167; Paul West, *SoR* NS 15 (Jan. 1979): 78-85; *Ch* 13 (Feb. 1977): 1589; also rev. in 583, 981, 1062.]

854 Guerra-DeBellis, Francesca. "Il talento drammatico di Charles Dickens (1812-1870)." *NA* 510 (Dec. 1970): 678-681. [Mentions *OliverTw, PickP.*]

855 Gupta, R. K. "Dickens's Development as Artist." *CalR* NS 2 (Oct.-Nov. 1970): 219-226.

856 Haberman, Melvyn. "The Courtship of the Void: The World of *Hard Times.*" In 306, pp. 37-55.

857 Haines, Charles. *Charles Dickens.* New York: F. Watts, 1969. x, 181 pp. [Juvenile biog.—Rev.: Michael Cart, *LJ* 95 (15 Feb. 1970): 787; also rev. in 314.]

858 Hall, William F. "Caricature in Dickens and James." *UTQ* 39 (Apr.

1970): 242-257. [Esp. *DavidC.*]

859 Halperin, John. "Dickens." *Egoism and Self-Discovery in the Victorian Novel: Studies in the Ordeal of Knowledge in the Nineteenth Century.* St. in Lit. and Crit., 1 (New York: B. Franklin, 1974), 81-123. [*DSon, GreatEx, TaleTwoC.*]

860 Hamblen, Abigail Ann. "Another Dickens come to Judgment." *Cresset* 33 (Jan. 1970): 12-15. [D and Monica Dickens compared.— Mentions *DavidC, OCShop, OliverTw.*]

861 Hamel, Günther. *Klassenbewusstsein und Charakterdarstellung im frühviktorianischen Sozialroman.* Europäische Hochschulschriften, Ser. 14: Angelsächsische Sprache und Literatur, 36 (Bern: Herbert Lang; Frankfurt and Munich: Peter Lang, 1976), passim. [Note earlier ed. in ser. Gesellschaft im Wandel, 1970.—Esp. *HardT.*]

862 Hamer, Douglas. "Dickens: The Old Court of Chancery." *N&Q* NS 17 (Sept. 1970): 341-347. [*BleakH.*]

863 Hamilton, Morse. "Nature and the Unnatural in *Little Dorrit.*" *VIJ* no. 6 (1977): 9-20.

864 Hamra, Albert R. "Dickens in *A Tale of Two Cities:* An Appreciation of Technique." *Missouri Eng Bull* 27 (Jan. 1970): 10-16.

865 Handley, Graham. *Brodie's Notes on Charles Dickens's Little Dorrit.* Pan Study Aids. London, etc.: Pan Books, 1979. 96 pp.

866 —. *Brodie's Notes on Charles Dickens's Oliver Twist.* Pan Study Aids. London, etc.: Pan Books, 1978. 88 pp.

867 —. *Brodie's Notes on Charles Dickens's Our Mutual Friend.* Pan Study Aids. London, etc.: Pan Books, 1979. 128 pp.

868 —. *Hard Times.* Oxford: Blackwell, 1969. 102 pp.

869 — and Stanley King. *Brodie's Notes on Charles Dickens's Bleak House.* Pan Study Aids. London, etc.: Pan Books, 1978. 119 pp.

870 Hannaford, Richard. "Fairy-tale Fantasy in *Nicholas Nickleby.*" *Criticism* 16 (Summer 1974): 247-259.

871 —. "The Fairy World of *Oliver Twist.*" *DSN* 8 (June 1977): 33-36.

872 —. "Irony and Sentimentality: Conflicting Modes in *Martin Chuzzle-*

wit." *VN* no. 46 (Fall 1974): 26-28.

873 Hanson, R. P. C. "The Circus Manager Goes to the Root of the Matter." *Times* (London) 18 Feb. 1978: 16. [Christianity.]

874 Harbage, Alfred. *A Kind of Power: The Shakespeare-Dickens Analogy.* MAPS, 105. Philadelphia: Amer. Phil. Soc., 1975. xiv, 78 pp. [Rev.: Walter Allen, *DSN* 7 (Sept. 1976): 88-90; Ronald Berman, *SR* 84 (Fall 1976): 661; B[ryan] H[ulse], *Dkn* 71 (Sept. 1975): 174-175; James R. Kincaid, *NCF* 30 (Mar. 1976): 535-538; also rev. in 981.]

875 —. "Shakespeare and the Early Dickens," in *Shakespeare: Aspects of Influence,* ed. G. B. Evans. HES, 7 (Cambridge and London: Harvard UP, 1976), 109-134.

876 Hardwick, Michael and Mollie. *As They Saw Him: Charles Dickens.* London: Harrap, 1970. 192 pp. [Rev.: Arthur A. Adrian, *DSN* 4 (Mar. 1973): 21-23; P. S. Sundaram, *Times of India* 20 Sept. 1970: 10; also rev. in 314.]

877 —, comps. *The Charles Dickens Encyclopedia.* Reading: Osprey; New York: Scribners, 1973. xi, 531 pp. [Rev.: Charles A. Bunge, *Wilson Lib Bull* 48 (Jan.1974): 418; Thomas J. Galvin, *LJ* 98 (1 Dec. 1973): 3544; Charles Mann, *ARBA* 5 (1974): 519; Marie Peel, *B&B* 18 (June 1973): 118-119; Christopher Porterfield, *Time* 102 (24 Dec. 1973): 81; Craig Raine, *TES* 11 May 1973: 22; L[eslie] S[taples], *Dkn* 69 (Sept. 1973): 186-187; James Swinnen, *New Orleans Rev* 4, iv (1975): 377; *Booklist* 70 (15 Apr. 1974): 888; *Ch* 11 (Mar. 1974): 62; *LJ* 99 (15 Apr. 1974): 1098; *Obs* 11 Mar. 1973: 37; *TLS* 2 Mar. 1973: 235; also rev. in 981.]

878 —. *The Charles Dickens Quiz Book.* London: Luscombe; New York: Larousse, 1974. 87 pp.

879 —. *Dickens's England.* London: Dent; South Brunswick and New York: Barnes, 1970; rpt. London: Dent, 1976. xi, 172 pp. [Rev.: Joseph H. Gardner, *DSN* 2 (Sept. 1971): 84-86; Tony Warburton, *B&B* 22 (Dec. 1976): 30-32; Raymond Williams, *Guardian Weekly* 6 June 1970: 18; *ContempR* 229 (Dec. 1976): 335; also rev. in 314, 967 (Jan. 1977), 2237.]

880 Hardy, Barbara. *Charles Dickens: The Later Novels,* [rev. ed.]. Writers and Their Work, 205. London: Longman for British Council, 1977. 52 pp. [1st ed. 1968.—Rev.: J. C. Field, *RLV* 37, ii (1971): 231-232; also rev. in 2138.]

881 —. "The Complexity of Dickens." In 1786, pp. 29-51. [Esp. *BleakH, HardT, NichN, OurMF, PickP.*]

882 —. "Dickens and the Passions." In 1419, pp. 67-84. [Esp. *DSon, GreatEx, LittleDor, OliverTw.*]

883 —. "Charles Dickens." *Tellers and Listeners: The Narrative Imagination* (London: Univ. of London, Athlone Press, 1975), 165-174. [Rpt. from *Dkn* 69 (May 1973): 73-78.—Esp. *DavidC, GreatEx, MChuz, PickP.*—Rev.: W. F. Axton, *DSN* 10 (Mar. 1979): 27-29; Morris Beja, *Dkn* 72 (May 1976): 105-106.]

884 —. *The Moral Art of Dickens.* London: Univ. of London, Athlone Press; New York: Oxford UP, 1970. xiii, 155 pp. [Esp. *DavidC, GreatEx, MChuz, PickP.*—Chap. on *GreatEx* rpt. in 839, pp. 130-140 and in 2064, pp. 478-490.—Rev.: T. J. Cribb, *RES* NS 23 (Aug. 1972): 372-374; Keith Cushman, *MP* 70 (Nov. 1972): 166-168; Stephen Gill, *N&Q* NS 18 (Nov. 1971): 425-427; Paul Goetsch, *NS* 72 (Feb. 1973): 117; E. D. H. Johnson, *NCF* 26 (Dec. 1971): 349-352; Joachim Krehayn, *Deutsche Literaturzeitung* 92 (Dec. 1971): 1018-1021; Lauriat Lane, Jr., *DSN* 2 (June 1971): 47-49; Francis Noel Lees, *BJA* 11 (Summer 1971): 310-311; Kenneth Muir, *MLR* 67 (Apr. 1972): 405-407; Patricia Thomson, *DUJ* 64 (Dec. 1971): 76-77; J. M. S. Tompkins, *SN* 44, i (1972): 175-176; Angus Wilson, *Dkn* 67 (Jan. 1971): 45-47; *Ch* 8 (May 1971): 388; *Times* (London) 5 Nov. 1970: 14; *VQR* 47 (Summer 1971): cxi; also rev. in 198, 981, 1126, 1578, 1961, 1972, 2065, 2216, 2227.]

885 —. "[Toast at] The London Birthday Dinner." *Dkn* 73 (May 1977): 122-126.

886 Hargrave, Harry A. "Kind Hearts and Coronets." In 651, pp. 31-38. [Personal relations between D and Tennyson.]

887 Hark, Ina Rae. "Marriage in the Symbolic Framework of *The Mystery of Edwin Drood.*" *SNNTS* 9 (Summer 1977): 154-168.

888 Harris, Robert R. "Dickens in America." *Wilson Q* 3 (Autumn 1979): 172-185. [Incl. passages from letters, *AmerN, MChuz.*]

889 Harris, Wendell V. *British Short Fiction in the Nineteenth Century: A Literary and Bibliographic Guide* (Detroit: Wayne State UP, 1979), 60-62.

890 —. "Fiction and Metaphysics in the Nineteenth Century." In 462, pp.

53-65. [Incl. *HardT.*—Rpt. from *Mosaic* 4, iii (Spring 1971): 53-65.]

891 Harrison, A. C. and J. E. L. Caiger. "Charles Dickens's Well." *Archaeologica Cantiana* 86 (1971): 11-14. [At Gadshill.]

892 Harrison, Fraser. *The Dark Angel: Aspects of Victorian Sexuality* (London: Sheldon Press, 1977; New York: Universe Books, 1978), passim. [Esp. *DavidC.*—Rev.: Branwen Bailey Pratt, *DSN* 10 (June-Sept. 1979): 73-75.]

893 Harting, Emilie C. *A Literary Tour Guide to England and Scotland* (New York: Morrow, 1976), passim.

894 Harvey, John. "George Cruikshank: A Master of the Poetic Use of Line." In 1510, pp. 129-155.

895 —. "Tolstoy in England." *CQ* 5 (1970): 115-133. [Mentions *DavidC, DSon, OurMF.*]

896 —. *Victorian Novelists and Their Illustrators* (London: Sidgwick and Jackson, 1970; New York: New York UP, 1971), passim. [Note also diss., "The Concern of Serial Novelists with the Illustration of Their Work in the Nineteenth Century, with Particular Reference to Dickens" (Cambridge, 1969).—Rev.: W. F. Axton, *DSN* 5 (June 1974): 54-56; Anthony Burton, *Dkn* (May 1971): 105-109; also rev. in 2065.]

897 Harvey, William R. "Charles Dickens and the Byronic Hero." *NCF* 24 (Dec. 1969): 305-316. [Esp. Carton, Steerforth, Wrayburn.]

898 Hauck, Richard. "The Dickens Controversy in *The Spirit of the Times.*" *PMLA* 85 (Mar. 1970): 278-283.

899 Hawes, Donald. "David Copperfield's Names." *Dkn* 74 (May 1978): 81-87. [Note also Alan S. Watts's ltr. to ed., 75 (Spring 1979): 35.]

900 —. "Marryat and Dickens: A Personal and Literary Relationship." In 1490, pp. 39-68. [Note also "More on Dickens and Marryat," *DSN* 8 (June 1977): 46-47.]

901 [Hay, Eloise.] "Hawthorne-Dickens." *HSN* 4 (Spring 1978): 8. [Requests info. for comp. study.]

902 Hayman, Ronald. "Dickens." *Leavis* (London: Heinemann; Totowa,

N.J.: Rowman and Littlefield, 1976), 125-135; et passim. [Rev.: William J. Palmer, *DSN* 9 (Sept. 1978): 91-93; also rev. in 967 (May 1977).]

902a Hays, R. W. "A Note about Lewis Carroll." *ArmD* 7 (Feb. 1974): 95-96. [D's infl.]

903 Haywood, Charles. "Charles Dickens and Shakespeare; or, The Irish Moor of Venice, *O'Thello,* with Music." *Dkn* 73 (May 1977): 67-88.

904 Hazama, Jiro. [*GreatEx:* Analysis of Pip's situation.] In 1285, pp. 16-31. [In Jap.]

904a —. [*OliverTw.*] In 412a, pp. 72-74. [In Jap.]

905 Healey, Edna. "At Work with Charles Dickens." *Lady Unknown: The Life of Angela Burdett-Coutts* (London: Sidgwick and Jackson; New York: Coward, McCann and Geoghegan, 1978), 115-140; et passim. [Rev.: K. J. Fielding, *Dkn* 74 (May 1978): 108-109.]

906 —. "[Toast at] The London Birthday Dinner." *Dkn* 74 (May 1978): 122-125.

907 Heatley, Edward. "The Redeemed Feminine of *Little Dorrit.*" In 1492, pp. 153-166.

908 Hebley, Kate B. "The Dickens Fellowship." *Carnegie Mag* 49 (June 1970): 235-237.

909 Heck, Edwin J. "*Hard Times:* The Handwriting on the Factory Wall." *EJ* 61 (Jan. 1972): 23-27.

910 Heineman, Helen. *Mrs. Trollope: The Triumphant Feminine in the Nineteenth Century* (Athens: Ohio UP, 1979), passim.

911 Hemstedt, Geoffrey. "The Novel." *The Victorians,* ed. Lawrence Lerner (London: Methuen; New York: Holmes and Meier, 1978), 3-24.

912 Henderson, Heather. " 'To You Only. . .': Forster to C. E. Norton on Dickens's Death." *JFNL* 1 (Oct. 1979): 32-40.

913 Henderson, James P. "Charles Dickens's *Hard Times* and the Industrial Revolution." *Cresset* 43 (Mar. 1980): 13-17.

914 Henkle, Roger B. "Early Dickens: Metamorphosis, Psychic Disorien-

tation, and the Small Fry"; "Later Dickens: Disenchantment, Transmogrification, and Ambivalence." *Comedy and Culture: England 1820-1900* (Princeton and Guildford: Princeton UP, 1980), 111-144; 145-184. [All the novels except *BarnR, GreatEx, NichN, TaleTwoC,* esp. *MChuz.*]

915 —. "Structure and Plot: Fairy Tale Desires, Lost Expectations, Paranoia." *Reading the Novel: An Introduction to the Techniques of Interpreting Fiction* (New York: Harper and Row, 1977), 47-64; et passim. [*GreatEx,* Kafka's *Trial.*]

916 Hennelly, Mark M., Jr. "*David Copperfield:* 'The Theme of This Incomprehensible Conundrum Was the Moon'." *SNNTS* 10 (Winter 1978): 375-396.

917 Herbert, Christopher. "Converging Worlds in *Pickwick Papers.*" *NCF* 27 (June 1972): 1-20.

918 —. "De Quincey and Dickens." *VS* 17 (Mar. 1974): 247-263. [*DavidC, LittleDor, MEDrood, OCShop, OliverTw.*]

919 Herr, Linda L. "Dickens's Jaggers and Shaw's Bohun: A Study of 'Character-Lifting'." In 1593, pp. 110-118. [*GreatEx, You Never Can Tell.*]

920 Herring, Paul D. "The Number Plans for *Dombey and Son:* Some Further Observations." *MP* 68 (Nov. 1970): 151-187.

921 Hewett, Edward W. "Christmas Spirits in Dickens." *DSN* 7 (Dec. 1976): 99-106. [Incl. recipes.]

922 Hewitt, Douglas. "The Logical Prison: *Little Dorrit.*" *The Approach to Fiction: Good and Bad Readings of Novels* (London: Longman; Totowa, N.J.: Rowman and Littlefield, 1972), 85-102.

923 Hibbott, Yvonne. "Bart's and the City in Dickens's Tales." *St. Bartholomew Hospital J* 75 (May 1971): 148-152.

924 Hicks, Granville. "Dickens's Indictment of Victorian Society." *Granville Hicks in The New Masses,* ed. Jack Alan Robbins (Port Washington, N.Y. and London: Kennikat Press, 1974), 189-192. [Rptd. rev. of 31 May 1938 of T. A. Jackson, *Charles Dickens: The Progress of a Radical.*]

924a Higashida, Chiaki. [D's style.] In 412a, pp. 49-51. [In Jap.]

925 Hill, Nancy K. "Picturesque Satire in *Little Dorrit.*" *HSL* 11, iii (1979): 212-223. [Abst. in *BRMMLA* 30 (Summer 1976): 159.]

926 Hill, Susan. "The Ghost of 131 Christmases Past." *Daily Telegraph* (London) 17 Dec. 1977: 7. [Morality of *CCarol.*]

927 —. "The Novelists' Novelist." *Daily Telegraph* (London) 13 Jan. 1979: 5.

928 —. "Sinister, Sombre, but the Greatest." *Daily Telegraph* (London) 10 Feb. 1979: 9. [*OurMF.*]

929 Hillmann, Heinz. "*Amerika:* Literature as a Problem-Solving Game," trans. June V. Featonby et al., ed. Irmgard Hobson, in *The Kafka Debate: New Perspectives for Our Time,* ed. Angel Flores (New York: Gordian Press, 1977), 279-297. [Incl. infl. of *DavidC.*]

930 Hirsch, Gordon D. "Charles Dickens's 'Nurse's Stories'." *Psychoanalytic Rev* 62 (Spring 1975): 173-179. [*UncomTr.*]

931 —. "Mr. Pickwick's Impotence." *Sphinx* 9 (1979): 28-35.

932 —. "The Mysteries in *Bleak House:* A Psychoanalytic Study." In 1492, pp. 132-152.

933 —. "A Psychoanalytic Rereading of *David Copperfield.*" *VN* no. 58 (Fall 1980): 1-5.

934 Hisada, Harunori. [From little women to new women: A survey of D's heroines.] In 1287, pp. 3-34. [In Jap.; Eng. abst., pp. 253-255 and in 1285, pp. 53-54.]

935 Hjartar, Ólafur F. "Hefurthu sjeth Dickens?," in *Afmaelisrit Björns Sigfússonar,* ed. Björn Teitsson et al. (Reykjavik: Sögufélag, 1975), 194-210. [Icelandic reception.—Eng. abst., pp. 210-211.]

936 Hobbs, Charles C. "Skinning a Dickens of a Skimpole." *TPB* 10 (July 1973): 37-38. [Abst.]

937 Hobsbaum, Philip. "Charles Dickens and the Jews: A Centenary Essay." *Jewish Affairs* (Johannesburg) 26 (Feb. 1971): 17-20.

938 —. "The Principle of the Roving Criterion." *A Theory of Communication* (London: Macmillan, 1970), 73-89. [Amer. ed. *A Theory of Criticism* (Bloomington and London: Indiana UP, 1970).—Incl. 1865-1959 reception of *OurMF.*]

939 —. *A Reader's Guide to Charles Dickens.* London: Thames and Hudson; New York: Farrar, Straus and Giroux, 1973. 318 pp. [Rev.:

Gordon Cheesewright, *DSN* 5 (June 1974): 40-44; Keith Cushman, *LJ* 98 (July 1973): 2107; Robert Greacen, *B&B* 18 (July 1973): 88; Bill Grundy, *Spec* 231 (21 July 1973): 84-85; James R. Kincaid, *Dkn* 70 (Jan. 1974): 57-59; Dorothy E. Litt, *ARBA* 5 (1974): 519-520; Craig Raine, *TES* 11 May 1973: 22; *TLS* 27 Apr. 1973: 478.]

940   —. "The Two Faces of Dickens." *Jewish Chronicle Lit Supp* 4 Dec. 1970: i-ii. [Esp. *OliverTw.*—Attitude toward Jews.]

940a Hoffmann, Gerhard. "Die atmosphärische Stimmung des Raums: Ch. Dickens, *Bleak House*"; "Die Mensch-Ding-Gleichung: Ch. Dickens, *Bleak House, Little Dorrit*"; "Das Unheimliche und der halluzinative bzw. visionäre Raumentwurf im Roman des 19. Jahrhunderts: E. Brontë, Ch. Dickens, H. Melville"; "Die Enthüllungsszene: Ch. Dickens, *Little Dorrit*"; "Die Entwicklung einer korrelativen räumlichen Gesamtstruktur: Ch. Dickens." *Raum, Situation, erzählte Wirklichkeit: Poetologische und historische Studien zum englischen und amerikanischen Roman* (Stuttgart: Metzler, 1978), 62-64; 127-130; 171-174; 544-546; 602-607; et passim.

941   Holderness, Graham. "Imagination in *A Christmas Carol.*" *EA* 32 (Jan.-Mar. 1979): 28-45.

942   Hollington, Michael. "Dickens and the Dance of Death." *Dkn* 74 (May 1978): 67-75. [Infl. of Holbein's work.]

943   —. "Dickens's Conception of the Grotesque." *Dkn* 76 (Summer 1980): 91-99.

944   —. "The Fantastic Paradox: An Aspect of the Theory of Romantic Realism." *Comparison* no. 7 (Spring 1978): 33-44. [Balzac and *DSon, OCShop, SBoz.*]

945   —. "Time in *Little Dorrit*," in *The English Novel in the Nineteenth Century: Essays on the Literary Mediation of Human Values*, ed. George Goodin. ISLL, 63 (Urbana and London: Univ. of Illinois Press, 1972), 109-125. [Rev. of book: Robert E. Lougy, *DSN* 5 (Mar. 1974): 14-18.]

946   Hollinshead, Marilyn P. "Dickens in Pittsburgh: A Stereoscopic View." *Dkn* 74 (Jan. 1978): 33-41.

947   Holloway, John. "Dickens and the Symbol." In 1786, pp. 53-74. [Esp. *OCShop, OliverTw,* also *DSon, MChuz.*]

948 —. "Dickens's Word-World." *Enc* 34 (June 1970): 63-68. [Rev.-art. on 4, 102, 294, 592, 2128.]

949 Holoch, George. "Consciousness and Society in *Little Dorrit*." *VS* 21 (Spring 1978): 335-351.

950 Holt, Douglas Gordon. "Victorian Gothic: Dickens's *A Tale of Two Cities*." *PAPA* 2 (Fall 1975): 11. [Abst.]

951 Hood, Thomas. *Letters,* ed. Peter F. Morgan. Univ. of Toronto Dept. of Eng. St. and Texts, 18 (Toronto and Buffalo: Univ. of Toronto Press, 1973), passim. [Rev.: John Clubbe, *DSN* 7 (Mar. 1976): 16-19.]

952 Hopkins, Charles. *"Great Expectations."* In 1238, II, 685-689. [David Lean's 1947 film.]

953 Hornback, Bert G. "Dickens's Language of Gesture: Creating Character." *DSN* 9 (Dec. 1978): 100-106. [Esp. *DavidC.*]

954 —. "The Hero Self." In 1495, pp. 151-162. [*DavidC.*]

955 —. *"Noah's Arkitecture": A Study of Dickens's Mythology.* Athens: Ohio UP, 1972. x, 182 pp. [Esp. *BarnR, BleakH, DavidC, DSon, GreatEx, HardT, LittleDor, MChuz, OurMF, TaleTwoC.*—Incorporates "Dickens's Argument with the Law," *Dimensions* 1 (Oct. 1970): 8-15.—Rev.: Keith Cushman, *LJ* 97 (1 Nov. 1972): 3691; Avrom Fleishman, *MLQ* 34 (June 1973): 191-199; Joseph Gold, *DSN* 4 (June 1973): 58-60; B[ryan] H[ulse], *Dkn* 69 (May 1973): 129-130; R. D. McMaster, *NCF* 28 (June 1973): 107-110; Philip A. Milner, *NDEJ* 8 (Spring 1973): 115-117; George J. Worth, *JEGP* 72 (Apr. 1973): 246-249; *Ch* 9 (Jan. 1973): 1446; *TLS* 27 Apr. 1973: 478; also rev. in 981, 1026.]

956 Horne, Lewis B. "Hope and Memory in *Hard Times*." *Dkn* 75 (Autumn 1979): 167-174.

957 Horton, Susan R. *Interpreting Interpreting: Interpreting Dickens's Dombey.* Baltimore and London: Johns Hopkins UP, 1979. xiii, 162 pp. [Rev.: Roy Roussel, *Criticism* 22 (Summer 1980): 274-277; G. B. Tennyson, *SEL* 20 (Autumn 1980): 728-729; *Ch* 17 (Apr. 1980): 220-221.]

958 Houfe, Simon. *The Dictionary of British Book Illustrators and Caricaturists, 1800-1914* ([Woodbridge, Suffolk: Antique Collectors' Club], 1978), passim. [Rev.: Andrew Sanders, *Dkn* 75 (Autumn

1979): 177-178.]

959   Howard, Patsy C., comp. "Charles Dickens." *Theses in English Literature 1894-1970* (Ann Arbor: Pierian Press, 1973), 88-93. [International bibliog. of M.A. theses.]

960   Howard-Hill, T. H. "Dickens, Charles John Huffam, 1812-1870." *Index to British Literary Bibliography* (Oxford: Clarendon Press, 1969-1979), I, 306-311; II, 256-257; V, 132-147.

961   Howarth, Herbert. "Voices of the Past in Dickens and Others." *UTQ* 41 (Winter 1972): 151-162. [Incl. *Richard III, OCShop; Macbeth, DSon*.]

962   Howells, William Dean. *W. D. Howells as Critic,* ed. Edwin H. Cady (London and Boston: Routledge and Kegan Paul, 1973), passim.

963   Howitt, D. "Baroja's Preoccupation with Clocks and His Emphatic Treatment of Time in the Introduction to *La Busca,*" in *Hispanic Studies in Honour of Joseph Manson,* ed. Dorothy M. Atkinson and Anthony H. Clarke (Oxford: Dolphin, 1972), 139-147. [Questions John Dos Passos's 1923 claim of Dickens's infl.]

964   Hughes, Dean. "The Composition of *Caleb Williams:* Dickens's Misunderstanding." *DSN* 8 (Sept. 1977): 80.

965   Hughes, Felicity. "Narrative Complexity in *David Copperfield.*" *ELH* 41 (Spring 1974): 89-105.

966   Hulin, Jean-Paul. " 'Rus in Urbe': A Key to Victorian Anti-Urbanism?," in *Victorian Writers and the City,* ed. Jean-Paul Hulin and Pierre Coustillas (Lille: Univ. of Lille III, 1979), 11-40. [*HsldWds,* all novels except *DavidC, GreatEx, MChuz*.]

967   Hulse, Bryan. "Books in general." *Dkn* 71 (May 1975): 113-115; 72 (Jan. 1976): 44-45; 72 (May 1976): 110-112; 73 (Jan. 1977): 50-52; 73 (May 1977): 117-118. [May 1975 rev.-art. incl. 187, 188, 1463, 2000, 2118.—Jan. 1976 rev.-art. incl. 8, 1501, 1600.—May 1976 rev.-art. incl. 503, 1034.—Jan. 1977 rev.-art. incl. 306, 879, 1525, 1611.—May 1977 rev.-art. incl. 902, 1924.]

968   Humpherys, Anne. "*Dombey and Son:* Carker the Manager." *NCF* 34 (Mar. 1980): 397-413.

969   —. "Mayhew and the Literature of His Time." *Travels into the Poor Man's Country: The Work of Henry Mayhew* (Athens: Univ. of

Georgia Press, 1977), 159-194, et passim. [Esp. *AllYR, HsldWds, SBoz.*—Incorporates "Dickens and Mayhew on the London Poor," in 1492, pp. 78-90.—Rev.: Ivan Melada, *DSN* 10 (June-Sept. 1979): 83-88; Graham Parry, *Dkn* 75 (Spring 1979): 42-43.]

970 Hunt, John Dixon. "Dickens and the Traditions of Graphic Satire," in *Encounters: Essays on Literature and the Visual Arts*, ed. John Dixon Hunt (London: Studio Vista; New York: Norton, 1971), 124-155. [Incorporates "Dickens and the Graphic Imagination," *Times* (London) 6 June 1970: 19.—Esp. Hogarth and *NichN, OliverTw, SBoz.*]

971 Hurley, Edward. "Dickens's Portrait of the Artist." *VN* no. 38 (Fall 1970): 1-5. [*DavidC.*]

972 —. "A Missing Childhood in *Hard Times.*" *VN* no. 42 (Fall 1972): 11-16. [Stephen Blackpool.]

973 Hutchens, John K. "One Thing and Another." *SatR* 53 (19 Dec. 1970): 30. [*CCarol.*]

974 Hutchings, Richard J. *Dickens on an Island: A Biographical Study of Charles Dickens in the Isle of Wight*, fwd. John Greaves. Bath: Brodie, 1970. xv, 83 pp. [Rev. in 314, 2237.]

975 Hutter, Albert D. "Crime and Fantasy in *Great Expectations*," in *Psychoanalysis and Literary Process*, ed. Frederick Crews (Cambridge, Mass.: Winthrop, 1970), 25-65.

976 —. "The High Tower of His Mind: Psychoanalysis and the Reader of *Bleak House.*" *Criticism* 19 (Fall 1977): 296-316.

977 —. "Nation and Generation in *A Tale of Two Cities.*" *PMLA* 93 (May 1978): 448-462.

978 —. "Psychoanalysis and Biography: Dickens's Experience at Warren's Blacking." In 1247, pp. 23-37.

979 —. "Reconstructive Autobiography: The Experience at Warren's Blacking." In 1494, pp. 1-14.

980 Ide, Hiroyuki. [The world of *OCShop.*] *Igirisu shosetsu panfuletto* 3 (1972): 47-61. [Also incl. 731, 732, 988, 989, 1705, 1927, 1934.—All arts. in Jap.]

980a Iijima, Tadashi. [D literature and the cinema.] In 412a, pp. 67-69.

[In Jap.]

981   Ikeler, A. Abbott. "Dickens Studies since 1970." *British St Monitor* 9, iii (Winter 1980): 26-48. [Rev.-art. on some 70 items.]

982   Ingham, Patricia. "Speech and Non-Communication in *Dombey and Son.*" *RES* NS 30 (May 1979): 144-153.

983   Ireland, Kenneth R. "Urban Perspectives: Fantasy and Reality in Hoffmann and Dickens." *CL* 30 (Spring 1978): 133-156.

984   Cancelled.

985   Irving, John. "In Defense of Sentimentality." *NYTBR* 25 Nov. 1979: 3, 96 [*CCarol, GreatEx.*]

986   Irwin, Michael. *Picturing: Description and Illusion in the Nineteenth-Century Novel* (London, Boston, Sydney: Allen and Unwin, 1979), passim. [Mentions all novels except *BarnR.*—Rev.: Hugh Witemeyer, *DSN* 11 (June 1980): 55-56.]

987   —. "Readings of Melodrama." In 839, pp. 15-31. [Esp. *DavidC, OCShop, OliverTw, TaleTwoC.*]

988   Ito, Kinji. [About *OliverTw.*] In 980, pp. 8-35. [In Jap.]

989   Iwami, Takeo. [The gospel of D.] In 980, pp. 1-7. [In Jap.]

990   Izzo, Carlo. *Civiltà britannica.* Letture di pensiero e d'arte, 44-45 (Rome: Ed. di Storia e Letteratura, 1970), passim. [Incl. "Il circolo Pickwick," I, 217-228 (intro. to Spaventa Filippi trans. orig. pub. 1954); "La bottega dell'antiquario," I, 229-241 (intro. to Spaventa Filippi trans. orig. pub. 1954); "Charles Dickens oggi," I, 242-250 (orig. pub. 1961); "Dickens regista," II, 141-144 (orig. pub. 1958); "111 = 111," II, 145-148 (on *MEDrood*, orig. pub. 1966)].

991   Jackson, Arlene M. "Reward, Punishment, and the Conclusion of *Dombey and Son.*" In 1495, pp. 103-127.

992   Jackson, Rosemary. "The Silenced Text: Shades of Gothic in Victorian Fiction." *MinnR* NS no. 13 (Fall 1979): 98-112. [Esp. *DSon, PickP.*]

993   Jacobson, Dan. "Charles Dickens," in *Atlantic Brief Lives: A Biographical Companion to the Arts,* ed. Louis Kronenberger and

Emily Morison Beck (Boston: Little, Brown, 1971), 221-224.

994 Jacobson, Wendy S. "John Jasper and Thuggee." *MLR* 72 (July 1977): 526-537. [Note also Anne Lohrli, "Dickens and Meadows Taylor," *N&Q* NS 27 (June 1980): 211.]

995 James, Louis. "An Artist in Time: George Cruikshank in Three Eras." In 1510, pp. 157-168.

996 —. *"Pickwick in America!"* In 1489, pp. 65-80. [Plagiarism.]

997 James, W. L. G. "The Portrayal of Death and 'Substance of Life': Aspects of the Modern Reader's Response to 'Victorianism'." In 839, pp. 226-242. [*OCShop.*]

998 Jan, Isabelle. "Des créatures humaines." In 768, p. 12. [Appreciation.]

999 Jarrett, David. "The Fall of the House of Clennam: Gothic Conventions in *Little Dorrit.*" *Dkn* 73 (Sept. 1977): 154-161.

1000 Jauss, Hans Robert. "Komik der Unschuld—Unschuld des Komischen (Dickens's humoristischer Held)." *Ästhetische Erfahrung und literarische Hermeneutik* (Munich: Fink, 1977), I, 286-294. [*PickP.*]

1001 —. "Über den Grund des Vergnügens am komischen Helden," in *Das Komische,* ed. Wolfgang Preisendanz and Rainer Warning. Poetik und Hermeneutik, 7 (Munich: Fink, 1976), 103-132. [Incl. *PickP.*]

1002 Jay, Elisabeth. *The Religion of the Heart: Anglican Evangelicalism and the Nineteenth-Century Novel* (Oxford: Clarendon Press; New York: Oxford UP, 1979), passim. [Esp. *BleakH, LittleDor.*]

1003 Jefferson, D. W. "The Artistry of *Bleak House.*" *E&S* NS 27 (1974): 37-51.

1004 —. "The Moral Centre of *Little Dorrit.*" *EIC* 26 (Oct. 1976): 300-317.

1005 Jennings, John. *Hard Times.* Helicon Student Guides. Dublin: Helicon, 1977. 56 pp.

1006 Jiggens, Clifford. "Inspector Bucket's Rival." *ArmD* 12 (Summer 1979): 270-271. [Inspector Cutting of R. D. Blackmore's *Clara Vaughn.*]

1007 Cancelled.

1008 Johnson, Alan P. *"Hard Times:* 'Performance' or 'Poetry'?" *DiS* 5 (May 1969): 62-80. [Esp. fire imagery.]

1009 (Johnson, E. D. H. *Charles Dickens: An Introduction to his Novels.* 1969.) [Rev.: Richard D. Altick, *Dkn* 66 (Jan. 1970): 59.]

1010 —. "The George Cruikshank Collection at Princeton." In 1510, pp. 1-33.

1011 Johnson, Edgar. *Charles Dickens: His Tragedy and Triumph,* rev. and abrg. ed. New York: Viking Press; London: Allen Lane, 1977. 601 pp. [Note also pbk. ed. (Harmondsworth and New York: Penguin, 1979).—Rev.: Anatole Broyard, *NYTBR* 18 Dec. 1977: 15-16 and Johnson's ltr. to ed. and Broyard's reply, 5 Feb. 1978: 45; *Mitzi M. Brunsdale, *Houston Post* 29 Jan. 1978; Douglas Bush, *New Republic* 178 (25 Mar. 1978): 25-26; John Carey, *STimes* (London) 9 Apr. 1978: 41; A. O. J. Cockshut *THES* 26 May 1978: 13; Philip Collins, *TLS* 21 Apr. 1978: 446; *Monica Dickens, *Boston Globe* 8 Jan. 1978; Angus Easson, *Dkn* 75 (Spring 1979): 37-38; Paul Gray, *Time* 110 (19 Dec. 1977): 98-99; Geoffrey Grigson, *CnL* 163 (6 Apr. 1978): 937-938; Mollie Hardwick, *B&B* 23 (July 1978): 48-50 and (a diff. rev.) 24 (Sept. 1979): 64; Selina Hastings, *Sunday Telegraph Mag* 12 Aug. 1979: 15; C. T. Houpt, *CSM* 11 Jan. 1978: 23; Dan Jacobson, *Guardian* 9 Apr. 1978: 23; *E. C. Kiessling, *Milwaukee J* 29 Jan. 1978; *Robert Kirsch, *St. Petersburg Times* 5 Feb. 1978; *Jonathan Lardley, *San Francisco Examiner* 3 Jan. 1978; Christopher Lehmann-Haupt, *NYT* 21 Dec. 1977: C19; Kerry McSweeney, *QQ* 85 (Summer 1978): 373; Michael Malone, *Harper's* 255 (Dec. 1977): 107; *Jonathan Megibow, *St. Louis Globe-Democrat* 25-26 Feb. 1978; Jo Modert, *St. Louis Post-Dispatch* 5 Feb. 1978: C4; Edward Neill, *TES* 8 Sept. 1978: 23; James Olney, *DSN* 10 (Mar. 1979): 23-27; Robert L. Patten, *Book World* (supp. to *Washington Post*) 25 Dec. 1977: H1, H6; Hilary Spurling, *TES* 30 Nov. 1979: 20; Ruth Walker, *Virginian-Pilot and Ledger-Star* (Norfolk) 22 Jan. 1978: C6; David Williams, *Punch* 277 (29 Aug. 1979): 338; *Ch* 15 (Mar. 1978): 70-71; *Christian Century* 94 (18 Jan. 1978): 60; *Denver Post* 22 Jan. 1978; *Grand Rapids Press* 15 Jan. 1978; also rev. in 981, 1538.]

1012 —. "Dickens's Anti-Chauvinism." In 1683, pp. 201-210.

1013 Johnson, Pamela Hansford. "The Sexual Life in Dickens's Novels." In 1786, pp. 173-194. [*GreatEx, LittleDor, MChuz, MEDrood,*

NichN, OCShop, OliverTw.]

1014 Johnson, Spencer. *The Value of Imagination: The Story of Charles Dickens,* illus. Pileggi. La Jolla, Cal.: Value Communications, 1977. 63 pp. [Juvenile biog.]

1015 Johnson, Wendell Stacy. "Victorian Triangles." *Living in Sin: The Victorian Sexual Revolution* (Chicago: Nelson-Hall, 1979), 69-123. [Mentions *HsldWds, SBoz,* all novels except *HardT, MEDrood, NichN, OCShop, TaleTwoC.*]

1016 Johnson, William C. "Dickens and Demons: A Comparative Approach." *EngR* 22 (Spring 1972): 33-40. [All novels except *BarnR, LittleDor, MChuz, MEDrood, NichN, OliverTw.*]

1017 Johnston, Arnold. "*The Pyramid:* Innovation, Rediscovery, Challenge." *Of Earth and Darkness: The Novels of William Golding* (Columbia and London: Univ. of Missouri Press, 1980), 83-97. [Incl. parallels with *GreatEx.*]

1018 Johnston, William R. "Alfred Jacob Miller—Would-Be Illustrator." *Walters Art Gallery Bull* 30 (Dec. 1977): 2-3. [*BarnR, LittleDor, MChuz, OCShop.*—19th-century Baltimore artist's sketches of D characters and a painting of The Marchioness.]

1019 Johnstone, Tom. "Decidedly this Side Idolatry: Dr. John Brown and Dickens." *Dkn* 74 (May 1978): 96-102.

1020 Jones, P. G. "Dickens's Literary Children." *Australian Paediatric J* 8 (1972): 233-245.

1021 Jordan, John. "What the Dickens!" *Hibernia* 12 Dec. 1975: 19. [Scrooge.]

1022 Jordan, John E. "Recent Studies in the Nineteenth Century." *SEL* 15 (Autumn 1975): 673, 688-689. [Rev.-art. incl. 103, 187, 1492, 1830.]

1023 Jordis, Christine. "Charles Dickens: *La maison d'apre-vent.*" *NRF* no. 327 (1 Apr. 1980): 127-130. [Rev.-art. on Sylvère Monod trans. *BleakH.*—Note also Richard Bales, *Dkn* 76 (Summer 1980): 107-109.]

1024 —. "Dickens revisité." *NL* 10 Jan. 1980: 26. [On reissue of earlier trans., rev. Jean Gattégno and new Sylvère Monod trans.]

1025 Jorgensen, Ove. "Charles Dickens: Indledning til Dickens's *Store Forventninger.*" *Udvalgte Skrifter: Ballet—Klassik—Litteratur—Kunst,* ed. Henning Krabbe, intro. Thure Hastrup (Copenhagen: Thaning og Appel, 1971), 163-185. [Intro. to his trans. of *GreatEx* orig. pub. 1929.]

1026 Joseph, Gerhard. "Recent Studies in the Nineteenth Century." *SEL* 13 (Autumn 1973): 720-722. [Rev.-art. incl. 65, 802, 955, 1103, 1438, 1490.]

1027 Joyce, James. "The Centenary of Charles Dickens." *James Joyce in Padua,* ed. and intro. Louis Berrone (New York: Random House, 1977), 33-37. [Recently-discovered exam paper (reproduced in facs.) for Univ. of Padua, 1912.—Rpt. from *JML* 5 (Feb. 1976): 1013.—Note also Israel Shenker, "Unpublished Work by Joyce Is Found," *NYT* 19 Sept. 1975: 39, 49.—Note also Louis Berrone, "Dos viajes a Padua," *RO* ser. 3, no. 3 (Jan. 1976): 4-9; "El centenario de Charles Dickens," [ed. and trans. (?) Louis Berrone], *RO* ser. 3, no. 8 (June 1976): 3-5; "Il centenario di Charles Dickens," ed. Louis Berrone, trans. Gianfranco Corsini and Giorgio Melchiori, in Joyce's *Scritti italiani,* ed. Gianfranco Corsini and Giorgio Melchiori ([Milan] : Arnoldo Mondadori, 1979), 187-193.]

1028 Jump, J. D. "Dickens and His Readers." *BJRL* 54 (Spring 1972): 384-397.

1029 Kabel, J. J. C. "Godfried Bomans en Charles Dickens vergeleken." *Dutch Dkn* 6, xv (Dec. 1976): 52-57. [Incl. commentary on Ronald Soetaert's thesis (Ghent).]

1030 —. "James Steerforth: Enkele opmerkingen bij Dickens's beeld van de romantiek." *Dutch Dkn* 6, xv (Dec. 1976): 3-23.

1031 [— and J. C. van Kessel.] "Ten geleide"; "Verantwoording." *Dutch Dkn* 6, xv (Dec. 1976): 1-2; 7, xvi (Dec. 1978): 2-3.

1032 Kaczmarek, Bozydar. "Relacja K. Dickensa o Metodach Ksztalto-wania Jezyka u Gluchociemnych w Instytucie Perkinsa." *Logopedia* (Lublin) 10 (1971): 111-115. [Perkins Institute for the Blind from *AmerN.*]

1033 Kanaguchi, Yoshiaki. [On the translation of *CCarol.*] *ELLS* 7 (1970): 110-122. [In Jap.]

1034 Kaplan, Fred. *Dickens and Mesmerism: The Hidden Springs of Fiction.* Princeton: Princeton UP, 1975. xiv, 249 pp. [Esp. *BleakH,*

LittleDor, MEDrood, NichN, OliverTw, OCShop, OurMF.—Rev.:
C. C. Barfoot, *ES* 58 (Dec. 1977): 542; Charles Bishop, *LJ* 101 (1
Mar. 1976): 718; John Carey, *NewSt* 91 (27 Feb. 1976): 262;
Larry Clipper, *Arnoldian* 6 (Winter 1979): 24-28; T. J. Cribb, *RES*
NS 28 (Nov. 1977): 514-515; Charles L. Crow, *JPC* 11 (Winter
1977): 622; Edwin M. Eigner, *MLR* 73 (Apr. 1978): 416-417; Mat-
thew Hodgart, *TLS* 2 Apr. 1976: 397; Hans Lindström, *Samlaren*
98 (1977): 179-180; Thomas McFarland, *SEL* 16 (Autumn 1976):
722-723; Sylvère Monod, *EA* 30 (Oct.-Dec. 1977): 500; Terry M.
Parssinen, *VPN* 11 (Mar. 1978): 31-32; Sam Pickering, *SR* 85
(Oct.-Dec. 1977): 657-658; Branwen Bailey Pratt, *L&P* 27, i
(1977): 35-38; Eugene F. Quirk, *HSL* 8, i (1976): 50-59; Heinz
Reinhold, *Anglia* 98, i-ii (1980): 256-259; Charles I. Schuster, *DR*
56 (Summer 1976): 397-400; Michael Steig, *NCF* 33 (Mar. 1979):
505-508; Garrett Stewart, *DSN* 7 (Dec. 1976): 117-120; *Ch* 13
(May 1976): 367; also rev. in 584, 967 (May 1976), 981, 1062.]

1035 —. "Pickwick's 'Magnanimous Revenge': Reason and Responsibility
in the *Pickwick Papers.*" *VN* no. 37 (Spring 1970): 18-21.

1036 Kappel, Andrew J. "The Gurney Photograph Controversy." *Dkn* 74
(Sept. 1978): 167-172.

1037 — and Robert L. Patten. "Dickens's Second American Tour and His
'Utterly Worthless and Profitless' American Rights." In 1495, pp.
1-33.

1038 Karl, Frederick R. "Charles Dickens: The Victorian Quixote." *A
Reader's Guide to the Nineteenth Century British Novel*, rev. ed.
(New York: Noonday Press, 1972, rpt. New York: Octagon, 1975),
105-175. [1st pub. 1964 as *An Age of Fiction.*—Esp. *BleakH,
GreatEx, HardT, PickP.*]

1039 (Katarskii, I. *Dikkens v Rossii.* 1966). [Rev.: Jean-Louis Backès,
RLC 45 (Apr.-June 1971): 287-289.—Note also obit. by Mira Per-
per, *Dkn* 68 (Jan. 1972): 51-52 and *DSN* 2 (Dec. 1971): 99.]

1039a —. "Dostoevskii i Dikkens, 1860-1870-e gg." *Dostoevskii* no. 2
(1976): 277-284.

1040 —. "Velikoe nasledie." *Literaturnaya gazeta* (Moscow) 24 June 1970:
13. [Infl. esp. on Gogol, Dostoevski, Turgenev.]

1041 Katona, Anna. "A magyarországi Dickens—kritika." *FK* 17 (Jan.-
June 1971): 201-207. [Rev. of Hungarian criticism 1858-1968.]

1042 —. "The Dickens Centenary Year in Hungary." *DSN* 2 (Mar. 1971):

19-25.

1043 Kauffman, Linda. "The Madam and the Midwife: Reba Rivers and Sairey Gamp." *MissQ* 30 (Summer 1977): 395-401. [Faulkner's *Sanctuary, MChuz*.]

1044 Kawahara, Shigekiyo. "An Approach to the Style of *Great Expectations*." In 2064, p. 64. [Abst.]

1045 Kawai, Michio. [On Micawberism.] In 1287, pp. 139-152. [In Jap.— Eng. abst., pp. 269-271 and in 1285, pp. 58-60.]

1046 Kawamoto, Shizuko. [D: *OurMF*.] *EigoS* 117 (1971): 302-304. [In Jap.]

1047 —. [Image of the prostitute in D.] *EigoS* 124 (1978): 444-446, 521-523. [In Jap.]

1048 —. [Micawber's innocence.] *EigoS* 120 (1974): 52-54. [In Jap.]

1049 Cancelled.

1050 Cancelled.

1051 Kearney, Anthony. "A Borrowing from *In Memoriam* in *David Copperfield*." *N&Q* NS 26 (Aug. 1979): 306-307.

1052 —. "The Storm Scene in *David Copperfield*." *ArielE* 9 (Jan. 1978): 19-30.

1053 Keating, P. J. *The Working Classes in Victorian Fiction* (London, etc.: Routledge and Kegan Paul, 1971; rpt. 1979), passim. [Rev.: Louis James, *DSN* 4 (Sept. 1973): 79-81; Sheila M. Smith, *Dkn* 68 (Jan. 1972): 61-62.]

1054 Kelley, Alice VanBuren. "The Bleak Houses of *Bleak House*." *NCF* 25 (Dec. 1970): 253-268. [Symbolism.]

1055 Kelly, Thomas. "Character in Dickens's Late Novels." *MLQ* 30 (Sept. 1969): 386-401.

1056 Kemp, Walter H. "*The Haunted Man* and Muscial Meaning." *Dkn* 74 (May 1978): 76-79.

1057 Kennard, Jean E. "Emerson and Dickens: A Note on Conrad's *Victory*." *Conradiana* 6, iii (1974): 215-219.

1058 Kennedy, Alan. "The Thread in the Garment"; "Agents and Patients in Dickens." *Meaning and Signs in Fiction* (London: Macmillan; New York: St. Martin's Press, 1979), 30-57; 70-104; et passim. [Incl. *BleakH, DSon, LittleDor, OurMF.*]

1059 Kennedy, George E., II. "Dickens's Manipulators of Righteousness." *DSN* 9 (Mar. 1978): 15-19. [Esp. *DavidC, MChuz, OurMF.*]

1060 —. "The Weakened Will and Dickens's Techniques of Redemption." *PAPA* 4 (Fall 1977): 12. [Abst.—*BleakH, GreatEx, LittleDor, OurMF.*]

1061 —. "Women Redeemed: Dickens's Fallen Women." *Dkn* 74 (Jan. 1978): 42-47. [Esp. Nancy and Lady Dedlock.]

1062 Kennedy, G. W. *VS* 20 (Spring 1977): 343-345. [Rev. of 92, 393, 853, 1034.]

1063 —. "Dickens's Endings." *SNNTS* 6 (Fall 1974): 280-287. [All novels except *BleakH, MEDrood.*]

1064 —. "Naming and Language in *Our Mutual Friend.*" *NCF* 29 (Sept. 1973): 165-178.

1065 —. "Terror and Dream: Nell and *The Old Curiosity Shop.*" *Eng St Coll* ser. 1, no. 3 (Sept. 1976): 1-7.

1066 —. "The Two Worlds of *Dombey and Son.*" *Eng St Coll* ser. 1, no. 4 (Sept. 1976): 1-11. [Family and individual.]

1067 —. "The Uses of Solitude: Dickens and *Robinson Crusoe.*" *VN* no. 52 (Fall 1977): 25-30. [*CCarol, DavidC, DSon, GreatEx, MChuz, OurMF.*]

1068 Kennedy, Valerie. "*Bleak House:* More Trouble with Esther?" *JWSL* 1 (Autumn 1979): 330-347.

1069 Kennedy, Veronica M. S. "Mrs. Gamp as the Great Mother: A Dickensian Use of the Archetype." *VN* no. 41 (Spring 1972): 1-5.

1070 Kenney, Blair G. "Carlyle and *Bleak House.*" *Dkn* 66 (Jan. 1970): 36-41.

1070a Kenny, Thomas Michael. *Who Wrote the Pickwick Papers, Dickens? The Answer.* Sydney: Trenear, 1976. xvi, 135 pp. [Attributes authorship of novel to Thomas Griffiths Wainewright.]

1071 Kessel, J. C. van. "Dickens in het Nederlands." *Dutch Dkn* 6, xv (Dec. 1976): 31-51. [Lists Dutch trans. of D's works.]

1072 Kestner, Joseph. "Elements of Epic in *The Pickwick Papers*." *UDR* 9 (Summer 1972): 15-24.

1073 —. *The Spatiality of the Novel* (Detroit: Wayne State UP, 1978), passim. [Esp. *GreatEx.*]

1074 Kettle, Arnold. "Balzac and Dickens," in *The Modern World, II: Realities*, ed. David Daiches and Anthony Thorlby. Lit. and Western Civ., [5] (London: Aldus Books, 1972), 239-266. [Esp. *BleakH, GreatEx, OurMF.*]

1075 —. "Dickens and the Popular Tradition," in *Marxists on Literature: An Anthology*, ed. David Craig (Harmondsworth, Baltimore, etc.: Penguin, 1975), 214-244. [Rpt. from *ZAA*, 1961.]

1076 Keyte, J. M. and M. L. Robinson. "Mr. Dick the Schizophrenic." *Dkn* 76 (Spring 1980): 37-39.

1077 Khatchadourian, Haig. "Fictional Sentences." *Ratio* 20 (Dec. 1978): 103-115. [Incl. *PickP.*]

1078 Kilian, Crawford. "In Defence of Esther Summerson." *DR* 54 (Summer 1974): 318-328.

1079 Kincaid, James R. " 'Be Ye Lukewarm!': The Nineteenth-Century Novel of Social Action." *MMLA Bull* 6 (Spring 1973): 88-95. [*DavidC, MChuz, OCShop.*]

1080 —. *Dickens and the Rhetoric of Laughter*. Oxford: Clarendon Press, 1971. ix, 264 pp. [Chaps. on *BarnR, DavidC, LittleDor, MChuz, OCShop, OliverTw, OurMF, PickP.*—Incorporates "The Education of Mr. Pickwick," *NCF* 24 (Sept. 1969): 127-141 and "Laughter and Pathos: *The Old Curiosity Shop*," in 1496, pp. 65-94.—Rev.: C. C. Barfoot, *ES* 54 (Aug. 1973): 365-366; Angus Easson, *N&Q* NS 22 (Mar. 1975): 131-132; K. J. Fielding, *RES* NS 24 (Feb. 1973): 100-102; Margaret Ganz, *DSN* 4 (Sept. 1973): 89-93; William H. Magee, *LJ* 97 (15 May 1972): 1812; William Myers, *VS* 17 (Sept. 1973): 108-110; E. F. Quirk, *JEGP* 73 (Apr. 1974): 260-262; Heinz Reinhold, *Anglia* 92, i-ii (1974): 254-256; Paul Schlicke, *Dkn* 69 (Jan. 1973): 51-53; Harvey Peter Sucksmith, *YES* 4 (1974): 323-325; Gilbert Thomas, *English* 21 (Summer 1972): 72; Alexander Welsh, *YR* 62 (Winter 1973): 281-287; *Ch* 9 (Sept. 1972): 814; also rev. in 981, 1956.]

1081 Kinkead-Weekes, Mark. "The Voicing of Fictions." In 839, pp. 168-192. [*DavidC.*]

1082 Klein, Karl L. "Die interpolierten Geschichten in Charles Dickens's *The Pickwick Papers:* Überlegungen gegen eine Integration," in *Miscellanea Anglo-Americana: Festschrift für Helmut Viebrock,* ed. Kuno Schuhmann et al. (Munich: Pressler, 1974), 320-334.

1083 Klieneberger, H. R. "Charles Dickens and Wilhelm Raabe." *Oxford Germ St* 4 (1969): 90-117. [D's infl.]

1084 Kligerman, Charles. "The Dream of Charles Dickens." *J of the Amer Psychoanalytic Assn* 18 (Oct. 1970): 783-799. [Esp. *Chimes,* "HTree."]

1085 Klimenko, E. I. "Angliiskaia literatura v period reform parlamenta i chartistskogo dvizheniia (20-40-e gody)." *Angliiskaia literatura pervoi poloviny XIX veka* ([Leningrad]: Izdatel'stvo Leningradskogo Univ., 1971), 81-139. [*OCShop, OliverTw, PickP, SBoz.*]

1086 Klotz, Kenneth. "Dostoevsky and *The Old Curiosity Shop.*" *YULG* 50 (Apr. 1976): 237-247.

1087 Knight, Everett. "The Case of Dickens." *A Theory of the Classical Novel* (London: Routledge and Kegan Paul, 1969; New York: Barnes and Noble, 1970), 106-143. [Esp. *BleakH, DSon, HardT, LittleDor.*]

1088 Knight, H. L. "Dickens and Mrs. Stowe." In 1493, pp. 43-58.

1089 Knoepflmacher, U. C. "*Our Mutual Friend:* Fantasy as Affirmation." *Laughter and Despair: Readings in Ten Novels of the Victorian Era* (Berkeley, etc.: Univ. of California Press, 1971), 137-167.

1090 Knowlton, Edgar C., Jr. " 'The Italian Dickens'." *AN&Q* 10 (Mar. 1972): 104. [Reply to query on Salvatore Farina, Italian novelist.]

1091 Kogztur, Gizella. "Dickens en Hongrie." In 743, pp. 124-130.

1092 Cancelled.

1093 Koike, Shigeru. [Attractiveness of novels read aloud.] *EigoS* 118 (1972): 84-85. [In Jap.]

1094 —. [D—his trivialism and 'camera-eye'.] In 1287, pp. 99-120. [in Jap.—Eng. abst., pp. 263-264 and in 1285, pp. 60-61.]

1094a — et al. [D, our contemporary?] In 412a, pp. 16-29. [In Jap.]

1095 Kolbuszewski, Jacek. "Przycznek do dziezów znajomosći Dickensa w Polsce." *KN* 21, ii (1974): 231-234. [Tripplin's 1852 sketch of D's life and work.—Engl. abst., p. 234.]

1096 Komatsubara, Shigero. [D and the Great Exhibition.] *EigoS* 116 (1970): 269-271.

1096a —. [D as a social novelist.] In 412a, pp. 40-42. [In Jap.]

1097 Korg, Jacob. "Society and Community in Dickens," in *Politics in Literature in the Nineteenth Century* (Lille: Univ. de Lille III; Paris: Éds. Univ., 1974), 83-11. [*BleakH, DavidC, DSon, GreatEx, LittleDor, MChuz, NichN, OliverTw, PickP.*]

1098 —. "A Stroll in London with Pip, Fagin and Oliver." *NYT* 17 Apr. 1977: X7. [Tour of surviving sites.]

1099 (—, ed. *Twentieth Century Interpretations of Bleak House.* 1968.) [Rev.: Trevor Blount, *Dkn* 66 (Jan. 1970): 57-59; Sylvère Monod, *EA* 23 (Apr.-June 1970): 218.]

1100 Kortländer, Bernd. "Kritik der Droste an Dickens *Oliver Twist:* Ein Brief an Luise v. Bornstedt vom 3. 5. 1839." *KBDF* 1971: 16-24.

1101 Kostelnick, Charles. "Dickens's Quarrel with the Gothic: Ruskin, Durdles, and *Edwin Drood.*" *DSN* 8 (Dec. 1977): 104-108.

1102 Cancelled.

1103 Kotzin, Michael. *Dickens and the Fairy Tale.* Bowling Green, Ohio: Bowling Green Univ. Popular Press, 1972. 123 pp. [Incorporates "The Fairy Business in *Oliver Twist* and *Great Expectations,*" in *Univ Teachers of Eng: Proc of the Conf at Bar Ilan Univ, April 1970,* ed. Ruth Nevo (Ramat Gan, Israel: Bar Ilan UP, 1970), 21-33.—Rev.: K. M. Briggs, *Folklore* 83 (Autumn 1972): 258; Russell M. Goldfarb, *DSN* 3 (Dec. 1972): 111-112; R. D. McMaster, *NCF* 28 (June 1973): 107-110; William Myers, *VS* 17 (Sept. 1973): 108-110; Harry Stone, *Dkn* 69 (May 1973): 121-123; *Ch* 9 (Dec. 1972): 1293; also rev. in 981, 1026.]

1104 Kovacević, Ivanka. *Fact into Fiction: English Literature and the Industrial Scene, 1750-1850* ([Leicester] : Leicester UP/Univ. of Belgrade Faculty of Philology, 1975), passim. [*HardT.*—Rev.: Sheila M. Smith, *Dkn* 73 (Sept. 1977): 170-171.]

1105 —. "William Godwin, the Factory Children and Dickens's *David Copperfield.*" *FP* 3-4 (1970): 29-43.

1106 Koviloska-Poposka, Ivanka. "Carls Dikens: Golemite iscekwanja." *Sovremenost* 21 (1971): 724-738. [*GreatEx.*]

1107 Kreimerman, Norma. "Elementos estructurales en la novela de Dickens." In 813, pp. 37-57.

1108 Kripalani, Sajni. "A Post-Colonial Perspective on Dickens." In 262, pp. 72-80. [*BleakH, NicbN.*]

1109 Kroeber, Karl. "Recent Studies in the Nineteenth Century." *SEL* 19 (Autumn 1979): 733-735. [Rev.-art. incl. 1495, 1504, 1559, 1728, 1733.]

1110 Kubiak, Richard, comp. "Oliver Twist, or The Parish Boy's Progress." *George Cruikshank: Printmaker (1792-1878): Selections from the Richard Vogler Collection* ([Santa Barbara: Santa Barbara Museum of Art, 1978]), 41-44; et passim. [Exhib. cat.—At the Museum Apr.-May 1978 and to be shown at 8 other museums through Feb. 1980.—Rev.: Joseph H. Gardner, *DSN* 11 (June 1980): 58-61.]

1111 Kucich, John. "Action in the Dickens Ending: *Bleak House* and *Great Expectations.*" *NCF* 33 (June 1978): 88-109. [Rev. of issue: F. S. Schwarzbach, *DSN* 11 (Sept. 1980): 89-92.]

1112 —. "Death Worship among the Victorians: *The Old Curiosity Shop.*" *PMLA* 95 (Jan. 1980): 58-72. [Note also F. S. Schwarzbach's ltr. to ed. and Kucich's reply, Oct. 1980, pp. 875-877.]

1113 Kulczycka-Saloni, Janina. "Dickens w Polsce." *PHum* 14, v (1970): 27-40. [Reception.]

1114 Kunzle, David. "*Mr. Lamkin:* Cruikshank's Strike for Independence." In 1510, pp. 169-187.

1115 Kupcenko, M. L. "Problema nravstvennogo 'voskresenija' v proizvedenijax C. Dikkensa." *VF* 4 (1979): 164-176. [Moral revelation.]

1116 Kurrik, Maire Jaanus. "Dickens." *Literature and Negation* (New York and Guildford: Columbia UP, 1979), 162-183; et passim. [*GreatEx.*]

1117 La Cour, Tage and Harald Mogensen. *The Murder Book: An Illustrat-*

ed History of the Detective Story, trans. Roy Duffell, fwd. Julian Symons (London: Allen and Unwin; New York: Herder and Herder, 1971), 24-33. [*BleakH, MEDrood.*—Orig. pub. as *Mordbogen*, Copenhagen, 1969.]

1118 Lahiri, K. "Of Gastronomical Humour in Dickens and in Others." In 262, pp. 29-40.

1119 Lamb, Virginia K. "Nerval, Dickens et. . .Sala." *RLC* 53 (Jan.-Mar. 1979): 84-86. [Sala's misattribution of "The Key of the Street" to D.]

1120 Landor, Walter Savage. *Landor as Critic,* ed. Charles L. Proudfit (London and Henley: Routledge and Kegan Paul, 1979), passim. [Mentions *BleakH, OCShop.*]

1121 Lane, Lauriat, Jr. "Dickens and Melville: Our Mutual Friends." *DR* 51 (Autumn 1971): 315-331. [Esp. *BleakH, GreatEx, MEDrood, OurMF.*]

1122 —. "Dickensian Iconography: 1970." *DR* 54 (Spring 1974): 130-135.

1123 —. "Dickens's Phenomenological Reality." *IFR* 7 (Summer 1980): 129-134. [Rev.-art. on 9, 1415, 1659, 1859, 2101.]

1124 —. "From Dingley Dell to Cloisterham: Dickens and Kent." *Atlantic Advocate* 60 (Aug. 1970): 33-36. [*GreatEx, MEDrood, PickP.*]

1125 —. "Melville and Dickens's *American Notes.*" *Extracts* (Melville Soc.) 12 (1972): 3-4. [D's infl.]

1126 —. "Satire, Society, and Symbol in Recent Dickens Criticism." *SNNTS* 5 (Spring 1973): 125-138. [Rev.-art. on 509, 592, 884, 1150, 1253, 1917, 2093, 2128.]

1127 —. "Theory and Practice of Dickensian Source Study: 1970." *DSN* 4 (June 1973): 34-39.

1128 Lane, Margaret. "Dickens on the Hearth." In 1786, pp. 153-171. [*CBooks, CrickH, DavidC, DSon, OurMF, PickP, SBoz.*]

1129 —. "Prologue: The Last Months." *Dkn* 66 (May 1970): 83-84. [Special no. on D's reputation 1870-1970.—For revs. see 448.]

1130 Langbaum, Robert. "The Art of Victorian Literature," in *The Mind and Art of Victorian England,* ed. Josef L. Altholz (Minneapolis:

Univ. of Minnesota Press; Don Mills, Ont.: Burns and MacEacharn, 1976), 16-34. [*GreatEx.*]

1131 Lange, Bernd-Peter. "Dickens und der historische Roman: *A Tale of Two Cities.*" *GRM* NS 20, iv (1970): 427-442. [Rev. in 1961.]

1132 Langman, Larry and Milt Fajans. "*A Tale of Two Cities.*" *Cinema & the School: A Guide to 101 Major American Films* (Dayton: Pflaum, 1975), 127-128. [Conway's 1935 prod.]

1133 Lankford, William T. " 'The Deep of Time': Narrative Order in *David Copperfield.*" *ELH* 46 (Fall 1979): 452-467.

1134 —. " 'The Parish Boy's Progress': The Evolving Form of *Oliver Twist.*" *PMLA* 93 (Jan. 1978): 20-32. [Note Michael Lund's response, 93 (Oct. 1978): 1007; Sidney Thomas, pp. 1009-1010; Lankford's answer, pp. 1010-1011.]

1135 Lansbury, Coral. "A Cry from Bergman—A Whisper from Dickens." *Meanjin* 32 (Sept. 1973): 323-327. [Refs. from *DSon, GreatEx* in *Cries and Whispers.*]

1136 —. "Dickens's Romanticism Domesticated." *DSN* 3 (June 1972): 36-46. [*MChuz.*]

1137 —. "Mr. Micawber." *Arcady in Australia: The Evocation of Australia in Nineteenth-Century English Literature* ([Carlton, Vic.]: Melbourne UP, 1970), 92-107; et passim. [Esp. *DavidC, GreatEx.*—Rev.: J. Miriam Benn, *DSN* 2 (Sept. 1971): 80-84; Donald H. Simpson, *Dkn* 68 (May 1972): 119-121.]

1138 —. "Terra Australis Dickensia." *MLS* 1 (Summer 1971): 12-20.

1139 Lapouge, Gilles. "Charles Dickens." In 768, pp. 9-10.

1140 Larson, Janet Karsten. "Identity's Fictions: Naming and Renaming in *Hard Times.*" *DSN* 10 (Mar. 1979): 14-19.

1141 Lary, N. M. *Dostoevsky and Dickens: A Study of Literary Influence.* London and Boston: Routledge and Kegan Paul, 1973. xvii, 172 pp. [Esp. *BarnR, DavidC, DSon, LittleDor, MChuz, NichN, OCShop, PickP.*—Note also diss., "Dickens and Dostoevsky" (Sussex, 1969).—Rev.: C. C. Barfoot, *ES* 55 (Aug. 1974): 374; Ellen Chances, *CL* 29 (Spring 1977): 172-175; Donald M. Fiene, *Bull of the Intl Dostoevsky Soc* no. 5 (Nov. 1975): 14-17; Gene Fitzgerald, *SEEJ* 20 (Winter 1976): 472-473; Joseph Frank, *DSN* 6

(Dec. 1975): 119-123; Robert Greacen, *B&B* 18 (Aug. 1973): 92; Militsa Greene, *SEER* 52 (Apr. 1974): 315; B[ryan] H[ulse], *Dkn* 70 (Jan. 1974): 54-55; M. V. J[ones], *JES* 4 (Mar. 1974): 98-99; Susan Knight, *NewSt* 85 (1 June 1973): 816; Willis Konick, *SlavR* 34, i (1975): 195-196; Annegret Maack, *N&Q* NS 22 (Mar. 1975): 133-134; Sylvère Monod, *EA* 26 (Oct.-Dec. 1973): 484-485; Rosemary Neiswender, *LJ* 99 (15 Feb. 1974): 487; R. A. Peace, *MLR* 69 (Apr. 1974): 478-479; Rado Pribić, *Kritikon litterarum*, 3, iv (1974): 308-309; D. H. Stewart, *WHR* 27 (Autumn 1973): 418-421; Harvey Peter Sucksmith, *NCF* 29 (June 1974): 101-104; Edward Wasiolek, *VS* 17 (Mar. 1974): 342-343; *Cb* 10 (Nov. 1973): 1377; *TLS* 10 Aug. 1973: 923; also rev. in 981, 2158.]

1142 Laski, Marghanita. "Dickens Today." *Times* (London) 30 May 1970: 19.

1143 Lauran, Annie. "Dickens dans ma nuit." In 743, pp. 23-26. [*DavidC.*]

1144 Laurence, Dan H., comp. *Shaw: An Exhibit* (Austin: Humanities Research Center, Univ. of Texas, 1977), items #126, 242, 623; et passim. [Quotes various Shaw documents on D's infl.]

1145 Cancelled.

1146 Lazarus, Mary. *A Tale of Two Brothers: Charles Dickens's Sons in Australia.* [Sydney and London] : Angus and Robertson, 1973. viii, 220 pp. [Incorporates "The Problem of Plorn: Edward Dickens's First Days in Australia," *Dkn* 68 (May 1972): 90-99; see also "Plorn's Australian Uncles," Sept., p. 172.—Rev.: Arthur A. Adrian, *Dkn* 70 (Jan. 1974): 60-62; Philip Collins, *TLS* 25 Oct. 1974: 1184; Mollie Hardwick, *B&B* 21 [i.e. 20] (Jan. 1975): 42-43; George Wing, *DSN* 6 (June 1975): 58-61; note also J. Miriam Benn, "A New Biography of the Dickens Sons in Australia," *DSN* 2 (June 1971): 56-58.]

1147 Leach, Elsie. "Lolita and Little Nell." *SJS* 3 (Feb. 1977): 71-78.

1148 Leavis, F. R. *Letters in Criticism,* ed. John Tasker (London: Chatto and Windus, 1974), 96; 140-141; et passim. [Ltrs. to eds., one rpt. from 1587.]

1149 —. " 'Literalism' versus 'Scientism': The Misconception and the Menace." *TLS* 23 Apr. 1970: 441-444. [Note also 1821.]

1150 — and Q. D. *Dickens: The Novelist*. London: Chatto and Windus; New York: Pantheon, 1970. xviii, 371 pp. [Note 2nd ed., rev. and enl., London: Chatto and Windus, 1970; 3rd ed., rev. and enl., London: Chatto and Windus, 1973; New Brunswick: Rutgers UP, 1979; pbk. ed. Harmondsworth: Penguin, 1972.—Chaps. on *BleakH, DavidC, DSon* (rpt. with changes from *SR*, 1962), *GreatEx, HardT* (diff. version pub. in *Scrutiny*, 1947, and rpt. in *The Great Tradition*, 1948), *LittleDor*.—Note also 197, 235.—Rev.: Alberto Adell, *Insula* 27 (Jan. 1972): 13; A[rnold] B[eichman], *CSM* 16 Sept. 1971: 11; Michael Black, *Human World*, no. 5 (Nov. 1971): 88-90; John Braine, *National Rev* 23 (13 July 1971): 763-764; Piers Brendan, *B&B* 16 (Dec. 1970): 27-28; Hugh Buckingham, *Harvard Advocate* 105 (Apr. 1971): 21-23; A. S. Byatt, *Times* (London) 1 Oct. 1970: 16; John Carey, *Lstr* 84 (29 Oct. 1970): 591-592; John Casey, *Spec* 225 (24 Oct. 1970): 477-478; Shirley Chew, *Enc* 36 (Feb. 1971): 74-77; R. C. Churchill, *Humanist* (England) 86 (Jan. 1971): 9-11; Keith Cushman, *LJ* 96 (July 1971): 2320; K. J. Fielding, *DSN* 2 (June 1971): 37-39; George H. Ford, *NCF* 26 (June 1971): 95-113; Barbara Hardy, *NewSt* 80 (9 Oct. 1970): 456-457; J. R. Harvey, *CQ* 6 (July 1972): 77-93; D. A. N. Jones, *New Society* 16 (26 Nov. 1970): 962-963; Sylvère Monod, *EA* 24 (Jan.-Mar. 1971): 59-72; Marvin Mudrick, *HudR* 24 (Summer 1971): 346-354 (see 1383); Edward Neill, *TES* 8 Feb. 1980: 27; W. W. Robson, *Dkn* 67 (May 1971): 99-104; D. R. G. Shayer, *Stand* 12, ii (1971): 74-75; Alan Shelston, *CritQ* 13 (Spring 1971): 89-91; Harvey Peter Sucksmith, *SoRA* 5 (Mar. 1972): 68-77; John Tasker, *B&B* 18 (Dec. 1972): 16; Dennis Walder, *New Edinburgh Rev* no. 15 (Nov. 1971): 33-34; Ian Watt, *Lstr* 85 (11 Mar. 1971): 298-301; Brian Wicker, *Commonweal* 94 (25 June 1971): 337-339 and Brian M. Barbour's ltr. to ed. and Wicker's reply, 6 Aug. 1971: 415; Angus Wilson, *Obs* 18 Oct. 1970: 34; *BBkN* (Dec. 1970): 965-966; *New Republic* 164 (22 May 1971): 33; also rev. in 182 (Aug. 1971), 981, 1126, 1578, 1961, 2065, 2205, 2216, 2227.]

1151 Lebowitz, Naomi. "The Structure of Disappointment in Balzac and Dickens," in *Essays on European Literature in Honor of Liselotte Dieckmann*, ed. Peter U. Hohendahl et al. (St. Louis: Washington UP, 1972), 53-60. [Esp. *LittleDor, MChuz*.—Rev.: Ann Humpherys, *DSN* 7 (Dec. 1976): 125-126.]

1152 Lecker, Barbara. "The Split Characters of Charles Dickens." *SEL* 19 (Autumn 1979): 689-704. [Public and private lives of esp. Bucket, Pancks, Lorry, Wemmick, Jaggers.]

1153 —. "Walter Gay and the Theme of Fancy in *Dombey and Son*." *Dkn*

67 (Jan. 1971): 21-30.

1154 LeComte, Edward. "Rubinstein, the Lady in Spain, and Miss Havisham." *Greyfriar* 17 (1976): 13-19. [Sex and symbolism.]

1155 Lee, B. R. L. "The Damp Souls of Housemaids: Class, Dickens, and the English Novel." *Haltwhistle Q* no. 1 (Spring 1973): 36-51.

1156 (Lee, James W., ed. *SNNTS* 1 [Summer 1969].) [D special no.— Rev.: K. J. Fielding, *Dkn* 66 (Jan. 1970): 50-51; Jerome Meckier, *DSN* 1 (Dec. 1970): 9-11; also rev. in 981, 1808.]

1157 Leimberg, Ingeborg. "*Hard Times:* Zeitbezug und überzeitliche Bedeutung: Zeitkritische Fakten im fiktionalen Zusammenhang." *GRM* NS 21, iii (1971): 269-296. [Rpt. in 848, pp. 269-308.]

1158 — and Lothar Cerny. *Charles Dickens: Methoden und Begriffe der Kritik*. Erträge der Froschung, 99. Darmstadt: Wissenschaftliche Buchgesellschaft, 1978. ix, 366 pp. [Reception 1844-1975.—Eng. abst., *EASG* 1979: 75-78.]

1159 Lelchuk, Alan. "Self, Family, and Society in *Great Expectations*." *SR* 78 (July-Sept. 1970): 407-426. [Rev. in 1961.]

1160 Lempruch, Nils-Göran von. "Some Grotesque Characters in Dickens's *Great Expectations*." *MSpr* 67, iv (1973): 328-332.

1161 Lengyel, Miklós. "Dickens hatása Magyarország elbeszélo müvészetére." *Palócföld* 6 (1972): 24-34. [Infl. on Hungarian lit.]

1162 Lennie, Campbell. *Landseer, the Victorian Paragon* (London: H. Hamilton, 1976), passim.

1163 Lerner, Laurence. "An Essay on *Dombey and Son*," in *The Victorians*, ed. Laurence Lerner (London: Methuen; New York: Holmes and Meier, 1978), 195-208.

1164 —. "Literature and Social Change." *JES* 7 (Dec. 1977): 231-252. [Incl. *GreatEx*.]

1165 —. *Love and Marriage: Literature and Its Social Context* (London: Edward Arnold; New York: St. Martin's, 1979), passim. [*BleakH, DavidC, NichN*.]

1166 — and Barry Supple. "Novelists and Social Change," in *The English*

Novel, ed. Cedric Watts (London: Sussex, 1976), 31-52. [Dialogue incl. *GreatEx, HardT, LittleDor*.]

1167 Lesser, M. J. "Dickens and the Chair-Bound." *Dkn* 73 (Jan. 1977): 25-32. [*BarnR, BleakH, DSon, GreatEx, LittleDor, NicbN*.]

1168 Levi, Laurina, Sr. "The Origin of Mr. Scrooge." *Family Digest* 30 (Dec. 1974): 9-11.

1169 Levin, Harry. "Dickens after a Century." *Grounds for Comparison*, HSCL, 32 (Cambridge: Harvard UP, 1972): 339-350. [Rpt. from *ASch* 39 (Autumn 1970): 670-676; in Span. as "Charles Dickens (1812-1870)," trans. Aída Fajardo, *SinN* 2, i (July-Sept. 1971): 24-33.]

1170 —. "The Uncles of Dickens." In 306, pp. 1-35. [Esp. *PickP*.]

1171 Levine, Richard A. "Reviews—Paperback Editions: *Dombey and Son*." *DSN* 3 (June 1972): 53-57. [Incl. 41.]

1172 Levitchi, Leon D. "Dickens, contemporanul nostru." In 588, pp. 11-20. [Eng. abst., p. 20.]

1173 Levy, Diane Wolfe. "Dickens's *Bleak House*." *Expl* 38 (Spring 1980): 40-42. [As detective fiction.]

1174 Lewis, Peter. "The Waste Land of *Our Mutual Friend*." *DUJ* NS 39 (Dec. 1977): 15-28.

1175 Lewis, Sinclair. "Detective Stories and Mr. Dickens." *YULG* 45 (Jan. 1971): 88-92. [Here 1st pub.; orig. intended for his aborted condensation of *BleakH*.—Note also 1532.]

1176 Ley, Charles David. "Galdós como novelista europeo." *Letras de Deusto* 4 (July-Dec. 1974): 95-113. [Infl. of D, Balzac, Tolstoy.]

1177 —. "Galdós comparado con Balzac y Dickens, como novelista nacional." Congreso Internacional de Estudios Galdosianos, *Actas* 1 (1977): 291-295.

1178 Librach, Ronald S. "Burdens of Self and Society: Release and Redemption in *Little Dorrit*." *SNNTS* 7 (Winter 1975): 538-551.

1179 Linehan, Tom. "The Importance of Plot in *Little Dorrit*." *JNT* 6 (Spring 1976): 116-131.

1180 —. "Rhetorical Technique and Moral Purpose in Dickens's *Hard Times.*" *UTQ* 47 (Fall 1977): 22-36.

1181 Lloyd, Eric. "Mr. Dickens: Some Great Expectations Fulfilled." *Wall Street J* 21 Aug. 1970: 6. [Rev. of 3, 448, 2005, 2128.]

1182 Locker, Kitty O. "Social Criticism as Theme: A Strategy for Teaching *Hard Times* and *Great Expectations.*" *Illinois Eng Bull* 67 (Fall 1979): 35-43.

1183 Lodge, David. "Types of Description." *The Modes of Modern Writing: Metaphor, Metonymy, and the Typology of Modern Literature* (London: Edward Arnold; Ithaca: Cornell UP, 1977), 93-103. [Incl. *BleakH.*—Method partly derived from Jakobson.]

1184 Lohrli, Anne. " 'Dickens on Beards'." *DSN* 11 (Mar. 1980): 16-17. [*HsldWds.*]

1185 —. "George Ballentine: *Household Words* Contributor." *Dkn* 72 (Jan. 1976): 30-33.

1186 —, comp. *Household Words, a Weekly Journal, 1850-1859, Conducted by Charles Dickens: Table of Contents, List of Contributors and Their Contributions.* Toronto and Buffalo: Univ. of Toronto Press, 1974. x, 534 pp. [Note also 383.—Rev.: Alec W. C. Brice, *DSN* 6 (June 1975): 56-58; Philip Collins, *VPN* 7 (Sept. 1974): 30-32; K. J. Fielding, *YES* 6 (1976): 308-310; Anthony Laude, *RES* NS 26 (May 1975): 232-234; Harry Stone, *Dkn* 70 (Sept. 1974): 209-211; Robert H. Tener, *ArielE* 5 (Oct. 1974): 82-83; *Cb* 11 (Sept. 1974): 913-914; *TLS* 19 Apr. 1974: 410; also rev. in 504.]

1187 —. "*Household Words:* Its Editor and Its Sub-Editor." *Dkn* 74 (Jan. 1978): 30-32.

1188 —. "A Note on Mr. Thoms." *N&Q* NS 25 (June 1978): 205-206. [William John Thoms, founder of *N&Q.*]

1189 Long, Richard W. "The England of Charles Dickens," photos. Adam Woolfitt. *National Geographic* 145 (Apr. 1974): 443-483.

1190 Longford, Lord. "[Toast at] 65th Annual Conference." *Dkn* 67 (Sept. 1971): 182-184.

1191 Lonoff, Sue. "Charles Dickens and Wilkie Collins." *NCF* 35 (Sept. 1980): 150-170. [Personal relations and co-infl.]

1192 López Ortega, Ramón. "*Hard Times* (1854), de Charles Dickens." *Movimiento obrero y novela inglesa.* Acta salmanticensia; Ensayos y textos de lengua y literatura inglesa, Ensayos, 2 (Salamanca: Univ. de Salamanca, 1976), 47-52.

1193 Lorent, Angela. "*A Tale of Two Cities:* Die Revolution als mythischer Kampf zwischen Individuum und Kollektiv"; "Die Massendarstellung als Kulturkritik in *Hard Times.*" *Funktionen der Massenszene im viktorianischen Roman.* NSAA, 18 (Frankfurt a.M., Bern, Cirencester: Peter Lang, 1980), 78-99; 177-185; et passim. [Freiburg diss.]

1194 Lorinczy, Huba. "A magyar századelo Twist Olivéje (Dickens-reminiszcenciák a gólyakalifában)." *Literatura* 3, iii-iv (1976): 25-30. [Infl. on Mihaly Babits.]

1195 Lougy, Robert E. "Dickens's *Hard Times:* The Romance as Radical Literature." In 1490, pp. 237-254.

1196 —. "Pickwick and 'The Parish Clerk'." *NCF* 25 (June 1970): 100-103.

1197 —. "Remembrances of Death Past and Future: A Reading of *David Copperfield.*" In 1494, pp. 72-101.

1198 Love, Theresa R. *Dickens and the Seven Deadly Sins,* [fwd. Lucien Fournier]. Danville, Ill.: Interstate, 1979. xxvi, 160 pp. [All the novels except *MEDrood.*]

1199 Lucas, John. "Dickens and Arnold." *RMS* 16 (1972): 86-111. [*BleakH, DavidC, LittleDor, OliverTw* used to show Arnold's marginal status.]

1200 —. "Dickens and Shaw: Women and Marriage in *David Copperfield* and *Candida.*" *ShawR* 22 (Jan. 1979): 13-22.

1201 —. *The Melancholy Man: A Study of Dickens's Novels.* London: Methuen; New York: Barnes and Noble, 1970. xiii, 353 pp. [Esp. *BleakH, DavidC, DSon, GreatEx, LittleDor, MChuz, NichN, OCShop, OurMF, PickP.*—Note also 2nd ed. (Totowa, N.J.: Barnes and Noble; Brighton: Harvester Press, 1980), xv, 366 pp.—Rev.: T. J. Cribb, *RES* NS 23 (Aug. 1972): 372-374; Ruth Etchells, *DUJ* 64 (Dec. 1971): 75-76; K. J. Fielding, *Dkn* 67 (May 1971): 115-116; Margaret Ganz, *VS* 15 (Dec. 1971): 234-236; Angela M. Lucas, *Studies* 61 (Summer 1972): 197-198; Jerome Meckier, *DSN* 2 (Dec. 1971): 100-102; Sylvère Monod, *EA* 24 (Jan.-Mar. 1971): 97-98; Kenneth Muir, *MLR* 67 (Apr. 1972):

405-407; Genevieve L. Quigley, *CEA* 34 (Nov. 1971): 38-39; *BBkN* (Jan. 1971): 61-62; *Ch* 8 (Nov. 1971): 1179; also rev. in 981, 1961, 1972, 2065, 2205, 2216.]

1202 Lucas, Victor. *Tolstoy in London* (London: Evans Brothers, 1979), 35-36. [On Tolstoy's alleged attendance in 1861 at a lecture on education by D.]

1203 Luedtke, Luther S. "Harold Frederic's Satanic Soulsby: Interpretation and Sources." *NCF* 30 (June 1975): 82-105. [Incl. Mrs. Jellyby as source for Sister Soulsby in *Damnation of Theron Ware*.]

1204 —. "System and Sympathy: The Structural Dialectic of Dickens's *Bleak House*." *LWU* 3, i (1970): 1-14.

1205 Lund, Michael. "Teaching Long Victorian Novels in Parts." *VN* no. 58 (Fall 1980): 29-32. [Incl. *DavidC*.]

1206 Lutman, Stephen. "Reading Illustrations: Pictures in *David Copperfield*." In 839, pp. 196-225.

1207 Lyons, John O. "Into Our Age." *The Invention of the Self: The Hinge of Consciousness in the Eighteenth Century* (Carbondale and Edwardsville: Southern Illinois UP; London and Amsterdam: Feffer and Simons, 1978), 219-229. [*DavidC, GreatEx, MEDrood.*]

1208 M., F. "Dickens, 100 años después." *Indice* 25 (15 June 1970): 36.

1209 Maack, Annegret. "Angus Wilsons Auseinandersetzung mit Charles Dickens." *LWU* 12 (Dec. 1979): 267-286.

1210 MacAndrew, Elizabeth. "A Second Level of Symbolism in *Great Expectations*." *ELWIU* 2 (Spring 1975): 65-75. [Institutions, spiritual states.]

1211 McCarron, Robert M. "Folly and Wisdom: Three Dickensian Wise Fools." In 1494, pp. 40-56. [Barnaby Rudge, Tom Pinch, Dick Swiveller.]

1212 McCarthy, Patrick J. "The Language of *Martin Chuzzlewit*." *SEL* 20 (Autumn 1980): 637-649. [Animism, superlatives, odd collocations, lists, reworked clichés, animal imagery.]

1213 McCook, James. "Inspector Dickens, N.W.M.P." *Blackwood's Mag* 311 (Feb. 1972): 122-133. [Francis Jeffrey Dickens.]

1214 McCullen, Maurice L. "Turveydrop of *Bleak House:* Basis of Dickens's Redefinition of Dandyism." *DSN* 4 (Mar. 1973): 15-21.

1215 McDonald, Andrew. "The Preservation of Innocence in *Dombey and Son:* Florence's Identity and the Role of Walter Gay." *TSLL* 18 (Spring 1976): 1-19.

1216 MacDonald Allen, D. G. "The Mystery of *The Mystery of Edwin Drood.*" *The Janus Sex: The Androgynous Challenge* (Hicksville, N.Y.: Exposition Press, 1975), 165-186.

1217 McDougal, Edwin D. "Lost New York." *TLS* 11 June 1971: 677. [Ltr. to ed. on D, Washington Irving, and a gin cocktail; see also Brendan Gill's ltr. to ed., 16 Apr. 1971: 449.]

1218 Macey, Samuel L. *Clocks and the Cosmos: Time in Western Life and Thought* (Hamden, Conn.: Archon Books, 1970), passim. [Esp. *GreatEx, MH'sClock.*]

1219 McGowan, John P. "*David Copperfield:* The Trial of Realism." *NCF* 34 (June 1979): 1-19.

1220 McGowan, Mary. "Arthur Ryland of Birmingham and Some New Dickens Letters." *Dkn* 74 (Sept. 1978): 148-156.

1221 Machin, Roger, comp. *Bibliotheca Dickensiana.* Kyoto: Kyoto Univ. of Foreign St. Lib., 1975. [Exhib. cat.—Rev.: M[ichael] S[later], *Dkn* 73 (Jan. 1977): 52.]

1222 MacKenzie, Norman. "Dickens on the Move." *ILN* 267 (May 1979): 47-49, 51. [Residences.]

1223 — and Jeanne. *Dickens: A Life.* Oxford, New York, etc.: Oxford UP, 1979. xi, 434 pp. [Rev.: Phoebe-Lou Adams, *Atlantic* 244 (July 1979): 82; John Bayley, *Lstr* 101 (3 May 1979): 627; *Valerie Brooks, *Chicago Sun-Times* 8 July 1979; E[dward] B[utscher], *Booklist* 75 (15 May 1979): 1414; *William J. Clew, *Hartford Courant* 17 June 1979; Philip Collins, *NewSt* 97 (25 May 1979): 761-762; P. J. Coveney, *BBkN* Aug. 1979: 686; C. B. C[ox], *CritQ* 21 (Autumn 1979): 91; William R. Evans, *Best Sellers* 39 (Aug. 1979): 178; Benny Green, *Spec* 242 (19 May 1979): 30-31; John Jordan, *Hibernia* 2 Aug. 1979: 14, 16; Peter Keating, *TLS* 7 Dec. 1979: 90; *Jacob Korg, *Seattle Times* 12 Aug. 1979; Margaret Lane, *Daily Telegraph* (London) 10 May 1979: 14; Marghanita Laski, *CnL* 165 (1979): 1315; Mary McBride, *LJ* 104 (1 June 1979): 1258; Elizabeth Muther, *CSM* 10 Sept. 1979: B3;

Joseph H. O'Mealy, *Biography* 3 (Spring 1980): 180-183; David Parker, *MLQ* 40 (Sept. 1979): 319-322; Robert L. Patten, *Houston Post* 17 June 1979: AA16; Sam Pickering, *SR* 88 (Spring 1980): xxxiv, xxxvi; V. S. Pritchett, *NYRB* 19 July 1979: 3-4; John Romano, *SatR* [NS] 6 (21 July 1979): 46-50; Lorna Sage, *Guardian Weekly* 13 May 1979: 22; Andrew Sanders, *Dkn* 76 (Spring 1980): 44-45; Michael Slater, *VS* 23 (Summer 1980): 520-522; Hilary Spurling, *TES* 30 Nov. 1979: 20; Harry Stone, *NCF* 34 (Mar. 1980): 438-443; John Sutherland, *New Society* 48 (10 May 1979): 342-343; John Wain, *NYTBR* 24 June 1979: 7; Rebecca West, *Sunday Telegraph* (London) 6 May 1979: 12; *AB Bookman's Weekly* 5 May 1980: 3488; *Ch* 16 (Nov. 1979): 1173; *Ecn* 271 (12 May 1979): 128-129; *NY* 55 (23 July 1979): 96; *Publishers Weekly* 215 (16 Apr. 1979): 65; also rev. in 217.]

1224 McLean, Hugh. *Nikolai Leskov: The Man and His Art* (Cambridge and London: Harvard UP, 1977), passim. [D's infl.]

1225 McLean, Robert Simpson. "Another Note on Nickleby." *DSN* 9 (Mar. 1978): 6-9. [Ralph Nickleby's villainy.—Note also George Wing's response, pp. 9-10.]

1226 —. "Another Source for Quilp." *NCF* 26 (Dec. 1971): 337-339.

1227 —. "Tory Noodles in Sydney Smith and Charles Dickens: An Unnoticed Parallel." *VN* no. 38 (Fall 1970): 24-25. [*BleakH, LittleDor.*]

1228 McMaster, R. D. "Collections of Centennial Essays on Dickens." *NCF* 26 (Sept. 1971): 219-228. [Rev.-art. on 448 (all essays), 1419, 1496, 1786, 2005.]

1229 —. "Reviews—Paperback Editions: *A Tale of Two Cities*." *DSN* 3 (Mar. 1972): 16-21. [Incl. 92.]

1230 —. " 'Society: (Whatever that was)': Dickens and Society as an Abstraction." In 154, pp. 125-135. [*HardT, LittleDor, OurMF.*]

1231 McMurtry, Jo. *Victorian Life and Victorian Fiction: A Companion for the American Reader* (Hamden, Conn.: Archon, 1979), passim.

1232 McPherson, Brian, comp., with Ada H. Fache and Mary A. Ronnie. *Charles Dickens, 1812-1870: Catalogue*, Centenary [i.e. 2nd, enl.] ed., ed. Mary A. Ronnie. Wellington, N.Z.: Reed for Dunedin Pub. Lib., 1970. 108 pp. Supp. 1971. 27 pp. [Alfred and Isabel Reed Coll. at Dunedin, N.Z., Pub. Lib.; 1st ed. 1965.]

1233 McWilliams, John P., Jr. "*Great Expectations:* The Beacon, the Gibbet, and the Ship." In 1490, pp. 255-266.

1234 —. "Progress without Politics: *A Tale of Two Cities.*" *ClioI* 7 (Fall 1977): 19-31.

1235 Madaule, Jacques. "Un univers fantastique et vrai." In 743, pp. 26-37. [*BarnR, CCarol, DSon, GreatEx, OCShop.*]

1236 Madden, David. *A Primer of the Novel: For Readers and Writers* (Metuchen, N.J., and London: Scarecrow Press, 1980), passim. [Esp. *BleakH.*]

1237 Maddocks, John. "Dickens and Lawson." *Quadrant* 22 (Feb. 1978): 42-46. [Infl. on Henry Lawson.]

1238 Magill, Frank N., ed. *Magill's Survey of Cinema: English Language Films,* 1st ser. (Englewood Cliffs, N.J.: Salem Press, 1980), I-IV, passim. [Incl. 242, 952, 1652, 2029.]

1239 Magnet, Myron. "Lord Chesterfield, *Barnaby Rudge,* and the History of Conscience." *BNYPL* 80 (Summer 1977): 474-502.

1240 Magoun, F. P., Jr. "Charles Dickens: Two Analogues." *NM* 72 (June 1971): 302-303. [Words and phrases in *OurMF, PickP.*]

1241 Mahalanobis, Shanta. "The Adult World of *Dombey and Son.*" In 262, pp. 59-71. [Compared to James's *Golden Bowl.*]

1242 Major, Gwen. "The Magwitch Hide-Out." *Dkn* 67 (Jan. 1971): 31-33. [Actual site.]

1243 Makowiecki, Stefan et al., comps. "Dickens, Ch." *Bibliografia anglistyki polskiej, 1945-1975: Jezykoznawstwo-Literaturoznawstwo,* ed. Jacek Fisiak (Warsaw: Państwowe Wydawn. Naukowe, 1977), 122-124. [Bibliog. of Polish criticism with 29 entries.]

1244 Man, Glenn K. S. "Affirmation in Dickens's *Little Dorrit.*" *ELWIU* 6 (Spring 1979): 43-56.

1245 Manchel, Frank. "Dickens in the Film: The Adaptation of Three Books." *Exercise Exchange* 19 (Fall 1974): 20-28. [Lean's 1947 *GreatEx,* Conway's 1935 *TaleTwoC,* Cukor's 1935 *DavidC.*—Rpt. with revisions from *Film Study: A Resource Guide* (Rutherford, Madison, Teaneck: Farleigh Dickinson UP, 1973), 149-158.]

1246 Manheim, Leonard. "Dickens's Fools and Madmen." In 1490, pp. 69-97. [Esp. *BarnR, DavidC, NichN, OCShop, OliverTw, PickP.*]

1247 —, ed. *Hartford Studies in Literature* 8, i (1976). "Proceedings of [1975 MLA] Seminar 255: Psychoanalytic Criticism of Dickens." [Ed., "Introduction to the Seminar," 1-3; Richard Dunn, ed., "Discussion Notes," 46-49 (by participants).—Incl. 978, 1569, 1860.— Rev.: Helen Storm Corsa, *DSN* 7 (Dec. 1976): 113-117; Bryan Hulse, *Dkn* 73 (Sept. 1977): 171-172.]

1248 —. "HEROES, *heroes,* and heroids." In 1493, pp. 1-22. [Esp. *DavidC, MChuz, PickP.*]

1249 —. "The Law as 'Father': An Aspect of the Dickens Pattern." *HSL* 9, ii-iii (1977): 100-109. [Enl. from *AI*, 1955.—Esp. *BleakH.*]

1250 —. "The Personal History of David Copperfield: A Study in Psychoanalytic Criticism." In 1955, pp. 75-94. [Rpt. from *AI*, 1952.]

1251 —. "A Tale of Two Characters: A Study in Multiple Projection." In 1489, pp. 225-237.

1252 Mankowitz, Wolf. *Dickens of London.* London: Weidenfeld and Nicolson, 1976; New York: Macmillan, 1977. 252 pp. [Based on 2906.—Note also *Het leven van Charles Dickens, 1812-1870,* trans. A. Hoevers (Wageningen: Veen, 1977), 251 pp.—Rev.: Philip Collins, *Dkn* 73 (May 1977): 114-116; Robert Giddings, *DSN* 8 (Sept. 1977): 81-84; Doris Grumbach, *NYTBR* 9 Oct. 1977: 16-17; Mollie Hardwick, *B&B* 22 (Nov. 1976): 32-33; [Albert H. Johnston], *Publishers Weekly* 212 (18 July 1977): 130; Colin McLeod, *LJ* 102 (1 Oct. 1977): 2066; Jonathan Megibow, *St. Louis Globe-Democrat* 10-11 Sept. 1977: H8; Jo Modert, *St. Louis Post-Dispatch* 5 Feb. 1978: C4; Sylvère Monod, *MLR* 74 (Jan. 1979): 174-175; Robert L. Patten, *Book World* (supp. to *Washington Post*) 25 Dec. 1977: H1, H6; Stephen P. Ryan, *Best Sellers* 37 (Nov. 1977): 244; *Booklist* 74 (15 Oct. 1977): 349; *Ch* 15 (Mar. 1978): 72; also rev. in 981, 1538, 1568.]

1253 Manning, Sylvia Bank. *Dickens as Satirist.* YSE, 176. New Haven and London: Yale UP, 1971. 256 pp. [Chap. on early novels plus chaps. on *BleakH, DSon, GreatEx, HardT, LittleDor, MChuz, OurMF, TaleTwoC.*—Rev.: Richard J. Allen, *VS* 15 (June 1972): 492-494; T. J. Cribb, *RES* NS 24 (May 1973): 230-233; Keith Cushman, *LJ* 96 (15 Apr. 1971): 1370; Duane DeVries, *DSN* 2 (June 1971): 51-53; Stephen Gill, *N&Q* NS 21 (Jan. 1974): 29-30; Michael S. Helfand, *Novel* 5 (Winter 1972): 186-189; Kenneth

Muir, *MLR* 67 (Apr. 1972): 405-407; Edgar Rosenberg, *ELN* 12 (Mar. 1975): 214-220; Rachel Trickett, *Dkn* 68 (Jan. 1972): 54-56; *Ch* 8 (June 1971): 552; also rev. in 182 (Aug. 1972), 981, 1126, 1578, 1956.]

1254 —. "Dickens, January, and May." *Dkn* 71 (May 1975): 67-75. [Esp. *CrickH, DavidC, DSon, LittleDor.*]

1255 —. "Families in Dickens," in *Changing Images of the Family,* ed. Virginia Tufte and Barbara Myerhoff (New Haven and London: Yale UP, 1979), 141-153. [Esp. *GreatEx.*]

1256 —. "Masking and Self-Revelation: Dickens's Three Autobiographies." *DSN* 7 (Sept. 1976): 69-75. [*DavidC, GreatEx, OliverTw.*]

1257 Marceau, Marcel interviewed by Barbara Lecker. *New Rev* 3 (Mar. 1977): 21-27. [D's infl., incl. description of Marceau's mime version of *CCarol* for BBC-TV.—See 2917.]

1258 Marcus, David D. "The Carlylean Vision of *A Tale of Two Cities.*" *SNNTS* 8 (Spring 1976): 56-68.

1259 —. "*Martin Chuzzlewit:* The Art of the Critical Imagination." *VN* no. 54 (Fall 1978): 10-16.

1260 —. "Symbolism and Mental Process in *Dombey and Son.*" In 1494, pp. 57-71.

1261 Marcus, Steven. "Dickens After One Hundred Years." *NYTBR* 7 June 1970: 1, 46-49, 51.

1262 —. *Engels, Manchester, and the Working Class* (New York: Random House; London: Weidenfeld and Nicolson, 1974), passim. [Rev.: Harvey Peter Sucksmith, *DSN* 8 (June 1977): 51-54.]

1263 —. "Language into Structure: *Pickwick Papers.*" *Representations: Essays on Literature and Society* (New York: Random House, 1975), 214-246. [Rpt. from *Daedalus* 101 (Winter 1972): 183-202.]

1264 Marković, Borivoje. "The Nature of the Novel Criticism in England, 1845-1860 (Part I)." *Blue Guitar* 1 (Dec. 1975): 117-146.

1265 Marks, Patricia. "Light and Dark Imagery in *Barnaby Rudge.*" *DSN* 9 (Sept. 1978): 73-76.

1266 —. "O. Henry and Dickens: Bleak House of Moral Decay." *ELN* 12 (Sept. 1974): 35-37. ["Elsie in New York."]

1267 —. "Time in *Nicholas Nickleby*." *VN* no. 55 (Spring 1979): 23-26.

1268 Marlow, James E. "Dickens and Carlyle's 'Way'." In 651, pp. 15-22. [*TaleTwoC.*]

1269 —. "Dickens's Romance: The Novel as Other." In 1493, pp. 23-42.

1270 —. "Memory, Romance, and the Expressive Symbol in Dickens." *NCF* 30 (June 1975): 20-32. [*Chimes.*]

1271 —. "The Solecism in *Our Mutual Friend*." *DSN* 5 (Mar. 1974): 7-9. [Faulty plot.]

1272 Marten, Harry. "Exaggerated Character: A Study of the Works of Dickens and Hogarth." *CentR* 20 (Summer 1976): 290-308. [*BleakH, LittleDor, MChuz, NichN, OCShop, OurMF.*]

1273 —. "Gestural Evil: Techniques of Characterization in Dickens's Early Work." *BSUF* 17 (Autumn 1976): 20-27.

1274 —. "The Visual Imaginations of Dickens and Hogarth: Structure and Scene." *SNNTS* 6 (Summer 1974): 145-164. [*BleakH, NichN.*]

1275 Martens, Johanne. "Gustav Brosings samlinger av bergensiana og Jacob Christensens Dickens-samling til Universitetsbiblioteket i Bergen." *Bibliotek og forskning* 19 (1973): 113-129.

1276 Martin, Augustine. *Charles Dickens: Hard Times.* Study-Guide Ser. Dublin: Gill; London: Macmillan, 1974. 37 pp.

1277 Martin, Graham. *A Study Guide to Great Expectations.* Arts, a Third Level Course: The Nineteenth Century Novel and Its Legacy, Units 6-7. [Milton Keynes] : Open UP, 1973. 2 vols. [Rev.: Robin Gilmour, *Dkn* 70 (May 1974): 132-133.]

1278 Martin, Jean-Paul. "Les classes sociales dans *David Copperfield*," in *Affrontements de classes et création littéraire.* Centre de Recherches d'Histoire et Littérature aux XVIIIe et XIXe Siècles, 2; Annales Littéraires de l'Univ. de Besançon, 129 (Paris: Belles Lettres, 1971), I, 85-99.

1279 Martin, John S. "Copperfield and Caulfield: Dickens in the Rye."

NMAL 4 (Fall 1980): no. 29.

1280 Martin, Richard. "Dickens's Mr. Jaggers: A Process of Abstraction."
LWU 7 (Oct. 1974): 142-153.

1281 Cancelled.

1282 Cancelled.

1283 Cancelled.

1284 Massie, Jo Ann. "Implications of the Disguise: A Psychological Analysis of Charles Dickens's *Hard Times.*" *PAPA* 4 (Fall 1977): 13.
[Abst.]

1285 Masui, Michio. "Dickens in Hiroshima." *HSELL* 17, ii (1970): 1-5.
[Discusses 2163; "Postscript," 81-82.—D no. incl. 904, 1044,
1346, 1435, 2007, and absts. of 137, 934, 1045, 1094, 1289,
1436, 1944, 2019, 2166.]

1286 —. [The language of D: Some recent approaches.] In 1287, pp. 207-
222. [In Jap.—Eng. abst., pp. 276-281.]

1287 — and Masami Tanabe. *Literature and Language of Dickens: Essays
and Studies in Commemoration of the Centenary of the Death of
Dickens.* Tokyo: Sanseido, 1972. 297 pp. [Incl. 137, 934, 1045,
1094, 1286, 1289, 1436, 1941, 1944, 2019, 2166.—Absts. for all
of these except 1286, 1941 in 1285.]

1288 Materassi, Mario. "A un secolo dalla morte: Verso un nuovo Dickens." *Ponte* 26 (July 1970): 867-878. [Esp. characterization,
humor, pessimism.]

1289 Matsumura, Masaie. [Ambiguity of evil in *DavidC.*] In 1827, pp. 53-
73. [In Jap.—Eng. abst., pp. 259-260 and in 1285, pp. 56-57.]

1290 —. [*Botchan* and *NichN*], in *Gengo to buntai: Higashida Chiaki kyoju
kanreki kinen ronbunshu,* ed. Chiaki Higashida (Osaka: Osaka
Kyoiku Tosho, 1975), 306-315. [Soseki Natsume and D.]

1290a —. [D and Japan.] In 412a, pp. 70-71. [In Jap.]

1291 —. [D and painting], in *Eikoku shosetsu kenkyu* (Tokyo: Shinozaki
Shorin, 1977), XII, 122-139. [In Jap.]

1292 —. "The Dickens Centenary Year in Japan." *DSN* 2 (Mar. 1971): 25-
28.

1293 —. [D's characters as seen in newly discovered letters.] *EigoS* 120 (Oct. 1974): 334-335.

1294 —. "Dickens in Japan." *Michi* 1 (1978): 34-54.

1295 Matthews, Maleen. "Illustrators of *A Christmas Carol*." *CnL* 156 (5 Dec. 1974): 1730-1732.

1296 —. "Illustrators of Dickens's *Chimes*." *CnL* 160 (2 Dec. 1976): 1626-1627.

1297 —. "Seen through Various Eyes: Illustrators of *The Cricket on the Hearth*." *CnL* 162 (1 Dec. 1977): 1604, 1606.

1298 Maxwell, J. C. " 'Filling Up a Form'." *N&Q* NS 18 (Sept. 1971): 336. [*LittleDor*.]

1299 Maxwell, Richard. *VS* 22 (Winter 1979): 216-219. [Rev. of 543, 1415, 1494, 1659, 2101.]

1300 —. "City Life and the Novel: Hugo, Ainsworth, Dickens." *CL* 30 (Spring 1978): 157-171. [*Nôtre-Dame de Paris, Old Saint Paul's* and *Revelations of London, MChuz*.]

1301 —. "Crowds and Creativity in *The Old Curiosity Shop*." *JEGP* 78 (Jan. 1979): 49-71.

1302 —. "Dickens's Omniscience." *ELH* 46 (Summer 1979): 290-313. [Omniscient narrator esp. in *GreatEx, LittleDor*.]

1303 —. "G. M. Reynolds, Dickens, and the Mysteries of London." *NCF* 23 (Sept. 1977): 188-213. [*BleakH, HsldWds*.]

1304 Maxwell-Mahon, W. D. "Charles Dickens: *Hard Times*." *Crux* 5 (Jan.-Mar. 1971): 20-24.

1305 Mayer, Hans. "Im Raritätenladen von Charles Dickens." *Aussenseiter* (Frankfurt: Suhrkamp, 1975), 391-396. [Jewish characters.]

1306 Mayes, Herbert R. "A Dickens Ferment." *SatR* 53 (4 Apr. 1970): 14, 66. [On celebrations planned for England.]

1307 Meckier, Jerome. "Charles Dickens: Research in Progress (1971)." *DSN* 2 (Dec. 1971): 111-121.

1308 —. "Dickens and *King Lear*: A Myth for Victorian England." *SAQ*

71 (Winter 1972): 75-90. [*DSon, HardT, OCShop.*]

1309 —. "Dickens and the Dystopian Novel: From *Hard Times* to *Lady Chatterley*." In 462, pp. 51-58.

1310 —. "The Faint Image of Eden: The Many Worlds of *Nicholas Nickleby*." In 1489, pp. 129-146. [Serialization and structure.]

1311 —. "*Hard Times*: A Seminal Dystopia." *SCB* 30 (Oct. 1970): 112. [Abst.]

1312 —. "How Modern the Victorians? A Plea to Have It Both Ways." *DSN* 8 (Dec. 1977): 109-118. [Rev.-art. on 306.]

1313 —. "Some Household Words: Two New Accounts of Dickens's Conversation." *Dkn* 71 (Jan. 1975): 5-20. [Reading, friends, current events.]

1314 —. "Suspense in *The Old Curiosity Shop*: Dickens's Contrapuntal Artistry." *JNT* 2 (Sept. 1972): 199-207.

1315 —. "Why the Man Who Liked Dickens Read Dickens Instead of Conrad: Waugh's *A Handful of Dust*." *Novel* 13 (Winter 1980): 171-187.

1316 Mehl, Dieter. "Dickens und die neuere Literaturkritik." *Archiv* 205 (July 1968): 102-118.

1317 Mehring, Franz. "Charles Dickens," in *Marxism and Art: Writings in Aesthetics and Criticism*, ed. Berel Lang and Forrest Williams (New York: David McKay; London: Longman, 1972), 438-442. [Eng. trans. of essay orig. pub. in *Neue Zeit*, 1912.—Mentions *BleakH, NichN, OliverTw, PickP.*]

1318 Meinke, A. "Das Werk Dickens und die bewusstseinsbildende Rolle des kulturellen Erbes." *WZUR* 20, vii (1971): 493-498. [Esp. *BleakH, DSon, LittleDor.*]

1319 Melada, Ivan. "*Nicholas Nickleby*"; "*Hard Times*." *The Captain of Industry in English Fiction, 1821-1871* (Albuquerque: Univ. of New Mexico Press, 1970), 103-110; 110-115. [Rev.: Rodger L. Tarr, *DSN* 4 (Sept. 1973): 84-86.]

1320 Mendez, Charlotte Walker. "Scriveners Forlorn: Dickens's Nemo and Melville's Bartleby." *DSN* 11 (June 1980): 33-38. [Infl. of *BleakH.*]

1321 [Merwe, Pieter van der and Roger Took.] "The Dickens Theatricals." *The Spectacular Career of Clarkson Stanfield, 1793-1867: Seaman, Scene-Painter, Royal Academician* ([Sunderland] : Tyne and Wear Co. Council Museums, 1979), 156-161. [Exhib. cat.—Note also slightly diff. *Clarkson Stanfield, 1793-1867: Die erstaunliche Karriere eines viktorianischen Malers,* trans. Ingeborg Krueger [?] (Bonn: Rheinisches Landesmuseum, 1979).]

1322 Metz, Nancy Aycock. "The Artistic Reclamation of Waste in *Our Mutual Friend.*" *NCF* 34 (June 1979): 59-72.

1323 —. "Science in *Household Words:* 'The Poetic. . .Passed into Our Common Life'." *VPN* 11 (Winter 1978): 121-133.

1324 Meyers, Jeffrey. "Charles Dickens (1939)." *A Reader's Guide to George Orwell* (London: Thames and Hudson, 1975; Totowa, N.J.: Littlefield, Adams, 1977), 50-54; et passim. [On Orwell's essay.]

1325 Michaelson, L. I. "Defoe and Dickens: Two London Journeys." *Dkn* 74 (May 1978): 103-107. [Use of setting in *Moll Flanders* and *OliverTw.*]

1326 Michel-Michot, Paulette. "The Fire Motif in *Great Expectations.*" *ArielE* 8 (Apr. 1977): 49-69.

1327 Middlebro', Tom. "Esther Summerson: A Plea for Justice." *QQ* 77 (Summer 1970): 252-260.

1328 Mikdadi, F. H. "*David Copperfield* in Arabic." *Dkn* 75 (Summer 1979): 85-93.

1329 Mikhal'skaia, N. P. "Nravstvenno-esteticheskii ideal i sistema avtorskikh otsenok v romane Dikkensa *Dombi i syn.*" *FN* no. 107 (1978): 88-97. [Moral-esthetic.]

1330 Miller, George Eric. "Postcard Dickensiana, 1900-1920." *Dkn* 71 (May 1975): 91-99. [Rpt. in *Deltiology* 15, vi [1975] : 1, 3; 16, i [1976] : 3.]

1331 Miller, J. Hillis. "Charles Dickens's *Great Expectations,*" trans. Regina Wolf, in *Englische Literatur von William Blake bis Thomas Hardy,* ed. Willi Erzgräber. Interpretationen, 8 (Frankfurt: Fischer, 1970), 230-260. [From 2384.]

1332 —. "The Fiction of Realism: *Sketches by Boz, Oliver Twist,* and Cruikshank's Illustrations." In 1419, pp. 85-153. [Rpt. from 261, pp. 1-69.]

1333 —. "The Sources of Dickens's Comic Art: From *American Notes* to *Martin Chuzzlewit.*" In 1419, pp. 467-476 (of periodical version).

1334 Miller, James Nathan. "Inimitable Charles Dickens." *Reader's Digest* 101 (Nov. 1972): 223-230.

1335 Miller, Jonathan. "In Praise of Fear." *Lstr* 83 (28 May 1970): 704-705. [Mentions *BleakH, DavidC, DSon, LittleDor, OCShop.*]

1336 Miller, Michael G. "Murdstone, Heep, and the Structure of *David Copperfield.*" *DSN* 11 (Sept. 1980): 65-70.

1337 Millhauser, Milton. "*David Copperfield:* Some Shifts of Plan." *NCF* 27 (Dec. 1972): 339-345.

1338 —. "*Great Expectations:* The Three Endings." In 1490, pp. 267-277.

1339 Mills, Nicolaus. "Charles Dickens and Mark Twain." *American and English Fiction of the Nineteenth Century: An Antigenre Critique and Comparison* (Bloomington and London: Indiana UP, 1973), 92-109. [Incorporates "Social and Moral Vision in *Great Expectations* and *Huckleberry Finn,*" *JAmS* 4 (July 1970): 61-72.]

1340 Milner, Ian. "The Dickens Drama: Mr. Dombey." In 1419, pp. 155-165.

1341 —. "Dickens's Style: A Textual Parallel in *Dombey and Son* and *Daniel Deronda.*" *PP* 17, iv (1974): 209-210.

1341a Mindra, Mihail. "Tema 'mesagerului' la Dickens si Dickens si Dostoievski." *St de literatura universala* 19 (1977): 111-114. [Theme of messenger.]

1342 Miyazaki, Koichi. *Capsules in Space—Little Dorrit.* Seijo Eng. Monographs, 12. Tokyo: Seijo Univ., 1973. 21 pp.

1343 —. "Disguise and Identity in *Our Mutual Friend.*" *SELit* 50 (1973): 211-230.

1343a —. [The history of D criticism.] In 412a, pp. 101-102. [In Jap.]

1344 —. *The Inner Structure of Charles Dickens's Later Novels.* Tokyo: Sanseido, 1974. iii, 163 pp. [Rev.: Angus Easson, *Dkn* 71 (May 1975): 111-112; S[ylvère] M[onod], *EA* 28 (Jan.-Mar. 1975): 115.]

1345 —. *A Study of Two of Dickens's Later Novels.* Seijo Eng. Monographs, 7. Tokyo: Seijo Univ., 1971. 47 pp. [*BleakH, HardT.*]

1346 Mizunoe, Ariyoshi. "Dickens's Youth in *David Copperfield.*" In 1285, pp. 51-53. [Abst.]

1346a —. [Studies in D's period.] In 412a, pp. 30-31. [In Jap.]

1347 Moers, Ellen. "*Bleak House:* The Agitating Women." *Dkn* 69 (Jan. 1973): 13-24.

1348 Cancelled.

1349 Monod, Sylvère. " 'Between Two Worlds': Editing Dickens," in *Editing Nineteenth-Century Fiction,* ed. Jane Millgate. Papers of the Conf. on Editorial Problems, 13th (New York and London: Garland, 1978), 17-39. [Esp. *BleakH.*]

1350 —. "Bilan et perspective d'une recherche dickensienne française." In 154, pp. 197-207.

1351 —. "Charles Dickens." *Histoire de la littérature anglaise de Victoria à Élisabeth II* (Paris: Armand Colin, 1970), 39-45. [Survey of life and works.]

1352 —. "Charles Dickens, ou la genèse d'un art moderne." In 743, pp. 12-23.

1353 —. "Confessions of an Unrepentant Chestertonian." In 1491, pp. 214-228. [Paper from 2180.]

1354 M[onod], S[ylvère]. "Dickens," in *La raison et l'imaginaire.* Soc. des Anglicistes de l'Enseignement Supérieur, Actes du Congrès de Rennes, 1970; EA, 45 (Paris: Didier, [1973?]), 163-164. [Summary of discussion of workshop on Victorian era.]

1355 Monod, Sylvère. "The Dickens Centenary Year in France." *DSN* 2 (Mar. 1971): 12-14.

1356 (—. *Dickens the Novelist.* 1968.) [Excerpt rpt. in 2064, pp. 519-527.—Rev.: T. J. Cribb, *RES* NS 21 (May 1970): 251-252; Michael Slater, *EA* 23 (Apr.-June 1970): 212-214; also rev. in 2138, 2204.]

1357 —. "Dickens's Attitudes in *A Tale of Two Cities.*" In 1419, pp. 166-183.

1358 —. "Entre l'arbre et l'écorce: T. S. Eliot chez les Victoriens," in *De Shakespeare à T. S. Eliot: Mélanges offrets à Henri Fluchère*. EA, 63 (Paris: Didier, 1976), 263-273. [Collins's supposed infl. on *BleakH*.]

1359 —. "Esther Summerson, Charles Dickens and the Reader of *Bleak House*." *DiS* 5 (May 1969): 5-25.

1360 —. "G. K. Chesterton on Dickens's Treatment of Language." *CRev* 3 (Spring-Summer 1977): 195-210.

1361 —. "*Hard Times:* An Undickensian Novel?" In 131, pp. 71-92.

1362 —. "The Need for a Dickens Concordance." *DSN* 9 (Sept. 1978): 65-69. [Intro. note by Joseph Gold.]

1363 —. "1900-1920: The Age of Chesterton." *Dkn* 66 (May 1970): 101-120. [Special no. on D's reputation 1870-1970.—For revs. see 448.]

1364 —. "Some Stylistic Devices in *A Tale of Two Cities*." In 1496, pp. 165-186.

1365 —. "*A Tale of Two Cities:* A French View." *Dkn* 66 (Sept. 1970): supp. 23-37. [Special no. of D Memorial Lectures 1970.—Also includes 1997, 2122.—Rev. in 1808, 1961, 2216.]

1366 —. [Toast at 71st annual conf. of D Fellowship.] *Dkn* 73 (Sept. 1977): 186-190.

1367 —. "Views and Reviews." In 846, pp. 68-71. [In Fr.]

1368 —. " 'When the Battle's Lost and Won. . .': Dickens *v.* the Compositors of *Bleak House*." *Dkn* 69 (Jan. 1973): 3-12.

1369 Moore, Katharine. "Victorian Wives in Fiction." *Victorian Wives* (London: Allison and Busby; New York: St. Martin's Press, 1974), 115-156. [D, Trollope, Thackeray, George Eliot, Gaskell, Yonge, Meredith.—Mentions *BleakH, DavidC, DSon, GreatEx, LittleDor, NichN, OurMF*.]

1370 More, Paul Elmer. "The Praise of Dickens." *The Essential Paul Elmer More*, ed. Byron C. Lambert (New Rochelle, N.Y.: Arlington, 1972), 159-174. [Rpt. from *Nation* 13 Dec. 1906; also in *Shelburne Essays*, 5th ser., 1908.—Esp. *DavidC*.]

1371 Morris, Patricia. "Some Notes on the Women in *David Copperfield:* Eleven Crude Categories and a Case for Miss Mowcher." *ESA* 21 (Mar. 1978): 17-21.

1372 Morrow, Patrick D. *Bret Harte: Literary Critic* (Bowling Green, Ohio: Bowling Green State Univ. Popular Press, 1979), 48-50; et passim. [D's infl.]

1373 Morse, J. Mitchell. "Prejudice and Literature." *Prejudice and Literature* (Philadelphia: Temple UP, 1976), 151-193. [Incl. Fagin.— Incorporates "Prejudice and Literature," *CE* 37 (Apr. 1976): 780-793.]

1374 Mortimer, John. "*Great Expectations.*" *Obs Mag* (supp. to the weekly) 5 Aug. 1979: 55. [Part of ser. on authors' favorite novels.]

1375 Morton, Lionel. "Allegories of Silence: Dickens's Use of the Word 'Allegory'." *ESC* 4 (Winter 1978): 430-449. [*BleakH, DavidC, OCShop.*]

1376 —. " 'His Truncheon's Length': A Recurrent Allusion to *Hamlet* in Dickens's Novels." *DSN* 11 (June 1980): 47-49. [Esp. *DavidC.*]

1377 Moss, Sidney P. "The American Press Assigns Dickens to Queen's Bench Prison." *Dkn* 75 (Summer 1979): 67-74.

1378 —. "Longfellow's Uncollected 'Letter to the Editor': Defending Dickens's *American Notes.*" *DSN* 10 (Mar. 1979): 4-7.

1379 —. "Poe's 'Two Long Interviews' with Dickens." *PoeS* 11 (June 1978): 10-12.

1380 Mott, Graham. "Was There a Stain upon Little Dorrit?" *Dkn* 76 (Spring 1980): 31-39. [Contra Leavis, idea of debt unreal to Amy Dorrit.]

1381 Mottershead, Mary. "Letter to the Editor." *Dkn* 72 (Jan. 1976): 46. [Parallel to Jasper Packlemerton of *OCShop.*]

1382 Mouchard, Claude. "L'ange de l'intime." In 768, pp. 13-14. [*PickP.*]

1383 Mudrick, Marvin. "Leavis on Dickens." *The Man in the Machine* (New York: Horizon Press, 1977), 111-122. [Rev.-art. on 1150.— Slightly rev. rpt. from *HudR* 24 (Summer 1971): 346-354.]

1384 —. "Mrs. Harris and the Hend of All Things." *Books Are Not Life but*

Then What Is? (New York: Oxford UP, 1979), 337-348. [Slightly rev. rpt. of afwd. to 1965 NAL ed. of *MChuz.*]

1385 Muir, Percy. *Victorian Illustrated Books* (London: Batsford; New York: Praeger, 1971), passim. [Rev.: W. F. Axton, *DSN* 5 (June 1974): 54-56; A[nthony] B[urton], *Dkn* 69 (May 1973): 125-127.]

1386 Mullaly, Edward J. "When Dickens Didn't." *Atlantic Advocate* 62 (Nov. 1971): 39, 41. [Failed attempt to bring D to St. John's, Newfoundland, in 1867.]

1387 Müllenbrock, Heinz-Joachim. "Der historische Roman der frühviktorianischen Epoche zwischen Vergangenheit und Gegenwart: Eine Analyse unter dem Aspekt seiner zeitgeschichtlichen Orientierung." *Anglia* 94, iii-iv (1976): 404-430. [Incl. *TaleTwoC.*]

1388 Muller, C. H. "Charles Dickens: *Great Expectations.*" *Crux* 8 (Feb. 1974): 5-13.

1389 —. "Dickens's *Hard Times:* The Gradgrind Educational System , Coketown, and the Circus." *Crux* 9 (Aug. 1975): 45-48, 52.

1390 —. "Victorian Sensationalism: The Short Stories of Wilkie Collins." *UES* 11 (Mar. 1973): 12-24. [Mentions *BleakH*, "HHouse," *HsldWds, LittleDor, PickP.*]

1391 Mulvey, Christopher. "*David Copperfield:* The Folk-Story Structure." In 1493, pp. 74-94.

1392 —. "A Surreal Image in *Bleak House:* A Landlord and His Tenants." *DSN* 8 (Sept. 1977): 68-72. [Krook, Miss Flite, Nemo.]

1393 Munch-Peterson, Erland, comp. "Dickens, Charles." *Bibliografi over oversaettelser til dansk 1800-1900 af prosafiktion fra de germanske og romanske sprog* (Copenhagen: Rosenkilde og Bagger for the Kongelige Bibliotek, Nationalbibliografisk afdeling, 1976), 74-84.

1394 Mundhenk, Rosemary. "The Education of the Reader in *Our Mutual Friend.*" *NCF* 34 (June 1979): 41-58.

1395 Munn, Carol. "Dickens and Gissing as Radical Feminists." *Gissing NL* 8 (Apr. 1972): 1-17. [*BleakH, DavidC, DSon, MEDrood, LittleDor, OurMF.*]

1396 Munro, Hector. "Curious Affair of the Cognovit." *Dkn* 74 (May 1978): 88-90. [Plot of *PickP*.]

1397 Murray, Christopher. "A Dickens Parallel." *SORev* 6 (1980): 42-44. [Capt. Boyle in O'Casey's *Juno and the Paycock* and Capt. Cuttle in *DSon*.]

1398 Murray, Isobel. *"Great Expectations* and *The Critic."* *N&Q* NS 18 (Nov. 1971): 414.

1399 Musselwhite, David. "The Novel as Narcotic," in *1848: The Sociology of Literature*, ed. Francis Barker et al. Proc. of Essex Conf. on the Sociology of Lit., July 1977 ([Colchester] : Univ. of Essex, 1978), 207-224. [Incl. *DSon*.]

1399a Mutis C., Guido. "El mundo onérico de *Little Dorrit."* *Estudios filológicos* 13 (1978): 187-202. [Esp. fantasy.]

1400 Myers, William. "The Radicalism of *Little Dorrit,"* in *Literature and Politics in the Nineteenth Century,* ed. John Lucas (London: Methuen, 1971), 77-104.

1401 Nabokov, Vladimir. *"Bleak House* (1852-1853)." *Lectures on Literature,* ed. Fredson Bowers, intro. John Updike (New York and London: Harcourt Brace Jovanovich/Bruccoli Clark, 1980), 62-124. [Brief excerpt in *Esquire* 94 (Sept. 1980): 67.]

1402 — and Edmund Wilson. *The Nabokov-Wilson Letters,* ed., annot., intro. Simon Karlinsky (New York etc.: Harper, 1979), passim. [Esp. late novels.]

1403 Nadel, Ira Bruce. " 'Wonderful Deception': Art and the Artist in *Little Dorrit."* *Criticism* 19 (Winter 1977): 17-33.

1404 Nakanishi, Toshikazu. *Charles Dickens no Eikoku.* Tokyo: Kaibunsha, 1977. 309 pp. [D's England.]

1405 Nalecz-Wojtczak, Jolanta. "Mystery in the Composition of Dickens's Novels." *KN* 17 (Mar. 1970): 239-251. [*BarnR, BleakH, GreatEx, LittleDor, MEDrood, OliverTw, OurMF, TaleTwoC.*]

1406 Naumenko, T. K. "Charl'z Dikkens v vospriiatii L. N. Tolśtogo." *Nauchnye trudy Novosibirskogo Pedagogocheskogo Instituta* 65 (1971): 232-250.

1407 (Naumov, Nicifor. *Dikens kod Srba i Hrvata.* 1968.) [Rev.: Edgar

Rosenberg, *Dkn* 66 (Jan. 1970): 52-54.]

1408 Nelson, Harland S. "Stagg's Gardens: The Railway Through Dickens's World." In 1491, pp. 41-53. [Esp. *DSon.*]

1409 Nelson, Michael. "Charles Dickens in America." *Coll of William and Mary Alumni Gazette* 47 (July-Aug. 1979): 2-8.

1410 Nersesova, M. A. *Kholodnii dom Dikkensa.* Moscow: Khudozh. Lit., 1971. 112 pp. [*BleakH.*–Rev.: Laurence Senelick, *Dkn* 69 (Jan. 1973): 56-57.]

1411 Neuhaus, Volker. "Das Verhältnis des Herausgebers zum Archiv– Charles Dickens *The Pickwick Papers.*" *Typen multiperspektevischen Erzählens.* LuL, NS 13 (Cologne and Vienna: Bohlau, 1971), 93-96.

1412 Newby, Richard L. "Dickensian Foibles." *AN&Q* 15 (Jan. 1977): 72-73. [Query on Mr. Creakle's whispering.–Answered by Robert F. Fleissner, 16 (Jan. 1978): 30.]

1413 Newman, S. J. "*Barnaby Rudge:* Dickens and Scott," in *Literature of the Romantic Period, 1750-1850,* ed. R. T. Davies and B. G. Beatty (Liverpool: Liverpool UP; New York: Barnes and Noble, 1976), 171-188. [Rev.: Richard Dunn, *DSN* 10 (Mar. 1979): 19-21.]

1414 Newman, Stephen. *Great Expectations (Charles Dickens).* Notes on Eng. Lit., 53. Oxford: Blackwell, 1975. 115 pp.

1415 Newsom, Robert. *Dickens on the Romantic Side of Familiar Things: Bleak House and the Novel Tradition.* New York and Guildford: Columbia UP, 1977. xiv, 173 pp. [Note also "Bleak House and the Romantic Side of Familiar Things," *DAI* 35 (June 1975): 7916A-7917A (Columbia).–Rev.: W. F. Axton, *MLQ* 39 (Sept. 1978): 309-312; Jean Gattégno, *EA* 32 (July-Sept. 1979): 346-347; [Roger Howell, Jr.], *British St Monitor* 9 (Summer 1979): 79-80; Sylvère Monod, *YES* 10 (1980): 316-317; Bill Overton, *Dkn* 74 (May 1978): 109-110; Michael Steig, *TLS* 22 Sept. 1978: 1051; Michael Ullman, *DSN* 10 (June-Sept. 1979): 68-71; *Ch* 15 (Apr. 1978): 233; also rev. in 531, 583, 981, 1123, 1299, 1538, 1568, 2094.]

1416 Nichols, Duane, ed. *Kansas English,* 56 (Dec. 1970). [Papers from 18th Annual Conf. on Comp. and Lit., Univ. of Kansas.–Incl. 455, 528, 565, 623, 639, 1880, 2144.]

1417 Nielsen, Jorgen Erik. "Bulwer, Marryat, Dickens og deres samtidige"; "Bibliografi," *Den samtidige engelske litteratur og Danmark, 1800-1840.* Pubs. of the Dept. of Eng. Univ. of Copenhagen, 3-4 (Copenhagen: Nova, 1976), I, 440-457; et passim; II, passim. [Note also sep. issued Eng. and Danish abst.—*NichN, OliverTw, PickP.*]

1418 Nisbet, Ada, ed. "Charles Dickens: International Guide to Study and Research." [Projected bibliog.—Description: D[uane] D[eVries], *DSN* 4 (Dec. 1975): 128.]

1419 — and Blake Nevius, eds. *Dickens Centennial Essays.* Berkeley and Los Angeles: Univ. of California Press, 1971. [Ada Nisbet, "Preface," v-vii.—Incl. 563, 660, 699, 882, 1332, 1340, 1357, 1776, 1899.—Issued as special D no. of *NCF* 24 (Mar. 1970), which incl. 1333 in place of 1332.—Note also Blake Nevius, "Tribute to Ada Nisbet," *NCF* 29 (June 1974): 1-2.—Rev.: C. C. Barfoot, *ES* 54 (Aug. 1973): 365-366; Rachel Bennett, *RES* NS 24 (Nov. 1973): 508-510; Keith Cushman, *LJ* 97 (15 June 1972): 2188; Angus Easson, *N&Q* NS 22 (Mar. 1975): 129-131; Robin Gilmour, *DSN* 4 (Sept. 1973): 76-79; Dana Guran-Albu, *RITL* 22 (1973): 141-143; James R. Kincaid, *Dkn* 68 (Sept. 1972): 186-188; Ivanka Kovacević, *FP* 10 (1972): 98-101; Jerome Meckier, *DSN* 1 (Dec. 1970): 9-11; Marie Peel, *B&B* 18 (Mar. 1973): 57; L. Pothet, *EA* 28 (Apr.-June 1975): 231-232; Heinz Reinhold, *Anglia* 92, iii-iv (1974): 503-507; Harvey Peter Sucksmith, *YES* 4 (1974): 325-326; *Booklist* 69 (1 Nov. 1972): 225; *Ch* 9 (Dec. 1972): 1293; *TLS* 27 Apr. 1973: 478; also rev. in 981, 1228, 1537, 1808, 1961.]

1420 Nishimae, Yoshimi. "The Loving Ballad of Lord Bateman: Dickens's Only Ballad." *HSELL* 18, ii (1972): 60-74. [In Jap.—Eng. abst., pp. 75-77.—Poem with pref. and mock-critical notes by D, illus. Cruikshank.]

1421 Noakes, Aubrey. "Dickens and Frith." *William Frith, Extraordinary Victorian Painter: A Biographical and Critical Study* (London: Jupiter, 1978), 141-145; et passim.

1422 Cancelled.

1423 Noffsinger, John W. "The Complexity of Ralph Nickleby." *DSN* 5 (Dec. 1974): 112-114.

1424 —. "Dream in *The Old Curiosity Shop.*" *SAB* 42 (May 1977): 23-34.

1425 Noll-Wiemann, Renate. "Charles Dickens, *David Copperfield* (1849/

50)." *Der Künstler im englischen Roman des 19. Jahrhunderts.* AF, 117 (Heidelberg: Winter, 1977), 77-88; et passim.

1426 Norman, Geraldine. "British Museum Buys Original Dickens Manuscript for £12,000." *Times* (London) 24 Nov. 1971: 16. [Ms of Chap. XV of *NichN* from Suzannet sale.]

1427 —. "Collector to Sell Early Love Letter by Dickens." *Times* (London) 11 Mar. 1972: 1. [1st love letter from D to Maria Beadnell (1831?).]

1428 —. "A Two-Day Feast for Dickens Lovers." *Times* (London) 23 Nov. 1971: 17. [Sale of Suzannet Coll. at Sotheby's.]

1429 Norrman, Ralf. *"Hard Times och North and South:* Parallelromaner." *FT* 190, viii-ix (1971): 376-391.

1430 — and Jon Haarberg. *Nature and Language: A Semiotic Study of Cucurbits in Literature* (London, Boston, Henley: Routledge and Kegan Paul, 1980), 134-139; et passim. [Esp. sex and cucumbers in *NichN*.]

1431 Nowell-Smith, Simon. "Editing Dickens." *TLS* 4 June 1970: 615-616.

1432 Obermeier, Thomas F. *Characters of Charles Dickens.* [Deerfield, Ill.?] : Privately Printed, 1970. vii, 233 pp.

1433 O'Brien, Anthony. "Benevolence and Insurrection: The Conflicts of Form and Purpose in *Barnaby Rudge*." *DiS* 5 (May 1969): 26-44.

1434 O'Brien, Conor Cruise. "Charles Dickens as Typhoid Mary." *Obs* (London) 23 Dec. 1979: 9.

1435 Ochi, Michio. [Harmon's transfiguration.] In 1285, pp. 32-47. [In Jap.–Eng. abst., pp. 48-49.]

1436 —. [Transfiguration and Micawber.] In 1287, pp. 75-98. [In Jap.–Eng. abst., pp. 261-262 and in 1285, pp. 57-58.]

1437 Oddie, William. "Charles Dickens and the Indian Mutiny." *Dkn* 68 (Jan. 1972): 3-15. ["Perils."]

1438 —. *Dickens and Carlyle: The Question of Influence.* London: Centenary Press, 1972. x, 165 pp. [Esp. *HardT, TaleTwoC.*–Note also diss. of same title (Leicester, 1970).–Rev.: J[erry] A.

D[ibble], *ELN* 11 (Sept. 1973): supp. 41-42; K. J. Fielding, *Dkn* 69 (May 1973): 111-118; Clive J. Gammon, *Spec* 230 (20 Jan. 1973): 79; Barry V. Qualls, *SSL* 12 (Oct. 1974): 146-153; Edward Sharples, *Criticism* 16 (Spring 1974): 180-183; Michael Slater, *VS* 17 (Mar. 1974): 328-330; Rodger L. Tarr, *Costerus*, NS 3 (1975): 171-176; G. B. Tennyson, *DSN* 5 (Mar. 1974): 24-28 and (a diff. rev.) *NCF* 23 (June 1973): 115-116, *TLS* 2 Mar. 1973: 235; also rev. in 981, 1026.]

1439 Oliver, John. *Dickens's Rochester*. Rochester: John Hallewell, 1978. 127 pp. [Rev.: David Parker, *Dkn* 75 (Summer 1979): 108-109.]

1440 Olmsted, John Charles, ed. *A Victorian Art of Fiction: Essays on the Novel in British Periodicals*. GRLH, 100, 165 (New York and London: Garland, 1979), passim. [For contents see this number in Appendix.]

1441 — and Jeffrey Egan Welch, comps. *Victorian Novel Illustrations: A Selected Checklist, 1900-1979*. GRLH, 164 (New York and London: Garland, 1979), passim. [Rev.: Andrew Sanders, *Dkn* 75 (Autumn 1979): 177-178.]

1442 Olofson, Harold. "The Birds and the Barber: An Anthropological Analysis of a Joke in Charles Dickens's *Martin Chuzzlewit*," in *Play: Anthropological Perspectives*, ed. Michael A. Salter. Proc. of Assn. for the Anthropological St. of Play, 1977 (West Point, N.Y.: Leisure Press, 1978), 104-112.

1443 Olsen, Stein Haugom. *The Structure of Literary Understanding* (Cambridge etc.: Cambridge UP, 1978), passim. [*BleakH, DavidC, DSon, HardT, OliverTw.*]

1444 Olshin, Toby A. " 'The Yellow Dwarf' and *The Old Curiosity Shop*." *NCF* 25 (June 1970): 96-99.

1445 Oppel, Horst. "Charles Dickens: *Our Mutual Friend*," in *Der moderne englische Roman*, ed. Horst Oppel, 2nd rev. ed. (Berlin: Schmidt, 1971), 15-34. [1st ed. 1965.]

1446 —. *Englisch-deutsche Literaturbeziehungen, II Von der Romantik bis zur Gegenwart*. Grundlagen der Anglistik und Amerikanistik, 2 (Berlin: Schmidt, 1971), passim.

1447 Organ, Dennis. "Compression and Explosion: Pattern in *Hard Times*." *SCB* 36 (Fall 1976): 94. [Abst.]

1448 Orozco Emerson, Ricardo. "*A Christmas Carol* en la enseñanza del inglés en México." In 813, pp. 183-192.

1449 Orton, Diana. "Mr. Dickens and Other Friends." *Made of Gold: A Biography of Angela Burdett Coutts* (London: Hamish Hamilton, 1980), 77-93; et passim.

1450 Otten, Kurt. "Charles Dickens (1812-1870)"; "Dickens Spätwerk." *Der englische Roman vom 16. zum 19. Jahrhundert.* Grundlagen der Anglistik und Amerikanistik, 4 (Berlin: Schmidt, 1971), 124-132; 132-135.

1451 Ousby, Ian. "The Broken Glass: Vision and Comprehension in *Bleak House.*" *NCF* 29 (Mar. 1975): 381-392. [Rpt. in 24, pp. 974-984.]

1452 —. "Charles Dickens." *Bloodhounds of Heaven: The Detective in English Fiction from Godwin to Doyle* (Cambridge and London: Harvard UP, 1976), 79-110. [Esp. *BleakH, HsldWds.*—Note also 765.—Note also diss. of same title (Chicago, 1973).—Rev.: James W. Christie, *DSN* 10 (June-Sept. 1979): 79-82.]

1453 —. "Language and Gesture in *Great Expectations.*" *MLR* 72 (Oct. 1977): 784-793.

1454 Owen, W. J. B. "Mrs. Gamp's Poetic Diction." *Dkn* 67 (May 1971): 91-96.

1455 Page, H. M. " 'A More Seditious Book than *Das Kapital*': Shaw on *Little Dorrit.*" In 1593, pp. 171-177.

1456 Page, Norman. "Convention and Consistency in Dickens's Cockney Dialect." *ES* 51 (Aug. 1970): 339-344. [*MChuz, PickP.*]

1457 —. "Dickens and Speech." *Speech in the English Novel.* Eng. Lang. Ser., 1 (London: Longman, 1973), 133-160; et passim. [Esp. dialect, idiolect, forms of address in *BleakH, DavidC, HardT, LittleDor, MChuz, NichN, OliverTw, OurMF, PickP.*—Incorporates "Forms of Address in Dickens," *Dkn* 67 (Jan. 1971): 16-20.—Excerpt rpt. in 839, pp. 195-202.—Rev.: Marghanita Laski, *Dkn* 70 (Jan. 1974): 59-60; John M. Robson, *DSN* 8 (June 1977): 55-56; also rev. in 504.]

1458 —, ed. *Dickens: Hard Times, Great Expectations, and Our Mutual Friend: A Casebook.* London: Macmillan, 1979. 211 pp. [For contents see this number in Appendix.]

1459 —. "Dickensian Elements in *Victory*." *Conradiana* 5, i (1973): 37-42. [Infl. of *DSon, HardT, OurMF.*]

1460 —. "Eccentric Speech in Dickens." *Critical Survey* 4 (Summer 1969): 96-100. [Esp. Sarah Gamp.]

1461 —. "*Ruth* and *Hard Times:* A Dickens Source." *N&Q* NS 18 (Nov. 1971): 413.

1462 —. "Silas Wegg Reads Gibbon." *Dkn* 68 (May 1972): 115. [Speed-reading and realism.]

1463 —, ed. *Wilkie Collins: The Critical Heritage* (London and Boston: Routledge and Kegan Paul, 1974), passim. [Rev. in 967 (May 1975).]

1464 Pagetti, Carol. "F. R. Leavis e Raymond Williams a Canossa: Alcuni aspetti della critica dickensiana." *Trimestre* (Pescara) no. 3-4 (1972): 516-529.

1465 —. *Hard Times e Great Expectations: Problemi di critica dickensiana.* Pescara: Lib. dell'Univ., 1979. 115 pp.

1466 —. "*Little Dorrit:* Dickens e il labirinto del linguaggio." *St inglesi* 2 (1975): 155-178.

1467 Palmer, Helen H. and Ann Jane Dyson, comps. "Charles Dickens." *English Novel Explication: Criticisms to 1972* (Hamden, Conn.: Shoe String Press; London: Clive Bingley, 1973), 67-84. [Bibliog. 1958-1972.—For supp. (1972-1974) see Peter L. Abernethy et al., "Charles Dickens," *English Novel Explication,* supp. 1 (Hamden, Conn.: Shoe String Press; London: Clive Bingley, 1976), 52-66.]

1468 Palmer, William J. "Dickens and the Eighteenth Century." In 1494, pp. 15-39. [Esp. *LittleDor, OCShop, PickP.*]

1469 —. "*Hard Times:* A Dickens Fable of Personal Salvation." *DR* 52 (Spring 1972): 67-77.

1470 —. "The Movement of History in *Our Mutual Friend*." *PMLA* 89 (May 1974): 487-495.

1471 Panter-Downes, Mollie. "Letter from London." *NY* 46 (25 July 1970): 75-76. [Centenary events.]

1472 Pantuckova, Lidmila. *W. M. Thackeray as a Critic of Literature.* BSE,

10/11; Opera Univ. Purkynianae Brunensis Facultas Philosophica, 177 (Brno: Univ. J. E. Purkyne, 1972), passim.

1473 Papu, Edgar. "Mitul Dickens." *RoLit* 3 (July 1970): 23.

1474 Paraf, Pierre. "Charles Dickens et Hans Christian Andersen." In 743, pp. 105-109.

1475 Parker, David. "Dickens's Archness." *Dkn* 67 (Sept. 1971): 149-158.

1476 —. "Mr. Dickens Sets up a Carriage." *Dkn* 75 (Spring 1979): 32-34. [At Doughty Street, 1838.]

1477 — and Michael Slater. "The Gladys Storey Papers." *Dkn* 76 (Spring 1980): 3-16. [Note also Katharine M. Longley's ltr. to ed., pp. 17-19.]

1478 Parker, Dorothy. "Allegory and the Extension of Mr. Bucket's Forefinger." *ELN* 12 (Sept. 1974): 31-35.

1479 Parker, Michael St. John. *Charles Dickens.* London: Pitkin Pictorials, 1973. 24 pp. [Trans. Eva Hemmer Hansen (Copenhagen: Hernov, 1976), 54 pp.—Rev.: *Dkn* 70 (Jan. 1974): 65.]

1480 Paroissien, David. *DSN* 4 (Dec. 1973): 105-109. [Rev.-art. on 2322, 2370, 2414, 2434, 2446.]

1481 —. "Charles Dickens and the Weller Family." In 1490, pp. 1-38.

1482 —. "Dickens and the Cinema." In 1495, pp. 68-80.

1483 —. "Dickens's *Pictures from Italy:* Stages of the Work's Development and Dickens's Method of Composition." *EM* 22 (1971): 243-262.

1484 —. "Dickens's Ralph Nickleby and Bulwer Lytton's William Brandon: A Note on the Antagonists." *DSN* 9 (Mar. 1978): 10-15.

1485 —. "*The Life and Adventures of Nicholas Nickleby:* Alberto Cavalcanti Interprets Dickens." *HSL* 9, i (1977): 17-28. [Cavalcanti's 1947 film.—Note also 368.]

1486 —. "Mr. Jingle: Another Bell." *DSN* 8 (Sept. 1977): 79.

1487 —. "*Pictures from Italy* and Its Original Illustrator." *Dkn* 67 (May 1971): 87-90.

1488 —. "The Victorian Experience." *DSN* 10 (June-Sept. 1979): 61-65. [Rev.-art. on 161.]

1489 Partlow, Robert B., Jr., ed. *Dickens Studies Annual.* Vol. 1. Carbondale: Southern Illinois UP; London: Feffer, 1970. [Ed., "Preface," ix-x.—Incl. 187 (chap. on *GreatEx*), 212, 237, 409, 543 (material on *Monthly Mag* tales), 605, 749, 818, 996, 1251, 1310, 1515, 1609, 1711, 1859 (material on *DSon*), 1902, 1938.—Rev.: T. J. Cribb, *RES* NS 24 (May 1973): 230-233; H. M. Daleski, *NCF* 26 (Mar. 1972): 486-491; T. J. Galvin, *LJ* 96 (1 Apr. 1971): 1270; Michael S. Helfand, *Novel* 5 (Winter 1972): 186-189; [Leonard F. Manheim?], *HSL* 3, i (1971): 67; Sylvère Monod, *EA* 24 (Jan.-Mar. 1971): 100-102; Howard Sergeant, *English* 21 (Spring 1972): 29-30; M[ichael] S[later], *Dkn* 67 (Sept. 1972): 177-178; *Ch* 8 (Oct. 1971): 1018; *Christian Century* 87 (2 Dec. 1970): 1455; *TLS* 19 Feb. 1971: 270; also rev. in 1808.]

1490 —, ed. *Dickens Studies Annual.* Vol. 2. Carbondale: Southern Illinois UP; London: Feffer, 1972. [Ed., "Preface," ix-x.—Incl. 163, 300, 455, 798 (chap. on *MChuz*), 900, 1195, 1233, 1246, 1338, 1481, 1505, 1667, 1689, 1859 (material on *MChuz*), 2054, 2143.—Rev.: Steven V. Daniels, *HAB* 24 (Spring 1973): 148-150; Earle Davis, *DSN* 4 (Mar. 1973): 24-26; Harvey Peter Sucksmith, *YES* 5 (1975): 317-319; G. B. Tennyson, *NCF* 28 (June 1973): 115; *Ch* 10 (Apr. 1973): 290; also rev. in 1026, 1537.]

1491 —, ed. *Dickens Studies Annual.* Vol. 3. Carbondale: Southern Illinois UP; London: Feffer, 1974. [Incl. papers from 2180.—Ed., "Preface," ix-xi.—Incl. 312, 440, 603, 829, 1353, 1408, 1651, 1663, 1712, 1940, 1971, 1988, 2081, 2140.—Rev.: Malcolm Andrews, *DSN* 7 (June 1976): 57-59; Rachel Bennett, *RES* NS 26 (Nov. 1975): 486-488; Michael Slater, *Dkn* 71 (Sept. 1975): 176-177; Harry Stone, *NCF* 29 (Mar. 1975): 474-477; *TLS* 5 July 1974: 733; also rev. in 504.]

1492 —, ed. *Dickens Studies Annual.* Vol. 4. Carbondale: Southern Illinois UP; London: Feffer, 1975. [Ed., "Preface," vii-xiii.—Incl. 511, 713, 714, 748, 907, 932, 969 (portion of this chap.), 1919.—Rev.: Angus Easson, *Dkn* 73 (Jan. 1977): 49-50; P. F. Fairclough, *YES* 7 (1977): 294-295; Barbara Hardy, *TLS* 23 Jan. 1976: 86; also rev. in 1022.]

1493 —, ed. *Dickens Studies Annual.* Vol. 5. Carbondale: Southern Illinois UP; London: Feffer, 1976. [Ed., "Preface," vii-xvi.—Incl. 156, 328, 631, 712, 1088, 1248, 1269, 1391, 1989.—Rev.: Rachel Bennett, *RES* NS 29 (May 1978): 232-235; Edwin M. Eigner, *MLR*

74 (Jan. 1979): 172-174; Sylvère Monod, *EA* 31 (Apr.-June 1978): 229-230; George J. Worth, *NCF* 32 (Dec. 1977): 348-351; also rev. in 583.]

1494 —, ed. *Dickens Studies Annual*. Vol. 6. Carbondale: Southern Illinois UP; London: Feffer, 1977. [Ed., "Preface," vii-xix.—Incl. 309, 391, 979, 1197, 1211, 1260, 1468, 1807, 1844, 1970.—Rev.: Rachel Bennett, *RES* NS 29 (Nov. 1978): 497-499; Angus Easson, *Dkn* 76 (Spring 1980): 45-47; Jo Modert, *St. Louis Post-Dispatch* 5 Feb. 1978: C4; Sylvère Monod, *EA* 31 (July-Dec. 1978): 398-400; Allen Samuels, *Library* ser. 5, 38 (June 1978): 183; also rev. in 531, 583, 1299, 1568.]

1495 —, ed. *Dickens Studies Annual*. Vol. 7. Carbondale: Southern Illinois UP; London: Feffer, 1978. [Ed., "Preface," vii-xvi.—Incl. 185, 524, 527, 582, 724, 954, 991, 1037, 1482, 1523, 1632, 2169.—Rev.: Rachel Bennett, *RES* NS 30 (Nov. 1979): 489-490; Angus Easson, *Dkn* 76 (Spring 1980): 45-47; Robert Giddings, *DSN* 11 (Mar. 1980): 19-24; Christopher Herbert, *NCF* 34 (Mar. 1980): 448-450; Sylvère Monod, *EA* 33 (Apr.-June 1980): 221-223; also rev. in 1109.]

1496 —, ed. *Dickens the Craftsman: Strategies of Presentation*. Carbondale: Southern Illinois UP; London: Feffer, 1970. [Ed., "Foreword," vii-xxiii.—Incl. 442, 579, 659, 1080 (chap. on *OCShop*), 1364, 1512, 1848, 1900.—Rev.: Earle Davis, *DSN* 1 (Dec. 1970): 7-8; K. J. Fielding, *RES* NS 22 (Aug. 1971): 364-366; Thomas J. Galvin, *LJ* 95 (1 Oct. 1970): 3286; [Leonard F. Manheim?], *HSL* 3, i (1971): 67; Michael Slater, *Dkn* 67 (May 1971): 112-114; *Ch* 8 (Apr. 1971): 222; *TLS* 5 Mar. 1971: 269-270; also rev. in 198, 981, 1228, 1808, 1961.]

1497 [— and Robert L. Patten.] "Opportunities for Research." *DSN* 1 (Mar. 1970): 6-7. [Note also 164.]

1498 Pascal, Roy. "Victorians: Dickens and Mimicry: *Bleak House*." *The Dual Voice: Free Indirect Speech and Its Functioning in the Nineteenth-Century European Novel* (Manchester: Manchester UP; New York: Rowman and Littlefield, 1977), 67-78. [Rev.: William J. Palmer, *DSN* 9 (Sept. 1978): 91.]

1499 Patán, Federico. "Los Estados Unidos del *Martin Chuzzlewit*." In 813, pp. 145-160.

1500 Pate, Janet. "Inspector Bucket." *The Book of Sleuths* (London: New Eng. Lib.; Chicago: Contemporary Books; Pickering, Ont.: Beaverbooks, 1977), 33-35. [Rev.: Thomas Jackson Rice, *DSN* 10 (June-Sept. 1979): 82-83.]

1501 —. "Uriah Heep." *The Black Book of Villains* (London and Newton Abbot: David and Charles; Indianapolis: Bobbs-Merrill, 1975), 116-119. [U.S. title *The Great Villains.*—Chiefly pictorial.—Rev. in 967 (Jan. 1976).]

1502 Patten, Robert L. "Autobiography into Autobiography: The Evolution of *David Copperfield*," in *Approaches to Victorian Autobiography*, ed. George P. Landow (Athens: Ohio UP, 1979), 269-291. [Esp. *DavidC, DSon.*]

1503 —. "Boz, Phiz, and Pickwick in the Pound." *ELH* 36 (Sept. 1969): 575-591.

1504 —. *Charles Dickens and His Publishers.* Oxford: Clarendon Press; New York: Oxford UP, 1978. xiv, 502 pp. [Incorporates "*Pickwick Papers* and the Development of Serial Fiction," *RUS* 61 (Winter 1975): 51-74.—Rev.: Richard D. Altick, *SAQ* 79 (Winter 1980): 107-108; Victor Bonham-Carter, *Author* 90 (Spring 1979): 30-31; Peter Bracher, *AEB* 4, ii (1980): 128-138; Philip Collins, *NCF* 34 (Mar. 1980): 444-448; J. D. F[leeman], *N&Q* NS 27 (Oct. 1980): 462-463; Donald Gray, *VS* 23 (Spring 1980): 416-418; Geoffrey Grigson, *CnL* 165 (1979): 99-100; Mollie Hardwick, *B&B* 24 (Feb. 1979): 34-36; Donald Hawes, *THES* 23 Nov. 1979: 17; Brian Jackson, *Guardian Weekly* 10 Dec. 1978: 21; Louis James, *VPR* 13 (Spring-Summer 1980): 72-74; Norman MacKenzie, *Sunday Telegraph* (London) 24 Dec. 1978: 12; Sylvère Monod, *EA* 33 (Apr.-June 1980): 223-224; Rosemary Mundhenk, *ABC* NS 1 (Mar.-Apr. 1980): 54-56; Harvey Peter Sucksmith, *JEGP* 79 (Jan. 1980): 136-139; John Sutherland, *BBkN* April 1979: 356; E. S. Turner, *Lstr* 100 (14 Dec. 1978): 793; Barry Westburg, *AUMLA* no. 53 (May 1980): 82-83; *Ch* 16 (June 1979): 532; *Ecn* 269 (30 Dec. 1978): 60; also rev. in 182 (Dec. 1979), 1109.—Note also interview by *Charlotte Phelan, *Houston Post* 25 Mar. 1979.]

1505 —. "Dickens Time and Again." In 1490, pp. 163-196.

1506 —. "The Fight at the Top of the Tree: *Vanity Fair* versus *Dombey and Son.*" *SEL* 10 (Autumn 1970): 759-773.

1507 —. "The London Centenary Celebrations." *DSN* 1 (Sept. 1970): 6-10. [Note also 2181.]

1508 —. "Pickwick's Picaresque Pilgrimage." *SCB* 31 (Oct. 1971): 119. [Abst.]

1509 —. "Portraits of Pott: Lord Brougham and the *Pickwick Papers.*" *Dkn* 66 (Sept. 1970): 205-224.

1510 —, ed. *Princeton University Library Chronicle* 35 (Autumn-Winter 1973-1974). ["George Cruikshank: A Revaluation."—Ed., "Foreword," vii-xii.—John Fowles, "Introduction: Remembering Cruikshank," xiii-xvi.—Incl. 315, 644, 894, 995, 1010, 1114, 1517, 1863, 1898, 2053.—Rev.: W. F. Axton, *NCF* 29 (Mar. 1975): 477-480; Peter Conrad, *TLS* 26 July 1974: 798-799; Edward Costigan, *VPN* 10 (Mar. 1977): 36-40; Celina Fox, *Burlington Mag* 118 (June 1976): 435; Joseph H. Gardner, *DSN* 7 (Sept. 1976): 83-88; Jonathan E. Hill, *VS* 18 (Dec. 1974): 237-238; John Dixon Hunt, *Dkn* 71 (Jan. 1975): 51-52; Paul Veyriras, *EA* 28 (Oct.-Dec. 1975): 485-486; Geoffrey Wakeman, *Library* ser. 5, 30 (Sept. 1975): 256-258.]

1511 —. "Reviews—Paperback Editions: *Oliver Twist.*" *DSN* 3 (Sept. 1972): 84-92. [All eds. prior to 1970.]

1512 —. " 'The Story-Weaver at His Loom': Dickens and the Beginning of *The Old Curiosity Shop.*" In 1496, pp. 44-64.

1513 —. " 'A Surprising Transformation': Dickens and the Hearth," in *Nature and the Victorian Imagination*, ed. U. C. Knoepflmacher and G. B. Tennyson (Berkeley, Los Angeles, London: Univ. of California Press, 1977), 153-170; et passim. [Rev. of book: John Clubbe, *DSN* 10 (Dec. 1979): 122-123; C. G. Worth, *Dkn* 75 (Spring 1979): 44-46.]

1514 —. "The Unpropitious Muse: *Pickwick's* 'Interpolated' Tales." *DSN* 1 (Mar. 1970): 7-10.

1515 Patterson, Annabel M. "*Our Mutual Friend:* Dickens as the Compleat Angler." In 1489, pp. 252-264.

1516 Pattison, Robert. "The Children of Dickens, George Eliot, and Henry James"; "Through the Child's Eyes: Gosse, Dickens, and Henry James." *The Child Figure in English Literature* (Athens: Univ. of Georgia Press, 1978), 76-107; 108-134; et passim. [*DavidC, DSon, OCShop.*—Note also "The Little Victims: The Child Figure and Original Sin in English Literature," *DAI* 37 (Dec. 1976): 3647A (Columbia).—Rev.: Arthur M. Adrian, *DSN* 10 (June-Sept. 1979): 78-79; Andrew Lincoln, *Dkn* 75 (Spring 1979):

43-44.]

1517 Paulson, Ronald. "The Tradition of Comic Illustration from Hogarth to Cruikshank." In 1510, pp. 35-60.

1518 Pavese, Cesare. "Preface to Dickens, *David Copperfield.*" *American Literature: Essays and Opinions,* trans. Edwin Fussell (Berkeley and Los Angeles: Univ. of California Press, 1970), 206-210. [From Pavese's trans. of *DavidC,* 1939.]

1519 Pearce, Richard. "The *Alazon:* The Theme of Intrusion in *Great Expectations* and *The Trial.*" *Stages of the Clown: Perspectives on Modern Fiction from Dostoevsky to Beckett* (Carbondale: Southern Illinois UP; London: Feffer and Simons, 1970), 26-46.

1520 Pearce, T. S. "*Bleak House.*" *George Eliot* (London: Evans; Totowa, N.J.: Rowman and Littlefield, 1973), 62-66.

1521 Pearl, Cyril. "Mr. Dickens and Mr. [G. W. M.] Reynolds." *Victorian Patchwork* (London: Heinemann, 1973), 67-94; et passim. [Incl. *HsldWds, OCShop,* but chiefly on Reynolds, the Victorian Mickey Spillane.]

1522 Pearlman, E. "David Copperfield Dreams of Drowning." In 1955, pp. 105-117. [Rpt. from *AI* 28 (Winter 1971): 391-403.]

1523 —. "Inversion in *Great Expectations.*" In 1495, pp. 190-202.

1524 —. "Two Notes on Religion in *David Copperfield.*" *VN* no. 41 (Spring 1972): 18-20.

1525 Pearsall, Ronald. *Collapse of Stout Party: Victorian Wit and Humour* (London: Weidenfeld and Nicolson, 1975), passim. [Touches on *MChuz, NichN, OliverTw, PickP.*—Rev.: David Paroissien, *DSN* 8 (Sept. 1977): 90-91; also rev. in 967 (Jan. 1977).]

1526 —. *Public Purity, Private Shame: Victorian Sexual Hypocrisy Exposed* (London: Weidenfeld and Nicolson, 1976), passim. [Rev.: William Gordon, *DSN* 8 (Sept. 1977): 91-92.]

1527 Pearson, Edmund L. *Sherlock Holmes and the Drood Mystery,* intro., afwd. Tom Schantz, illus. Enid Schantz. Freeville, N.Y.: Aspen Press, 1973. ix, 39 pp. [Rpt. from his *Secret Book* (1914).—Rev.: A[llen] J. R[ubin], *ArmD* 6 (May 1973): 191.]

1528 Pearson, Gabriel. "Towards a Reading of *Dombey and Son,*" in *The*

Modern English Novel: The Reader, the Writer and the Work, ed.
Gabriel Josipovici (London: Open Books; New York: Barnes and
Noble, 1976), 54-76.

1529 Peel, Marie. *"Little Dorrit:* Prison or Cage?" *B&B* 17 (Sept. 1972):
38-42.

1530 Pei, Lowry. "Mirrors, the Dead Child, Snagsby's Secret, and Esther."
ELN 16 (Dec. 1978): 144-156.

1531 Petrie, Graham. "Dickens, Godard, and the Film Today." *YR* 64
(Winter 1975): 185-201.

1532 Petrullo, Helen B. "Sinclair Lewis's Condensation of Dickens's *Bleak
House.*" *YULG* 45 (Jan. 1971): 85-87. [See 1175.]

1533 Pettingell, Phoebe. "Ambiguous Expectations," in *Poems and Essays
in Honor of Francis Golffing*, ed. Wesley Clymer ([Rindge, N.H.] :
n.p., 1977), 15-17.

1534 Phelps, Gilbert. *"The Posthumous Papers of the Pickwick Club"*;
"Great Expectations"; *"Our Mutual Friend."* An Introduction to
Fifty British Novels, 1600-1900 (London and Sydney: Pan Books,
1979), 213-228; 385-395; 396-406. [Summaries and critical commentaries.—Also pub. as *A Reader's Guide to Fifty British Novels,
1600-1900* (London: Heinemann; New York: Barnes and Noble,
1979).]

1535 Phelps, Wayne H. "Dickens to Bradbury and Evans: An Unnoted
Letter, and Cruikshank to Chapman and Hall: A Letter concerning
Sketches by 'Boz'." *Dkn* 75 (Spring 1979): 30-31.

1536 Phillips, Virginia. " 'Brought up by Hand': Dickens's Pip, Little Paul
Dombey, and Oliver Twist." *Dkn* 74 (Sept. 1978): 144-147.

1537 Pickering, Samuel F. *GaR* 27 (Fall 1973): 455-463. [Rev.-art. on
798, 802, 1419, 1490.]

1538 —. "The Critical Rule of Thumb." *GaR* 32 (Fall 1978): 662-667.
[Rev.-art. on 1011, 1252, 1415, 2052.]

1539 —. *"The Old Curiosity Shop,* and Legh Richmond's Tracts"; "Protestantism in *Barnaby Rudge*"; *"Dombey and Son* and Unitarianism." *The Moral Tradition in English Fiction, 1785-1850* (Han-
over, N.H.: UP of New England for Dartmouth Coll., 1976), 107-
122; 123-148; 149-168. [Incorporates *"Dombey and Son* and

Dickens's Unitarian Period," *GaR* 26 (Winter 1972): 438-454 and "*The Old Curiosity Shop:* A Religious Tract?," *IllinoisQ* 36 (Sept. 1973): 5-20.—Rev.: Thomas Jackson Rice, *DSN* 10 (June-Sept. 1979): 82-83.]

1540 Piellerr, Evelyne. "Rêvez lecteur!" In 768, pp. 10-11. [*GreatEx, MEDrood*.]

1541 Pimentel y A., Luz Aurora. "El encuentro fortuito y la casualidad aparente como fuente de conocimiento interno en *Great Expectations*." In 813, pp. 109-144.

1542 Pinsker, Sanford. "Charles Dickens and Nathanael West: Great Expectations Unfulfilled." *Topic* 19 (Fall 1969): 40-52. [Esp. satire in *GreatEx* and *Miss Lonelyhearts, MChuz* and *Cool Million*.]

1543 Piscopo, Ugo. "Dickens e l'Italia." *CeS* 10 (Apr.-June 1971): 79-92. [*PictIt*.]

1544 —. "Dickens en Italie," trans. Camille Sinaï. In 743, pp. 116-124. [Reception.]

1545 Pittman, Philip McM. "*A Christmas Carol:* Review and Assessment." *VIJ* no. 4 (Summer 1975): 25-34.

1546 —. "Time, Narrative Technique, and the Theme of Regeneration in *A Christmas Carol*." *BWVACET* 2, ii (1975): 34-49.

1547 Pochoda, Elizabeth. "Sense and Sentimentality." *Nation* 223 (18 Dec. 1976): 661-663. [Christmas in *PickP*.]

1548 Pocock, D. C. D. *The Novelist and the North.* Univ. of Durham, Dept. of Geography, Occasional Pubs., NS 12 (Durham: Univ. of Durham, Dept. of Geography, 1978), passim. [*HardT, OCShop*.]

1549 Podeschi, John. "Gimbel Collection." *TLS* 7 Jan. 1972: 15. [At Yale.—Note also anon. ltr. to ed., *TLS* 14 Jan. 1972: 40.]

1550 Poe, Edgar Allan. "L'idéalité (à propos de récits de Charles Dickens)." *L'Herne* no. 26 [1974]: 101-107. [1st French trans. of rev. of *OCShop* in *Graham's Mag*, 1841.—Eng. orig. rpt. in 2331, pp. 19-24 and in 438, pp. 105-111.]

1551 Pointer, Michael. "A Dickens Garland." *Amer Film* 1 (Dec. 1975): 14-19. [D films surveyed.]

1552 Polikarpov, Iu. "Russkii prototip personazha Dikkensa." *VLit* 16 (Mar. 1972): 184-185. [Russian Imperial Army officer prototype of Sam Weller.]

1553 Politi, Jina. "Past and Present: The Ethical Implications of Tense." *The Novel and Its Presuppositions: Changes in the Conceptual Structure of Novels in the 18th and 19th Centuries* (Amsterdam: Hakkert; Athens: Harvey, 1976), 197-229. [*BleakH.*]

1554 Pollin, Burton R. "*Nicholas Nickleby* in 'The Devil in the Belfry'." *PoeS* 8 (June 1975): 23.

1555 Pollock, Zailig. " 'Partings Welded Together': Parting and Coming Together in the Structure of *Great Expectations*." *DSN* 8 (June 1977): 40-44.

1556 Pook, John. "Allegory and Thematic Imagery in *Dombey and Son* and *Hard Times*." *AWR* 20 (Autumn 1971): 101-108.

1557 —. "*Bleak House* and *Little Dorrit*: A Comparison." *AWR* 19 (Autumn 1970): 154-159.

1558 Poole, Adrian. *Gissing in Context* (London: Macmillan; Totowa, N.J.: Rowman and Littlefield, 1975), passim.

1559 Pope, Norris. *Dickens and Charity.* London: Macmillan; New York: Columbia UP, 1978. xi, 303 pp. [Esp. *BleakH, HsldWds, PickP, SBoz.*—Note also diss., "Charitable Activity and Attitudes in Early Victorian England, with Special Reference to Dickens and the Evangelicals" (Oxford, 1975).—Rev.: Asa Briggs, *Enc* 52 (Apr. 1979): 75-76; Philip Collins, *NewSt* 96 (15 Dec. 1978): 823-824; Charmazel Dudt, *C&L* 28 (Summer 1979): 64-65; Avrom Fleishman, *NCF* 35 (June 1980): 105-109; Ruth Glancy, *BBkN* Apr. 1979: 325; Robert Greacen, *Tablet* 233 (6 Jan. 1979): 9; Geoffrey Grigson, *CnL* 165 (1979): 99-100; Mollie Hardwick, *B&B* 24 (Sept. 1979): 43-44; Edgar Johnson, *NYRB* 22 Mar. 1979: 24-25, 28; Margaret Lane, *Daily Telegraph* (London) 28 Dec. 1978: 7; Sylvère Monod, *EA* 33 (Apr.-June 1980): 224-225; Daniel Pals, *Church Hist* 49 (Sept. 1980): 342-343; Robert L. Patten, *Amer Hist Rev* 85 (Feb. 1980): 127-128; Michael Slater, *VS* 23 (Summer 1980): 520-522; Alan S. Watts, *Dkn* 75 (Summer 1979): 111-113; Judith Wilt, *Criticism* 21 (Summer 1979): 273-276; *Ch* 16 (Apr. 1979): 225; *Ecn* 269 (30 Dec. 1978): 60; also rev. in 1109, 1751.]

1560 Pope-Hennessy, Una. *Charles Dickens.* Harmondsworth: Pelican, 1970. xii, 476 pp. [Orig. pub. 1945.]

1561 Popescu, Petru. "Londra într-o nuca." *RoLit* 3 (16 Apr. 1970): 19. [Esp. *SBoz.*]

1562 Poston, Laurence. "Uriah Heep, Scott, and a Note on Puritanism." *Dkn* 71 (Jan. 1975): 43-44.

1563 Pothet, Lucien. " 'The Haunted Man' de Charles Dickens, ou: Les déguisements d'une confidence," in *Littérature-linguistique-civilisation-pédagogie.* Soc. des Anglicistes de l'Enseignement Supérieur, Actes du Congrès de Grenoble, 1973; EA, 65 (Paris: Didier, 1976), 151-168.

1564 —. *Mythe et tradition populaire dans l'imaginaire dickensien,* ed. Jean Burgos, pref. Sylvère Monod, fwd. Jean Perrin. Bibliothèque Circé, 1. Paris: Lettres Modernes, 1979. 281 pp. [Posthumous pub. of unfinished Sorbonne diss.]

1565 —. "Sur quelque images d'intimité chez Dickens." In 154, pp. 136-157.

1566 Powell, Dilys. "Postscript: Dickens on Film." *Dkn* 66 (May 1970): 183-185. [Special no. on D's reputation 1870-1970.—For revs. see 448.]

1567 Pratley, Gerald. "*Great Expectations* (1946)"; "*Oliver Twist* (1948)." *The Cinema of David Lean* (South Brunswick, N.J. and New York: S. Barnes; London: Tantivy Press, 1974), 59-71; 72-81. [Rev.: Ana Laura Zambrano, *DSN* 8 (June 1977): 58-59.]

1568 Pratt, Branwen Bailey. *NCF* 33 (Sept. 1978): 262-268. [Rev. of 1252, 1415, 1494, 2052.]

1569 —. "Dickens and Father: Notes on the Family Romance." In 1247, pp. 4-22.

1570 —. "Dickens and Freedom: Young Bailey in *Martin Chuzzlewit.*" *NCF* 30 (Sept. 1975): 185-199.

1571 —. "A Note on a Character Who Does Not Appear in *Martin Chuzzlewit.*" *DSN* 8 (June 1977): 45-46. [Young Bailey's mother in a ballad.]

1572 —. "Sympathy for the Devil: A Dissenting View of Quilp." *HSL* 6, ii (1974): 129-146. [Note also Michael Steig's response, iii, pp. 282-283.]

1573 Prause, Gerhard. "Charles Dickens." *Genies in der Schule: Legende und Wahrheit über den Erfolg im Leben* (Düsseldorf and Vienna: Econ, 1974), 269-272. [Note also "Charles Dickens," *School Days of the Famous: Do School Achievements Foretell Success in Life?*, trans. and adap. Susan Hecker Roy (New York: Springer, 1978), 192-195.]

1574 Prawer, S. S. *Karl Marx and World Literature* (Oxford: Clarendon Press, 1976), passim. [Marx's uses and opinions of D.]

1575 Praz, Mario. "Nascita e tramonto del sentimentalismo." *NA* 514 (Apr. 1972): 441-462.

1576 Prendergast, Christopher. *Balzac: Fiction and Melodrama* (London: E. Arnold; New York: Holmes and Meier, 1978), passim.

1577 Prettejohns, Graham, Brenda Mann, and Larry Ilott. *Charles Dickens and Southwark*, illus. David Burch. London: Council of the London Borough of Southwark, 1974. 28 pp. [Rev.: *Dkn* 70 (May 1974): 136.]

1578 Price, Martin. "Taking Dickens Seriously." *YR* 61 (Dec. 1971): 271-279. [Rev.-art. on 509, 884, 1150, 1253, 2093, 2128.]

1579 Prickett, Stephen. "Christmas at Scrooge's." *Victorian Fantasy* (Hassocks: Harvester Press; Bloomington: Indiana UP, 1979), 38-74. [Also *Chimes.*—Rev.: Malcolm Andrews, *Dkn* 76 (Summer 1980): 109-110.]

1580 Priestley, J. B. "[Toast at] 64th Annual Conference." *Dkn* 66 (Sept. 1970): 260-261.

1581 —. *Victoria's Heyday* (London: Heinemann; New York: Harper, 1972), passim. [Mentions *AllYR, BleakH, DavidC, DSon, HardT, HsldWds, LittleDor, MChuz, OCShop.*—Rev.: James D. Barry, *DSN* 4 (Dec. 1973): 103-105; B[ryan] H[ulse], *Dkn* 68 (Sept. 1972): 194-195.]

1582 —. "The Wonderful World of Dickens." *English Humour* (London: Heinemann; New York: Stein and Day, 1976), 66-77; et passim. [Esp. *MChuz, NichN, OurMF, PickP.*—Diff. from his 1929 book of same title.]

1583 Pringle, John Douglas. "Literary Migrants." *On Second Thoughts: Australian Essays* (Sydney and London: Angus and Robertson, 1971), 126-133. [On *DavidC.*]

1584 Proshkina, E. P. "O vnutrennem monologe v romanakh Dikkensa."
     VLU no. 1 (1977): 90-94. [Eng. abst., p. 94.]

1585 Purton, Valerie. "Dickens and Bulwer Lytton: The Dandy Re-
     claimed?" *Dkn* 74 (Jan. 1978): 25-29. [Infl. of Bulwer's plays.]

1586 —. "Dickens and 'Cheap Melodrama'." *EA* 28 (Jan.-Mar. 1975): 22-
     26. [Esp. *NichN, OurMF*.]

1587 Putt, S. Gorley. "Henry James and Dickens." *TLS* 19 Feb. 1971:
     213. [Ltr. to ed.—Note also F. R. Leavis, 5 Mar. 1971: 271 (rpt.
     in 1148); S. Gorley Putt, Arthur Freeman, 12 Mar. 1971: 296,
     F. R. Leavis, 19 Mar. 1971: 325; S. Gorley Putt, 26 Mar. 1971:
     353.]

1588 Qualls, Barry V. "Savages in a 'Bran-New' World: Carlyle and *Our
     Mutual Friend*." *SNNTS* 10 (Summer 1978): 199-217.

1589 Quayle, Eric. "Charles Dickens and Wilkie Collins." *The Collector's
     Book of Detective Fiction* (London: Studio Vista, 1972), 42-50.
     [Esp. *BarnR, BleakH, HsldWds, MEDrood*.]

1590 Quinn, Martin. "Dickens and *Misalliance*." *ShawR* 17 (Sept. 1974):
     141-143.

1591 —. "Dickens as Shavian Metaphor." *ShawR* 18 (May 1975): 44-56.

1592 —. "The Dickensian Presence in *Heartbreak House*." In 1593, pp.
     119-125.

1593 —, ed. *Shaw Review* 20 (Sept. 1977). [Special no. on Shaw and D.—
     Incl. 710, 803, 919, 1455, 1592, 1668.—Rev.: Charles A. Berst,
     DSN 9 (Sept. 1978): 89-91.]

1594 Quirk, Eugene F. "Tulkinghorn's Buried Life: A Study of Character
     in *Bleak House*." *JEGP* 72 (Oct. 1973): 526-535.

1595 Quirk, Randolph. "Charles Dickens, Linguist." *The Linguist and the
     English Language* (London: Arnold; New York: St. Martin's Press,
     1974), 1-36. [All novels except *BarnR, OliverTw, TaleTwoC*.—
     Based upon 2407 and "Some Observations on the Language of
     Dickens," *REL*, 1961.—Rev.: Norman Page, *Dkn* 72 (Jan. 1976):
     43-44.]

1596 Rabkin, Eric S. "The Comedy and the Melodrama." *Narrative Sus-
     pense: "When Slim Turned Sideways. . ."* (Ann Arbor: Univ. of

Michigan Press, 1973), 139-149. [*BleakH.*]

1597 Ragussis, Michael. "The Ghostly Signs of *Bleak House*." *NCF* 34 (Dec. 1979): 253-280. [Language and naming.]

1598 Raimond, Jean. "Le roman de l'ère victorienne triomphante: 1832-1870"; "Charles Dickens: *Great Expectations*," in *Le roman anglais aux XIXe siècle,* by Pierre Coustillas, Jean-Pierre Petit, and Jean Raimond (Paris: Presses Univs. de France, 1978), 87-111; 210-223; et passim. [Symbolism, realism.]

1599 Raine, Craig. "Dickens and Language." *TES* 12 Jan. 1973: 21.

1600 Rance, Nicholas. "Charles Dickens: *A Tale of Two Cities* (1859)." *The Historical Novel and Popular Politics in Nineteenth-Century England* (London: Vision Press; New York: Barnes and Noble, 1975), 83-101; et passim. [Rev. in 967 (Jan. 1976).]

1601 Rapin, René. "Le centenaire de la mort de Dickens." *Gazette littéraire* 25-26 July 1970: 31.

1602 Rares, Ana Maria. "Charles Dickens: Aventura—carte." *ViR* 23 (June 1970): 86-89. [*GreatEx, OliverTw, PickP.*]

1603 Rataboul, Louis J. "Dickens." *Le pasteur anglican dans le roman victorien: Aspects sociaux et religieux.* EA, 70 (Paris: Didier Érudition, 1978), 132-141; et passim. [Esp. Charles Timson (*SBoz*), Bishop (*LittleDor*), Frank Milvey (*OurMF*), Septimus Crisparkle (*MEDrood*).]

1604 Ray, Gordon N. *The Illustrator and the Book in England from 1790 to 1914* (New York, London, etc.: Pierpont Morgan Lib. [and] Oxford UP, 1976), passim. [Note also accompanying monochrome microfiche reproduction of plates from *CCarol, OliverTw* (plus titles), *PickP* issued by Chadwyck-Healey (Cambridge) and Somerset House (Teaneck, N.J.).]

1605 Ray, Laura Krugman. "Dickens and 'The Magic Barrel'." *SAJL* 4 (Spring 1978): 35-40. [*GreatEx* as source for Malamud.]

1606 —. "Kenneth Grahame and the Literature of Childhood." *ELT* 20 (1977): 3-12. [Mentions *DavidC, GreatEx.*]

1607 Razumovskaia, T. F. "Problema tipicheskogo kharaktera v tvorchestve Ch. Dikkensa i D. Golsuorsi: Romany *Dombey i syn, Sob-*

stvennik." *Literaturnye sviazi i traditsii* 4 (1974): 117-123. [Typical character in *DSon, Man of Property*.]

1608 Reed, A. H. *Charles Dickens: A Centenary Tribute.* Wellington, N.Z.: Reed for Dunedin Pub. Lib., 1970. 30 pp.

1609 Reed, John R. "Confinement and Character in Dickens's Novels." In 1489, pp. 41-54. [Esp. *DavidC, DSon, GreatEx, LittleDor, PickP.*—Note also Robert F. Fleissner's ltr. to ed., *DSN* 2 (June 1972): 58-59.]

1610 —. "Freedom, Fate, and the Future in *Bleak House.*" *ClioI* 8 (Winter 1979): 175-194.

1611 —. *Victorian Conventions* ([Athens] : Ohio UP, 1975), passim. [Esp. conventions of the return in *OurMF*, of Judith and Griselda types in *DavidC, DSon, GreatEx, LittleDor*, of disguise in *BleakH, Little-Dor, OurMF, TaleTwoC.*—Incorporates "Emblems in Victorian Literature," *HSL* 2, i (1970): 19-39.—Rev.: Sylvia Manning, *DSN* 8 (Mar. 1977): 22-25; also rev. in 967 (Jan. 1977).]

1612 Rees, John O. " 'What Price Dotheboys Hall?': Some Dickens Echoes in Waugh." *KanQ* 7 (Fall 1975): 14-18.

1613 Reeves, William J. "Blake and Dickens: The Similar Vision." *AN&Q* 17 (Nov. 1978): 37-40.

1614 —. "Chimney Sweeps and Charter'd Streets: The Teaching of *Oliver Twist*, with an Assist from William Blake." *J of Eng Teaching Techniques* 7 (Spring 1974): 32-35.

1615 Reibetanz, J. M. "Villain, Victim, and Hero: Structure and Theme in *David Copperfield.*" *DR* 59 (Summer 1979): 321-337.

1616 Reichert, John. *Making Sense of Literature* (Chicago and London: Univ. of Chicago Press, 1977), passim. [*DavidC, GreatEx. PickP.*]

1617 (Reid, John C. *Dickens: Little Dorrit.* 1967.) [Rev.: Edward Davies, *UES* 11 (Mar. 1973): 53.]

1618 Reinhold, Heinz. "Charles Dickens: *Bleak House*," in *Der englische Roman im 19. Jahrhundert: Interpretationen*, ed. Paul Goetsch et al. (Berlin: Schmidt, 1973), 106-123.

1619 —. "Charles Dickens (1812-1870)." *Der englische Roman des 19. Jahrhunderts.* Studienreihe Englisch, 31 (Düsseldorf: Bagel;

Bern and Munich; Francke, 1976), 36-47. [General survey of novels.]

1620 (–, ed. *Charles Dickens: Sein Werke im Lichte neuer deutscher Forschung.* 1969.) [Eng. abst. in *EASG* 1969: 63-66.—Rev.: J. M. Blom, *Neophil* 56 (July 1972): 375-376; C. A. Bodelsen, *ES* 53 (June 1972): 264-266; Frederick L. Burwick, *NCF* 26 (Dec. 1971): 358-362; Werner Faulstich, *Lit, Music, Fine Arts* (*Germ St,* sec. 3) 10, i (1977): 50-52; Annegret Maack, *NS* 71 (Sept. 1972): 554-555; John A. S. Phillips, *DSN* 2 (Sept. 1971): 73-76; W. D. Robson-Scott, *Dkn* 67 (Jan. 1971): 52-54; Georg Seehase, *ZAA* 21, ii (1973): 209-211; J. M. S. Tompkins, *SN* 42 (1970): 478-480.]

1621 –. "The Dickens Centenary Year in German-Speaking Countries," trans. Pamela Reilly. *DSN* 2 (Mar. 1971): 12-19.

1622 –. "Die Helden und Heroinen der ersten Schaffensperiode von Charles Dickens im Wandel der deutschen Kritik des 19. Jahrhunderts," in *Grossbritannien und Deutschland: Europäische Aspeckte der politischkulturellen Beziehungen beider Länder in Geschichte und Gegenwart,* ed. Ortwin Kuhn (Munich: Goldmann, 1974), 414-420. [*PickP* through *DavidC.*]

1623 –. "[Toast at] The London Birthday Dinner." *Dkn* 71 (May 1975): 122-124.

1624 Rekowski, Peter-Jurgen. *Die Erzählhaltung in den historischen Romanen von Walter Scott und Charles Dickens.* Europäische Hochschulschriften, Ser. 14: Angelsächsische Sprache und Literatur, 30. Bern: Herbert Lang; Frankfurt: Peter Lang, 1975. 272 pp. [Eng. abst. in *EASG* 1977: 102-104 (Marburg diss.).]

1625 Remash, Hugh and James Flynn. "Letter and Reply (on *Great Expectations*)." *RecL* 1 (Winter 1972): 29-42.

1626 Revol, E. L. "Dickens y la mitología victoriana." *Literatura inglesa del siglo XX.* Nuevos esquemas, 29 (Buenos Aires: Columba, 1973), 21-40. [Esp. *TaleTwoC.*—Rev. and enl. from *RO* 94 (Jan. 1971): 36-48.]

1627 Rexroth, Kenneth. *"Pickwick Papers." The Elastic Retort: Essays in Literature and Ideas* (New York: Seabury Press, 1973), 98-102. [Slightly rev. rpt. from *SatR,* 7 Dec. 1968.]

1628 Rey, Henri-François. "Dickens, c'était un Jean-Jacques Rousseau ami des hommes." *FL* 22 June 1970: 20-21.

1629 Reynolds, Graham. "Charles Dickens and the World of Art." *Apollo* 91 (June 1970): 422-429.

1630 —. "Radio Dickens." *Guardian* (Manchester) 6 June 1970: 8. [Surveys commemorative broadcasts.]

1631 Rhöse, Franz. "Kritik an den 'Tendenzgeschichten' von Dickens." *Konflikt und Versöhnung: Untersuchungen zur Theorie des Romans von Hegel bis zum Naturalismus.* GA, 47 (Stuttgart: Metzlersche Verlagsbuchhandlung, 1978), 149-152; et passim. [1856-1874.]

1632 Rice, Thomas J. "*Barnaby Rudge:* A Vade Mecum for the Theme of Domestic Government in Dickens." In 1495, pp. 81-102.

1633 —. "Dickens, Poe and the Time Scheme of *Barnaby Rudge.*" *DSN* 7 (June 1976): 34-38.

1634 —. "The End of Dickens's Apprenticeship: Variable Focus in *Barnaby Rudge.*" *NCF* 30 (Sept. 1975): 172-184.

1635 —. "*Oliver Twist* and the Genesis of *Barnaby Rudge.*" *DSN* 4 (Mar. 1973): 10-15.

1636 Rickards, Maurice. "Charles Dickens (1812-70)." *Where They Lived in London* (Newton Abbot: David and Charles; New York: Taplinger, 1972), 96-97.

1637 Riley, Michael M. "Dickens and Film: Notes on Adaptation." *DSN* 5 (Dec. 1974): 110-112.

1638 Riviere, François. "Où Dickens retrouve sa vigueur." *NL* 10 Jan. 1980: 26. [On new Sylvère Monod trans.]

1639 Rizzati, Maria Luisa and Donatella Bisutti. *Charles Dickens.* Milan: Periodici Mondadori, 1974. 136 pp. [Rev.: E. W. F. Tomlin, *Dkn* 71 (May 1975): 109-110.]

1640 Roazen, Deborah Heller. "A Peculiar Attraction: *Bleak House, Der Prozess,* and the Law." *ELWIU* 5 (Fall 1978): 251-266.

1641 Robert, P.-E. *Marcel Proust, lecteur des Anglo-Saxons* (Paris: Nizet, 1976), 141-152; et passim.

1642 Roberts, David. "Dickens and the Arctic." *Horizon* 23 (Jan. 1980): 64-68, 70-71. [*FDeep.*]

1643 —. "Paternalism and Rebellion in the Early Victorian Novel." *Paternalism in Early Victorian England* (New Brunswick, N.J.: Rutgers UP; London: Croom Helm, 1979), 85-101. [Incl. *Chimes, CCarol, HardT, NichN, PickP.*]

1644 Robertson, D. S. *A Study Guide to Charles Dickens's Great Expectations.* Brisbane: William Brooks, 1969. 93 pp.

1645 Robinson, Frank. "Dickens, the Schoolmaster and the Clock." *Northern Notes* 3, iii-iv (1971): supp. [Incl. sources of *MH's-Clock.*]

1646 Robinson, Roger. "The Influence of Fielding on *Barnaby Rudge.*" *AUMLA* no. 40 (Nov. 1973): 183-197.

1647 Robison, Roselee. "Dickens and the Sentimental Tradition: Mr. Pickwick and My Uncle Toby." *UTQ* 39 (Apr. 1970): 258-273.

1648 —. "Dickens's Everlastingly Green Garden." *ES* 59 (Oct. 1978): 409-424.

1649 —. "The Several Worlds of *Great Expectations.*" *QQ* 78 (Spring 1971): 54-59.

1650 —. "Time, Death and the River in Dickens's Novels." *ES* 53 (Oct. 1972): 436-454. [Esp. *DSon, GreatEx, OurMF, MEDrood.*]

1651 Robson, John M. "*Our Mutual Friend:* A Rhetorical Approach to the First Number." In 1491, pp. 198-213. [Paper from 2180.]

1652 Roddick, Nick. "*Oliver!*" In 1238, III, 1252-1255. [Carol Reed's 1968 film.]

1653 Rodway, Allan. *English Comedy: Its Role and Nature from Chaucer to the Present Day* (London: Chatto and Windus; Berkeley: Univ. of California Press; Toronto: Clarke Irwin, 1975), passim. [Esp. *MChuz.*—Rev.: Elliot Engel, *DSN* 8 (Dec. 1977): 118-120.]

1654 Rogers, Frederick R. S. "Charles Dickens and Horology." *Antiquarian Horology and the Proc of the Antiquarian Horological Soc* (London) 7 (1970): 60-65.

1655 Rogers, Henry N., III. "Shadows of Irony: The Comic Structure of

Little Dorrit." *PAPA* 5 (Fall 1979): 58-63. [Abst. in *PAPA* 5 (Fall 1978): 20.]

1656 Rogers, Philip. "The Dynamics of Time in *The Old Curiosity Shop.*" *NCF* 28 (Sept. 1973): 127-144.

1657 —. "Mr. Pickwick's Innocence." *NCF* 27 (June 1972): 21-37.

1658 Rohrberger, Mary. "The Daydream and the Nightmare: Surreality in *Oliver Twist.*" *StHum* 6 (Mar. 1978): 21-28.

1659 Romano, John. *Dickens and Reality.* New York and Guildford: Columbia UP, 1978. viii, 187 pp. [Esp. *OurMF, DSon, Little-Dor, OCShop, OliverTw.*—Note also "Dickens and the Form of the Realist Novel," *DAI* 37 (July 1976): 338A-339A (Yale).—Rev.: William Burgan, *SNNTS* 10 (Winter 1978): 471-473; Ross H. Dabney, *NCF* 33 (Mar. 1979): 513-515; Robin Gilmour, *Dkn* 75 (Spring 1979): 38-39; Cicely Palser Havely, *N&Q* NS 27 (Oct. 1980): 461-462; Linda K. Hughes, *Criticism* 21 (Spring 1979): 167-171; Ruth Mathewson, *New Leader* 61 (22 May 1978): 4; Sylvère Monod, *EA* 33 (Jan.-Mar. 1980): 86-88; Robert O'Kell, *QQ* 86 (Winter 1979-1980): 712-714; Robert L. Patten, *Novel* 12 (Spring 1979): 254-259; F. S. Schwarzbach, *DSN* 10 (June-Sept. 1979): 66-68; Michael Steig, *Arnoldian* 6 (Winter 1979): 28-31; Alan Thomas, *TLS* 10 Nov. 1978: 1317; *Ch* 15 (July-Aug. 1978): 693; also rev. in 583, 981, 1123, 1299, 2094.]

1660 Ron, Moshe. "Autobiographical Narration and Formal Closure in *Great Expectations.*" *HUSL* 5 (Spring 1977): 37-66.

1661 Ronald, Ann. "Dickens's Gloomiest Gothic Castle." *DSN* 6 (Sept. 1975): 71-75. [*BleakH.*]

1662 Rooke, Patrick. *The Age of Dickens.* New York: Putnam; London: Wayward, 1970. 128 pp. [Rev.: Louis James, *DSN* 2 (Dec. 1971): 106; also rev. in 314.]

1663 Roopnaraine, R. Rupert. "Time and the Circle in *Little Dorrit.*" In 1491, pp. 54-76.

1664 Roos, David A. "Dickens at the Royal Academy of Arts: A New Speech and Two Eulogies." *Dkn* 73 (May 1977): 100-107. [Incl. speeches by D, Trollope, Forster.]

1665 Rosenberg, Devra Braun. "Contrasting Pictorial Representations of Time: The Dual Narration of *Bleak House.*" *VN* no. 51 (Spring

1977): 10-16.

1666 Rosenberg, Edgar. "Dating *Edwin Drood.*" *Dkn* 76 (Spring 1980): 42-43.

1667 —. "A Preface to *Great Expectations:* The Pale Usher Dusts His Lexicons." In 1490, pp. 294-335.

1668 —. "The Shaw/Dickens File: 1885-1950: Two Checklists." In 1593, pp. 148-170 and in *ShawR* 21 (Jan. 1978): 2-19.

1669 —. "Small Talk in Hammersmith: Chapter 23 of *Great Expectations.*" *Dkn* 69 (May 1973): 90-101.

1670 —. "Wopsle's Consecration." *DSN* 8 (Mar. 1977): 6-11. [Source of Waldengarver, his stage-name.]

1671 Rosenberg, John D. "Varieties of Infernal Experience." *HudR* 23 (Autumn 1970): 454-480. [London.]

1672 Rosenblatt, Roger. "*A Christmas Carol.*" *New Republic* 172 (27 Dec. 1975): 33-34.

1673 Rosenwater, Irving. "Charles Dickens and Cricket." *London Mag* 19 (June 1970): 45-56.

1674 Rosner, Mary. " 'The Siren-Like Delusions of Art.' "*DSN* 10 (June-Sept. 1979): 47-51. [Opening of *MChuz.*]

1674a Rothstein, Eric. "The Historical Hypothesis." *Systems of Order and Inquiry in Later Eighteenth-Century Fiction* (Berkeley, Los Angeles, London: Univ. of California Press, 1975), 243-265. [Late novels.]

1675 Rotundo, Barbara. "The Literary Lights Were Always Bright at 148 Charles Street." *AH* 22 (Feb. 1971): 10-15. [American friends Annie and James Fields.]

1676 Roudy, Pierre. "Dickens en Angleterre." In 743, pp. 110-116.

1677 Rounds, Stephen R. "Naming People: Dickens's Technique in *Hard Times.*" *DSN* 8 (June 1977): 36-40.

1678 Roussel, Roy. "The Completed Story in *The Mystery of Edwin Drood.*" *Criticism* 20 (Fall 1978): 383-402.

1679 Rubin, Abba. "The Antisemitism of Charles Dickens: A Re-Examination." *Univ of Portland Rev* 31 (Spring 1979): 22-37. [Fagin, Riah.]

1680 Rubin, Stan S. "Spectator and Spectacle: Narrative Evasion and Narrative Voice in *Pickwick Papers.*" *JNT* 6 (Fall 1976): 188-203.

1681 Ruer, Jean. "Charles Dickens, Wilkie Collins et *The Frozen Deep.*" In 154, pp. 183-189.

1682 Ruff, Lillian M. "How Musical was Charles Dickens?" *Dkn* 68 (Jan. 1972): 31-42. [Esp. *DSon,MChuz, NichN, OCShop, OurMF.*]

1683 Ryals, Clyde de L., ed. *Nineteenth-Century Literary Perspectives: Essays in Honor of Lionel Stevenson.* Durham, N. C.: Duke UP, 1974. [Incl. 125, 202, 1012, 2153.—Rev.: Michael Slater, *Dkn* 71 (Sept. 1975): 175-176; George J. Worth, *DSN* 6 (Dec. 1975): 124-127.]

1684 Ryan, A. P. "The Full Life." *TES* 22 May 1970: 15-16. [Appreciation.]

1685 Ryan, Alan. "Mill and Dickens." *J. S. Mill* (London and Boston: Routledge and Kegan Paul, 1974), 23-26. [*HardT.*]

1686 Ryan, Sr. M. Rosario. "Dickens and Shakespeare: Probable Sources for *Barnaby Rudge.*" *English* 19 (Summer 1970): 43-48. [*Macbeth, King Lear.*]

1687 Sabbadini, Silvano. "Noterelle vittoriane." *St inglesi* 3-4 (1976-1977): 257-279. [Marxist.]

1688 Sackett, S. J. and Herman A. Dreifke, comps. "Master's Theses in Literature Presented at American Colleges and Universities Sept. 1, 1967-Aug. 31, 1970." *LIT* 10, ii/11, ii (1971-1973): passim. [Bibliog.]

1689 Sadock, Geoffrey Johnston. "Dickens and Dr. Leavis: A Critical Commentary on *Hard Times.*" In 1490, pp. 208-216.

1690 Sadoff, Dianne F. "Change and Changelessness in *Bleak House.*" *VN* no. 46 (Fall 1974): 5-10.

1691 —. "Storytelling and the Figure of the Father in *Little Dorrit.*" *PMLA* 95 (Mar. 1980): 234-245.

1692 Sadrin, Anny. "The Perversion of Desire: A Study of Irony as a Structural Element in *Hard Times*." In 131, pp. 93-110.

1693 —. "A Plea for Gradgrind." *YES* 3 (1973): 196-205.

1694 —. "La Ville dans *Hard Times*," in *La raison et l'imaginaire*. Soc. des Anglicistes de l'Enseignement Supérieur, Actes du Congrès de Rennes, 1970; EA, 45 (Paris: Didier, [1973?]), 151-162.

1695 Sage, Victor. "Dickens and Beckett: Two Uses of Materialism." *J of Beckett St* no. 2 (Summer 1977): 15-39. [*DavidC, DSon, Little-Dor, OurMF.*]

1696 Saha, Narayan. "Dickens's Treatment of Child-Psychology—and David Copperfield." In 262, pp. 26-28.

1697 Said, Edward W. "Molestation and Authority in Narrative Fiction," in *Aspects of Narrative*, ed. J. Hillis Miller. Sel. Papers from the Eng. Inst., 1970 (New York and London: Columbia UP, 1971), 47-69. [Incl. *GreatEx.*]

1697a —. "The Problem of Textuality: Two Exemplary Positions." *CritI* 4 (Summer 1978): 673-714. [Incl. *GreatEx.*—Positions of Derrida and Foucault.]

1698 Saijo, Takao. "Unity and *The Pickwick Papers*." *HSELL* 16, i-ii (1969): 30-40.

1699 Saint Victor, Carol de. "*Master Humphrey's Clock:* Dickens's 'Lost' Book." *TSLL* 10 (Winter 1969): 569-584.

1700 Sakhaltuyev, Arsen. "Leo Tolstoy Reads Charles Dickens." *Sputnik* 12 (Dec. 1970): 144-145. [Trans. from *Inostrannaya Literatur.*]

1701 Sakuraba, Nobuyuki. *Hogarth to Dickens.* Seijo Eng. Monographs, 17. Tokyo: Seijo Univ., 1977. 49 pp. [*BleakH, DavidC, HsldWds, MChuz, PickP.*]

1701a —. [The humor of D.] In 412a, pp. 43-45. [In Jap.]

1702 Sampson, Edward. "The Problem of Communication in *Bleak House*," in *Twenty-Seven to One: A Potpourri of Humanistic Material Presented to Dr. Donald Gale Stillman...*, ed. Bradford B. Broughton [Potsdam, N.Y.: Clarkson Coll. of Technology, 1972], 121-124.

1702a Samsel, John. *The Money Question in Our Mutual Friend.* Northwest Missouri State Univ. St., 38, i. Maryville: Northwest

Missouri State Univ., 1979. 25 pp.

1703 Sanders, Andrew. " 'Come Back and Be Alive': Living and Dying in *Our Mutual Friend.*" *Dkn* 74 (Sept. 1978): 131-143.

1704 —. "The Track of a Storm: Charles Dickens's Historical Novels." *The Victorian Historical Novel, 1840-1880* (London: Macmillan, 1978; New York: St. Martin's Press, 1979), 68-69; et passim. [*BarnR, TaleTwoC.*—Rev.: Harry Edmund Shaw, *Dkn* 76 (Summer 1980): 103-104.]

1705 Sano, Akira. [The decline of the father in *LittleDor.*] In 980, pp. 73-87. [In Jap.]

1706 Santaló, Joaquín. "Galdós and Dickens." *The Tragic Import in the Novels of Pérez Galdós* (Madrid: Playor, 1973), 35-38. [Esp. *GreatEx, La desheredada.*]

1707 Santelli, Claude interviewed by Jacqueline Beaulieu. "Dickens à la télévision." In 743, pp. 55-61. [Adaptations of *DavidC, GreatEx, LittleDor, OCShop, OliverTw, PickP.*]

1708 Sauerberg, Annette Juel. "On the Literariness of Illustrations: A Study of Rowlandson and Cruikshank." *Semiotica* 14, iv (1975): 364-386. [*OliverTw.*]

1709 Saunders, John K. "The Case of Mrs. Nickleby: Humor and Negligent Parenthood." *DSN* 10 (June-Sept. 1979): 56-58.

1710 Sayers, Dorothy L. *Wilkie Collins: A Critical and Biographical Study,* ed. E. R. Gregory ([Toledo:] Friends of the Univ. of Toledo Libs., 1977), passim. [Rev.: Ian Ousby, *DSN* 10 (Dec. 1979): 119.]

1711 Schachterle, Lance. "*Bleak House* as a Serial Novel." In 1489, pp. 212-224.

1712 —. "*Oliver Twist* and Its Serial Predecessors." In 1491, pp. 1-13.

1713 Schazmann, Paul-Émile. *Charles Dickens, ses sejours en Suisse.* Lausanne: Swiss National Tourist Office, 1972. 47 pp. [Note also *Charles Dickens in Switzerland,* trans. H. P. B. Betlem, and *Charles Dickens in der Schweiz,* trans. Bee Jucker.—Rev. of Eng. trans.: Robert F. Fleissner, *DSN* 5 (Dec. 1974): 119-121; *Dkn* 69 (May 1973): 130.]

1714 Schilling, Bernard N. "Balzac, Dickens and 'This Harsh World'." *Adam* nos. 331-333 (1969): 109-122. [*GreatEx, Les illusions perdues.*]

1715 Schimmelpenninck-Verbeek, C. "De eerste Dickens-fellow was een Dordtenaar." *Dutch Dkn* 7, xvi (Dec. 1978): 63-65. [Ary Scheffer.]

1716 Schippers, J. G. "So Many Characters, So Many Words: Some Aspects of the Language of *Little Dorrit.*" *DQR* 8, iv (1978): 242-265.

1717 Schlicke, Paul. "Bumble and the Poor Law Satire of *Oliver Twist.*" *Dkn* 71 (Sept. 1975): 149-156.

1718 —. "A 'Discipline of Feeling': Macready's *Lear* and *The Old Curiosity Shop.*" *Dkn* 76 (Summer 1980): 78-90.

1719 Schmidt, A. V. C. "Crumpets in 'Coriolan,' Muffins in *Pickwick.*" *N&Q* NS 23 (July 1976): 298-299. [Allusion in T. S. Eliot.]

1720 Schmidt, Johann N. *Charles Dickens in Selbstzeugnissen und Bilddokumenten.* Reinbek bei Hamburg: Rowholt, 1978. 153 pp.

1721 Schrero, Elliot M. "Intonation in Nineteenth-Century Fiction: The Voices of Paraphrase." *QJS* 60 (Oct. 1974): 289-295. [Incl. *BleakH.*]

1722 Schücking, Levin. [Über Charles Dickens], in Karl Gutzkow, *Liberale Energie: Eine Sammlung seiner kritischen Schriften,* ed. Peter Demetz (Frankfurt: Ullstein, 1974), 288-292. [Rev. of *NichN* from *Telegraph für Deutschland,* 1839.—Incl. Gutzkow's comments (as ed. of *Telegraph*), p. 292.]

1723 Schulz, Siegfried A. "Premchand's Novel *Godan:* Echoes of Charles Dickens in an Indian Setting," in *Studies in Honor of Tatiana Fotich,* ed. Josep M. Sola-Solé, Allessandro S. Crisafulli, and Siegfried A. Schulz (Washington: Catholic UP in assn. with Consortium Press, 1973), 341-366.

1724 Schuster, Charles I. "Dickens and the Language of Alienation." *ELN* 16 (Dec. 1978): 117-128. [Esp. *DSon, GreatEx, LittleDor, NichN, OurMF, PickP.*]

1725 Schwartz, Roberta C. "The Moral Fable of *Great Expectations.*" *NDQ* 47 (Winter 1979): 55-66.

1726 Schwarzbach, F. S. "The Burning of Francis L. McIntosh: A Note to a Dickens Letter from America." *DSN* 11 (June 1980): 38-41. [Corrects Pilgrim ed. annot. to ltr. of 1842.]

1727 —. "Dickens and Carlyle Again: A Note on an Early Influence." *Dkn* 73 (Sept. 1977): 149-153.

1728 —. *Dickens and the City.* London: Univ. of London, Athlone Press, 1979. xii, 258 pp. [Incorporates "A Note on *Bleak House:* John Jarndyce and the East Wind," *DSN* 6 (Sept. 1975): 82-84 (see also M. J. Crump's response, 9 [June 1978] : 46-47) and "*Sketches by Boz:* Fiction for the Metropolis," *Dkn* 72 (Jan. 1976): 13-20.— Note also diss. of same title (London, 1977).—Rev.: Avrom Fleishman, *NCF* 35 (June 1980): 105-109; R. Glancy, *BBkN* July 1979: 606-607; Benny Green, *Spec* 242 (10 Mar. 1979): 21-22; Joachim Krehayn, *Deutsche Literaturzeitung* 101 (Apr. 1980): 287-290; Sylvère Monod, *EA* 33 (Jan.-Mar. 1980): 87-88; Lorna Sage, *Guardian Weekly* 13 May 1979: 22; Barry West-burg, *AUMLA* no. 53 (May 1980): 80-81; *Ch* 16 (Sept. 1979): 837; also rev. in 217, 1109.]

1729 —. "Dickens and the City: His and Ours." *Washington Univ Mag* 49 (Spring 1979): 4-10.

1730 —. "A New Theatrical Source for Dickens's *A Tale of Two Cities.*" *N&Q* NS 24 (Feb. 1977): 18-20. [Monk Lewis's *Castle Spectre.*]

1731 Scott, P. G. "Letter to the Editor." *Dkn* 71 (Sept. 1975): 172. [Possible source for word-play in *GreatEx.*]

1732 —. "*Pickwick Papers:* A Bibliographical Curiosity." *N&Q* NS 20 (Sept. 1973): 341. [Answers query on unrecorded ed., Mar., p. 100.]

1733 Scott, P. J. M. *Reality and Comic Confidence in Charles Dickens.* London: Macmillan, 1978; New York: Barnes and Noble, 1979. 216 pp. [Esp. *BleakH, LittleDor, OurMF.*—Note also same title, *DAI* 37 (Spring 1977): 472C (York).—Rev.: P. J. Coveney, *BBkN* June 1979: 524; Richard J. Dunn, *SNNTS* 11 (Fall 1979): 374-375; Christopher Herbert, *NCF* 34 (Mar. 1980): 450-452; Jean-Jacques Mayoux, *EA* 32 (Oct.-Dec. 1979): 483-485; Paul Schlicke, *Dkn* 75 (Autumn 1979): 178-179; *Ch* 16 (Sept. 1979): 837; also rev. in 182 (Dec. 1979), 217, 981, 1109, 1751.]

1734 Scribner, Margo. "Dickens's Use of Animals in *Martin Chuzzlewit.*"

DSN 10 (June-Sept. 1979): 40-44.

1735 Sedgley, Anne. "*Hard Times:* Facts or Fantasy?" *CR* no. 16 (1973): 116-132.

1736 Seiple, Jo Ann Massie. "Implications of the Disguise: A Psychological Analysis of Charles Dickens's *Hard Times.*" *PAPA* 4 (Fall 1978): 45-51.

1737 Sellers, Ian. "The Dickens Factor." *Nineteenth Century Liverpool and the Novelists* (Warrington, Ches.: Author, 1979), 17-22. [*MChuz, UncomTr.*]

1738 Sen, S. C. "Dickens the Conjurer." In 262, pp. 1-13. [Characterization in *SBoz.*]

1739 Senelick, Laurence. "Charles Dickens and 'The Tell-Tale Heart'." *PoeS* 6 (June 1973): 12-14.

1740 —. "Traces of *Othello* in *Oliver Twist.*" *Dkn* 70 (May 1974): 97-102.

1740a Senf, Carol A. "*Bleak House:* The Need for Social Exorcism." *DSN* 11 (Sept. 1980): 70-73. [Vampire-victim relationship.]

1741 Ser, Cary D. "The Functionof Chapter I of *Martin Chuzzlewit.*" *DSN* 10 (June-Sept. 1979): 45-47.

1742 Serlen, Ellen. "The Two Worlds of *Bleak House.*" *ELH* 43 (Winter 1976): 551-566.

1743 Serrano Poncela, Segundo. "Dickens, o la novela burguesa inglesa." *La literatura occidental* (Caracas: Eds. de la Biblioteca de la Univ. Central de Venezuela, 1971), 590-593.

1744 Shatto, Susan. "Byron, Dickens, Tennyson, and the Monstrous Efts." *YES* 6 (1976): 144-155. [Dinosaurs.—Incl. *AllYR, BleakH, HsldWds.*]

1745 —. " 'A complete course, according to question and answer'." *Dkn* 70 (May 1974): 113-120.

1746 —. "New Notes on *Bleak House.*" *DSN* 6 (Sept., Dec. 1975): 78-82, 108-115.

1747 Shattock, Joanne. "The Entertainers: Dickens and Thackeray on Tour." *Dkn* 74 (Jan. 1978): 17-21.

1748 Shaw, George Bernard. *Collected Letters, 1898-1910,* ed. Dan H. Laurence (London: Reinhardt; New York: Dodd, Mead, 1972), passim. [Ltr. to Chesterton rpt. *Dkn* 69 (Jan. 1973): 44-45.]

1749 —. *"Hard Times"; "Great Expectations." Bernard Shaw's Nondramatic Literary Criticism,* ed. Stanley Weintraub (Lincoln: Univ. of Nebraska Press, 1972), 40-48; 49-65. [Intros. to eds. of *HardT* (1912) and *GreatEx* (1937).—Former rpt. in 1458, pp. 38-45 and in 2331, pp. 125-135; latter in 2064, pp. 284-297.]

1750 Shelston, Alan. "Dickens," in *The Victorians,* ed. Arthur Pollard. Hist. of Lit. in the Eng. Lang., 6 (London: Barrie and Jenkins, 1970), 74-106. [Social vision.]

1751 —. "Recent Studies in Nineteenth-Century Fiction." *CritQ* 22 (Summer 1980): 47-51. [Rev.-art. incl. 139, 1559, 1733, 1896.]

1752 Sheppard, E. A. *Henry James and The Turn of the Screw* ([Auckland]: Auckland UP; [London]: Oxford UP, 1974), passim.

1753 Shereikis, Richard. "Selves at the Center: The Theme of Isolation in Dickens's *Martin Chuzzlewit." DSN* 7 (June 1976): 38-42.

1754 Sherer, Ray J. "Laughter in *Our Mutual Friend." TSLL* 13 (Fall 1971): 509-521.

1755 Sherif, Nur. *Dickens in Arabic (1912-1970).* [Beirut]: Jami'at Bayrut al-'Arabiyah, 1974. 36 pp.

1756 Shichi, Soroku. [The technique of D's short stories.] In 412a, pp. 46-48. [In Jap.]

1757 Cancelled.

1758 Schillingsburg, Peter L. "Reviews—Paperback Editions: *The Pickwick Papers." DSN* 3 (Dec. 1972): 119-123. [Incl. 80.]

1759 Shklovsky, Vikotr. "The Mystery Novel: Dickens's *Little Dorrit."* trans. Guy Carter, in *Readings in Russian Poetics: Formalist and Structuralist Views,* ed. Ladislav Matejka and Krystyna Pomorska (Cambridge and London: MIT Press, 1971), 220-226. [Excerpts from "Roman tajn," *O teorii prozy* (Moscow, 1925), 117-138.—Rev.: Alan Burke, *DSN* 4 (Sept. 1973): 86-89.]

1760 Shoemaker, William H. "Dickens, Carlos." *La crítica literaria de*

Galdós (Madrid: Insula, 1979), 21; 233-234. [On Galdós's essay in *Galería* 9 Mar. 1868.]

1761 Shores, Lucille P. "The Character of Estella in *Great Expectations*." *MSE* 3 (Fall 1972): 91-99.

1762 Showalter, Elaine. "Dickens's *Little Dorrit* and Holme Lee's *Gilbert Massenger*." *DSN* 10 (June-Sept. 1979): 59-60.

1763 —. "Guilt, Authority, and the Shadows of *Little Dorrit*." *NCF* 34 (June 1979): 20-40.

1764 Silman, T. I. "Dickens, Charles," in *Great Soviet Encyclopedia* (New York: Macmillan; London: Collier Macmillan, 1975), VIII, 206-207. [Trans. from *Bol'shaia sovetskaia entsiklopediia*, 3rd ed., 1970.]

1765 —. *Dikkens: Ocherki tvorchestva.* Leningrad: Izdatel'stvo 'Khudozhestvennaya Literatura,' 1970. 376 pp. [Rev. from 1958 ed. with two added chaps.—Rev.: Henry Gifford, *Dkn* 68 (Jan. 1972): 56-58.]

1766 Silver, Alain and James Ursini. "The Dickens Adaptations: *Great Expectations* (1946); *Oliver Twist* (1948)." *David Lean and His Films* (London: Frewin, 1974), 53-84. [Incorporates Alain Silver, "The Untranquil Light: David Lean's *Great Expectations*," *LFQ* 2 (Spring 1974): 140-152.]

1767 Singh, Amritjit. "The Ending of *Great Expectations*." *IJES* 18 (1978-1979): 43-53.

1768 Sinha, Amitabha. "Image and Symbol in Dickens." In 262, pp. 41-58. [*LittleDor, OurMF*.]

1769 Sipe, Samuel M. "The Intentional World of Dickens's Fiction." *NCF* 30 (June 1975): 1-19. [Esp. *BleakH, DSon, LittleDor, MChuz, OurMF*.]

1770 —. "Memory and Confession in *Great Expectations*." *ELWIU* 2 (Spring 1975): 53-64.

1771 Skilton, David. " 'Des êtres blets': Quelques techniques de récit dans la présentation de la grande bourgeoisie chez Dickens, Trollope, et Meredith," trans. Pierre Citron. *Romantisme* no. 17-18 (1977): 174-184. [*OurMF*.]

1772 —. "Dickens and the Literature of London." *The English Novel Defoe to the Victorians* (Newton Abbot, etc.: David and Charles; New York: Barnes and Noble, 1977), 99-119; et passim. [Esp. *BleakH, LittleDor, PickP, SBoz.*]

1773 Slater, Michael. "Appreciating Mrs. Nickleby." *Dkn* 71 (Sept. 1975): 136-139.

1774 —. "*The Bastille Prisoner:* A Reading Dickens Never Gave." In 154, pp. 190-196.

1775 S[later], M[ichael]. "The Birthplace Museum." *Dkn* 66 (Sept. 1970): 264-266.

1776 Slater, Michael. "Carlyle and Jerrold into Dickens: A Study of *The Chimes.*" In 1419, pp. 184-204.

1777 —, ed. *The Catalogue of the Suzannet Charles Dickens Collection.* London: Sotheby, 1975. xvi, 299 pp. [Rev.: Philip Collins, *TLS* 5 Dec. 1975: 1464; Mollie Hardwick, *B&B* 21 (Mar. 1976): 42-43; Timothy d'Arch Smith, *Dkn* 72 (Jan. 1976): 38-39; Harry Stone, *DSN* 7 (June 1976): 51-53.]

1778 —, comp. *Catalogue of Treasures from the Dickens Collection formed by the late Comte Alain de Suzannet on Exhibition at the Dickens House 1 June-12 Sept. 1970,* fwd. Leslie C. Staples. [London]: Dickens Fellowship, 1970. 42 pp. [Rev.: Malcolm Y. Andrews, *DSN* 1 (Sept. 1970): 11-12.]

1779 —. "The Centenary on Radio, Stage and Screen." *Dkn* 66 (May 1970): 237-239.

1780 —. *The Composition and Monthly Publication of Nicholas Nickleby.* [Menston, Yorks.]: Scolar Press, 1973. iv, 42 pp. [Issued with 2254.]

1781 S[later], M[ichael]. "Conference in Philadelphia." *Dkn* 72 (Sept. 1976): 183-186.

1782 Slater, Michael. "David to Dora: A New Dickens Letter." *Dkn* 68 (Sept. 1972): 162-166. [To Maria Beadnell.]

1783 —. "Dickens," in *The English Novel: Select Bibliographical Guides,* ed. A. E. Dyson (London, New York, etc.: Oxford UP, 1974), 179-199.

1784 S[later], M[ichael]. "Dickens at Christie's." *Dkn* 70 (Jan. 1974): 48.

1785 —. "Dickens at Sotheby's." *Dkn* 70 (Jan. 1974): 30; 70 (May 1974): 96, 120; 71 (May 1975): 102-103; 72 (Jan. 1976): 47-49; 73 (Sept. 1977): 163-164; 75 (Spring 1979): 53-55. [Note also 2198 and 2233.]

1786 Slater, Michael, ed. *Dickens 1970*. London: Chapman and Hall; New York: Stein and Day, 1970. [Incl. 199, 881, 947, 1013, 1128, 1788, 1823, 2119, 2123.—Rev.: John Bayley, *NYRB* 15 (8 Oct. 1970): 8; Keith Cushman, *LJ* 95 (1 Sept. 1970): 2084; K. J. Fielding, *RES* NS 22 (Aug. 1971): 364-366; E. D. H. Johnson, *DSN* 1 (Sept. 1970): 5-6; J. C. Maxwell, *N&Q* NS 18 (Nov. 1971): 427-428; Sylvère Monod, *EA* 24 (Jan.-Mar. 1971): 98-100; H. Reinhold, *Anglia* 91, i (1973): 131-135; Georg Seehase, *ZAA* 21, ii (1973): 209-211; William Kean Seymour, *ContempR* 217 (Sept. 1970): 161-162; F. Seymour Smith, *Aryan Path* 41 (Sept.-Oct. 1970): 330-331; Alexander Welsh, *Dkn* 66 (Sept. 1970): 248-250; *Cb* 7 (Dec. 1970): 1377-1378; *Ecn* 235 (20 June 1970): 67; also rev. in 182 (Aug. 1971), 198, 981, 1228, 1961, 1972, 2065, 2200, 2227.]

1787 S[later], M[ichael]. "Dickens Plays Revived." *Dkn* 67 (May 1971): 97-98. [*IsShe, SGent.*]

1788 Slater, Michael. "Dickens's Tract for the Times." In 1786, pp. 99-123. [*Chimes.*]

1789 S[later], M[ichael]. "The Editor in America." *Dkn* 68 (May 1972): 142-145.

1790 Slater, Michael. "How Dickens 'Told' Catherine about His Past." *Dkn* 75 (Spring 1979): 3-6.

1791 —. "New Letters at Dickens House." *Dkn* 69 (Sept. 1973): 148-152. [Esp. to Charles Coote 1851-1857 conductor at amateur theatricals.]

1792 S[later], M[ichael]. "[1970] Fellowship Birthday Dinner." *Dkn* 66 (May 1970): 186-187.

1793 Slater, Michael. "1920-1940: 'Superior Folk' and Scandalmongers." *Dkn* 66 (May 1970): 121-142. [Special no. on D's reputation 1870-1970.—For revs. see 448.]

1794 —. "On Reading *Oliver Twist*." *Dkn* 70 (May 1974): 75-81.

1795 —. "The Peyrouton Bequest." *Dkn* 72 (May 1976): 98-100.

1796 S[later], M[ichael]. "The W. J. Carlton Bequest." *Dkn* 70 (Jan. 1974): 46-47.

1797 Slater, Michael. "The Year's Work in Dickens Studies 1969." *Dkn* 66 (Sept. 1970): 225-230. [Note also 2239.]

1798 [Slayden, David.] "Dickens." *VS* 20 (1977): supp. 97-101. [Annot. checklist of arts. on D in *VS*, 1957-1977.]

1799 Sloane, David E. E. "Phrenology in *Hard Times:* A Source for Bitzer." *DSN* 5 (Mar. 1974): 9-12. [George Parker Bidder (1806-1878).]

1800 Smith, Anne. "*Hard Times* and *The Times* Newspaper." *Dkn* 69 (Sept. 1973): 153-162. [Unionism.]

1801 —. "The Ironmaster in *Bleak House*." *EIC* 21 (Apr. 1971): 159-169. [Note also 239 and Smith's reply, 22 (Apr. 1972): 218-220.]

1802 —. "The Martyrdom of Stephen in *Hard Times*." *JNT* 2 (Sept. 1972): 159-170.

1803 —. "Reviews—Paperback Editions: *Hard Times*." *DSN* 4 (Dec. 1973): 115-122. [All eds. prior to 1969.]

1804 Smith, D. H. F. *Narrator and Protagonist in Dickens's Great Expectations.* North Herts Coll. Occasional Papers, 1. Hitchin: North Herts Coll., 1979. 56 pp.

1805 Smith, David. "*Mary Barton* and *Hard Times:* Their Social Insights." *Mosaic* 5 (Winter 1971-1972): 97-112.

1806 Smith, F. Seymour. "Charles Dickens: The World's Novelist." *Aryan Path* 42 (Jan. 1971): 30-34.

1807 Smith, Frank Edmund. "Perverted Balance: Expressive Form in *Hard Times*." In 1494, pp. 102-118.

1808 Smith, Grahame. *VS* 14 (June 1971): 459-462. [Rev. of 448 (all essays), 1156, 1365 (all essays), 1419, 1489, 1496, 1786, 2005, 2188.]

1809 —. *Charles Dickens: Bleak House.* St. in Eng. Lit., 54. London: Edward Arnold, 1974. 64 pp. [Rev.: P. A. Burger, *UES* 14 (Apr.

1976): 60; Stephen Gill, *N&Q* NS 23 (Sept. 1976): 425; Sylvère Monod, *EA* 29 (Apr.-June 1976): 227; Robert Newsom, *Dkn* 71 (May 1975): 110-111.]

1810 (—. *Dickens, Money and Society.* 1968.) [Rev.: Richard C. Carpenter, *JPC* 4 (Fall 1970): 540-549; Clara Howe, *J of Human Relations* 18, ii (1970): 957-959; Arnold Kettle, *RES* NS 21 (May 1970): 233-235; Lauriat Lane, Jr., *SNNTS* 2 (Fall 1970): 377-378; R. D. McMaster, *VS* 13 (June 1970): 447-448; also rev. in 2138, 2204.]

1811 — and Angela. "Dickens as a Popular Artist." *Dkn* 67 (Sept. 1971): 131-144. [*LittleDor.*]

1812 Smith, John T. "The Two Endings of *Great Expectations:* A Re-Evaluation." *Thoth* 12 (Fall 1971): 11-17.

1813 Smith, Mary Daehler. " 'All Her Perfections Tarnished': The Thematic Function of Esther Summerson." *VN* 38 (Fall 1970): 10-14.

1814 Smith, Sheila M. "Blue Books and Victorian Novelists." *RES* NS 21 (Feb. 1970): 23-41. [Attitudes of D, Disraeli, and others to government reports.]

1815 —. " 'Captain Swing' Explained." *N&Q* NS 21 (Jan. 1974): 13-15. [John Overs and Chartism.]

1816 —. "John Overs to Charles Dickens: A Working-Man's Letter and Its Implications." *VS* 18 (Dec. 1974): 195-217.

1817 —. *The Other Nation: The Poor in English Novels of the 1840s and 1850s* (Oxford: Clarendon Press; New York: Oxford UP, 1980), passim. [Esp. *HardT, SBoz.*—Note also diss., "The Other Nation, in Fact and Fiction: The Poor in English Novels of the 1840s and 1850s, with Particular Reference to Disraeli's *Sybil,* Mrs. Gaskell's *Mary Barton,* Charles Kingsley's *Yeast* and *Alton Locke,* Dickens's *Hard Times* and Charles Reade's *It is Never too Late to Mend*" (London, 1976).]

1818 Smithers, David Waldron. *Dickens's Doctors.* Oxford, New York, etc.: Pergamon Press, 1979. xiii, 111 pp. [Rev.: Malcolm Andrews, *BBkN* Jan. 1980: 55-56; *AB Bookman's Weekly* 65 (28 Apr. 1980): 3296; *VQR* 56 (Summer 1980): 109-110.]

1819 —. "[Toast at] The London Birthday Dinner." *Dkn* 76 (Summer 1980): 120-126.

1820 Cancelled.

1821 Snow, C. P. "The Case of Leavis and the Serious Case." *TLS* 9 July 1970: 737-740. [Note also 1149 and responses by R. C. Churchill, 23 July 1970: 814 and by Michael Slater, 7 Aug. 1970: 878.]

1822 —. "Dickens." *The Realists: Portraits of Eight Novelists* (London: Macmillan, 1978), 62-83. [Note also *The Realists: Eight Portraits* (New York: Scribners, 1978), 72-101.]

1823 —. "Dickens and the Public Service." In 1786, pp. 125-149. [*Little-Dor.*]

1824 Sobel, Margaret. "Balzac's *Le Père Goriot* and Dickens's *Dombey and Son:* A Comparison." *RUS* 59 (Summer 1973): 71-81.

1825 Söderlind, Johannes. "En spraklig analys av en Dickensroman." Kungl. Humanistiska Vetenskaps-Samfundet i Uppsala. *Arbsbok* 1973-1974: 20-33. [Style of *DSon.*]

1826 Solberg, Sarah A. "Bull's-eye's 'Eyes' in *Oliver Twist.*" *N&Q* NS 27 (June 1980): 211-212.

1827 —. "Dickens and Illustration: A Matter of Perspective." *JNT* 10 (Spring 1980): 128-137. [Esp. *DSon.*]

1828 —. "A Note on Phiz's Dark Plates." *Dkn* 76 (Spring 1980): 40-41.

1829 Solinas Donghi, Beatrice. "Il principe povero, ovvero lo snobismo del trovatello." *Paragone* no. 266 (Apr. 1972): 120-127. [*GreatEx, OliverTw.*]

1830 Solomon, Pearl Chesler. *Dickens and Melville in Their Time.* New York: Columbia UP, 1975. 233 pp. [Esp. *CCarol, DavidC, Great-Ex,* Melville's "Bartleby the Scrivener."—Note also "A Correspondent Coloring: Dickens and Melville in Their Time," *DAI* 37 (July 1976): 294A (Columbia).—Rev.: W. D. Allen, *QQ* 81 (Autumn 1975): 468-469; C. C. Barfoot, *ES* 58 (Dec. 1977): 542-543; William B. Dillingham, *SR* 83 (Summer 1975): lxxxii-lxxxiii; H. Bruce Franklin, *NCF* 30 (Mar. 1976): 547-553; David Isaacson, *LJ* 100 (Mar. 1975): 586; Lauriat Lane, Jr., *Extracts* (Melville Soc.) no. 23 (Sept. 1975): 14 and (a diff. rev.) *DSN* 7 (June 1976): 46-48; Kerry McSweeney, *HAB* 26 (Summer 1975): 268-270; William Norris, *CEA Forum* 6 (Apr. 1976): 12-13; Joseph Schiffman, *AL* 47 (Nov. 1975): 457-458; G. R. Thompson, *MFS* 22 (Summer 1976): 300; *Ch* 12 (June 1975): 537; also rev. in 981, 1022.]

1831 Cancelled.

1832 Sossaman, Stephen. "Language and Communication in *Great Expectations.*" *DSN* 5 (Sept. 1974): 66-68.

1833 Spacks, Patricia Meyer. "Us or Them." *HudR* 31 (Spring 1978): 34-52. [Esp. *GreatEx.*—Adolescence.]

1834 Spanberg, Sven-Johan. "Education and Moral Insight in Dickens, Mrs. Gaskell, and Meredith." *SN* 48, i (1976): 76-89. [*HardT, Ruth, Ordeal of Richard Feverel.*]

1835 Spiers, John. *Poetry Towards Novel* (London: Faber and Faber; New York: New York UP, 1971), passim. [Esp. *Little-Dor.*]

1836 Spence, Gordon. *Charles Dickens as a Familiar Essayist.* Romantic Reassessment, 71. Salzburg: Institut für Englische Sprache und Literatur, Univ. Salzburg, 1977. vi, 159 pp. [Rev.: Dennis Walder, *Prose Studies 1800-1900* 2 (Feb. 1979): 126-128; *Ch* 15 (Sept. 1978): 875; also rev. in 981.]

1837 —. "Dickens as a Historical Novelist." *Dkn* 72 (Jan. 1976): 21-29. [*BarnR, TaleTwoC.*]

1838 Spencer, T. J. B. "A Case in the State Trials." *Dkn* 72 (sept. 1976): 140-147. [Material for possible story in D's memoranda book.]

1839 Spengemann, William C. *"David Copperfield." The Forms of Autobiography: Episodes in the History of a Literary Genre* (New Haven and London: Yale UP, 1980), 119-132. [Note also pp. 233-237 of bibliog. essay.]

1840 Spiess-Faure, Dominique. "Charles Dickens." *Écrivains britanniques de Chaucer aux Victoriens* (Paris: Larousse, 1979), 165-177. [Taken mainly from *La grande encyclopédie.*]

1841 Spilka, Mark. "Erich Segal as Little Nell, *or* The Real Meaning of *Love Story*," in *A Question of Quality: Popularity and Value in Modern Creative Writing*, ed. Louis Filler (Bowling Green, Ohio: Bowling Green Univ. Popular Press, 1976), 8-25. [Rpt. with added comment from *JPC* 5 (Spring 1972): 782-798. This version also rpt. in *Popular Culture and the Expanding Consciousness*, ed. Ray B. Browne (New York and London: John Wiley and Sons, 1973), 120-137. Another, slightly diff. version in *SoRA* 5 (Mar. 1972): 38-51.]

1842 —. "Kafka and Dickens: The Country Sweetheart." In 1955, pp. 95-104. [*DavidC, Amerika.*—Rpt. from *AI*, 1959.]

1843 —. "Leopold Bloom as Jewish Pickwick: A Neo-Dickensian Perspective." *Novel* 13 (Fall 1979): 121-146.

1844 Splitter, Randolph. "Guilt and the Trappings of Melodrama in *Little Dorrit.*" In 1494, pp. 119-133.

1845 Spodsberg, Jorgen *Familiens dodskamp: En analyse af Charles Dickens roman Bleak House.* Skriftraekke fra Institut for Litteraturvidenskab (Copenhagen), 8. Grena: GMT, 1976. vi, 170 pp.

1846 Stabler, A. P. "Dickens's *Household Words* and the Sources of *Hamlet.*" *EA* 24 (Jan.-Mar. 1971): 73-76.

1847 Stacey, Edward. *Great Expectations: Notes.* Toronto: Coles, 1976. 112 pp.

1848 Stang, Richard. "*Little Dorrit:* A World in Reverse." In 1496, pp. 140-164. [Novel as elaboration of a single metaphor.]

1849 Stange, G. Robert. "Expectations Well Lost: Dickens's Fable for His Time," in *The Nineteenth-Century Novel: Critical Essays and Documents,* ed. Arnold Kettle (London: Heinemann Ed. Books in assn. with Open UP, 1972), 127-139. [Rpt. from *CE*, 1954; also rpt. in 2082, pp. 110-122 and in 2331, pp. 294-308.]

1850 Stanzel, Franz K. "Unterschwellige Perspektivierung bei Dickens." *Theorie des Erzählens* (Göttingen: Vandenhoeck und Ruprecht, 1979), 182-188; et passim. [Esp. *CCarol.*]

1851 Staples, Leslie C. "Some Early Memories of the Dickens Fellowship." *Dkn* 73 (Sept. 1977): 131-137.

1852 Stapleton, Peter T. "*Hard Times:* Dickens's Counter Culture." *Clearing House* 47 (Feb. 1973): 380-381. [Teaching of.]

1853 Steele, Joan. "Steinbeck and Charles Dickens," in *Steinbeck's Literary Dimension: A Guide to Comparative Studies,* ed. Tetsumaro Hayashi (Metuchen, N.J.: Scarecrow Press, 1973), 16-27. [*BarnR* and *Of Mice and Men.*—Rpt. from *Steinbeck Q* 5 (Winter 1972): 8-17.]

1854 Steele, Peter. "Dickens and the Grotesque." *Quadrant* 17 (Mar.-Apr. 1973): 15-23. [Esp. *BleakH.*]

1855 Steig, Michael. *"Barnaby Rudge* and *Vanity Fair:* A Note on a Possible Influence." *NCF* 25 (Dec. 1970): 353-354.

1856 —. "A Chapter of Noses: George Cruikshank's Psyconography of the Nose." *Criticism* 17 (Fall 1975): 308-325. [*OliverTw.*]

1857 —. "Cruikshank's Nancy." *Dkn* 72 (May 1976): 87-92.

1858 —. "Cruikshank's Peacock Feathers in *Oliver Twist.*" *ArielE* 4 (Apr. 1973): 49-53.

1859 —. *Dickens and Phiz.* Bloomington and London: Indiana UP, 1978. x, 340 pp. [Esp. *BleakH, DavidC, DSon, LittleDor, MChuz, NichN, PickP.*—Incorporates "The Critic and the Illustrated Novel: Mr. Turveydrop from Gillray to *Bleak House,*" *HLQ* 36 (Nov. 1972): 55-67; "*David Copperfield,* Plate 1: A Note on Phiz and Hogarth," *DSN* 2 (June 1971): 55-56; "*Dombey and Son:* Chapter XXXI, Plate 20," *ELN* 7 (Dec. 1969): 124-127; "The Iconography of *David Copperfield,*" *HSL* 2, i (1970): 1-18; "The Iconography of Sexual Conflict in *Dombey and Son,*" in 1489, pp. 161-167; "*Martin Chuzzlewit's* Progress by Dickens and Phiz," in 1490, pp. 119-149.—Rev.: Anthony Burton, *VS* 23 (Winter 1980): 280-283; Joseph H. Gardner, *DSN* 11 (June 1980): 58-61; Joseph Gold, *UTQ* 49 (Spring 1980): 279-282; L. W. Griffin, *LJ* 103 (15 Oct. 1978): 2101-2102; Geoffrey Grigson, *CnL* 165 (1979): 99-100; Mollie Hardwick, *B&B* 24 (Feb. 1979): 34-36; John Dixon Hunt, *Dkn* 76 (Spring 1980): 51-52; Robert L. Patten, *NCF* 34 (Sept. 1979): 224-228; John R. Reed, *HSL* 11, iii (1979): 224-228; Graham Reynolds, *Apollo* 110 (July 1979): 82; Judith Wilt, *Criticism* 21 (Summer 1979): 273-276; *Ch* 15 (Jan. 1979): 1522; also rev. in 1123.]

1860 —. "Dickens's Characters and Psychoanalytic Criticism." In 1247, pp. 38-45.

1861 —. "Dickens's Excremental Vision." *VS* 13 (Mar. 1970): 339-355.

1862 —. "*Dombey and Son* and the Railway Panic of 1845." *Dkn* 67 (Sept. 1971): 145-148. [Note also H. W. Woodward's ltr. to ed., 75 (Spring 1979): 36.]

1863 —. "George Cruikshank and the Grotesque: A Psychodynamic Approach." In 1510, pp. 189-211.

1864 —. "Ghosts in *Master Humphrey's Clock:* Two Notes on Scholarly Errors." *DSN* 4 (June 1973): 40-41. [Note also Dennis Walder's ltr. to ed., Dec., p. 123.]

1865 —. "The Grotesque and the Aesthetic Response in Shakespeare, Dickens, and Günter Grass." *CLS* 6 (June 1969): 167-181. [*OCShop, Richard III, Tin Drum.*]

1866 —. "The Intentional Phallus: Determining Verbal Meaning in Literature." *JAAC* 36 (Fall 1977): 51-61. [Exs. from *MChuz* and *OCShop.*]

1867 —. "Structure and the Grotesque in Dickens: *Dombey and Son, Bleak House.*" *CentR* 14 (Summer 1970): 313-331.

1868 —. "*Ten Thousand a-Year* and the Political Content of *Barnaby Rudge.*" *DSN* 4 (Sept. 1973): 67-68. [Samuel Warren's Tittlebat Titmouse possible source for Sim Tappertit.]

1869 — and F. A. C. Wilson. "Hortense versus Bucket: The Ambiguity of Order in *Bleak House.*" *MLQ* 33 (Sept. 1972): 289-298.

1870 Steinecke, Hartmut. *Romantheorie und Romankritik in Deutschland: Die Entwicklung des Gattungsverständnisses von der Scott-Rezeption bis zum programmatischen Realismus,* 2 vols. (Stuttgart: Metzler, 1975), passim. [Esp. "Boz und die gegenwärtige Gestaltung des Volksromans," II, 146-151; rpt. from *Blätter für literarische Unterhaltung,* 1839.]

1871 Stella, Maria. "La traduzione di *David Copperfield.*" *Cesare Pavese, traduttore.* Univ. di Roma, Istituto di Letteratura Inglese e Americana, St. e ricerche, 6 (Rome: Bulzoni, 1977), 145-166.

1872 Stéphane, Nelly. "Chronologie de Dickens." In 743, pp. 147-156.

1873 —. "Double Dickens: Les *Contes de Noël.*" In 743, pp. 88-104.

1874 Sterrenburg, Lee. "Psychoanalysis and the Iconography of Revolution." *VS* 19 (Dec. 1975): 241-264. [Incl. *TaleTwoC.*]

1875 Stetz, Margaret Diane. "Charles Dickens and 'The Sanatorium': An Unpublished Letter and Manuscript." *Dkn* 76 (Spring 1980): 22-30.

1876 Stevenson, Lionel. "Letter to the Editor." *DSN* 2 (Sept. 1971): 86-87. [Actual parallel to Dedlock plot of *BleakH.*—Note also E[sther] J. E[vans], "Arthur Lionel Stevenson, 1902-1973," *Library Notes* (Duke Univ.) no. 45 (Dec. 1974): 45-51.]

1877 Stevenson, Lloyd G. " 'All According to the Constitooshun': Charles Dickens and Lead Poisoning," in *Healing and History: Essays for George Rosen,* ed. Charles E. Rosenberg (Folkestone: William Dawson and Sons; New York: Science Hist. Pubs., 1979), 137-148. [*UncomTr.*]

1878 Stevenson, R. W. *Charles Dickens: David Copperfield: Notes.* York Notes, 9. London: Longman, 1980. 77 pp.

1879 Stevick, Philip. "Sentimentality and Classic Fiction." In 462, pp. 41-49. [Incl. *DavidC.*—Rpt. from *Mosaic* 4, iii (Spring 1971): 23-31.]

1880 Stewart, Donald C. "Dickens's *Bleak House:* A Novel for Our Time." In 1416, pp. 84-88.

1881 Stewart, Garrett. *Dickens and the Trials of Imagination.* Cambridge: Harvard UP, 1974. xxiii, 260 pp. [Esp. *OCShop, OurMF, PickP.*— Incorporates "The 'Golden Bower' of *Our Mutual Friend*," *ELH* 40 (Spring 1973): 105-130.—Note also "The Trials of Imagination: Style in Dickens," *DAI* 32 (June 1973): 7008A (Yale).—Rev.: Philip Collins, *TLS* 19 Sept. 1975: 1066 and Randolph Stow's ltr. to ed., 3 Oct. 1975: 1141; Keith Cushman, *LJ* 100 (1 June 1975): 1132; K. J. Fielding, *RES* NS 28 (Feb. 1977): 102-103; Robin Gilmour, *Dkn* 72 (Jan. 1976): 39-40; Bert G. Hornback, *DSN* 7 (Sept. 1976): 81-83; James R. Kincaid, *NCF* 30 (Mar. 1976): 535-538; Lauriat Lane, Jr., *IFR* 3 (Jan. 1976): 62-64; John Lucas, *L&H* no. 6 (Autumn 1977): 270-271; Sylvère Monod, *EA* 30 (Jan.-Mar. 1977): 105-106; Margaret Myers, *VS* 19 (June 1976): 541-543; Sam Pickering, *SR* 85 (Oct.-Dec. 1977): 658; Charles I. Schuster, *PQ* 55 (Winter 1976): 142-144; Alexander Welsh, *Novel* 10 (Fall 1976): 79-84; *Cb* 12 (June 1975): 537; also rev. in 981, 584.]

1882 —. "Modern Hard Times: Chaplin and the Cinema of Self-Reflection." *CritI* 3 (Winter 1976): 295-314.

1883 —. "The New Mortality of *Bleak House*." *ELH* 45 (Fall 1978): 443-487.

1884 —. "Teaching Prose Fiction: Some 'Instructive' Styles." *CE* 37 (Dec. 1975): 383-401. [Incl. *GreatEx.*]

1885 Stewart, Ian. "Lord Boz in the New World: Charles Dickens's First Visit to America." *CnL* 156 (19 Dec. 1974): 1952.

1886 Stewart, R. F. *. . . And Always a Detective: Chapters on the History* *of Detective Fiction* (Newton Abbot, London, North Pomfrey, Vt.: David and Charles, 1980), passim. [Esp. *BleakH.*]

1887 Stigant, Paul and Peter Widdowson. *"Barnaby Rudge:* A Historical Novel?" *L&H* no. 2 (Oct. 1975): 2-44.

1888 Stiles, G. W. "Charles Dickens (1812-1870): The Centenary Year." *Crux* 4 (July-Sept. 1970): 5.

1889 —. "The Significance in *Great Expectations* of Pip's First Meeting with Miss Havisham." *Crux* 4 (July-Sept. 1970): 5-12.

1890 (Stoehr, Taylor. *Dickens: The Dreamer's Stance.* 1965.) [Rev. in 209.]

1891 Stokes, E. *"Bleak House* and *The Scarlet Letter." AUMLA* no. 32 (Nov. 1969): 177-189. [Esp. similarity between Chillingworth and Tulkinghorn.]

1892 Stokes, M. Veronica. "Charles Dickens: A Customer of Coutts & Co." *Dkn* 68 (Jan. 1972): 17-30.

1893 Stone, Donald D. "Death and Circuses: Charles Dickens and the Byroads of Romanticism." *The Romantic Impulse in Victorian Fiction* (Cambridge and London: Harvard UP, 1980), 249-283; et passim.

1894 Stone, Harry. *"A Christmas Carol:* The Ghost of Things to Come." *Angel's Flight* 4 (Fall-Spring 1978-1979): 48-54.

1895 —. "Dickens and Fantasy: The Case of Uriah Heep." *Dkn* 75 (Summer 1979): 95-103.

1896 —. *Dickens and the Invisible World: Fairy Tales, Fantasy, and Novel-Making.* Bloomington and London: Indiana UP, 1979; London: Macmillan, 1980. xii, 370 pp. [Esp. *CBooks, DavidC, DSon, GreatEx.*—Rev.: Charles Bishop, *LJ* 104 (1 Sept. 1979): 1700; Philip Collins, *THES* 8 Aug. 1980: 12; Peter Davalle, *Times* (London) 27 Mar. 1980: 11; Peter Keating, *TLS* 18 Apr. 1980: 444; Margaret Lane, *Daily Telegraph* (London) 10 Apr. 1980; Marion Lochhead, *Scotsman* (Edinburgh) 29 Mar. 1980; C. P. Snow, *Financial Times* 29 Mar. 1980; G. B. Tennyson, *SEL* 20 (Autumn 1980): 731; Lynne Truss, *TES* 9 May 1980: 27; *Ch* 16 (Feb. 1980): 1584; also rev. in 1751.]

1897 —. "Dickens and the Uses of Literature." *Dkn* 69 (Sept. 1973): 139-

147.

1898 —. "Dickens, Cruikshank, and Fairy Tales." In 1510, pp. 213-247.

1899 —. "Dickens Rediscovered: Some Lost Writings Retrieved." In 1419, pp. 205-226.

1900 —. "The Love Pattern in Dickens's Novels." In 1496, pp. 1-20. [*DavidC, DSon, GreatEx, HMan, TaleTwoC.*—Incl. infl. of Browning.]

1901 —. "*Oliver Twist* and Fairy Tales." *DSN* 10 (June-Sept. 1979): 34-39.

1902 —. "The Unknown Dickens: With a Sample of Uncollected Writings." In 1489, pp. 1-22.

1903 Stones, Sandi Brinkman. "Pollution and the Relevance of the Nineteenth Century." *EJ* 62 (Nov. 1973): 1177-1179. [*HardT, OliverTw.*]

1904 Storey, Graham. "An Unpublished Satirical Sketch by Dickens." *Dkn* 74 (Jan. 1978): 6-7. [On Crimean War written 1859.]

1905 Stow, Randolph. "The Australian Miss Havisham." *ALS* 6 (Oct. 1974): 418-419. [Note also A. F. Dilnot's response, 7 (Oct. 1975): 206-208.]

1906 Strange, Kathleen H. "Blacking-Polish." *Dkn* 75 (Spring 1979): 7-11.

1907 —. "Two of the Three Rs." *Dkn* 73 (May 1977): 108-112. [*BleakH, GreatEx, OCShop.*]

1908 Strauss, P. E. "Dickens and the Law in *Bleak House*." *Natal Univ Law Rev* 1, iv (1975): 142-146.

1909 Streiff, Eric. "Graphologisches bei Dickens." *Neue Zürcher Zeitung* 4 Apr. 1971: 51-52. [*BleakH, LittleDor.*]

1910 Strickland, Edward. "Dickens's 'A Madman's Manuscript' and 'The Tell-Tale Heart'." *PoeS* 9 (June 1976): 22-23.

1911 Subramanyam, Ka Naa. "Reading Dickens in 1978." *Perspective* (Calcutta) 2 (Oct. 1978): 61-63.

1912 Sucksmith, Harvey Peter. "Dickens among the Pre-Raphaelites: Mr. Merdle and Holman Hunt's 'The Light of the World'." *Dkn* 72

(Sept. 1976): 159-163.

1913 —. "Dickens and Mayhew: A Further Note." *NCF* 24 (Dec. 1969): 345-349. [*BleakH.*]

1914 —. "The Dust-Heaps in *Our Mutual Friend.*" *EIC* 23 (Apr. 1973): 206-212.

1915 —. "The Identity and Significance of the Mad Huntsman in *Pickwick Papers.*" *Dkn* 68 (May 1972): 109-114.

1916 —. "The Melodramatic Villain in *Little Dorrit.*" *Dkn* 71 (May 1975): 76-83.

1917 —. *The Narrative Art of Charles Dickens: The Rhetoric of Sympathy and Irony in His Novels.* Oxford: Clarendon Press, 1970. xiv, 374 pp. [Rev.: Peter Bryant, *UES* 9 (June 1971): 34-35; Duane DeVries, *JEGP* 71 (Jan. 1972): 152-154; K. J. Fielding, *VS* 14 (Dec. 1970): 211-212; Thomas J. Galvin, *LJ* 96 (1 Jan. 1971): 80; Stephen Gill, *N&Q* NS 18 (Nov. 1971): 425-427; H. F. Harding, *QJS* 58 (Feb. 1972): 110; Dieter Mehl, *Archiv* 123 (Apr. 1972): 401-404; Sylvère Monod, *EA* 24 (Jan.-Mar. 1971): 102-104; Robert B. Partlow, Jr., *NCF* 26 (Mar. 1972): 494-497; Grahame Smith, *Dkn* 67 (Jan. 1971): 49-51; G. W. Spence, *AUMLA* no. 35 (May 1971): 106-107; Richard Stang, *DSN* 1 (Dec. 1970): 5-7; Michael Steig, *Criticism* 13 (Summer 1971): 319-321; Christian W. Thomson, *Anglia* 91, iv (1973): 545-547; Patricia Thomson, *RES* NS 22 (Nov. 1971): 509-512; Kensuke Ueki, *HSELL* 17, ii (1970): 66-72; Dennis Walder, *New Edinburgh Rev* no. 15 (Nov. 1971): 33-34; *Ch* 7 (Jan. 1971): 1513; also. rev. in 182 (Aug. 1971), 981, 1126, 1961, 1972, 2065, 2205, 2216.]

1918 —. "The Secret of Immediacy: Dickens's Debt to the Tale of Terror in *Blackwood's.*" *NCF* 26 (Sept. 1971): 145-157. [*LittleDor, OliverTw, PickP, SBoz.*]

1919 —. "Sir Leicester Dedlock, Wat Tyler, and the Chartists: The Role of the Ironmaster in *Bleak House.*" In 1492, pp. 113-131.

1920 Suhamy, Henry. "Dickens, poète et naturaliste de la Ville," in *La raison et l'imaginaire.* Soc. des Anglicistes de l'Enseignment Supérieur, Actes du Congrès de Rennes, 1970; EA, 45 (Paris: Didier, [1973?]), 141-149.

1921 Sulfridge, Cynthia. "*Martin Chuzzlewit:* Dickens's Prodigal and the Myth of the Wandering Son." *SNNTS* 11 (Fall 1979): 318-325.

1922 Sullivan, Mary Rose. "Black and White Characters in *Hard Times*." *VN* 38 (Fall 1970): 5-10.

1923 Sullivan, Patricia Rosalind. "A Student Response to the Genuine: Fear and Pain in *Mort à crédit* and *David Copperfield*." *RecL* 7 (Fall-Winter 1979): 42-55.

1924 Sutherland, J. A. "Dickens as Publisher." *Victorian Novelists and Publishers* (London: Univ. of London, Athlone Press; Chicago: Univ. of Chicago Press, 1976), 166-187; et passim. [Esp. *AllYR*.—Rev.: Ian Ousby *DSN* 8 (Sept. 1977): 85-87; also rev. in 967 (May 1977).]

1925 —. "The Fiction Earning Patterns of Thackeray, Dickens, George Eliot, and Trollope." *BIS* 7 (1979): 71-92.

1926 —. "A *Vanity Fair* Mystery: The Delay in Publication." *Costerus* NS 2 (1974): 185-191. [Incl. conflict with *DSon*.]

1927 Suzuki, Ryohei. [Fragments about D.] In 980, pp. 97-109. [In Jap.]

1928 Swinburne, Algernon Charles. "Charles Dickens." *Swinburne as Critic*, ed. Clyde K. Hyder (London and Boston: Routledge and Kegan Paul, 1972), 223-242. [Rpt. from *Quarterly Rev*, 1902.]

1929 Swinden, Patrick. "Deaths and Entrances." *Unofficial Selves: Character in the Novel from Dickens to the Present Day* (London: Macmillan; New York: Barnes and Noble, 1973), 27-61. [Esp. *BleakH*.—Rev.: Ross H. Dabney, *DSN* 6 (Sept. 1975): 89-93.]

1930 Symons, Julian. *Charles Dickens*, 2nd ed. London: Arthur Barker, 1969. 94 pp. [Very little rev. from 1951 ed.—Rev. in 2204.]

1931 —. "Dickens, Collins, Gaboriau: The Pattern Forms." *Mortal Consequences: A History—From the Detective Story to the Crime Novel* (New York: Harper and Row, 1972; New York: Schocken Books, 1973), 36-53. [*BleakH, HsldWds*.—Note also *Bloody Murder: From the Detective Story to the Crime Novel: A History* (London: Faber and Faber; Harmondsworth: Penguin, 1972).]

1932 Szladits, Lola L. "Dickens and His Illustrators." *BNYPL* 74 (June 1970): 351-353. [Incl. *OliverTw, OurMF, PickP, SBoz*.—Incl. 7 plates.]

1933 Takami, Kotero. [Strolling rambles in D literature.] In 412a, pp. 55-62. [In Jap.]

1934 Taketani, Kikuo. [Death and rebirth in *OurMF.*] In 980, pp. 88-96. [In Jap.]

1934a Taketomo, Sofu. [The world of D.] In 412a, pp. 63-66. [In Jap.— Rpt. from *Eigo kenkyu,* 1929.]

1935 Takeuchi, Akira. [*MChuz* and *DSon:* On their themes and structures.] *SELit* 48, i (1971): 81-94. [In Jap.; Eng. abst., pp. 194-195.]

1936 —. "The Structure of *Little Dorrit.*" *Kenkyu shuroku* no. 21 (Mar. 1973): 39-65.

1937 Talbor, Norman. "The Naming and the Names of the Hero: A Study in *David Copperfield.*" *SoRA* 11 (Nov. 1978): 267-282.

1938 Talon, Henri. "*Dombey and Son:* A Closer Look at the Text." In 1489, pp. 147-160.

1939 —. "On Some Aspects of the Comic in *Great Expectations.*" *VN* no. 42 (Fall 1972): 6-11.

1940 —. "Space, Time, and Memory in *Great Expectations.*" In 1491, pp. 122-133.

1941 Tanabe, Masami. [The art of D.] In 1287, pp. 121-136. [In Jap.; Eng. abst., pp. 265-266.]

1941a —. [*DavidC.*] In 412a, pp. 75-77. [In Jap.]

1942 —. [D's art and view of life.] *Hiroshima daigaku bungakubu kiyo* 35, i (Jan. 1976): 137-151. [In Jap.; Eng. abst., supp. p. 7.]

1943 —. [A study of *HardT* as an example of the collapse of a novel.] *Hiroshima daigaku bungakubu kiyo* 29 (Mar. 1970): 125-142. [In Jap.; Eng. abst., supp. p. 7.]

1944 Tanaka, Toshiro. [Regional and occupational dialect of Joe Gargery.] In 1287, pp. 153-187. [In Jap.; Eng. abst., pp. 272-273 and in 1285, pp. 62-63.]

1945 Tanselle, G. Thomas. "Problems and Accomplishments in the Editing of the Novel." *SNNTS* 7 (Fall 1975): 344-350. [Incl. Clarendon ed.]

1946 Taplin, Kim. *The English Path* (Ipswich: Boydell Press, 1979), passim. [*DSon, HardT, LittleDor, OCShop, PickP, SBoz.*]

1947 Tarantelli, Carole Beebe. "The City in *Martin Chuzzlewit.*" *St inglesi* 3-4 (1976-1977): 231-255.

1948 Tarr, Rodger L. "Dickens's Debt to Carlyle's 'Justice Metaphor' in *The Chimes.*" *NCF* 27 (Sept. 1972): 208-215. [*Past and Present.*]

1949 —. "Foreign Philanthropy and the Thematic Art of *Bleak House.*" *DSN* 8 (Dec. 1977): 100-104.

1950 —. "The 'Foreign Philanthropy Question' in *Bleak House:* A Carlylean Influence." *SNNTS* 3 (Fall 1971): 275-283.

1951 Tate, E. "Dickens's Vanity Fair: The Show Image in *The Old Curiosity Shop.*" *Hong Kong Baptist Coll Academic J* 4 (July 1977): 167-171.

1952 Tate, Eleanor. "Kafka's *The Castle:* Another Dickens Novel?" *SoRA* 7 (July 1974): 157-168.

1953 Taxner-Tóth, Erno. *Dickens világa.* Budapest: Európa, 1972. 245 pp.

1953a Telen'ko, G. M. "A. V. Lunacharskii o Ch. Dikkense." *Voprosy russkoi literatury* no. 29 (1977): 29-37.

1954 Tendler, Stewart. "Legacy of Dickens's Snowy Childhood." *Times* (London) 28 Dec. 1977: 1. [D responsible for white Christmas myth.]

1955 Tennenhouse, Leonard, ed. *The Practice of Psychoanalytic Criticism.* Detroit: Wayne State UP, 1976. [Incl. 1250, 1522, 1842.—Rev.: Richard Dunn, *DSN* 10 (Mar. 1979): 19-21.]

1956 Tennyson, G. B. *NCF* 27 (Dec. 1972): 369-372. [Rev. of 294, 485, 670, 1080, 1253.]

1957 Teodoreanu, Lilliana. "Elemente fantastice în stilul lui Dickens." In 588, pp. 33-44. [Eng. abst., pp. 43-44.]

1958 —. "Romanticul Dickens." *Familia* 6 (Aug. 1970): 3.

1959 Terry, R. C. *Anthony Trollope: The Artist in Hiding* (London: Macmillan; Totowa, N.J.: Rowman and Littlefield, 1977), passim.

1960 Tetzeli von Rosador, Kurt. "Charles Dickens: *Great Expectations:* Das Ende eines Ich-Romans." *NS* 18 (Aug. 1969): 399-408.

1961 —. "Dickens 1970: 'These Goblin Volumes'." *Archiv* 208 (Apr. 1972): 298-309. [Rev.-art on some 25 items.]

1962 —. "Dickens und die Psychoanalyse." *Archiv* 216, i (1979): 52-67. [Esp. *GreatEx, HardT, MChuz, OurMF, TaleTwoC.*]

1963 Tewari, R. P. "Dickens and Democracy." *AUJR-L* 24 (Jan. 1976): 21-27. [*BleakH, HardT, NichN, PickP.*]

1964 —. "The Treatment of Fallen Women in the Novels of Dickens and Mrs. Gaskell." *AUJR-L* 19 (Jan. 1971): 43-52. [Incl. *DavidC, DSon, OliverTw.*]

1965 — and S. P. Jain. "Dickens and the Law." *AUJR-L* 21 (Jan. 1973): 41-46. [*BleakH, GreatEx, HardT, PickP.*]

1966 — and S. P. Jain. "Dickens and the Prison." *AUJR-L* 21 (July 1973): 49-52. [Esp. *LittleDor, PickP.*]

1967 Tharaud, Barry. "Two Film Versions of *Oliver Twist:* Moral Vision in Film and Literature." *DSN* 11 (June 1980): 41-46. [Lean's 1947 version and Cowen's 1933 version.]

1968 Thomas, Deborah A. "The Chord of the Chirstmas Season: Playing House at the Holly-Tree Inn." *DSN* 6 (Dec. 1975): 103-108.

1969 —. "Contributors to the Christmas Numbers of *Household Words* and *All the Year Round,* 1850-1867." *Dkn* 69 (Sept. 1973): 163-172; 70 (Jan. 1974): 21-29.

1970 —. "Dickens's Mrs. Lirriper and the Evolution of a Feminine Stereotype." In 1494, pp. 154-166.

1971 —. "The Equivocal Explanation of Dickens's George Silverman." In 1491, pp. 134-143.

1972 Thomas, Gilbert. *English* 20 (Spring 1971): 25-26. [Rev. of 509, 592, 884, 1201, 1786, 1917.]

1973 —. "Publishing Dickens 60 Years Ago." *Bookseller* 18 Apr. 1970: 2042-2043.

1974 Thomas, Gillian. "Dickens and *The Portfolio.*" *Dkn* 68 (Sept. 1972): 167-172.

1975 Thomas, L. H. C. "Otto Ludwig and Charles Dickens: A German Reading of *Great Expectations* and Other Novels." *Hermathena* no. 111 (1971): 35-50.

1976 —. "Otto Ludwig's *Die Heiteretei und ihr Widerspiel.*" *FMLS* 6 (July 1970): 226-234. [D's infl.]

1977 (Thomas, R. George. *Charles Dickens: Great Expectations.* 1964.) [Rev.: Edward Davis, *UES* 10 (Sept. 1972): 63; Robin Gilmour, *Dkn* 70 (May 1974): 132-133.]

1978 Thomsen, Christian W. "Charles Dickens: *Great Expectations,*" in *Der englische Roman im 19. Jahrundert: Interpretationen,* ed. Paul Goetsch et al. (Berlin: Erich Schmidt, 1973), 165-179.

1979 —. "Das Groteske in Charles Dickens's *Great Expectations.*" *Anglia* 92, i-ii (1974): 113-142.

1980 —. *Das Groteske und die englische Literatur.* Erträge zur Forschung, 64 (Darmstadt: Wissenschaftliche Buchgesellschaft, 1977), passim.

1981 Thomson, David T., Jr. "Pip: The Divided Self." *PsyculR* 1 (Winter 1977): 49-67. [Method derived from Laing.]

1982 Thro, A. Brooker. "An Approach to Melodramatic Fiction: Goodness and Energy in the Novels of Dickens, Collins and Reade." *Genre* 11 (Fall 1978): 359-374. [Incl. *OliverTw.*]

1983 Thundyil, Zacharias. "Dickens, Fagin, and Critics." *Thought* (Delhi) 26 (16 Feb. 1974): 15-17.

1984 Thurley, Geoffrey. *The Dickens Myth: Its Genesis and Structure.* London: Routledge and Kegan Paul; New York: St. Martin's Press; St. Lucia: Univ. of Queensland Press, 1976. xi, 379 pp. [Chap. on each novel except *NichN, PickP.*—Rev.: C. C. Barfoot, *ES* 58 (Dec. 1977): 542; Rachel Bennett, *RES* NS 29 (May 1978): 232-235; Maria Teresa Chialant, *AION-SG* 20, i (1977): 162-165; Peter Christmas, *DSN* 9 (June 1978): 50-52; A. O. J. Cockshut, *TLS* 29 Oct. 1976: 1359; Robin Gilmour, *Dkn* 73 (May 1977): 116-117; Barbara Hardy, *THES* 31 Dec. 1976: 11; Sylvère Monod, *EA* 30 (Oct.-Dec. 1977): 498-499; Robert L. Patten, *Novel* 12 (Spring 1979): 254-259; Peter Preston, *N&Q* NS 26 (Oct. 1979): 460-462; Robin Wood, *TES* 17 Dec. 1976: 21; *Ecn* 260 (21 Aug. 1976): 92-93; also rev. in 583, 981.]

1985 Tick, Stanley. "The Decline and Fall of Little Nell: Some Evidence from the Manuscripts." *PCP* 9 (Apr. 1974): 62-72.

1986 —. "*Hard Times,* Page One: An Analysis." *VN* no. 46 (Fall 1974): 20-22.

1987 —. "The Memorializing of Mr. Dick." *NCF* 24 (Sept. 1969): 142-153. [As metaphor for artist.]

1988 —. "The Sad End of Mr. Meagles." In 1491, pp. 87-99.

1989 —. "Toward Jaggers." In 1493, pp. 133-149.

1990 —. "The Unfinished Business of *Dombey and Son*." *MLQ* 36 (Dec. 1975): 390-402.

1991 Tigner, Steven S. "Charles Dickens in and about Magic: A Preliminary Sketch." *J of Magic Hist* 1 (July 1979): 89-117. [Incl. "Out-Conjuring Conjurors" from *HsldWds* 9 Apr. 1859.]

1992 Tillotson, Geoffrey. "Dickens." *A View of Victorian Literature,* [ed. Kathleen Tillotson] (Oxford: Clarendon Press, 1978), 112-151. [Esp. *BleakH, DavidC, DSon, MChuz, NichN, PickP, SBoz.*—Orig. intended for *OHEL*.]

1993 Tillotson, Kathleen. "Charles Dickens's Library." *BC* 28 (Autumn 1979): 436.

1994 —. "Dickens, Wilkie Collins and the Suicidal Curates." *Dkn* 69 (Sept. 1973): 173. [Infl. of *MChuz* on *Woman in White*.]

1995 —. "Eliza Acton and *Martin Chuzzlewit*." *Dkn* 75 (Autumn 1979): 143-144.

1996 —. "Louisa King and Cornelia Blimber." *Dkn* 74 (May 1978): 91-95. [Note also author's ltr. to ed., 75 (Summer 1979): 105.]

1997 —. "The Middle Years: From the *Carol* to *Copperfield*." *Dkn* 66 (Sept. 1970): supp. 7-19. [Special no. of D Memorial Lectures 1970.—For revs. see 1365.]

1998 — and Nina Burgis. "Forster's Reviews in the *Examiner,* 1840-1841." *Dkn* 68 (May 1972): 105-108. [Note also Alec W. C. Brice's ltr. to ed., 72 (Jan. 1976): 46-47.]

1999 Tjoa, Hock Guan. *George Henry Lewes: A Victorian Mind*. Harvard Hist. Monographs, 70 (Cambridge and London: Harvard UP, 1977), passim.

2000 Tobias, J. J. *Prince of Fences: The Life and Crimes of Ikey Solomons* (London: Valentine, Mitchell, 1974), passim. [Solomons not orig. for Fagin.—Rev. in 968 (May 1975).]

2001 Toliver, Harold. *Animate Illustrations: Explorations of Narrative Structure* (Lincoln: Univ. of Nebraska Press, 1974), passim. [*BarnR, NichN, OliverTw*.]

2002 Tolstoi, Catherine. "Le rendez-vous de Gad's Hill: Dickens cent ans après." *NL* 16 July 1970: 3.

2003 Tolstoy, Lev. *Letters,* sel., ed., trans. R. F. Christian, 2 vols. (London: Univ. of London, Athlone Press, 1978), passim. [Incl. *BleakH, DavidC, LittleDor, NichN, OliverTw, OurMF, TaleTwoC.*]

2004 Tomlin, E. W. F. "Charles Dickens and Henry Fothergill Chorley." *EA* 32 (Oct.-Dec. 1979): 434-448. [Incl. unpub. 23 Apr. 1865 ltr. from D to printer Birtles.]

2005 (—, ed. *Charles Dickens 1812-1870: A Centenary Volume.* 1969.) [Rev.: Trevor Blount, *DSN* 2 (June 1971): 49-51; Robert F. Fleissner, *SNNTS* 2 (Fall 1970): 384-386; Thomas J. Galvin, *LJ* 95 (1 Feb. 1970): 499; Sylvère Monod, *EA* 23 (Apr.-June 1970): 214-216; Leslie C. Staples, *Dkn* 66 (Jan. 1970): 54-57; *Cb* 7 (Mar. 1970): 70; also rev. in 981, 1181, 1228, 1808, 1961, 2138.—Note also *Die Welt des Charles Dickens,* trans. Eva Gärtner (Hamburg: Hoffmann und Campe, 1969), 279 pp.—Rev.: Alfred Starkman, *Welt der Literatur* 28 May 1970: 4.]

2006 —. "Dickens, Macready and George Sand." *EA* 28 (July-Sept. 1975): 331-333.

2007 —. "Dickens, the Supreme Entertainer." In 1285, pp. 10-15.

2008 —. "The Englishness of Dickens." In 154, pp. 113-124. [Humor, social vision.]

2009 Tomlinson, T. B. "Dickens: *Dombey and Son, Bleak House.*" *The English Middle-Class Novel* (London: Macmillan; New York: Barnes and Noble, 1976), 52-68; et passim. [Incorporates "Dickens and Individualism: *Dombey and Son, Bleak House,*" *CR* (Melbourne) no. 15 (1972): 64-81.]

2010 Toomre, Joyce S. "Dining with Dickens." *Harvard Mag* (Univ. Ed.) 81 (Jan.-Feb. 1978): 38-44. [Food in *PickP.*]

2011 Torrens, James. "Dickens a Century Later." *America* 122 (6 June 1970): 609-610.

2011a Tracy, G.-M. "Dickens le mal marié et les femmes." *Écrits de Paris* no. 356 (Mar. 1976): 88-97.

2012 Trautmann, Fredrick. "Philadelphia Bowled Clean Over: Public Readings by Charles Dickens." *PMHB* 98 (Oct. 1974): 456-468.

2013 Tremper, Ellen. "Commitment and Escape: The Fairy Tales of
Thackeray, Dickens, and Wilde." *L&U* 2, i (1978): 38-47.
["Magic Fishbone" from "HRom."]

2014 Trickett, Rachel. "Vitality of Language in Nineteenth-Century Fiction," in *The Modern English Novel: The Reader, the Writer and
the Work*, ed. Gabriel Josipovici (London: Open Books; New York:
Barnes and Noble, 1976), 37-53. [Esp. *BleakH.*]

2015 Trilling, Lionel. "The Dickens of Our Day." *A Gathering of Fugi-
tives*. His Works: Uniform Ed. (New York and London: Harcourt
Brace Jovanovich, [1978]), 45-52. [Rev.-art. on 1st ed. of Johnson's biog. orig. pub. in *Griffin*, 1952; this coll. 1st pub. 1956.]

2016 —. "*Little Dorrit.*" *The Opposing Self: Nine Essays in Criticism.* His
Works: Uniform Ed. (New York and London: Harcourt Brace
Jovanovich, 1978), 44-57. [Orig. pub. as intro. to New Oxford
Illus. ed. (also in *KR*, 1953); this coll. 1st pub. 1955.—Rpt. in
2331, pp. 279-293 and in 2064, pp. 363-375.]

2017 Trudgill, Eric. *Madonnas and Magdalens: The Origins and Development of Victorian Sexual Attitudes* (London: Heinemann; New
York: Holmes and Meier, 1976), passim.

2018 Tschumi, Raymond. "Dickens and Switzerland." *ES* 60 (Aug. 1979):
444-461. [Esp. *NoTho.*]

2019 Tsumura, Norifumi. [D: Centenary events in England.] In 1287, pp.
225-240. [In Jap.; Eng. abst., pp. 285-287 and in 1285, pp. 64-
65.]

2020 Tucker, David. "Dickens at Work on the MS of *A Tale of Two
Cities.*" *EA* 32 (Oct.-Dec. 1979): 449-457.

2021 —. "The Reception of *A Tale of Two Cities.*" *DSN* 10 (Mar., June-
Sept. 1979): 8-13, 51-56. [Contrary to opinion, a favorable contemporary reception.]

2022 —. "The Text of the Oxford Illustrated Dickens: *A Tale of Two
Cities*: Some Shortcomings Noted." *N&Q* NS 25 (Aug. 1978):
311-313.

2023 Turner, David R. *Charles Dickens's David Copperfield.* Arco Notes. New York: Arco, 1970. 60 pp.

2024 Turpin, John. "Maclise as a Dickens Illustrator." *Dkn* 76 (Summer 1980): 66-77.

2025 Twain, Mark. *Notebooks and Journals,* ed. Frederick Anderson, Robert Pack Browning, et al. 3 vols. (Berkeley, Los Angeles, London: Univ. of California Press, 1975-1979), passim. [Humor, dialect.]

2026 Tye, J. R. "Legal Caricature: Cruikshank Analogues to the *Bleak House* Cover." *Dkn* 69 (Jan. 1973): 39-41. [Note also Ian Gowan's ltr. to ed. (May), p. 78.]

2027 Tyler, Ralph and John F. Baker. "Classic Corner: The Works of Great Writers Available Today: Charles Dickens." *Bookviews* 2 (Dec. 1978): 24-25.

2028 Ullman, Michael A. "Where George Stopped Growing: Dickens's 'George Silverman's Explanation'." *ArielE* 10 (Jan. 1979): 11-23.

2029 Ursini, James. "*A Christmas Carol (Scrooge).*" In 1238, I, 336-338. [Brian Desmond Hurst's 1951 film.]

2030 Ussher, R. G. "Boz and the Character Tradition." *Hermathena* no. 120 (Summer 1976): 59-62.

2031 Valentry, Duane. "The Story Dickens Loved Most." *Modern Maturity* 20 (Dec. 1977-Jan. 1978): 25-26. [*CCarol.*]

2032 Vallance, Rosalind. "Forster's *Goldsmith.*" *Dkn* 71 (Jan. 1975): 21-29.

2033 Vallès, Jules. "Littérature anglaise, le roman." *Oeuvres,* ed. Roger Bellet (Paris: Gallimard, 1975), I, 548-559. [Orig. in *Courrier du Dimanche,* 17 Sept. and 1 Oct. 1865.]

2034 Van Heyningen, C. "Aspects of Dickens." *Theoria* 42 (June 1974): 65-77. [All novels except *BarnR, DSon, MEDrood, OCShop, PickP, TaleTwoC.*]

2035 —. "*Dombey and Son.*" *Theoria* 44 (May 1975): 11-19.

2036 Van Inwagen, Peter. "Creatures of Fiction." *Amer Phil Q* 14 (Oct. 1977): 299-308. [Fictitiousness of Pickwick and Sarah Gamp.—

Note also 359.]

2037 Vann, J. Don. "Dickens and Charley Bates," in *Of Edsels and Marauders*, ed. Fred Tarpley and Ann Moseley. South-Central Names Inst. Pub. 1 (Commerce, Texas: Names Inst. Press, 1970), 117-122. [Esp. *OliverTw.*]

2038 —. "Dickens to J. P. Collier: A Letter Re-Dated." *DSN* 8 (June 1977): 47-48. [Pilgrim ed., I, 220.]

2039 —. "The Early Success of *Pickwick.*" *Publishing Hist* 2 (1977): 51-55.

2040 —. "*Pickwick* and 'Bartleby'." *SAF* 6 (Autumn 1978): 235-237.

2041 —. "*Pickwick* in the London Newspapers." *Dkn* 70 (Jan. 1974): 49-52.

2042 Vega-Ritter, Max. "Étude psychocritique de *David Copperfield.*" In 131, pp. 23-70. [With Eng. abst., pp. 11-21.]

2043 Venner, R. H. *Charles Dickens: A Brief Reader's Guide*, intro. N. V. Tilley. [Nottingham: Nottinghamshire County Lib.], 1970. 18 pp.

2044 Veres, Grigore. "Charles Dickens." *ConLit* (Jassy) NS 1, iv (Aug. 1970): 76-78.

2045 —. "Perenitatea creatiei dickensiane." *Cronica* 5 (June 1970): 9.

2046 —. "Unele consideratii privind receptarea critica a operei lui Charles Dickens în România." *ASUI* 17 (1970): 97-101.

2047 —. "Viziunea dickensiana asupra lumii în *Casa umbrelor.*" *ASUI* 20 (1974): 109-115.

2048 Vermilye, Jerry. *"Great Expectations"; "Oliver Twist." The Great British Films* (Secaucus, N.J.: Citadel Press, 1978), 102-105; 117-120. [Lean films.]

2049 Vernon, Sally. *"Oliver Twist* and *The Golden Farmer." DSN* 8 (Sept. 1977): 65-68.

2050 Versfeld, Barbara. *Notes on Charles Dickens's Oliver Twist.* Study-Aid Ser. London: Methuen, 1976, 1978. 77, 67 pp.

2051 Visser, N. W. "Temporal Vantage Point in the Novel." *JNT* 7 (Spring

1977): 81-93. [Incl. *GreatEx.*]

2052 Vogel, Jane. *Allegory in Dickens.* St. in the Humanities, 17. University: Univ. of Alabama Press, 1977. xvi, 347 pp. [Esp. *DavidC,* with chap. on characters from that novel.—Rev.: C. C. Barfoot, *ES* 59 (Dec. 1978): 566; Charles Bishop, *LJ* 101 (15 Nov. 1976): 2375-2376; A. O. J. Cockshut, *TLS* 17 Mar. 1978: 308 and Alan S. Watts's ltr., 28 Apr. 1978: 475; Bert C. Hornback, *DSN* 9 (June 1978): 53-54; D. A. Miller, *VS* 22 (Summer 1979): 473-474; Robert O'Kell, *QQ* 86 (Winter 1979-1980): 712-714; Allen Samuels, *Dkn* 74 (May 1978): 111-113; *Ch* 15 (Mar. 1978): 74; *Christian Century* 94 (23 Nov. 1977): 1100; also rev. in 981, 531, 583, 1538, 1568.]

2053 Vogler, Richard A. "Cruikshank and Dickens: A Reassessment of the Role of the Artist and the Author." In 1510, pp. 61-91.

2054 —. *"Oliver Twist:* Cruikshank's Pictorial Prototypes." In 1490, pp. 98-118.

2055 —. *An Oliver Twist Exhibition: A Memento for the Dickens Centennial, 1970: An Essay.* Los Angeles: UCLA Lib., 1970. 15 pp.

2056 Waddington, Patrick. "Dickens, Pauline Viardot, Turgenev: A Study in Mutual Admiration." *NZSJ* NS no. 1 (Sept. 1974): 55-73. [Incl. "CrickH," *DavidC, DSon, HsldWds, LittleDor, OliverTw,* "SomeLug."]

2057 Wade, Rosalind. "Charles Dickens (1812-70): A Centenary Tribute: Some Sources of His Experience and Inspiration." *ContempR* 217 (Aug. 1970): 98-104.

2058 (Wagenknecht, Edward. *Dickens and the Scandalmongers: Essays in Criticism.* 1965.) [Rev. in 209.]

2059 (—. *The Man Charles Dickens: A Victorian Portrait,* rev. ed. 1966.) [Rev. in 209.]

2060 Wagner, Horst. "Zur Frage der Erzähleinschübe im *Don Quijote* und in dem *Pickwick Papers." Arcadia* 9, i (1974): 1-22.

2061 Wagner, Karl Heinz. "Charles Dickens oder die humane Qualität des humors." *NsM* 23, ii (1970): 102-103.

2062 Walder, Dennis. "Dickens and the Victorian Idea of Death." *New Edinburgh Rev* no. 9 (Nov. 1970): 4-8. [Mentions *DSon, GreatEx,*

OCShop, OliverTw, OurMF, PickP.]

2063 —. "The Novel and Religion: *Great Expectations.*" *Proteus* 1 (Nov. 1977): 7-20.

2064 Wall, Stephen, ed. *Charles Dickens: A Critical Anthology.* Harmondsworth: Penguin, 1970. 551 pp. [For contents see this number in Appendix.—Rev.: Edith Briard, *EA* 28 (Jan.-Mar. 1975): 100-101; Shirley Chew, *Enc* 36 (Feb. 1971): 74-77; Richard J. Dunn, *DSN* 3 (June 1972): 46-50; Ranga Kapoor, *EducationQ* (India) 23 (July 1971): 72-73; Irma Rantavaara, *Dkn* 67 (May 1971): 109-111; Dennis Walder, *New Edinburgh Rev* no. 15 (Nov. 1971): 33-34; also rev. in 182 (Aug. 1971), 2216.]

2065 —. "Dickens in 1970." *EIC* 21 (July 1971): 261-280. [Rev.-art. on some 12 items.]

2066 Wallins, Roger P. "Dickens and Decomposition." *DSN* 5 (Sept. 1974): 68-70. [Krook's death.]

2067 —. "Victorian Periodicals and the Emerging Social Conscience." *VPN* no. 8 (June 1975): 47-59. [*BleakH, DSon, OliverTw.*]

2068 Walsh, Jim. "Through the Stereoscope: The Centennial Observance of Charles Dickens's Death." *Hobbies* 75 (June 1970): 48-50, 129-130. [Tribute.]

2069 Walsh, Thomas P. "Yet Another Comment on Dickens's Two Endings for *Great Expectations.*" *PAPA* 3 (Fall 1976): 16. [Abst.]

2070 Walsh, William. "The Arnoldian Middle." *F. R. Leavis* (Bloomington and London: Indiana UP, 1980), 131-153; et passim.

2071 Ward, W. A. "On Dickens," in *Literary English since Shakespeare*, ed. George Watson (London and New York: Oxford UP, 1970), 339-346. [Esp. *MChuz.*—Rev. from *Lstr* 23 May 1963.]

2072 Warman, Christopher. "Dickens Relics on Show in His London House." *Times* (London) 12 June 1971: 2. [Suzannet Coll.]

2073 Warncke, Wayne. "George Orwell's Dickens." *SAQ* 69 (Summer 1970): 373-382.

2074 Warson, Yves. "De hekelutopie in de *Schetsen van Boz* door Charles Dickens." *Dialoog* (Antwerp) 14, i-ii (1973-1974): 367-373.

2075 Watkins, A. H. *Charles Dickens and H. G. Wells.* Wells Soc. Occ. Papers, 2 [Nottingham?] : H. G. Wells Soc., 1976. 8 pp.

2076 Watkins, G. M. "A Possible Source for Quilp." *N&Q* NS 18 (Nov. 1971): 411-413. [Grimaldi's *Memoirs.*]

2077 Watson, Garry. *The Leavises, the "Social" and the Left* (Brynmill, Swansea: Brynmill, 1977), passim.

2078 Watson, George. *The English Ideology: Studies in the Language of Victorian Politics* (London: Allen Lane, 1973), passim. [Esp. *BleakH, DavidC, GreatEx, HardT, LittleDor, TaleTwoC.*]

2079 Watson, J. L. "Dickens at Work on Manuscript and Proof: *Bleak House* and *Little Dorrit.*" *AUMLA* no. 45 (May 1976): 54-68.

2080 Watson, Thomas L. "The Ethics of Feasting: Dickens's Dramatic Use of Agape," in *Essays in Honor of Edmond Linworth Marilla,* ed. Thomas Austin Kirby and William John Olive. Louisiana State Univ. St. Humanities Ser., 19 (Baton Rouge: Louisiana State UP, 1970), 243-252. [*DSon, HardT, PickP.*—Rev.: Alan Burke, *DSN* 4 (Sept. 1973): 86-89.]

2081 Watt, Ian. "Oral Dickens." In 1491, pp. 165-181. [Esp. *GreatEx, MChuz.*—Paper from 2180.]

2082 —, ed. *The Victorian Novel: Modern Essays in Criticism.* Oxford: Oxford UP, 1971. [For items on D see this number in Appendix. —Rev.: Richard J. Dunn, *DSN* 3 (June 1972): 46-50.]

2083 Watts, Alan S. "Letter to the Editor." *Dkn* 76 (Spring 1980): 20-21. [Illustration in *OCShop.*]

2084 —. "Octavia Hill and the Influence of Dickens." *Hist Today* 24 (May 1974): 348-353. [Philanthropy.]

2085 Webster, Grant. *The Republic of Letters: A History of Postwar American Literary Opinion* (Baltimore and London: Johns Hopkins UP, 1979), 264-266. [On Marcus, *Dickens from Pickwick to Dombey,* 1965.]

2086 Wechter, Sidney. "Cruikshank's Fagin—The Illustrator as Creator." *Courier* (Syracuse Univ. Lib.) 14, iii (1977): 28-31.

2087 —. "Letter to the Editor." *Dkn* 71 (Sept. 1975): 169. [Verifies that Edmund Yates accompanied D to Britannia Theatre 29 January

1860.]

2088 Wees, William C. "Dickens, Griffith and Eisenstein: Form and Image in Literature and Film." *HAB* 24 (Fall 1973): 266-276.

2089 Weigel, James. *Pickwick Papers: Notes.* Lincoln, Neb.: Cliff's Notes, 1970. 97 pp.

2090 Weinberg, A. M. "*A Tale of Two Cities*: Death and Regeneration." *Crux* 5 (July-Sept. 1971): 10-16.

2091 Weinstein, Arnold L. "Solvable Mysteries: Balzac and Dickens." *Vision and Response in Modern Fiction* (Ithaca: Cornell UP, 1974), 25-49. [Incl. *BleakH, GreatEx, LittleDor, OurMF.*—Rev.: Anne Humpherys, *DSN* 7 (Dec. 1976): 125-126.]

2092 Weinstock, Donald J. "Jaggers in the Country." *NDQ* 47 (Summer 1979): 25-29. [Defense.]

2093 Welsh, Alexander. *The City of Dickens.* Oxford: Clarendon Press, 1971. xi, 233 pp. [Rev.: William Burgan, *VS* 16 (Sept. 1972): 122-123; C. Clarke, *JES* 2 (Mar. 1972): 85; T. J. Cribb, *RES* NS 24 (May 1973): 230-233; Keith Cushman, *LJ* 96 (1 Nov. 1971): 3615; Edward Davis, *UES* 10 (Mar. 1972): 76; Stephen Gill, *N&Q* NS 20 (July 1973): 277-278; Barbara Hardy, *Enc* 38 (Dec. 1971): 48-49; James R. Kincaid, *DSN* 3 (Sept. 1972): 81-84; Annegret Maack, *NS* 72 (Jan. 1973): 52-53; Sylvère Monod, *EA* 45 (Jan.-Mar. 1972): 165-166; Heinz Reinhold, *Anglia* 90, iv (1972): 545-546; Ruth Schrock, *ELN* 10 (Sept. 1972): 57-60; Michael Slater, *NCF* 26 (Mar. 1972): 492-494; Harvey Peter Sucksmith, *YES* 2 (1972): 310-312; Kurt Tetzeli von Rosador, *Archiv* 123 (Apr. 1972): 405-406; Raymond Williams, *Dkn* 68 (Jan. 1972): 53-54; George J. Worth, *JEGP* 71 (Oct. 1972): 551-554; *NY* 47 (6 Nov. 1971): 202; *TLS* 29 Oct. 1971: 1361; also rev. in 182 (Aug. 1972), 981, 1126, 1578.]

2094 —. "Novels and Letters of Dickens." *YR* 68 (Oct. 1978): 123-130. [Rev.-art. on 104, 1415, 1659, 2101.]

2095 —. "Realism as a Practical and Cosmic Joke." *Novel* 9 (Fall 1975): 23-39. [Incl. *PickP.*]

2096 —. "Time and the City in *The Chimes*." *Dkn* 73 (Jan. 1977): 8-17.

2097 Werkman, Evert and J. C. van Kessel. "Een betreurenswaardige Correspondentie." *Dutch Dkn* 6, xv (Dec. 1976): 58-60. [Mrs.

Squeers.]

2098 Werner, Craig. "Fugal Structure in *The Mystery of Edwin Drood.*"
DSN 9 (Sept. 1978): 77-80.

2099 Weseliński, Andrzej. "Glosy polskiej krytyki literackiej o twórczości
K. Dickensa w okresie modernizmu." *APh* 6 (1974): 261-282.
[Reception.]

2100 —. "Struktura powieści Karola Dickensa w świetle seryjnej formy
publikacji." *APh* 4 (1972): 59-86. [Eng. abst., p. 87.]

2101 Westburg, Barry. *The Confessional Fictions of Charles Dickens.*
Dekalb: Northern Illinois UP, 1977. xxiii, 223 pp. [Esp. *DavidC,
GreatEx, OliverTw.*—Incorporates " 'His Allegorical Way of Ex-
pressing It': Civil War and Psychic Conflict in *Oliver Twist* and *A
Child's History,*" *SNNTS* 6 (Spring 1974): 27-37.—Rev.: Jerome H.
Buckley, *NCF* 33 (Mar. 1979): 508-512; William Burgan, *SNNTS*
10 (Winter 1978): 471-473; Pierre Coustillas, *MLR* 75 (Oct. 1980):
860-862; Angus Easson, *THES* 29 Apr. 1978: 14; Felicity A.
Hughes, *SoRA* 12 (July 1979): 181-188; David D. Marcus, *DSN* 9
(Dec. 1978): 119-121; Sylvère Monod, *EA* 31 (July-Dec. 1978):
400-403; Robert O'Kell, *QQ* 86 (Winter 1979-1980): 712-714;
David Parker, *MLQ* 39 (Mar. 1978): 79-82; Robert L. Patten,
Novel 12 (Spring 1979): 254-259; Paul Schlicke, *Dkn* 74 (May
1978): 113-115; Michael Steig, *TLS* 22 Sept. 1978: 1051; G. B.
Tennyson, *SEL* 20 (Autumn 1980): 732; *Ch* 15 (Apr. 1978): 237;
also rev. in 182 (Dec. 1979), 531, 583, 981, 1123, 1299, 2094.]

2102 —. "How Poe Solved the Mystery of *Barnaby Rudge.*" *DSN* 5 (June
1974): 38-40. [In his reviews of the novel.]

2103 Wheale, J. W. "More Metempsychosis?: The Influence of Charles
Dickens on James Joyce." *JJQ* 17 (Summer 1980): 439-444.

2104 Wheeler, Michael. "Apocalypse in a Mechnical Age: *Hard Times.*"
The Art of Allusion in Victorian Fiction (London: Macmillan;
New York: Barnes and Noble, 1979), 61-77; et passim. [Also
Gaskell's *Mary Barton.*—Rev.: Steven Connor, *Dkn* 79 (Sum-
mer 1980): 113-114.]

2105 Whitaker, Muriel. "The Proper Bringing up of Young Pip." *ChildL*
2 (1973): 152-158.

2106 White, Allon H. "Language and Location in Charles Dickens's *Bleak
House.*" *CritQ* 20 (Winter 1978): 73-89.

2107 White, Colin. "La exploración moral del mundo urbanizado en la obra de Dickens." In 813, pp. 59-76.

2108 White, Gabriel. *Edward Ardizzone: Artist and Illustrator* (London, Sydney, Toronto: Bodley Head, 1979; New York: Schocken, 1980), 135-136.

2109 White, John. "Style and Meaning in *A Tale of Two Cities*." *Missouri Eng Bull* 27 (Mar. 1970): 1-5.

2110 Whitehill, Sharon. "Jonas Chuzzlewit: Archetype of the Self-Destroyer." *DSN* 9 (Sept. 1978): 70-73.

2111 Whitlow, Roger. "Animal and Human Personalities in Dickens's Novels." *CLAJ* 19 (Sept. 1975): 65-74. [*DavidC, DSon, HardT, OCShop, OliverTw*.]

2112 Whitridge, Arnold. "Dickens and Thackeray in America." *New York Hist Soc Q* 62 (1978): 219-237.

2113 Wilhelm, Albert E. "Law and Comic Pattern in Dickens's Late Novels." *SAB* 41 (Jan. 1976): 59-60. [Abst.]

2114 Wilkins, Michael. "Dickens's Portrayal of the Dedlocks." *Dkn* 72 (May 1976): 67-74.

2115 Williams, George G. *Guide to Literary London* (London: Batsford; New York: Hastings, 1973), passim.

2116 Williams, Ioan. "The Development of Realist Fiction: From Dickens to George Meredith"; "The Realism of Dickens." *The Realist Novel in England: A Study in Development* (London: Macmillan, 1974; Pittsburgh: Univ. of Pittsburgh Press, 1975), 115-138; 139-155; et passim. [Esp. *DavidC, DSon, GreatEx.*—Rev.: Richard Dunn, *DSN* 8 (June 1977): 56-58.]

2117 Williams, Nigel. "The Parish Boy's Progress." *Lstr* 94 (18 Dec. 1975): 819-820.

2118 Williams, Raymond. "Charles Dickens." *The English Novel from Dickens to Lawrence* (London: Chatto and Windus; New York: Oxford UP, 1970), 28-59; et passim. [Esp. *DSon.*—Note also ed. Frogmore, St. Albans: Paladin, 1974 and interview on this book in *Politics and Letters: Interviews with New Left Review* (London: NLB, 1979), 243-270.—Rev.: Philip Collins, *Dkn* 67 (Jan. 1971): 47-49; R. G. Collins, *DSN* 5 (June 1974): 48-53; also rev. in 198,

967 (May 1975), 1961.]

2119 —. "Dickens and Social Ideas," in *Sociology of Literature and Drama: Selected Readings,* ed. Elizabeth and Tom Burns (Harmondsworth and Baltimore: Penguin, 1973), 328-347. [Esp. *HardT* also *BleakH, DSon, GreatEx, LittleDor, NichN.*—Rpt. from 1786, pp. 77-98.]

2120 —. "People of the City." *The Country and the City* (London: Chatto and Windus; New York: Oxford UP, 1973), 153-164; et passim. [Incl. *DSon, HardT, LittleDor.*—Rev.: Malcolm Andrews, *Dkn* 70 (Jan. 1974): 56-57.]

2121 Wilson, Angus. "Charles Dickens Today." In 846, pp. 11-14. [Esp. style, alienation, similarity to Dostoevski.]

2122 —. "Dickens and Dostoevsky." *Dkn* 66 (Sept. 1970): supp. 41-61. [Special no. of D Memorial Lectures 1970.—For revs. see 1365.]

2123 —. "Dickens on Children and Childhood." In 1786, pp. 195-227.

2124 —. "Light and Dark in Dickens." *Lstr* 83 (28 May 1970): 701-703. [Incl. *BarnR, DavidC, GreatEx, OCShop, OliverTw, PickP.*]

2125 —. "Little Nell and *Derby Day.*" *DSN* 2 (Sept. 1971): 88-89. [Infl. on Frith's painting.]

2126 —. "On Dickens's Influence." *Dkn* 72 (Jan. 1976): 56-58. [D's infl. on Wilson's own novels; speech at 69th annual conf. of D Fellowship.]

2127 —. "[Toast at] The London Birthday Dinner." *Dkn* 70 (May 1974): 138-139.

2128 —. *The World of Charles Dickens.* London: Secker and Warburg; New York: Viking Press, 1970. 302 pp. [Note pbk. ed. (Harmondsworth: Penguin, 1972) and extracts, "The Macabre World of Young Dickens," *Obs Mag* (supp. to the weekly) 17 May 1970: 24-25 and "Charles Dickens: A Failed Middle-Class Marriage," 24 May 1970: 37-38, 41-43.—Rev.: Alberto Adell, *Insula* 27 (Jan. 1972): 13; Trevor Allen, *B&B* 18 (Jan. 1973): 124 and 18 (Mar. 1973): III-IV; Paul Bailey, *Nova* July 1970: 14, 17, 19; John Bayley, *NYRB* 15 (8 Oct. 1970): 8; Pearl K. Bell, *New Leader* 54 (25 Jan. 1971): 15-16; Elizabeth Bowen, *Spec* 224 (30 May 1970): 713; John Carey, *Lstr* 83 (28 May 1970): 724-725; Mary Silva Cosgrave, *Horn Book* 47 (Feb. 1971): 73-74; Denis Donoghue, *NCF* 27 (Sept. 1972): 216-218; M. A. Fido, *VS* 15 (Sept. 1971): 101-102; K. J. Fielding, *Dkn* 66 (Sept. 1970): 248 and (a diff. rev.) *NYTBR* 13 Sept. 1970: 7; John Fowles, *Life* 69 (4 Sept. 1970): 8-9; Thomas J. Galvin, *LJ* 95 (15 Sept. 1970): 2920; Christopher Hibbert, *Book World* 13 Sept. 1970: 5; John Holloway, *Enc* 34 (June 1970): 63; Anna Katona, *Helikon* 17, iii-iv (1971): 503-504; J. M. Lalley, *Modern Age* 15 (Spring 1971): 185-190; Neil Millar, *CSM* 1 Oct. 1970: 11; Sylvère Monod, *DSN* 2 (June 1971): 39-42; Christopher Porterfield, *Time* 96 (28 Dec. 1970): 59-60; V. S. Pritchett, *NewSt* 79 (June 1970): 807; Takao Saijo, *HSELL* 17, ii (1970): 72-79; Alfred Starkman, *Welt der Literatur* 28 May 1970: 4; G. W. Stiles, *Lantern* 20 (Dec. 1970): 46-53; Harvey Peter Sucksmith, *SoRA* 5 (Mar. 1972): 68-77; Raymond Williams, *Guardian Weekly* 6 June 1970: 6; Geoffrey Wolff, *Newsweek* 76 (31 Aug. 1970): 73; Helen Yglesias, *Nation* 211 (23 Nov. 1970): 540-541; *Best Sellers*, 30 (15 Sept. 1970): 236-237; *Blackwood's Mag* 308 (Dec. 1970): 569; *Ch* 7 (Dec. 1970): 1378; *Ecn* 235 (20 June 1970): 54, *NY* 46 (19 Sept. 1970): 137; *TLS* 4 June 1970: 597; also rev. in 198, 948, 981, 1126, 1181, 1578, 2065, 2138, 2200.—Note also London ed. issued in the Netherlands with an app. by Godfried Bomans, "De tijd van Dickens."—Rev.: K. Fens, *Streven* 24 (Oct. 1970): 54-57.— Note also *Le monde de Charles Dickens*, trans. Suzanne Nétillard (Paris: Gallimard, 1972).—Rev.: Annie Brierre, *RDM* no. 6 (June 1973): 764-765; Robert Kanters, *Bull de la Soc Littéraire des P. T. T.* no. 108 (Dec. 1972): 4-5; Guy Le Clec'h, *NL* 7 Jan. 1973: 4.]

2129 — and A. E. Dyson. "Charles Dickens," in *The English Novel,* [ed. Cedric Watts] (London: Sussex,1976), 53-75. [Transcription of discussion.—Note also 2891.]

2130 — interviewed by Diane Fernandez and Patrick Reumaux. "Angus Wilson parle de Dickens." *QL* 1-15 Jan. 1973: 5-6.

2131 Wilson, Colin. *The Craft of the Novel* (London: Gollancz, 1975), passim. [Incl. *BleakH, CCarol, DavidC, PickP*.]

2132 Wilson, John R. "Dickens and Christian Mystery." *SAQ* 73 (Autumn 1974): 528-540. [*BleakH, GreatEx, OliverTw, OurMF*.]

2133 Wilt, Judith. "Confusion and Consciousness in Dickens's Esther." *NCF* 32 (Dec. 1977): 285-309. [Incl. Pip and David Copperfield.]

2134 Winehouse, Bernard. "Israel Zangwill Dares to Do Down Dickens." *Dkn* 73 (Jan. 1977): 37-38.

2135 (Wing, George. *Dickens.* 1969.) [Rev.: James Kissane, *DSN* 3 (Mar. 1972): 12-14; *TLS* 23 Apr. 1970: 450; also rev. in 314, 981.]

2136 —. "*Edwin Drood* and *Desperate Remedies:* Prototypes of Detective Fiction in 1870." *SEL* 13 (Autumn 1973): 677-687.

2137 —. "Mr. F's Aunt: A Laughing Matter." *ESC* 3 (Summer 1977): 207-215.

2138 —. "Some Recent Dickens Criticism and Scholarship." *ArielE* 1 (Oct. 1970): 56-66. [Rev.-art. on some 15 items.]

2139 Winkgens, Meinhard. "Das Problem der 'historischen Wahrheit' in dem Roman *Hard Times* von Charles Dickens." *Poetica* 12, i (1980): 24-58.

2140 Winner, Anthony. "Character and Knowledge in Dickens: The Enigma of Jaggers." In 1491, pp. 100-121.

2141 Winslow, Joan D. "Esther Summerson: The Betrayal of the Imagination." *JNT* 6 (Winter 1976): 1-12.

2142 —. "The Number Plans for *Our Mutual Friend:* A Note." *DSN* 9 (Dec. 1978): 106-109.

2143 Winters, Warrington. "Dickens's *Hard Times:* The Lost Childhood." In 1490, pp. 217-236.

2144 Wolfe, Charles K. "Dickens and the Underground." In 1416, pp. 63-69. [Contemporary relevance.]

2145 Wolfe, Peter. "The Fictional Crux and the Double Structure of *Great Expectations.*" *SAQ* 73 (Summer 1974): 335-347.

2146 Wolff, Robert Lee. *Sensational Victorian: The Life and Fiction of Mary Elizabeth Braddon* (New York and London: Garland, 1979), passim.

2147 —. "*A Strange Story* (1862): Interpretations." *Strange Stories and Other Explorations in Victorian Fiction* (Boston: Gambit, 1971), 288-322. [D and Bulwer-Lytton.]

2148 Wolpers, Theodor. "Charles Dickens," in *Europäischer Realismus,* by Reinhard Lauer et al. Neues Handbuch der Literaturwissenschaft, 17 (Wiesbaden: Akademische Verlagsgesellschaft Athenaion,

1980), 128-157; et passim. [Esp. *BleakH, DavidC, HardT, Oliver-Tw, PickP, SBoz.*]

2149 Wood, Christopher. *Victorian Panorma: Paintings of Victorian Life* (London: Faber and Faber, 1976), passim. [Note also cat. of exhib. at Alexander Gallery (London), Oct.-Nov. 1976, to coincide with pub. of book.]

2150 Wood, Michael. "Portraits of Bobbies." *New Society* 37 (16 Sept. 1976): 609-610. [Incl. *BleakH, HsldWds, OurMF.*]

2151 Woodall, Robert. "The Public Readings of Charles Dickens." *Blackwood's Mag* 326 (Dec. 1979): 511-525.

2152 Woodhead, M. R. "De Quincey and *Little Dorrit.*" *N&Q* NS 19 (Nov. 1972): 409.

2153 Woodring, Carl. "Change in *Chuzzlewit.*" In 1683, pp. 211-218.

2154 Woodruff, Douglas. "The Christianity of Charles Dickens." *Tablet* 224 (June 1970): 542-544. [Incl. *AllYR, CHistEng, HsldWds, NichN, OliverTw, PickP, TaleTwoC.*—Note also the Rev. Tony Cross's ltr. to ed., 27 June 1970: 624.]

2155 Woodward, Kathleen. "Passivity and Passion in *Little Dorrit.*" *Dkn* 71 (Sept. 1975): 140-148.

2156 Woolley, David. "Forster's *Swift.*" *Dkn* 70 (Sept. 1974): 191-204.

2157 Worth, George J. *Dickensian Melodrama: A Reading of the Novels.* UKPHS, 50. Lawrence: Univ. of Kansas, 1978. 147 pp. [All novels except *MEDrood*, esp. *BleakH, DavidC, DSon, NichN, OliverTw, PickP.*—Incorporates "The Control of Emotional Response in *David Copperfield*," in *The English Novel in the Nineteenth Century: Essays on the Literary Mediation of Human Values*, ed.George Goodin, ISLL, 63 (Urbana and London: Univ. of Illinois Press, 1972), 97-108 (for rev. of this book see 945).—Rev.: Christopher Herbert, *NCF* 34 (Mar. 1980): 452; Jacob Korg, *JEGP* 79 (Jan. 1980): 139-140; Grahame Smith, *Dkn* 75 (Autumn 1979): 175-176; Jean Sudrann, *DSN* 11 (June 1980): 56-58.]

2158 —. "Five (More) on Dickens." *CEA* 37 (Nov. 1974): 32-35. [Rev.-art. on 798, 802, 830, 1141, 2322.]

2159 Wright, Chad C. "Artifacts and Effigies: The Porreño Household Revisited." *Anales Galdosianos* 14 (1979): 13-26. [D's infl., houses.]

2160 Wynn, Jones, Michael. "The Facts of Fiction (1830-1842)." *George Cruikshank: His Life and London* (London: Macmillan, 1978), 59-79; et passim. [*OliverTw.*—Rev.: Anthony Burton, *Dkn* 75 (Summer 1979): 114-116.]

2161 Wyslouch, Seweryna. "Anatomia widna." *Teksty* no. 32 (1977): 135-157. [Fantasy.]

2162 Yamamoto, Tadao. [D's use of language.] *EigoS* 116 (1970): 310-311. [In Jap.]

2162a —. [The English of D.] In 412a, pp. 52-54. [In Jap.]

2163 —. "Our Tortured Work." In 1285, pp. 6-9. [Progress of his D lexicon.]

2164 Yates, W. E. "Creative Adaptation." *Nestroy: Satire and Parody in Viennese Popular Comedy* (Cambridge: Cambridge UP, 1972), 120-148. [Incl. discussion of his play adap. of *Martin Chuzzlewit.*]

2165 Yelin, Louise. "Strategies for Survival: Florence and Edith in *Dombey and Son.*" *VS* 22 (Spring 1979): 297-319.

2166 Yoneda, Kazuhiko. [David's self-portrait: An aspect of *DavidC.*] In 1287, pp. 35-52. [In Jap.—Eng. abst., pp. 256-258 and in 1285, pp. 54-56.]

2167 —. [D and Thackeray: David and Pen], in *Eikoku shosetsu kenkyu* (Tokyo: Shinozaki Shorin, 1977), XII, 101-121. [In Jap.]

2168 —. [D and Thackeray: A return to *OliverTw*], in *Gengo to buntai: Higashida Chiaki kyoju kanreki kinen ronbunshu,* ed. Chiaki Higashida (Osaka: Osaka Kyoiku Tosho, 1975), 133-143. [In Jap.]

2168a —. [*GreatEx.*] In 412a, pp. 81-83. [In Jap.]

2169 Young, Melanie. "Distorted Expectations: Pip and the Problems of Language." In 1495, pp. 203-220.

2170 Zambrano, Ana Laura. "Audio-Visual Teaching Materials: A Dickensian Checklist." *DSN* 7 (June, Dec. 1976): 43-46, 110-113; 8 Mar. 1977): 17-19.

2171 —. *Dickens and Film.* New York: Gordon Press, 1977. ii, 442 pp. [Incorporates some material from "Charles Dickens and Sergei Eisenstein: The Emergence of Cinema," *Style* 9 (Fall 1975): 469-487; "*David Copperfield:* Novel and Films," *HSL* 9, 8 (1977): 1-16; "Dickens and Charles Mathews," *MSpr* 66, iii (1972): 235-242; "Dickens and the Rise of Dramatic Realism: The Problem of Social

Reform," *SJ* 21, i (1974): 66-82; "Feature Motion Pictures Adapted from Dickens: A Checklist," *DSN* 5 (Dec. 1974): 106-109, 6 (Mar. 1975): 9-13; "*Great Expectations:* Dickens and David Lean," *LFQ* 2 (Spring 1974): 154-161; "*Great Expectations:* Dickens's Style in Terms of Film," *HSL* 4, ii (1972): 104-113; "The Style of Dickens and Griffith: *A Tale of Two Cities* and *Orphans of the Storm.*" *Lang&S* 7 (Winter 1974): 53-61.—Note also "The Novels of Charles Dickens and the Modern Film: A Study in the Aesthetics of Visual Imagination," *DAI* 33 (Jan. 1973): 3682A (UCLA).—Rev.: *Cb* 15 (July-Aug. 1978): 699; also rev. in 981.]

2172 Zatonskii, D. "Tumany *Kholodnogo doma.*" *Iskusstvo romana i XX vek* (Moscow: Khudozhestvennaia Literatura, 1973), 174-185; et passim. [Esp. *BleakH, LittleDor.*]

2173 Zeiss, Cecilia. "Charles Dickens: *Oliver Twist.*" *Crux* 9 (May 1975): 31-35.

2174 —. "*Hard Times.*" *Crux* 7 (Nov. 1973): 19-23.

2175 Zentella Mayer, Arturo. "Carlos Dickens en México." In 813, pp. 161-182.

2176 Ziegler, Gilette. "Dickens et l'enfance malheureuse." In 743, pp. 77-80.

2177 Zubova, I. I. "Charl'z Dikkens: K 100-letiiu so dnia smerti." *Srednee spetsial'noe obrazovanie* (Moscow) 5 (1970): 49-51. [Centenary observance of D's death.]

2178 Zwerdling, Alex. "Esther Summerson Rehabilitated." *PMLA* 88 (May 1973): 429-439.

Unsigned, Special Events, etc.

2179 "Accessions to the Dickens House Museum." *Dkn* 70 (May 1974): 121-123.

2180 Alberta, University of, Dickens Conference, 1-2 Oct. 1970. [Papers incl. 26 (intro.), 440, 1263, 1353, 1651, 2081.—Reports: Norman Page, *Dkn* 67 (Jan. 1971): 43-44; Robert L. Patten, *DSN* 1 (Dec. 1970): 22-24.]

2181 Birbeck College, University of London,Discussion Meeting on Present and Future State of Dickens Studies, 6 June 1970. [Discussants incl. George Ford, Joseph Gold, Ian Milner, Sylvère Monod, Robert Patten, Angus Wilson.—Reports: M[ichael] S[later], *Dkn* 66 (Sept. 1970): 268-269; see also 1507.]

2182 Boulogne-sur-Mer Dickens Conference, 2-4 June 1978. [Reports: A[ndrew] S[anders], *Dkn* 74 (Sept. 1978): 188-190; Robert B. Sargent, *DSN* 9 (Sept. 1978): 86-88; Gérard Spiteri, *NL* 8 June 1978: 6.—See also Elizabeth Grice, *STimes* 14 May 1978: 37; *NL* 18 May 1978: 10.]

2183 Bridgeport, University of, Symposium on Victorian Literature and Culture, 3 Apr. 1976. [Report (incl. summary of E. D. H. Johnson's paper "Dickens and the Art of the Cinema"): David Paroissien, *DSN* 7 (June 1976): 59-60.]

2184 Broadstairs Dickens Festival. [Annual.—Report (sometimes incl. other minor festivals): J[ohn] G[reaves] et al., *Dkn* Sept. nos.]

2185 Camden Central Library Dickens Exhibition, June 1975. [Report: L[eslie] C. S[taples], *Dkn* 71 (Sept. 1975): 157-158.]

2186 *Catalogue of Autograph Manuscripts and Letters, Original Drawings and First Editions of Charles Dickens from the Collection of the Late Comte Alain de Suzannet. . .Which Will Be Sold by Auction by Sotheby & Co. . . .*, fwd. Michael Slater. [London: Sotheby, 1971.] 121 pp. [325 lots auctioned 22-23 Nov.—See also *BC* 21 (Spring 1972): 113-114; *TLS* 11 June 1971: 674; *TLS* 10 Dec. 1971: 1561.]

2187 *Charles Dickens: A Preliminary Catalogue of His Works and Books Relating to Him in the Rare Book Collection, Lockwood Memorial Library, State University of New York at Buffalo.* Buffalo: The Library, 1970. i, 26 pp.

2188 *Charles Dickens: An Exhibition to Commemorate the Centenary of His Death.* London: Victoria and Albert Museum, 1970. 121 pp. 60 pl. [Rev.: David Coombs, *Connoisseur* 175 (Sept. 1970): 75; Duane DeVries, *DSN* 1 (Sept. 1970): 12-16; William Gaunt, *Times* (London): 17 June 1970: 8; Richard A. Vogler, *DSN* 1 (Dec. 1970): 16-17; Mary Webster, *Pantheon* 28 (Nov.-Dec. 1970): 533; G. S. Whittet, *Art and Artists* 5 (Sept. 1970): 36; *BC* 19 (Winter 1970): 515; *TLS* 14 Aug. 1970: 906; also rev. in 1808, 1961.]

2189 *Charles Dickens, 1812-1870: A Centenary Book Exhibition.* London:

British Council, 1970. 18 pp.

2190 *Charles Dickens, 1812-1870: An Exhibition of His Works Held at the Wahlert Memorial Library, October 18 to November 20, 1970.* Dubuque, Iowa: Loras Coll., 1970. 15 pp.

2191 *Charles Dickens: 1812-1870: Exposition organisée par le British Council en commémoration du centième anniversaire de la mort de Dickens du 18 mars au 27 mars 1970.* Liège: Bibliothèque Générale de l'Université de Liège, 1970. 16 pp.

2192 *Charles Dickens: The J. F. Dexter Collection: Accessions to the General Catalogue of Printed Books, Manuscripts, Prints and Drawings.* London: British Museum Pubs. for the British Lib. Board, 1974. 120 cols. [Rev.: Philip Collins, *TLS* 5 Dec. 1975: 1464; Kathleen Tillotson, *Dkn* 72 (May 1976): 101-103.]

2193 Chelles Dickens Month, December 1974. [Report: S[ylvère] M[onod] , *Dkn* 71 (May 1975): 84.]

2194 Chugoku-Shikoku Branch of the English Literary Society, Dickens Centenary Symposium at Shikoku-Gakuin University, 23-24 Oct. 1970. [Report: [Michio Masui] , *HSELL*, 17, ii (1970): 50-51.— Note also 1292.—Abstrs. of papers read in 137, 934, 1044, 1045, 1094, 1289, 1346, 1436, 1944, 2019, 2166.]

2195 *Dickens,* [trans. from Italian] . Maidenhead: Low, 1977. [Orig. pub. Milan: Mondadori, 1968?—Rev.: Clive Porter, *Speech and Drama* 26 (Summer 1977): 36-37.]

2196 "Dickens and Doctors." *Med J of Australia* 57 (20 June 1970): 1235-1236.

2197 "Dickens and Others in New York." *TLS* 9 July 1970: 756. [Centennial events.]

2198 "Dickens at Sotheby's." *Dkn* 66 (Jan. 1970): 29; 67 (Jan., May, Sept. 1971): 20, 44, 90, 159; 68 (May 1972): 108; 69 (Jan. 1973): 46-47. [See also 1785 and 2233.]

2199 "Dickens 'Bores' Wykehamists." *Times* (London) 8 Nov. 1977: 2. [Winchester boys vote him most tedious author.—Note also ltrs. to ed. from A. W. Beer and Piers Jessop, 10 Nov., p. 17 and *Dkn* 74 (1978): 58.]

2200 "Dickens 1812-1870." *TLS* 4 June 1970: 597-598. [Rev.-art. incl.

448 (all essays), 592, 743, 1786, 2128.—Rpt. in *T. L. S.: Essays and Reviews from the Times Literary Supplement 1970* (London: Oxford Univ. Press, 1971), 1-7.]

2201 Dickens Fellowship, London. [Reports, notices, announcements, incl. news of Fellowship branches, obits., etc. regularly in *Dkn.*]

2202 "Dickens in Russia." *Sputnik* 12 (Dec. 1970): 142-143. [1838-1969.—Trans. from *Russkaya literatura.*]

2203 "Dickens in the Witness Box." *Dkn* 70 (May 1974): 103.

2204 "Dickens: New Words and Old Opinions." *TLS* 13 Nov. 1969: 1319. [Rev.-art. on 4, 591, 1356, 1810, 1930.—Note also ltrs. to ed. by Herbert van Thal, 20 Nov. 1969: 1339 and by Julian Symons, 27 Nov. 1969: 1363.]

2205 "The Dickens of a Year." *Ecn* 237 (21 Nov. 1970): xxi. [Rev.-art. on 509, 670, 1150, 1201, 1917.]

2206 "Dickens on Film." *Dkn* 66 (May 1970): 192. [Centenary program at National Film Theatre, London, 7 June-6 July 1970.]

2207 Cancelled.

2208 Dickens Society. [Reports of business meetings, notices of interest to members etc. regularly in *DSN.*]

2209 "Dickens Stamps." *Dkn* 66 (May, Sept. 1970): 193-194, 263. [Centenary commemorative issues 3 June 1970.]

2210 English Association Dickens Centenary Meeting, Southampton, 13 Mar. 1970. [Participants incl. Angus Easson, K. J. Fielding.—Report: *Dkn* 66 (May 1970): 188-189.]

2211 *A Guide to the Charles Dickens Birthplace Museum.* Portsmouth: City Museum and Art Gallery, 1970. 12 pp.

2212 Hansraj College (Delhi). "Dickens's Influence on Indian Novelists." *Times of India* 7 Feb. 1971: 3. [Report of centenary program incl. novelists Mulk Raj Anand, Nayantara Sehgal.]

2213 "In Search of a Lost Childhood: Scenes from Dickens's Kent." *CnL* 147 (25 June 1970): 1238-1240.

2214 *Katalog over Jacob Christensens Dickens-Samling.* Bergen: Universitetsbiblioteket, 1974. 25 pp.

2215 Knebworth House Bulwer Exhibition, Summer 1973. [Report: A[nthony] B[urton], *Dkn* 69 (Sept. 1973): 174-175.]

2216 "Last Days of a Centenary." *TLS* 25 Dec. 1970: 1521-1522. [Rev.-art. on 502, 509, 670, 884, 1150, 1201, 1365 (all essays), 1917, 2064.]

2217 Leicester University Conference on Dickens in His Time, 3-7 July 1970. [Participants incl. Asa Briggs, Philip Collins, K. J. Fielding, Michael Slater, Grahame Smith, Alexander Welsh.—Reports: Richard Allen, *VS* 14 (Mar. 1971): 339-340; Paul Schlicke, *DSN* 1 (Sept. 1970): 16-18; Patrick Scott, *Dkn* 66 (Sept. 1970): 240-241.]

2218 Liverpool Central Library Dickens Centenary Exhibition, opened 14 Jan. 1970. [Report: G. Chandler, *Dkn* 66 (May 1970): 187.]

2219 Liverpool University Dickens Centenary Lectures, Autumn 1969. [By Miriam Allott, Philip Collins, K. J. Fielding, Graham Storey, R. R. Wright.—Report: R. C. Barnes, *Dkn* 66 (1970): 189-190.]

2220 London University Dickens Centenary Lectures, Jan.-Mar. 1970. [By Isobel Armstrong, Gillian Beer, Geoffrey Best, Martin Dodsworth, Michael Slater, Katherine Worth, Alex Zwerdling.—Report: *Dkn* 66 (May 1970): 190.]

2221 "Magnificent Gift to the Dickens House." *Dkn* 67 (May 1971): 67-69. [Suzannet Coll.]

2222 Modern Language Association of America Annual Convention Meetings on Dickens.
   a. *1969.* "Dickens at Denver," *Dkn* 66 (May 1970): 187-188; "The Dickens Seminar 1969," *DSN* 1 (Mar. 1970): 4-5.
   b. *1970.* Jerome Meckier, "The Dickens Seminar at MLA," *DSN* 2 (Mar. 1971): 2-4; Lionel Stevenson, "Literary Forum II: 'Charles Dickens Now'," 2.
   c. *1971.* Deborah Allen Thomas, "MLA Seminar 71: *Dickens and the Romantic Tradition*," *DSN* 3 (Mar. 1972): 4-5.
   d. *1972.* David Paroissien, "MLA Seminar 44: *Dickens and Film: A Report*," *DSN* 4 (Mar. 1973): 7-9; Deborah Allen Thomas, "MLA Seminar 62: *Dickens and the Graphic Arts*," 5-7.
   e. *1973.* Katherine V. Pope, "MLA Seminar 73: Women in Dickens," *DSN* 4 (Mar. 1974): 4-7.
   f. *1974.* Deborah Thomas, "Two MLA Seminars: 'Carlyle Today'

and 'Dickens and Carlyle'," *DSN* 6 (Mar. 1975): 4-7.

g. *1975*. [See 451, 1247.]

h. *1976*. David Paroissien, "The Dickens Society Annual Meeting: Dickens and America," *DSN* 8 (Mar. 1977): 1-3; Deborah A. Thomas, "Special Session 92: A Computerized Concordance to Dickens," 4-6.

i. *1977*. Zelda Austen, "The Eighth Annual Dickens Society Meeting: Papers," *DSN* 9 (Mar. 1978): 2-4; Elliot D. Engel, "Special Session 333: Charles Dickens's Short Writings," 4-6.

j. *1978*. Robert McLean, "The Ninth Annual Dickens Society Meeting: Papers," *DSN* 10 (Mar. 1979): 1-3.

k. *1979*. David Paroissien, "The Tenth Annual Dickens Society Meeting: Papers," *DSN* 11 (Mar. 1980): 1-4.

2223 "The Mystery and its Manuscript." *TLS* 11 Aug. 1972: 946. [Rev.-art. on recent Clarendon Press and Penguin eds. of D's novels.—Incl. 19, 65, 70, 80.—See also ltrs. to ed. by Arnold Goldman and John S. Whitley, Stanley Bayliss, 18 Aug. 1972: 970; reviewer's reply, 25 Aug. 1972: 997; James Cochrane, Arnold Goldman, 15 Sept. 1972: 1060.]

2224 National Portrait Gallery, London, Dickens Centenary Lectures, Mar.-Apr. 1970. [By Philip Collins, F. R. Leavis, Gabriel Pearson, Graham Storey, J. C. Trewin.—Report: Barbara Lecker, *Dkn* 66 (May 1970): 191-192.]

2225 National Portrait Gallery, London, Maclise Exhibition, Mar.-Apr. 1972. [Report: A[nthony] B[urton], *Dkn* 68 (May 1972): 116-117.]

2226 "New News?" *Times* (London) 19 Mar. 1971: 20. [D as first editor of *Daily News,* 1846.]

2227 "Not the Last of Dickens." *Shavian* 4 (Spring 1971): 151-152. [Rev.-art on 448 (all essays), 884, 1150, 1786.]

2228 *Notes on Charles Dickens's Bleak House.* Study-Aid Ser. London: Methuen, 1975. 96 pp.

2229 *Notes on Charles Dickens's Hard Times.* Study Air Ser. London: Methuen Ed., 1970. 66 pp.

2230 "Our Australian Branches." *Dkn* 68 (May 1972): 136-138.

2231 "Our Mutual Friend Charles Dickens." *SovL* 272 (1970): 179-180. [Russian reception and infl.]

2232 Philadelphia Free Library Dickens Centenary Exhibition, 18 May-11 July 1970. [Report: *Dkn* 66 (May 1970): 193.]

2233 "Sales of Dickens Letters at Sotheby's." *Dkn* 66 (Sept. 1970): 236. [See also 1785 and 2198.]

2234 Sotheby's auction cat., 5-6 July 1977, lots 323 346. [Group of a.l.s. and memorabilia.]

2235 Southwark Dickens Festival, June-July 1971. [Announcement: *Dkn* 66 (Jan. 1970): 41; see also 70 (May 1974): 52.]

2236 Tokyo Branch, Dickens Fellowship, inaugural meeting, 22 Dec. 1970. [Report: Masaie Matsumura, *HSELL* 17, ii (1970): 79-80.]

2237 "The Topography of Dickens." *TLS* 4 June 1970: 618. [Rev.-art. on 6, 653, 690, 831, 879, 974.]

2238 Victorian and Albert Museum Cruikshank Exhibition, 28 Feb.-28 Apr. 1974, then at various sites. [Report: A[nthony] B[urton], *Dkn* 70 (May 1974): 124-126.]

2239 "The Year's Work in Dickens Studies. . . ." *Dkn* Sept. nos. 1971-1977, 1979. [Incl. 143; see also 1797.]

REPRINTS

Dickens's Works

Anthologies, Collections, etc.

2240 *Character Portraits from Dickens,* ed. Charles Welsh. 1908; rpt. New York: Haskell, 1972. 348 pp.

2241 *Charles Dickens,* ed. Richard Burton. 1919; rpt. Folcroft, Pa.: Folcroft Lib. Eds., 1978. 308 pp. [Selections from novels.]

2242 *Charles Dickens: The Writer and His Work,* ed. M. and P. Floyd. 1948; rpt. Plainview, N.Y.: Books for Libs. Press, 1975. 111 pp.

2243 *The Humour of Dickens,* comp. R. J. Cruikshank. 1952; rpt. Folcroft, Pa.: Folcroft Lib. Eds., 1975; Norwood, Pa.: Norwood Eds., 1978. xiv, 145 pp.

2244 *The Poems and Verses,* ed. F. A. Kitton. 1903; rpt. Boston: Milford, 1974. viii, 205 pp.

2245 *The Religious Sentiments of Charles Dickens,* comp. Charles H. McKenzie. 1884; rpt. New York: Haskell, 1973. 171 pp.

2246 *Wit and Wisdom from Dickens: A Treasury of Choice Passages,* comp. Adelaide Rawnsley Fossard. 1912; rpt. Folcroft, Pa.: Folcroft Lib. Eds., 1977. 248 pp.

Individual Titles

A Christmas Carol

2247 *A Christmas Carol,* pref. Henry Charles Dickens, fwd. Cedric C. Dickens, afwd. John Greaves, illus. Charles Wilton. 1965; rpt. London: Routledge and Kegan Paul, 1972. 64 pp. [Rpt. of D House ed.— Rev.: Angus Easson, *DSN* 4 (Sept. 1973): 68-71; *TLS* 15 Dec. 1972: 1525.]

2248 *A Christmas Carol,* illus. John Leech. 1843; rpt. Chicago: J. G. Ferguson, 1976. 166 pp. [Facs. of 1st ed.—See also 2256.]

2249 *A Christmas Carol,* illus. John Leech. [London: David Paradine, 1978.] 166 pp. [Facs. of 1st ed.]

2250 *A Christmas Carol: A Facsimile of the Manuscript in the Pierpont Morgan Library,* pref. Frederick B. Adams, Jr., intro. Monica Dickens, illus. John Leech. 1967; rpt. London: Folio Press, 1970; New York: Dover; London: Constable, 1971. xi, 142 pp. [Text from 1st ed. and facs. of ms on facing pp.; Dover and Constable title varies slightly.—Rev.: M[ichael] S[later], *Dkn* 67 (May 1971): 118.]

Martin Chuzzlewit

2251 *The Life and Adventures of Martin Chuzzlewit,* ed. P. N. Furbank, illus. Hablot K. Browne. 1968; rpt. Harmondsworth and Baltimore: Penguin, 1975. 941 pp. [Rev.: J. C. Field, *RLV* 37, ii (1971): 231-232.]

The Mystery of Edwin Drood

2252 *Dickens's Mystery of Edwin Drood,* completed by a Loyal Dickensian. 1925; rpt. New York: Haskell, 1976. 262 pp.

2253 *Mystery of Edwin Drood,* intro. C. Day-Lewis. 1956; rpt. London: Collins, 1970. 352 pp. [Rev.: C. H. Muller, *UES* 13 (June 1975): 42-44.]

Nicholas Nickleby

2254 *Nicholas Nickleby.* 1838-1839; rpt. Menston: Scolar Press, 1972-1973. [Facs. of orig. issue in parts.—See also 1780.—Rev.: Elizabeth M. Brennan, *Dkn* 69 (Sept. 1973): 187-189; Jerome Meckier, *DSN* 6 (Sept. 1975): 96-98; *BBkN* Sept. 1973: 616; *TLS* 22 June 1973: 723.]

2255 *Nicholas Nickleby at the Yorkshire School: A Reading.* 1861 or 1862; rpt. Ilkley, Yorks.: Ilkley Lib. Festival, 1973. 71 pp. [Facs. of unique reading copy, pp. 34-53 deleted.—Rev.: *TLS* 22 June 1973: 723; see also ltrs. to ed. from John Commander and Your Reviewer, 6 July 1973: 779.]

Oliver Twist

2256 *Oliver Twist; A Christmas Carol,* intro. (in Jap.) Masumi Yuki and Shigeru Koike. 1837-1839; 1843; rpt. Tokyo: Yushodo, 1977. [Facs. of orig. issues.]

The Pickwick Papers

2257 *Bardell v. Pickwick,* ed. Percy Fitzgerald. 1902; rpt. Folcroft, Pa.: Folcroft Lib. Eds., 1976. 116 pp.

2258 *The Posthumous Papers of the Pickwick Club,* illus. Robert Seymour and Hablot K. Browne. 1837; rpt. London: Nottingham Court Press in Assn. with Dickens Fellowship, 1979. xiv, 609 pp.

Letters

2259 *Charles Dickens and Maria Beadnell: Private Correspondence,* ed. George Pierce Baker. 1908; rpt. Folcroft, Pa.: Folcroft Lib. Eds., 1974; Philadelphia: R. West, 1977. xxx, 152 pp.

2260 *Charles Dickens as Editor: Being Letters Written by Him to William Henry Wills, His Sub-Editor,* ed. R. C. Lehmann. 1912; rpt. New York: Kraus, 1971; Haskell, 1972. xvi, 404 pp.

2261 *Dickens to His Oldest Friend: The Letters of a Lifetime from Charles Dickens to Thomas Beard,* ed. Walter Dexter. 1932; rpt. New York: Haskell, 1973. xiii, 295 pp.

2262 *The Earliest Letters of Charles Dickens (Written to His Friend Henry Kolle),* ed. Harry B. Smith. 1910; rpt. Folcroft, Pa.: Folcroft Lib. Eds., 1976; Norwood, Pa.: Norwood Eds., 1977. xi, 90 pp.

2263 *The Heart of Charles Dickens as Revealed in His Letters to Angela Burdett-Coutts,* ed. Edgar Johnson. 1952; rpt. Westport, Conn.: Greenwood Press, 1976. xiv, 415 pp.

2264 *Letters of Charles Dickens to Wilkie Collins 1851-1870,* sel. Georgina Hogarth, ed. Laurence Hutton. 1892; rpt. New York: Haskell, 1974. 171 pp.

2265 *The Love Romance of Charles Dickens Told in His Letters to Maria Beadnell (Mrs. Winter),* ed. Walter Dexter. 1936; rpt. New York: Kraus, 1971; Folcroft, Pa.: Folcroft Lib. Eds., 1974; Norwood,

Pa.: Norwood Eds., 1977. 125 pp.

2266 *Mr. and Mrs. Charles Dickens: His Letters to Her*, ed. Walter Dexter. 1934; rpt. New York: Haskell, 1972. xvii, 298 pp.

2267 *The Story of a Great Friendship: Charles Dickens and Clarkson Stanfield*, intro. Cumberland Clark. 1918; rpt. Folcroft, Pa.: Folcroft Lib. Eds., 1973; Norwood, Pa.: Norwood Eds., 1975; Philadelphia: R. West, 1977. 31 pp.

2268 *The Unpublished Letters of Charles Dickens to Mark Lemon*, ed. Walter Dexter. 1927; rpt. New York: Haskell, 1971; Folcroft, Pa.: Folcroft Lib. Eds., 1974; Norwood, Pa.: Norwood Eds., 1976; Philadelphia: R. West, 1977. vii, 164 pp.

Secondary Sources

2269 Adrian, Arthur A. *Georgina Hogarth and the Dickens Circle.* 1957; rpt. New York: Kraus, 1971. 320 pp.

2270 Allbut, Robert. *London Rambles "en zigzag," with Charles Dickens.* 1886(?); rpt. New York: Haskell, 1974. iv, 118 pp.

2271 —. *Rambles in Dickens's Land*, intro. Gerald Brenan, illus. Helen M. James. 1899; rpt. Brooklyn: Haskell, 1977. xxvii, 174 pp. [London.]

2272 Amerongen, J. B. van. *The Actor in Dickens: A Study of the Histrionic and Dramatic Elements in the Novelist's Life and Works.* 1926; rpt. New York: Haskell, 1970. ix, 301 pp.

2273 Andersen, Hans Christian. *The Fairy Tale of My Life: An Autobiography* (1871; rpt. London: Paddington Press; New York: Two Continents, 1975), passim.

2274 Barlow, George. *The Genius of Dickens.* 1909(?); rpt. New York: Haskell, 1975; Folcroft, Pa.: Folcroft Lib. Eds., 1976. 60 pp.

2275 Bloor, R. H. U. "The Victorian Novel: Thackeray and Dickens." *The English Novel from Chaucer to Galsworthy* (1935; rpt. Folcroft, Pa.: Folcroft Press, 1970), 199-219.

2276 Brewer, Luther A. *Leigh Hunt and Charles Dickens: The Skimpole Caricature.* 1930; rpt. Folcroft, Pa.: Folcroft Press, 1971; Folcroft, Pa.: Folcroft Lib. Eds., 1974; Norwood, Pa.: Norwood, 1976; Philadelphia: R. West, 1977. 35 pp.

2277 Brown, John Mason. "Mr. Dickens Reads Again." *As They Appeared* (1952; rpt. Westport, Conn.: Greenwood Press, 1971), 132-137. [Orig. in *SatR* 23 Feb. 1952 as rev. of Emlyn Williams's readings.]

2278 Browne, Edgar A. *Phiz and Dickens as They Appeared to Edgar Browne.* 1914; rpt. New York: Haskell, 1972. xiv, 320 pp.

2279 Chancellor, E. Beresford. "Charles Dickens—Novelist"; "The Pathos of Dickens (A Note)." *Literary Types* (1895; rpt. Port Washington, N. Y.: Kennikat Press, 1970), 140-163; 164-171.

2280 —. *Dickens and His Times.* 1932; rpt. Folcroft, Pa.: Folcroft Lib. Eds., 1976; Norwood, Pa.: Norwood Eds., 1977; Philadelphia: R. West, 1978. 160 pp.

2281 —. *The London of Charles Dickens: Being an Account of the Haunts of His Characters and the Topographical Setting of His Novels.* 1924; rpt. Folcroft, Pa.: Folcroft Lib. Eds., 1978. 317 pp.

2282 Chesterton, G. K. *Appreciations and Criticisms of the Works of Charles Dickens.* 1911; rpt. New York: Haskell, 1970; Folcroft, Pa.: Folcroft Lib. Eds., 1974; Norwood, Pa.: Norwood, 1977. xxx, 243 pp. [Excerpts rpt. in 23, pp. 988-992 and in 24, pp. 942-946.—See also 467.]

2283 —. *Charles Dickens.* 1906; rpt. London: Burns and Oates, 1975. xiv, 216 pp. [Portions on *PickP* and D and Christmas rpt. in 2331, pp. 109-121, 122-125 and, with diff. omissions, in 2064, pp. 244-250.—Excerpts also rpt. in 1458, p. 102 and in 384.—See also 467.—Rev.: Sylvère Monod, *Dkn* 72 (Jan. 1976): 42-43; Terence de Vere White, *Irish Times* 28 June 1975: 10.]

2284 —. "On Dickens and After." *Come to Think of It* (1931; rpt. Freeport, N.Y.: Books for Libs. Press, 1971), 250-260.

2285 Chevalley, Abel. "Dickens, Thackeray, and Their Contemporaries." *The Modern English Novel,* trans. Ben Ray Redman (1925; rpt. New York: Haskell, 1973), 30-38.

2286 Christie, O. F. *Dickens and His Age.* 1939; rpt. New York: Phaeton Press, 1974. 240 pp.

2287 Clare, Maurice. *A Day with Charles Dickens.* 1910(?); rpt. Folcroft,

Pa.: Folcroft Lib. Eds., 1977. 44 pp.

2288 Clark, Cumberland. *Charles Dickens and the Begging-Letter Writer, with Publication of Dickens's Original Letter.* 1923; rpt. New York: Haskell, 1972. 31 pp.

2289 —. *Charles Dickens and the Yorkshire Schools, with His Letter to Mrs. Hall.* 1918; rpt. Folcroft, Pa.: Folcroft Lib. Eds., 1975; Norwood, Pa.: Norwood Eds., 1975; Philadelphia: R. West, 1977. 33 pp.

2290 —. *Dickens's London.* 1923; rpt. New York: Haskell, 1973, Folcroft, Pa.: Folcroft Lib. Eds., 1974; Norwood, Pa.: Norwood Eds., 1977. 103 pp.

2291 —. *The Dogs in Dickens.* 1926; rpt. New York: Haskell, 1973. 63 pp.

2292 —. *Shakespeare and Dickens: A Lecture as Delivered to the Dickens Fellowship.* 1918; rpt. New York: Haskell, 1973. 39 pp.

2293 Crotch, W. Walter. *The Pageant of Dickens.* 1915; rpt. New York: Haskell, 1972. x, 261 pp.

2294 —. *The Secret of Dickens.* 1919; rpt. New York: Haskell, 1972. xv, 254 pp.

2295 —. *The Soul of Dickens.* 1916; rpt. New York: Haskell, 1974. xii, 227 pp.

2296 Dark, Sidney. *Charles Dickens.* 1919; rpt. Folcroft, Pa.: Folcroft Lib. Eds., 1973; New York: Haskell, 1975. 123 pp.

2297 Darton, F. J. Harvey, ed. *Vincent Crummles: His Theatre and His Times.* 1926; rpt. New York: Blom, 1972. lxx, 230 pp.

2298 Darwin, Bernard. *Dickens.* 1933; rpt. New York: Haskell, 1973. 134 pp.

2299 —, ed. *The Dickens Advertiser: A Collection of the Advertisements in the Original Parts of Novels by Charles Dickens.* 1930; rpt. New York: Haskell, 1971. vii, 208 pp.

2300 Davey, Samuel. "Charles Dickens." *Darwin, Carlyle, and Dickens* (1876; rpt. New York: Haskell, 1971), 121-156.

2301 Davis, George W. *The Posthumous Papers of the Pickwick Club:*

Some New Bibliographical Discoveries. 1928; rpt. Folcroft, Pa.: Folcroft Press, 1971; New York: Haskell, 1972; Folcroft, Pa.: Folcroft Lib. Eds., 1973; Norwood, Pa.: Norwood Eds., 1976; Philadelphia: R. West, 1977. 20 pp.

2302 Dexter, Walter. *Days in Dickensland.* 1933; rpt. New York: Haskell, 1972. xi, 256 pp.

2303 —. *Dickens: The Story of the Life of the World's Favourite Author.* 1937; rpt. Folcroft, Pa.: Folcroft Lib. Eds., 1977; Norwood, Pa.: Norwood Eds., 1978. 85 pp.

2304 —. *The Kent of Dickens.* 1924; rpt. New York: Haskell, 1972. 245 pp.

2305 —. *Mr. Pickwick's Pilgrimage.* 1926; rpt. New York: Haskell, 1972. xvi, 224 pp.

2306 — and J. W. T. Ley. *The Origin of Pickwick: New Facts now First Published in the Year of the Centenary.* 1936; rpt. Folcroft, Pa.: Folcroft Lib. Eds., 1974; Philadelphia: R. West, 1977. 158 pp.

2307 Dickens, Charles C. B. *A London Dictionary and Guide Book for 1879.* 1879; rpt. London: Howard Baker Press, 1972. 352 pp. [Rev.: J[ohn] G[reaves], *Dkn* 69 (Sept. 1973): 189-190.]

2308 —. *Reminiscences of My Father*, fwd. Mary Angela Dickens. 1934; rpt. New York: Haskell, 1972. 31 pp.

2309 Dickens, Henry F. *Memories of My Father.* 1928; rpt. New York: Haskell, 1972. 30 pp.

2310 Dickens, Mary. *Charles Dickens, by His Eldest Daughter.* 1889; rpt. Brooklyn: Haskell, 1977. 128 pp.

2311 —. *My Father as I Recall Him.* 1896; rpt. New York: Haskell, 1974. 128 pp.

2312 Dolby, George. *Charles Dickens as I Knew Him: The Story of the Reading Tours in Great Britain and America, 1866-1870.* 1885; rpt. New York: Haskell, 1970. xiii, 466 pp. [Portion on final farewell reading rpt. in 2064, pp. 218-220.]

2313 DuCann, Charles G. *The Love Lives of Charles Dickens.* 1961; rpt. Westport, Conn.: Greenwood Press, 1972. 288 pp.

2314 Eckel, John C. *The First Editions of the Writings of Charles Dickens and Their Values: A Bibliography.* 1913; rpt. Folcroft, Pa.: Folcroft Lib. Eds., 1973; Havertown, Pa.: R. West, 1976; Norwood, Pa.: Norwood Eds., 1976. xviii, 296 pp. [Note also *The First Editions of the Writings of Charles Dickens: Their Points and Values,* rev. and enl. ed. (1932; rpt. New York: Haskell, 1972), xvi, 272 pp.—Rev.: Edwin S. Gleaves, *ARBA* 5 (1974): 517-518.]

2315 Ellis, S. M. *William Harrison Ainsworth and His Friends* (1911; rpt. New York: Garland, 1979), passim.

2316 Elton, Oliver. "Charles Dickens, Wilkie Collins, Charles Reade." *A Survey of English Literature, 1830-1880* (1932; rpt. Folcroft, Pa.: Folcroft Lib. Eds., 1977; New York: AMS Press, 1978), II, 195-230.

2317 —. *Dickens and Thackeray.* 1924; rpt. Folcroft, Pa.: Folcroft Press, 1969; New York: Haskell, 1970; Folcroft, Pa.: Folcroft Lib. Eds., 1971; Norwood, Pa.: Norwood Eds., 1975; Philadelphia: R. West, 1976. vi, 96 pp. [Separate issue of chaps. from his *Survey of English Literature, 1830-1880,* 1920, with some additions.—Rev.: W. F. Axton, *DSN* 2 (Sept. 1971): 78-80.]

2318 Farr, Chester N., Jr. *Random Thoughts on Dickens.* 1931; rpt. Folcroft, Pa.: Folcroft Lib. Eds., 1977. 11 pp. [Speech at Philadelphia branch of D Fellowship.]

2319 Fields, James T. "Dickens." *Yesterdays with Authors* (1900; rpt. New York: AMS Press; St. Clair Shores, Mich.: Scholarly Press, 1970), 125-250.

2320 —. *In and Out of Doors with Charles Dickens.* 1876; rpt. New York: AMS Press, 1976. 170 pp.

2321 Figgis, Darrell. "Charles Dickens and the Novel." *Studies and Appreciations* (1912; rpt. [Norwood, Pa.]: Norwood Eds., 1977), 199-221.

2322 Fitzgerald, Percy. *Bozland: Dickens's Places and People.* 1895; rpt. Detroit: Gale, 1970; Ann Arbor; Gryphon, 1971. 254 pp. [Rev.: *Library* ser. 5, 29 (Mar. 1974): 123; also rev. in 1480, 2158.]

2323 —. *The History of Pickwick: An Account of Its Characters, Localities, Allusions, and Illustrations.* 1891; rpt. Folcroft, Pa.: Folcroft Lib. Eds., 1977. viii, 375 pp.

2324 —. *The Life of Charles Dickens as Revealed in His Writings.* 2 vols. 1905; rpt. New York: Haskell, 1973.

2325 —. *Memories of Charles Dickens, with an Account of Household Words and All the Year Round, and of the Contributors Thereto.* 1913; rpt. New York: B. Blom, 1971; New York: AMS, 1973. xiv, 383 pp.

2326 —. *The Pickwickian Dictionary and Cyclopaedia.* 1902; rpt. Folcroft, Pa.: Folcroft Lib. Eds., 1974; New York: AMS, 1975; Norwood, Pa.: Norwood Eds., 1976. viii, 359 pp.

2327 —. *Pickwickian Manners and Customs.* 1897; rpt. Folcroft, Pa.: Folcroft Lib. Eds., 1974; New York: Haskell, 1974; Norwood, Pa.: Norwood Eds., 1976; Philadelphia: R. West, 1978. 128 pp.

2328 —. *Pickwickian Studies.* 1899; rpt. Folcroft, Pa.: Folcroft Lib. Eds., 1977; Norwood, Pa.: Norwood Eds., 1978. 114 pp.

2329 Fitz-Gerald, S. J. Adair. *Dickens and the Drama: Being an Account of Charles Dickens's Connection with the Stage and the Stage's Connection with Him.* 1910; rpt. New York: Blom, 1971. xiii, 351 pp.

2330 Ford, George H. *Dickens and His Readers: Aspects of Novel Criticism since 1836.* 1955; rpt. New York: Gordian Press, 1974. xviii, 318 pp. [Excerpt on D and Kafka rpt. in 24, pp. 946-947.—Rev. in 133.]

2331 — and Lauriat Lane, Jr., eds. *The Dickens Critics.* 1961; rpt. Westport, Conn.: Greenwood Press, 1972. x, 417 pp. [For contents see this number in Appendix.]

2332 Forster, John. *Charles Dickens.* (?); rpt. Folcroft, Pa.: Folcroft Lib. Eds., 1977. 38 pp.

2333 Freymond, Roland. *Der Einfluss von Charles Dickens auf Gustav Freytag mit besonderer Berücksichtigung der Romane David Copperfield und Soll und Haben.* Prager deutsche St., 19. 1912; rpt. Hildesheim: Gerstenberg, 1973. xii, 98 pp.

2334 Fyfe, Thomas Alexander, comp. *Who's Who in Dickens: A Complete Dickens Repertory in Dickens's Own Words,* 2nd ed. 1913; rpt. Detroit: Gryphon, 1971; Folcroft, Pa.: Folcroft Lib. Eds., 1971; New York: Haskell, 1971; Norwood, Pa.: Norwood Eds., 1975; Philadelphia: R. West, 1977. 352 pp. [Rev.: *Reprint Bull* 19

(Spring 1974): 50.]

2335 Gissing, George. *Charles Dickens: A Critical Study.* 1898; rpt. St. Clair Shores, Mich.: Scholarly Press, 1972. 293 pp. [Chap. 4 rpt. in 2331, pp. 76-94, chap. 5 in 2064, pp. 222-239, excerpts in 23, pp. 987-988 and in 1458, p. 37.—Note also *Charles Dickens: A Critical Study* (1903; rpt. Folcroft, Pa.: Folcroft Lib. Eds.; London: Blackie; New York: Haskell, 1974), vi, 244 pp.]

2336 Green, Frank. *London Homes of Dickens.* 1928; rpt. Folcroft, Pa.: Folcroft Press, 1970. 32 pp.

2337 Grubb, Gerald Giles. "Dickens and the *Daily News:* The Origin of the Idea," in *Booker Memorial Studies: Eight Essays on Victorian Literature in Memory of John Manning Booker,* ed. Hill Shine (1950; rpt. Folcroft, Pa.: Folcroft Lib. Eds., 1978), 60-77.

2338 Gummer, Ellis N. *Dickens's Works in Germany, 1837-1937.* 1940; rpt. New York: Octagon Books, 1976. 200 pp.

2339 Hall, Hammond. *Mr. Pickwick's Kent: A Photographic Record of a Tour. . . .* 1899; rpt. Folcroft, Pa.: Folcroft Lib. Eds., 1974; Norwood, Pa.: Norwood Eds., 1975; Philadelphia: R. West, 1977. 92 pp.

2340 Hammond, R. A. *The Life and Writings of Charles Dickens: A Memorial Volume,* intro. Elihu Burritt. 1871; rpt. New York: Haskell, 1972. 426 pp.

2341 Hardy, Thomas John. "The Boyhood of Charles Dickens." *Books on the Shelf* (1934; rpt. Freeport, N.Y.: Books for Libs. Press, 1970), 86-107.

2342 Harrison, Michael. *Charles Dickens: A Sentimental Journey in Search of an Unvarnished Portrait.* 1953; rpt. New York: Haskell, 1976. 269 pp.

2343 Hatton, Thomas and Arthur H. Cleaver. *A Bibliography of the Periodical Works of Charles Dickens.* 1933; rpt. New York: Haskell, 1973. xix, 383 pp.

2344 Holdsworth, William Searle. *Charles Dickens as a Legal Historian.* 1928; rpt. New York: Haskell, 1972. 157 pp.

2345 Holland, Norman N. *The Dynamics of Literary Response* (1968; rpt. New York: Norton, 1975), passim.

2346 Horsman, Ernest Alan. *Dickens and the Structure of the Novel.* 1959; rpt. Folcroft, Pa.: Folcroft Press, 1970; Folcroft Lib. Eds., 1977; Norwood, Pa.: Norwood Eds., 1978. 11 pp.

2347 Hotten, J. C. *Charles Dickens: The Story of His Life.* 1870; rpt. Folcroft, Pa.: Folcroft Lib. Eds., 1978. 110 pp.

2348 House, Humphry. "Dickens." *All in Due Time: The Collected Essays and Broadcast Talks* (1955; rpt. Folcroft, Pa.: Folcroft Lib. Eds., 1978), 181-236. [Rpts. 5 book revs., arts., and talks.—"The Macabre Dickens" rpt. in 2064, pp. 351-357, in 2082, pp. 40-46, and in 2331, pp. 190-197.]

2349 Howe, M. A. DeWolfe. "With Dickens in America." *Memories of a Hostess: A Chronicle of Eminent Friendships Drawn Chiefly from the Diaries of Mrs. James T. Fields* (1922; rpt. New York: Arno Press, 1974), 135-195.

2350 Hughes, James L. *Dickens as an Educator.* 1902; rpt. New York: Haskell, 1971. xi, 319 pp.

2351 Jackson, Henry. *About Edwin Drood.* 1911; rpt. Folcroft, Pa.: Folcroft Lib. Eds., 1973; New York: Haskell, 1974; Norwood, Pa.: Norwood Eds., 1976; Philadelphia: R. West, 1977. ix, 90 pp.

2352 Jackson, T. A. *Charles Dickens: The Progress of a Radical.* 1937; rpt. New York: Haskell, 1971. x, 302 pp.

2353 Jaques, Edward T. *Charles Dickens in Chancery: His Proceedings in Respect of the Christmas Carol.* 1914; rpt. New York: Haskell, 1972. 95 pp.

2354 Kavanagh, Mary. *A New Solution of the Mystery of Edwin Drood.* 1919; rpt. Folcroft, Pa.: Folcroft Lib. Eds., 1973; Norwood, Pa.: Norwood Eds., 1976; Philadelphia: R. West, 1977. 82 pp.

2355 Keim, Albert and Louis Lumet. *Charles Dickens,* trans. Frederic Tabor Cooper. 1914; rpt. Folcroft, Pa.: Folcroft Lib. Eds., 1979. viii, 237 pp.

2356 Kent, Charles. *Charles Dickens as a Reader.* 1872; rpt. Farnborough: Gregg, 1971; New York: Haskell, 1973. xv, vii, 271 pp. [Gregg ed. incl. intro. Philip Collins.—Rev.: J[ohn] G[reaves], *Dkn* 68 (May 1972): 130-131.]

2357 Kent, William R. *London for Dickens Lovers.* 1935; rpt. New York:

Haskell, 1972. xi, 177 pp.

2358 Kingsmill, Hugh. *The Sentimental Journey: A Life of Charles Dickens.* 1935; rpt. Folcroft, Pa.: Folcroft Lib. Eds., 1978. 246 pp.

2359 Kitton, Frederic G. *Dickens and His Illustrators.* 1899; rpt. Amsterdam: Emmering, 1972; New York: AMS Press, 1973. xvi, 256 pp. [Rev.: A[nthony] B[urton], *Dkn* 68 (Sept. 1972): 196.]

2360 —. *The Dickens Country.* 1911; rpt. Folcroft, Pa.: Folcroft Lib. Eds., 1979. xiv, 235 pp.

2361 —. *Dickensiana: A Bibliography of the Literature Relating to Charles Dickens and His Writings.* 1886; rpt. New York: Haskell, 1971. xxxii, 510 pp.

2362 —. *The Minor Writings of Charles Dickens: A Bibliography and Sketch.* 1900; rpt. New York: Haskell, 1970; New York: AMS Press, 1975. xi, 260 pp. [Rev.: Joseph Gold, *DSN* 3 (Mar. 1972): 14-16.]

2363 —. *The Novels of Charles Dickens: A Bibliography and Sketch.* 1897; rpt. New York: AMS Press, 1975. ix, 245 pp.

2364 —. *"Phiz" (Hablot Knight Browne): A Memoir.* 1882; rpt. New York: Haskell, 1974. 32 pp.

2365 Lambert, Samuel W. *When Mr. Pickwick Went Fishing,* illus. Robert Seymour. 1924; rpt. New York: Haskell, 1974. 83 pp. [D-Seymour controversy.]

2366 Lang, Andrew. *The Puzzle of Dickens's Last Plot.* 1905; rpt. Folcroft, Pa.: Folcroft Lib. Eds., 1976; Norwood, Pa.: Norwood Eds., 1977. xii, 100 pp.

2367 Langton, Charles. *The Childhood and Youth of Charles Dickens.* 1891; rpt. New York: AMS Press, 1975. 260 pp.

2368 Leatham, James. *The Dual Purpose of the Dickens Novels: A Note on Style in General and the Style of Charles Dickens in Particular.* 1928; rpt. Folcroft, Pa.: Folcroft Lib. Eds., 1977. 24 pp.

2369 Ley, J. W. T. *The Dickens Circle: A Narrative of the Novelist's Friendships.* 1919; rpt. New York: Haskell, 1972. xix, 424 pp.

2370 Lightwood, James T. *Charles Dickens and Music.* 1912; rpt. New

York: Haskell, 1970. xiv, 177 pp. [Rev. in 1480.]

2371 Lindsay, Jack. *Charles Dickens.* 1950; rpt. New York: Kraus, 1970. 459 pp. [Concl. rpt. in 2331, pp. 233-243, excerpts in 23, pp. 992-995 and in 1458, pp. 158-159.]

2372 Lockwood, Frank. *The Law and Lawyers of Pickwick.* 1894; rpt. New York: Haskell, 1972. 108 pp.

2373 Lodge, David. "The Rhetoric of *Hard Times.*" *Language of Fiction: Essays in Criticism and Verbal Analysis of the English Novel* (1966; rpt. London etc.: Routledge and Kegan Paul, 1979), 144-163. [Rpt. in 1458, pp. 69-87.]

2374 Lupton, Edward Basil. *Dickens, the Immortal.* 1923; rpt. Folcroft, Pa.: Folcroft Lib. Eds., 1976; Norwood, Pa.: Norwood Eds., 1977. 117 pp.

2375 McCullough, Bruce. "Comedy of Character." *Representative English Novelists: Defoe to Conrad* (1946; rpt. Freeport, N.Y.: Books for Libs. Press, 1972), 131-151.

2376 McKenzie, Gordon. "Dickens and Daumier," in *Studies in the Comic.* Univ. of California Pubs. in Eng., 8, ii (1941; rpt. Darby, Pa.: Arden Lib., 1978), 273-298.

2377 McNulty, J. H. *Concerning Dickens and Other Literary Characters.* 1933; rpt. Folcroft, Pa.: Folcroft Lib. Eds., 1977. 111 pp.

2378 McSpadden, Joseph W. *Synopses of Dickens's Novels.* 1904; rpt. Folcroft, Pa.: Folcroft Lib. Eds., 1971; Norwood, Pa.: Norwood Eds., 1975; Philadelphia: R. West, 1978. xvi, 208 pp.

2379 Maly-Schlatter, Florence. *The Puritan Element in Victorian Fiction, with Special Reference to the Works of G. Eliot, Dickens and Thackeray.* 1940; rpt. Norwood, Pa.: Norwood Eds., 1975. 112 pp. [Zurich diss.]

2380 Marzials, Frank T. *Life of Charles Dickens.* 1887; rpt. Folcroft, Pa.: Folcroft Lib. Eds., 1973. xxxiii, 166 pp.

2381 Masson, Flora. "Mainly about Dickens and Thackeray." *Victorians All* (1931; rpt. Port Washington, N.Y., and London: Kennikat Press, 1970), 7-14.

2382 Matz, B. W. *The Inns & Taverns of Pickwick with Some Observations*

on Their Other Associations. 1922; rpt. New York: Haskell, 1973.
xii, 250 pp.

2383 Maugham, W. Somerset. "Charles Dickens and *David Copperfield.*"
*The Art of Fiction: An Introduction to Ten Novels and Their
Authors* (1955; rpt. New York: Arno Press, 1977), 135-161.

2384 Miller, J. Hillis. *Charles Dickens: The World of His Novels.* 1958;
rpt. Bloomington and London: Indiana UP, 1969. xvi, 346 pp.
[Excerpts rpt. in 23, pp. 995-1011, in 24, pp. 947-959, in 591,
pp. 157-191, in 2064, pp. 391-405, and in 2331, pp. 366-373.—
Rev.: Silvian Iosifescu, *Luceafarul* 26 (3 Oct. 1973): 41; Sylvère
Monod, *EA* 23 (Apr.-June 1970): 219.]

2385 —. *The Form of Victorian Fiction: Thackeray, Dickens, Trollope,
George Eliot, Meredith, and Hardy.* 1968; rpt. Cleveland: Arete
Press, 1979. xiii, 151 pp. [Esp. *OurMF.*—With additional pref. to
this ed.]

2386 Moreland, Arthur. *Dickens in London: Forty-Seven Drawings, with
Descriptive Notes,* intro. Frank S. Johnson. 1928; rpt. Folcroft,
Pa.: Folcroft Lib. Eds., 1974; Norwood, Pa.: Norwood Eds., 1978.
93 pp.

2387 —. *Dickens Landmarks in London,* fwd. Henry F. Dickens. 1931; rpt.
New York: Haskell, 1973. xiv, 82 pp.

2388 Murray, David Christie. "First the Critics, and then a Word on Dickens." *My Contemporaries in Fiction* (1897; rpt. Folcroft, Pa.: Folcroft Lib. Eds., 1973), 1-15.

2389 Neale, Charles M. *An Index to Pickwick.* 1897; rpt. Folcroft, Pa.:
Folcroft Lib. Eds., 1974; Norwood, Pa.: Norwood Eds., 1976;
Philadelphia: R. West, 1977. iv, 75 pp.

2390 Nicoll, William Robertson. *Dickens's Own Story: Side-Lights on His
Life and Personality.* 1923; rpt. Folcroft, Pa.: Folcroft Lib. Eds.,
1976. xii, 244 pp.

2391 —. *The Problem of Edwin Drood: A Study in the Methods of Dickens.*
1912; rpt. New York: Haskell, 1972. xviii, 212 pp.

2392 O'Faolain, Sean. "Dickens and Thackeray," in *The English Novelists:
A Survey of the Novel by Twenty Contemporary Novelists,* ed.
Derek Verschoyle (1936; rpt. Folcroft, Pa.: Folcroft Press, 1970),
149-159.

2393 Orwell, George. "Charles Dickens." *Dickens, Dali, and Others* (1946; rpt. New York: Harcourt Brace Jovanovich, 1970), 1-75. [Orig. in his *Inside the Whale,* 1940.—Partially rpt. in 205, pp. 96-100, in 2064, pp. 297-313 and in 2331, pp. 157-171.]

2394 Parrott, Thomas Marc and Robert Bernard Martin. "Dickens." *A Companion to Victorian Literature* (1955; rpt. Clifton, N. J.: Kelley, 1974), 178-185.

2395 Pemberton, T. Edgar. *Dickens's London.* 1876; rpt. New York: Haskell, 1972. 260 pp.

2396 Perkins, Frederic B. *Charles Dickens: A Sketch of His Life and Works.* 1870; rpt. Folcroft, Pa.: Folcroft Lib. Eds., 1973; New York: Haskell, 1973; Norwood, Pa.: Norwood Eds., 1976. 264 pp.

2397 Philip, Alex J. *Dickens's Honeymoon and Where He Spent It.* 1934; rpt. New York: Haskell, 1973; Norwood, Pa.: Norwood Eds., 1976. 47 pp.

2398 — and W. Laurence Gadd. *A Dickens Dictionary,* 2nd ed., rev. and enl. 1928; rpt. New York: B. Franklin, 1970. xxii, 375 pp.

2399 Phillips, Walter C. *Dickens, Reade, and Collins: Sensation Novelists.* Fiction of Popular Culture, 10. 1919; rpt. New York: Garland, 1979. ix, 230 pp.

2400 Pierce, Gilbert A. *The Dickens Dictionary: A Key to the Characters and Principal Incidents in the Tales of Charles Dickens.* 1872; rpt. New York: Haskell, 1972. xv, 573 pp. [Rev.: Kenyon C. Rosenberg, *ARBA* 5 (1974): 520.]

2401 Powys, John Cowper. "Dickens." *Visions and Revisions: A Book of Literary Devotions* (1915; rpt. Great Neck, N. Y.: Core Collection Books, 1978), 119-131.

2402 Priestley, J. B. *Charles Dickens and His World.* 1961; rpt. New York: Viking Press; London: Thames and Hudson, 1969; New York: Scribners; London: Thames and Hudson, 1978. 144 pp. [Orig. pub. as *Charles Dickens: A Pictorial Biography.*—Rev.: Sylvère Monod, *EA* 23 (Apr.-June 1970): 223.]

2403 —. "Dickens and Thackeray." *The English Novel* (1931; rpt. St. Clair Shores, Mich.: Scholarly Press, 1971; Folcroft, Pa.: Folcroft Lib. Eds., 1974), 56-77.

2404 —. "The Two Wellers"; "Dick Swiveller"; "Mr. Micawber." *The English Comic Characters* (1925; rpt. Staten Island: Phaeton, 1972), 198-223; 224-240; 241-276.

2405 Pugh, Edwin. *The Charles Dickens Originals.* 1912; rpt. New York: AMS Press, 1975. 346 pp.

2406 —. *Charles Dickens: The Apostle of the People.* 1908; rpt. New York: Haskell, 1971; New York: AMS Press, 1975. vi, 316 pp.

2407 Quirk, Randolph. *Charles Dickens and Appropriate Language.* 1959; rpt. Folcroft, Pa.: Folcroft Lib. Eds., 1974; Norwood, Pa.: Norwood Eds., 1976; Philadelphia: R. West, 1977. 26 pp. [Rpt. in part in 2064, pp. 409-422.—See also 1595.]

2408 Rantavaara, Irma. *Dickens in the Light of English Criticism.* 1944; rpt. Folcroft, Pa.: Folcroft Lib. Eds., 1971; Norwood, Pa.: Norwood Eds., 1976; Philadelphia: R. West, 1977. 240 pp.

2409 Reid, J. C. *The Hidden World of Charles Dickens.* 1962; rpt. Folcroft, Pa.: Folcroft Lib Eds., 1977. 47 pp.

2410 Rideal, Charles F. *Charles Dickens's Heroines and Womenfolk: Some Thoughts concerning Them,* 2nd. rev. ed. 1896; rpt. New York: Haskell, 1974. vi, 64 pp.

2411 Ritchie, Anne Thackeray. "Charles Dickens as I Remember Him." *From the Porch* (1913; rpt. Freeport, N.Y.: Books for Libs. Press, 1971), 31-45.

2412 Saintsbury, George. "Dickens"; "Dickens *(concluded).*" *Corrected Impressions: Essays on Victorian Writers* (1895; rpt. Freeport, N.Y.: Books for Libs. Press, 1972; Folcroft, Pa.: Folcroft Lib. Eds., 1974), 117-126; 127-137.

2413 —. *The English Novel* (1913; rpt. Folcroft, Pa.: Folcroft Lib. Eds., 1974), passim.

2414 Sala, George A. *Charles Dickens.* 1870; rpt. Farnborough: Gregg, 1970. x, 144 pp. [Rev. in 1480.]

2415 Saunders, Montagu. *The Mystery in the Drood Family.* 1914; rpt. Folcroft, Pa.: Folcroft Lib. Eds., 1974; New York: Haskell, 1974; Norwood, Pa.: Norwood Eds., 1978. xiii, 159 pp.

2416 S[awyer], C[harles] J. and F. J. H[arvey] D[arton]. *Dickens v.*

Barabbas, Forster Intervening. 1930; rpt. New York: Haskell, 1972; Folcroft, Pa.: Folcroft Lib. Eds., 1973; Philadelphia: R. West, 1977. 79 pp.

2417 Seale, Alfred A., comp. *List of Books, Prints, Autograph Letters and Memorials Exhibited at Dickens's Birthplace Museum.* 1923; rpt. Folcroft, Pa.: Folcroft Lib. Eds., 1975; Norwood, Pa.: Norwood Eds., 1975; Philadelphia: R. West, 1977. 71 pp.

2418 Shepherd, Richard Herne. *The Bibliography of Dickens: A Bibliographical List, Arranged in Chronological Order, of the Published Writings in Prose and Verse of Charles Dickens (from 1834 to 1880).* 1880; rpt. Folcroft, Pa.: Folcroft Press, 1970; Norwood, Pa.: Norwood Eds., 1976; Philadelphia: R. West, 1977. viii, 107 pp.

2419 Shore, W. Teignmouth. *Dickens.* 1904; rpt. Folcroft, Pa.: Folcroft Lib. Eds., 1977; Norwood, Pa.: Norwood Eds., 1978. 83 pp.

2420 Simons, J. B. *The Romance and Humanity of Charles Dickens.* 1956; rpt. Folcroft, Pa.: Folcroft Lib. Eds., 1972, 1977; Norwood, Pa.: Norwood Eds., 1978. 36 pp.

2421 Sitwell, Osbert. *Dickens.* 1932; rpt. Folcroft, Pa.: Folcroft Lib. Eds.; New York: Haskell, 1973; Philadelphia: R. West, 1977. 47 pp.

2422 —. "Dickens and the Modern Novel," in *Trio: Dissertations on Some Aspects of National Genius,* by Osbert, Edith and Sacheverell Sitwell (1938; rpt. Freeport, N.Y.: Books for Libs. Press, 1970), 3-45.

2423 Smith, Mabel S., ed. *Studies in Dickens.* 1910; rpt. New York: Haskell, 1972. 295 pp.

2424 Spring, Howard. "Dickens." *Book Parade* (1938; rpt. Port Washington, N.Y., and London: Kennikat Press, 1970), 47-50. [Orig. rev. of Stephen Leacock book in *Evening Standard* 7 Dec. 1933.]

2425 Stevens, James Stacy. *Quotations and References in Charles Dickens.* 1929; rpt. Folcroft, Pa.: Folcroft Lib. Eds., 1973; Norwood, Pa.: Norwood Eds., 1978. 102 pp.

2426 Stevenson, Lionel. *The English Novel: A Panorama* (1960; rpt. Westport, Conn.: Greenwood Press, 1978), passim.

2427 Stonehouse, John H. *Green Leaves: New Chapters in the Life of Charles Dickens.* 1931; rpt. New York: Haskell, 1973; Norwood,

Pa.: Norwood Eds., 1978. 123 pp.

2428 Storey, Gladys. *Dickens and Daughter.* 1939; rpt. New York: Haskell, 1971. 236 pp.

2429 Swinburne, Algernon. *Charles Dickens,* [ed. Theodore Watts-Dunton]. 1913; rpt. Folcroft, Pa.: Folcroft Lib. Eds., 1977. xx, 84 pp. [Excerpt rpt. in 2064, pp. 244-250.]

2430 Symons, Julian. *Charles Dickens.* 1951; rpt. New York: Haskell, 1974. 94 pp.

2431 Thomson, Patricia. *The Victorian Heroine: A Changing Ideal, 1837-1873* (1956; rpt. Westport, Conn.: Greenwood Press, 1978), passim.

2432 Thomson, W. R. *In Dickens Street.* 1912; rpt. Brooklyn: Haskell, 1977; Folcroft, Pa.: Folcroft Lib. Eds., 1978. vii, 193 pp.

2433 Trollope, Anthony. *An Autobiography,* intro. Bradford Booth (1947; rpt. Berkeley and Los Angeles: Univ. of California Press, 1979), passim. [Portion rpt. in 2331, pp. 74-76.]

2434 Walters, J. Cuming. *Clues to Dickens's Mystery of Edwin Drood.* 1905; rpt. New York: Haskell, 1970. 116 pp. [Rev. in 1480.]

2435 —. *The Complete Mystery of Edwin Drood by Charles Dickens: The History, Continuations, and Solutions (1870-1912).* 1912; rpt. Folcroft, Pa.: Folcroft Press, 1974; Norwood, Pa.: Norwood Eds., 1978. xxxiv, 267 pp.

2436 —. *Phases of Dickens: The Man, His Message, and His Mission.* 1911; rpt. New York: Haskell, 1971. xxiv, 288 pp.

2437 Watt, James Crabb. "Dickens." *Great Novelists: Scott, Thackeray, Dickens, Lytton* (1880; rpt. Folcroft, Pa.: Folcroft Press, 1974), 163-218.

2438 Whipple, Edwin Percy. *Charles Dickens, the Man and His Work,* intro. Arlo Bates. 2 vols. 1912; rpt. New York: AMS Press, 1975.

2439 Wilkins, William Glyde, ed. *Charles Dickens in America.* 1911; rpt. New York: Haskell, 1970. xii, 318 pp.

2440 Williams, Mary. *The Dickens Concordance.* 1907; rpt. Folcroft, Pa.: Folcroft Press; New York: Haskell, 1970; Folcroft, Pa.: Folcroft

Lib. Eds., 1974; Norwood, Pa.: Norwood Eds., 1978. 162 pp. [Rev.: Joseph Gold, *DSN* 3 (Mar. 1972): 14-16.]

2441 Williams, Orlo. *"Martin Chuzzlewit:* Studies in the Art of Fiction." *Some Great English Novels* (1926; rpt. St. Clair Shores, Mich.: Scholarly Press, 1970), 26-52.

2442 Wilson, Edmund. "Dickens: The Two Scrooges." *The Wound and the Bow,* [corr. ed.] (1965; rpt. New York: Farrar, 1978), 3-85. [1st ed. 1941; orig. in *New Republic,* 1940.]

2443 Wright, Thomas. *The Life of Charles Dickens.* 1935; rpt. Folcroft, Pa.: Folcroft Lib. Eds., 1973; Norwood, Pa.: Norwood Eds., 1978. 392 pp.

Unsigned

2444 *Bookman, February 1912; Dickens Centenary Number.* 1912; rpt. Folcroft, Pa.: Folcroft Lib. Eds., 1977; Norwood, Pa.: Norwood Eds., 1978. 35 pp.

2445 *Dickens Memento,* intro. Francis Phillimore. 1884; rpt. Folcroft, Pa.: Folcroft Lib. Eds., 1978. 11 pp. [Cat. of Christie's sale of D's art coll. 9 July 1870.]

2446 *A Pickwick Portrait Gallery.* 1936; rpt. Port Washington, N.Y., and London: Kennikat Press, 1970. 243 pp. [16 arts. by diverse hands on *PickP.*—Rev. in 1480.]

DOCTORAL DISSERTATIONS

See also 65, 115, 146, 229, 333, 362, 371, 643, 648, 770, 821, 845, 896, 1141, 1193, 1415, 1438, 1452, 1516, 1559, 1564, 1624, 1659, 1728, 1733, 1817, 1830, 1881, 2171, 2379, add13, add14.

2447 Adamowski, Thomas Henry. "The Dickens World and Yoknapatawpha County: A Study of Character and Society in Dickens and Faulkner." *DAI* 30 (Jan. 1970): 2995A-2996A (Indiana). [Incl. *BleakH, DSon, GreatEx, LittleDor, OCShop, OurMF.*]

2448 Aldemeyer, Barrett Albert. "The Pursuit of Happiness: A Study of the Celebrations in Selected Works of Dickens." *DAI* 36 (Sept. 1975): 1514A-1515A (Fordham). [*BarnR, CStories, LittleDor, OurMF, PickP, TaleTwoC.*]

2449 Allen, Richard Julian. "The Rise and Decline of Conscientious Realism in English Fiction: A Contextual Study of Novels by Charles Dickens and George Gissing." *DAI* 39 (Jan. 1979): 4263A (Indiana). [Esp. *LittleDor.*]

2450 Andrews, Malcolm Y. "The Composition and Design of *The Old Curiosity Shop:* A Study in the Working of Dickens's Imagination" (London, 1973).

2451 Arakawa, Steven Ryoichi. "The Relationship of Father and Daughter in the Novels of Charles Dickens." *DAI* 38 (Dec. 1977): 3507A-3508A (Yale). [*DSon, LittleDor, OCShop, OurMF.*]

2452 Armstrong, Nancy Bowes. "Character and Closure in Selected Nineteenth-Century Novels." *DAI* 38 (May 1978): 6736A (Wisconsin). [*GreatEx, HardT, OliverTw, OurMF.*—Method partly derived from Greimas.]

2453 Austen, Zelda. "Dickens's Ambivalence: The Two *Oliver Twists.*" *DAI* 33 (Nov. 1972): 2359A-2360A (SUNY, Stony Brook). [Crime.]

2454 Axelrod, Rise Borenstein. "The Urban Elegy: Dickens's *Our Mutual Friend* and Eliot's *The Waste Land.*" *DAI* 38 (Feb. 1978): 4799A

(UCLA).

2455 Bailey, William Knox, Jr. "Charles Dickens and the Grotesque: A Study of Five Novels." *DAI* 37 (Oct. 1976): 2191A (South Carolina). [*BarnR, GreatEx, MChuz, OurMF, TaleTwoC.*]

2456 Barickman, Richard Bruce. "Mind-Forg'd Manacles: Dickens's Late Heroes and Heroines." *DAI* 31 (Dec. 1970): 2903A (Yale).

2457 Barstow, Jane Missner. "Childhood Revisited and Revised: Perspective in the First Person Novels of Dickens, Grass and Proust." *DAI* 34 (Oct. 1973): 1848A (Michigan). [*DavidC, Blechtrommel, À la recherche du temps perdu.*]

2458 Bathurst, Robert Barrie. "Dickens's Liberal Russian Readers." *DAI* 38 (Mar. 1978): 5448A (Brown).

2459 Belden, Daniel Morgan, Jr. "The Hero as Failure in an Age of Hero Worship: Five Victorian Writers." *DAI* 35 (July 1974): 393A-394A (Michigan). [Esp. *GreatEx.*]

2460 Belmont, Anthony Michael, Jr. "An Analysis of the Structure of the Chapters and Serial Divisions of Charles Dickens's *Bleak House.*" *DAI* 40 (Sept. 1979): 1478A (Arkansas).

2461 Bengel, Jane Walters. "The Rhetoric of Characterization: A Study of Dickens's Mr. Dombey and Arthur Clennam." *DAI* 39 (Dec. 1978): 3591A (North Carolina, Greensboro).

2462 Bennett, Joseph T. "The Critical Reception of the English Novel, 1830-1880." *DAI* 30 (July 1969): 272A (New York). [Incl. *GreatEx.*]

2463 Bernard, Catherine Adelaide. "Dickens and Dreams: A Study of the Dream Theories and Dream Fiction of Charles Dickens." *DAI* 38 (Oct. 1977): 2134A (New York).

2464 Bernard, Stephen Joel. "The Fairy-Tale Imagination: A Study of Charles Dickens and William Makepeace Thackeray." *DAI* 35 (Aug. 1974): 1039A (New York).

2465 Berndt, David Edward. " 'This Hard, Real Life': Self and Society in Five Victorian Bildungsromane." *DAI* 33 (Apr. 1973): 5713A-5714A (Cornell). [Incl. *DavidC, GreatEx.*]

2466 Berrone, Louis C., Jr. "Faulkner's *Absalom, Absalom!* and Dickens:

A Study of Time and Change Correspondences." *DAI* 34 (Feb. 1974): 5158A (Fordham). [*BleakH, DSon, GreatEx.*]

2467 Bethke, Frederick John. "Elements of Autobiography in Six Continental Travelogues by Victorian Novelists." *DAI* 35 (Apr. 1975): 6702A-6703A (Columbia). [Incl. *PictIt.*]

2468 Bevan, Ernest Richard, Jr. "Pasts and Presents: The Uses of the Past in Nineteenth and Early-Twentieth Century British Fiction." *DAI* 37 (Jan. 1977): 4362A (Virginia). [Esp. *GreatEx, OCShop, OurMF.*]

2469 Beyer, Manfred. "Zufall und Fügung im Romanwerk von Charles Dickens: Ein Beitrag zu Dickens Realismus." *EASG* 1976: 88-90 (Düsseldorf). [Esp. *BleakH, GreatEx, OliverTw.*]

2470 Bishop, Charles Williams. "Fire and Fancy: Dickens's Theories of Fiction." *DAI* 31 (Apr. 1971): 5351A (Duke). [Esp. *BarnR, NichN, OCShop, OliverTw, PickP.*]

2471 Blasky, Andrew Henry. "Once a Month, All the Year Round: The English Serial Novel." *DAI* 39 (Aug. 1978): 890A (California).

2472 Bogaty, Lewis. "Dickens's America: A Study of the Backgrounds and of Dickens's Use of America in *American Notes* and *Martin Chuzzlewit.*" *DAI* 37 (Nov. 1976): 2887A (Ohio State).

2473 Boone, William Francis. "Into the Labyrinth: The Daydream Mode in Literature." *DAI* 32 (Mar. 1972): 5219A-5220A (SUNY, Buffalo). [Incl. *BleakH, DSon, MChuz, OCShop, OliverTw, OurMF, PickP.*]

2474 Breslow, Julian William. "*Sketches by Boz:* Dickens's First Formulation of the Problem of Communication." *DAI* 35 (Dec. 1974): 3726A (Johns Hopkins).

2475 Brind, Frederica Wolf. " 'Mind-Forg'd Manacles': Verbal Satire in *Bleak House, Little Dorrit* and *Our Mutual Friend.*" *DAI* 33 (Apr. 1973): 5671A (Bryn Mawr).

2476 Briner, Karl Dean. "The Symbolic Design of Charles Dickens's *Bleak House.*" *DAI* 34 (July 1973): 267A-268A (Nebraska).

2477 Brown, Earl Benedict, Jr. "The Rhetoric of Charles Dickens: A Study of *David Copperfield.*" *DAI* 32 (May 1972): 6367A-6368A (Emory).

2478 Brown, J. M. "A Sociological Analysis of the Novels of Charles Dickens" (London School of Economics, 1977).

2479 Brown, Robert Edwards. "Dickensian Allegory: The Dynamics of Abstraction." *DAI* 40 (Jan. 1980): 4049A (Iowa). [All the novels except *BarnR, DSon, MEDrood. PickP, TaleTwoC.*]

2480 Browne, Gerald Duane. "The Significance of Time in the Novels of Charles Dickens." *DAI* 31 (June 1971): 6541A-6542A (Wisconsin).

2481 Brueck, Katherine Trace. "Treatments of Poverty in Realistic Fiction." *DAI* 40 (Apr. 1980): 5431A (Illinois). [Incl. *OliverTw.*]

2482 Bühler, Hildegund. "Kombinierte Methoden der semantischen Strukturanalyse: Am Beispiel der Verben des Zustimmens bei Charles Dickens." *EASG* 1978: 18 (Vienna).

2483 Buitenhuis, Elspeth MacGregor. "Fractions of Man: Doubles in Victorian Fiction." *DAI* 32 (July 1971): 381A (McGill). [Incl. *TaleTwoC.*]

2484 Burgan, William Marcellus. "Dickens's Use of Setting in *Little Dorrit.*" *DAI* 31 (Aug. 1970): 752A (Princeton).

2485 Burt, Della Ann. "The Widening Arc and the Closed Circle: A Study of Problematic Novel Endings." *DAI* 40 (Jan. 1980): 4011A (Indiana). [Incl. *GreatEx.*]

2486 Burton, Carl Taylor. "The Hero as Detective." *DAI* 34 (Nov. 1973): 2549A (Columbia). [Incl. *BleakH,* "HDown," *LittleDor, MChuz, MEDrood, PickP.*]

2487 Buttram, Sara Mac. "A Content Analysis of Eight Major Literary Selections Studied by High School Students to Discover the Nature and Frequency of Biblical Allusion: With Implications for Teaching Literature." *DAI* 31 (Feb. 1971): 4113A (Auburn). [Incl. *GreatEx, TaleTwoC.*]

2488 Bystrom, Valerie Ann. "*Dombey and Son*: How to Read It." *DAI* 34 (Nov. 1973): 2612A (Washington).

2489 Cahill, Patricia Ann Ellen. "Beginning the World: Women and Society in the Novels of Dickens." *DAI* 39 (Sept. 1978): 1581A (Massachusetts). [*BleakH, DSon, HardT, LittleDor, OliverTw, OCShop.*]

2490 Carlisle, Janice Margaret. "The Moral Imagination: Dickens, Thackeray, and George Eliot." *DAI* 34 (Apr. 1974): 6630A (Cornell). [Incl. *CCarol, DSon, HardT, LittleDor.*]

2491 Carmichael, Thomas Arthur. "Self and Society: Marriage in the Novels of Charles Dickens." *DAI* 38 (Dec. 1977): 3511A-3512A (Illinois). [*DavidC, DSon, HardT, LittleDor.*]

2492 Carolan, Katherine Ashenburg. "A Study of Christmas in the Works of Charles Dickens, with Special Attention to the Christmas Books." *DAI* 33 (Oct. 1972): 1717A (Washington Univ.).

2493 Carr, Jean Ferguson. "Autobiographical Narration in Dickens and Trollope." *DAI* 40 (Apr. 1980): 5449A (Michigan). [Incl. *BleakH, DavidC, GreatEx.*]

2494 Casey, Ellen M. "Novels in Teaspoonfuls: Serial Novels in *All the Year Round*, 1859-1895." *DAI* 30 (Oct. 1969): 1521A (Wisconsin).

2495 Castronovo, David A. "Dickens and the Idea of the Gentleman." *DAI* 36 (Sept. 1975): 1518A-1519A (Columbia). [Incl. *GreatEx, LittleDor, MChuz, NichN, OliverTw, OurMF, PickP.*]

2496 Cheesewright, Gordon Paul. "Authority From Crisis: Patterns of Conversion in Five Major Victorians." *DAI* 33 (Feb. 1973): 4335A (UCLA). [Late novels.]

2497 Christie, James W. "Satiric and Sentimental Modes in Dickens's Later Novels: *Dombey and Son, Bleak House, Little Dorrit, Our Mutual Friend.*" *DAI* 35 (Feb. 1975): 5390A (Pennsylvania).

2498 Citino, David John. "From Pemberley to Eccles Street: Families and Heroes in the Fiction of Jane Austen, Charles Dickens, and James Joyce." *DAI* 35 (Aug. 1974): 1090A-1091A (Ohio State). [Esp. *DavidC, DSon.*—Method partly derived from Campbell and Laing.]

2499 Clayton, John Bunyan, IV. "Romanticism and the English Novel: Visionary Experience in Narrative." *DAI* 40 (Mar. 1980): 5063A (Virginia). [Incl. Wordsworth and *LittleDor.*]

2500 Clews, D. "The Dickens-Thackeray Debate" (Warwick, 1972-1973).

2501 Clift, Jean Dalby. "Little Nell and the Lost Feminine: An Archetypal Analysis of Some Projections in Victorian Culture." *DAI* 39 (Dec. 1978): 3593A-3594A (Denver).

2502 Cohan, Steven Michael. "Fiction and the Creation of Character." *DAI* 35 (Sept. 1974): 1616A-1617A (UCLA). [Incl. *OurMF.*]

2503 Collins, Angus Paul. "Three Apocalyptic Novels: *Our Mutual Friend, The Princess Casamassima, Tender is the Night.*" *DAI* 37 (Feb. 1977): 5109A (Indiana).

2504 Comer, Irene Forsyth, ed. "Little Nell and the Marchioness: Milestone in the Development of American Musical Comedy." *DAI* 40 (Sept. 1979): 1151A (Tufts). [Recently discovered mss of John Brougham musical, popular ca. 1867-1885, starring Lotta Crabtree.]

2505 Cordery, Gareth. "The Gothic and the Sentimental in Charles Dickens." *DAI* 36 (Apr. 1976): 6697A-6698A (Wisconsin). [*DSon, GreatEx, MChuz, MEDrood, OCShop, OliverTw.*]

2506 Cotsell, M. "A Commentary on Dickens's *Our Mutual Friend*" (Birmingham, 1976-1977).

2507 Cox, Don Richard. "The Beast Within: The Development of Dickens's Moral Vision." *DAI* 36 (Apr. 1976): 6698A (Missouri).

2508 Craig, David Martin. "A Study of Endings of Selected Nineteenth Century Novels." *DAI* 36 (Dec. 1975): 3675A (Notre Dame). [Incl. *BleakH.*]

2509 Crew, Erman Louie. "Dickens's Use of Language for Protest." *DAI* 32 (Aug. 1971): 913A-914A (Alabama).

2510 Daniels, Steven V. "The History of Mr. Pickwick: A Study in Artistic Development" (Harvard, 1971).

2511 David, Deirdre Ada. "Fictions of Resolution in Three Victorian Novels." *DAI* 41 (Aug. 1980): 678A (Columbia). [Incl. *OurMF.*]

2512 Davis, Robert Con. "Revenge against Time: The Father in Fiction." *DAI* 40 (Aug. 1979): 835A-836A (California, Davis). [Incl. *GreatEx, HardT.*]

2513 Davison, Ann. "Guilt in the Novels of Charles Dickens." *DAI* 40 (Nov. 1979): 2692A (New York).

2514 DeBacco, Ronald Eugene. "Dickens and the Mercantile Hero." *DAI* 41 (Sept. 1980): 1062A-1063A (Indiana of Pennsylvania). [*DavidC, DSon, GreatEx, HardT, LittleDor, MChuz, NichN,*

OurMF.]

2515 DeMille, Barbara Munn. "The Imperatives of the Imagination: Dickens, James, Conrad, and Wallace Stevens." *DAI* 39 (Mar. 1979): 5522A-5523A (SUNY, Buffalo). [*BleakH, DSon, GreatEx, HardT, LittleDor, OurMF, PickP.*]

2516 Den Hartog, P. D. "The Novels of Charles Dickens: Their Relation to Certain Aspects of Romanticism" (Leicester, 1975).

2517 Detter, Howard Montgomery. "The Female Sexual Outlaw in the Victorian Novel: A Study in the Conventions of Fiction." *DAI* 32 (Aug. 1971): 915A-916A (Indiana). [Incl. *DavidC, OliverTw.*]

2518 Diedrick, James Keith. "The 'Aspect of Destiny' in the Mid-Victorian Novel: A Study of Fictional Endings." *DAI* 39 (Nov. 1978): 2951A-2952A (Washington). [Incl. *BleakH, LittleDor.*]

2519 Dilnot, A. F. "The Relationship in Dickens's Fiction between a Character's Moral Status and the Way in Which He Earns His Living" (Oxford, 1973-1974).

2520 Dobrin, David Neil. " 'Veels vithin Veels': The Secret Self and the World in the Novels of Charles Dickens." *DAI* 38 (May 1978): 6740A (California, San Diego). [*DavidC, OliverTw, OurMF, PickP.*]

⅄ 2521 Duda, Eleanor Joan. "The Family in the Later Novels of Dickens." *DAI* 39 (Sept. 1978): 1584A-1585A (Toronto).

2522 Dunn, Albert Anthony. "The Articulation of Time in Dickens's Later Novels." *DAI* 33 (Jan. 1973): 3581A (Virginia).

2523 Durlin, William Kenneth. "The Apprenticeship Romance." *DAI* 38 (Sept. 1977): 1406A (Emory). [Incl. *GreatEx.*]

⅄2524 Durling, Linda Niemann. "Dickens's Family Romance: A Study of Identity in *David Copperfield* and *Great Expectations*" (California, 1975).

2525 Dvorak, Wilfred Paul. "Dickens and Money: *Our Mutual Friend* in the Context of Victorian Monetary Attitudes and *All the Year Round.*" *DAI* 33 (Feb. 1973): 4339A (Indiana).

2526 Ellis, Julie Wren Rothwell. "A Critical Analysis of Charles Dickens's *The Old Curiosity Shop.*" *DAI* 37 (July 1976): 329A (Ball State).

2527 Emery, Helen LaVerne. "The Interrelation of Literature and So-
ciology in the Explication of Three English Novels." *DAI* 34
(Apr. 1974): 6588A-6589A (Middle Tennessee State). [Incl.
BleakH.]

2528 Engel, Elliot David. "Comic Technique in Dickens: An Assessment
of the Early Fiction and Its Critics." *DAI* 36 (Dec. 1975): 3728A-
3729A (UCLA).

2529 Erskine, Jeffrey Paul. "Narrators, Novelists, and Readers: Studies in
the Rhetoric of the Nineteenth Century British First Person
Novel." *DAI* 40 (Dec. 1979): 3313A (Pennsylvania). [Incl.
GreatEx.]

2530 Fajans, Elizabeth. "Melodrama in Victorian Fiction: Studies in
Charles Dickens, Charlotte Brontë, George Eliot." *DAI* 40 (Jan.
1980): 4051A-4052A (Rutgers).

2531 Faville, John Nye. "The Rhetoric of Characterization in the Novels
of Charles Dickens, George Eliot, and Joseph Conrad" (California,
1973).

2532 Fenster, Alan Richard. "The Other Tradition: An Essay on Forms
of Realism in the Novel." *DAI* 38 (Aug. 1977): 802A-803A (California). [Incl. *OurMF, PickP.*]

2533 Fischer, David John. "John Harmon, the Emblematic Hero of *Our
Mutual Friend:* One Aspect of Characterization in Dickens's
Novels." *DAI* 34 (Oct. 1973): 1855A-1856A (Tulane).

2534 Fletcher, Robert Pearson. "The Convention of the Double-Self in
Nineteenth-Century English Fiction." *DAI* 37 (Oct. 1976): 2195A
(Delaware). [Incl. *BleakH, GreatEx, HMan, LittleDor, MChuz,
MEDrood, OliverTw, OurMF.*]

2535 Flower, Linda Stevenson. "Fantasy Perception and the Myth of Innocence in Dickens." *DAI* 34 (Dec. 1973): 3340A-3341A (Rutgers).
[*DavidC, DSon, GreatEx.*]

2536 Flower, Timothy Frank. "Charles Dickens and Gothic Fiction."
DAI 32 (June 1972): 6927A (Rutgers). [Esp. *GreatEx.*]

2537 Flynn, Thomas E. "Imaginative Conceptions of Evil in the Victorian
Novel, with Special Reference to Dickens, the Brontës, James,
Stevenson and Wilde" (London, 1972).

2538 Ford, Jane M. "The Father/Daughter/Suitor Triangle in Shakespeare, Dickens, James, Conrad, and Joyce." *DAI* 36 (Jan. 1976): 4507A (SUNY, Buffalo). [*BleakH, OurMF, PickP.*]

2539 Fortune, Ronald John. "Dialectical Characterization in Victorian Literature." *DAI* 39 (Aug. 1978): 895A-896A (Purdue). [Incl. *BleakH.*]

2540 Franklin, Stephen Lyle. "The Dilemma of Time: Time as a Shaping Force in the Writings of Carlyle, Arnold, Browning, Dickens, and Tennyson." *DAI* 34 (Mar. 1974): 5966A (Illinois). [Incl. *BleakH, GreatEx, MEDrood, OCShop.*]

2541 Freedman, Nadezhda. "Essays by Boz: The Eighteenth-Century Periodical Essay and Dickens's *Sketches by Boz.*" *DAI* 38 (July 1977): 277A (Columbia).

2542 Freeman, Ann. "A Comparative Study of Hans Christian Andersen and Charles Dickens: The Relationship between Spiritual and Material Value Systems as Defined by Their Treatment of the Child." *DAI* 41 (July 1980): 236A-237A (California).

2543 Freeman, Janet Helfrich. "Story, Teller, and Listener: A Study of Six Victorian Novels." *DAI* 36 (Feb. 1976): 5315A (Iowa). [Incl. *DavidC, GreatEx.*]

2544 Fulkerson, Richard Paul. "The Dickens Novel on the Victorian Stage." *DAI* 31 (Jan. 1970): 3502A (Ohio State).

2545 Gardner, Joseph Hogue. "Dickens in America: Mark Twain, Howells, James, and Norris." *DAI* 30 (Apr. 1970): 4409A-4410A (California). [Infl.]

2546 Garland, Barbara Carolyn. "Comic Form in Nineteenth Century English Fiction." *DAI* 33 (Feb. 1973): 4412A (Indiana). [Incl. *HardT, PickP.*]

2547 Genet, George Malcolm. "Charles Dickens and the Magazine World: The Periodical Author in the Eighteen Thirties." *DAI* 37 (July 1976): 330A (California). [Esp. *SBoz.*]

2548 Gibson, Katherine Measamer. "The Changing Function of the Characters' Memories in the Fiction of Charles Dickens." *DAI* 39 (Oct. 1978): 2288A-2289A (Drew). [Esp. *BleakH, DavidC, GreatEx, LittleDor, OurMF.*]

2549 Giddings, R. "Charles Dickens before 1850, with Especial Reference to the Child Figure in *Barnaby Rudge, The Old Curiosity Shop* and *Dombey and Son*" (Keele, 1974-1975).

2550 Gifford, James Allen. "Symbolic Settings in the Novels of Charles Dickens." *DAI* 38 (July 1977): 277A-278A (California, Riverside). [All novels except *DavidC, MChuz, MEDrood, NichN, PickP.*]

2551 Gilmour, Robin. "The House of Memory: A Study of the Relation between Retrospection and Contemporary Satire in the Evolution of Dickens's Later Novels, 1846-1865" (Edinburgh, 1969).

2552 Glancy, R. F. "Dickens and the Framed Tale" (Queen Mary, 1978).

2553 Goldfarb, William. "The Hoofs of the Scoundrels: Mr. Pickwick and the Law." *DAI* 35 (Mar. 1975): 6137A (Columbia).

2554 Goode, Alice. "Mothers and Daughters and the Novel." *DAI* 40 (Sept. 1979): 1447A (SUNY, Stony Brook). [Incl. *DSon.*]

2555 Gordon, Felicia Mary Morris. " 'The Wonderful Immensity': A Comparative Study of the City in Dickens and Balzac" (California, 1974).

2556 Green, Charlotte Krack. "The Great Exhibition of 1851 and the Mid-Century Works of Dickens, Kingsley, and Carlyle." *DAI* 39 (Apr. 1979): 6141A (Ohio State). [Incl. *BleakH, HsldWds.*]

2557 Griffin, Barbara Jean. "Naming as a Literary Device in the Novels of Charles Dickens." *DAI* 31 (Jan. 1971): 3504A (Indiana). [Esp. *BleakH, OurMF.*]

2558 Haberman, Melvyn. "Freedom and Form: A Study of the Law and the Laws of Society in *Pickwick Papers* and *Bleak House*." (Harvard, 1971).

2559 Hagwood, Thomas Richard. "Dickens and the Power of Goodness: The Portrayal of the 'Positively Good Man' in Dickens." *DAI* 36 (June 1976): 8073A-8074A (Iowa). [*DSon, GreatEx, PickP.*]

2560 Hale, Norman Leclair. "Views from Outside: Five Studies in Victorian Omniscience." *DAI* 37 (Dec. 1976): 3641A-3642A (Oregon). [Incl. *LittleDor.*]

2561 Hamilton, Robert Morse, Jr. "Uses of the Pastoral in Dickens and

Dostoevsky." *DAI* 37 (Dec. 1976): 3612A (Columbia). [*DavidC, GreatEx, LittleDor, MChuz, NichN, OCShop, OurMF, PickP.*]

2562 Hannaford, Richard Gordon. "Fairy Tale in the Early Novels of Charles Dickens." *DAI* 31 (Mar. 1971): 4771A-4772A (Indiana).

2563 Harlow, Nancy Rex. "Dickens's Cinematic Imagination." *DAI* 35 (May 1975): 7307A (Brown). [Incl. index of available data on 94 film adaptations.]

2564 Hass, Robert Louis. "Reason's Children: Economic Ideology and the Themes of Fiction, 1720-1880." *DAI* 36 (June 1976): 8033A-8034A (Stanford). [Incl. *HardT, OurMF.*]

2565 Hayes, Edward Daniel. "Two Satirists of the Apocalypse: A Comparative Study of the Grotesque Satire of Charles Dickens and Philippe-Auguste Villiers de l'Isle-Adam." *DAI* 32 (June 1972): 6977A (South Carolina).

2566 Hazen, Lynn Shuford. "Vessels of Salvation: Fathers and Daughters in Six Dickens Novels." *DAI* 39 (Sept. 1978): 1587A-1588A (Wisconsin). [*DSon, HardT, LittleDor, OCShop, OurMF, TaleTwoC.*]

2567 Heagney, Anice Julienne. "Structure and Characterization in Dickens's *Bleak House*." *DAI* 39 (Sept. 1978): 1588A (Boston College).

2568 Helfand, Michael Steven. "Liberalism and the Form of the Novel." *DAI* 31 (Mar. 1971): 4773A (Iowa). [Incl. *DavidC.*]

2569 Hemstedt, Geoffrey Colin. "Some Victorian Novels and Their Illustrations." *DAI* 35 (Dec. 1974): 3682A-3683A (Princeton). [Incl. *DavidC, OliverTw.*]

2570 Herbert, Christopher Clarke. "Dickens's House of Mirrors: Studies of Stylized Design in a Series of Novels." *DAI* 31 (Dec. 1970): 2918A (Yale). [*DavidC, LittleDor, MChuz, OCShop, PickP.*]

2571 Herzog, Tobey Church. "Dickens and Hardy: The Architectonics of Characterization." *DAI* 36 (Mar. 1976): 6114A (Purdue). [*BleakH, GreatEx, LittleDor, OliverTw, OurMF, PickP.*]

2572 Heung, Marina May-chun. "Strategies of Discontinuity: Balzac, Dickens, Sterne, Proust and the Realistic Novel." *DAI* 40 (Apr. 1980): 5429A-5430A (Northwestern). [Incl. *BleakH.*]

2573 Higbie, Robert Griggs. "Characterization in the English Novel: Richardson, Jane Austen, and Dickens." *DAI* 34 (Jan. 1974): 4263A-4264A (Indiana). [Incl. *OCShop.*]

2574 Hill, Nancy Klenk. "Visual Art in the Imagery of Charles Dickens." *DAI* 33 (Dec. 1972): 2936A (Northwestern). [*DSon, GreatEx, HardT, LittleDor, MEDrood, OCShop, OliverTw, PickP.*]

2575 Hirsch, Gordon Dan. "Hero and Villain in the Novels of Charles Dickens: A Psychoanalytic Study." *DAI* 32 (Feb. 1972): 4612A (California).

2576 Hodge, Jan Douglas. "The Gospel Influences on Dickens's Art." *DAI* 38 (Aug. 1977): 805A-806A (New Mexico). [*Chimes, CStories, DSon, HardT.*]

2577 Holoch, George Andrew, Jr. "Self and Society in Balzac and Dickens." *DAI* 35 (Dec. 1974): 3745A (Columbia). [Incl. *BleakH, DSon, LittleDor, OurMF.*]

2578 Horton, Susan R. "The Feeling of Meaning in the Novels of Dickens." *DAI* 33 (June 1973): 6872A (Brandeis).

2579 Hudson, Samuel, Jr. "Victims or Parasites?: Attitudes about the Poor in the Early Victorian Novel." *DAI* 33 (Nov. 1972): 2329A-2330A (Wayne State). [Incl. *BleakH, Chimes, HardT, LittleDor, OliverTw.*]

2580 Huff, Roland Kenneth. "The Dickensian Imagination: A Generative Analysis of the Evolution of the Canon." *DAI* 39 (May 1979): 6775A (Indiana).

2581 Hutter, Albert D. "From Autobiography to Style: A Psychoanalytic Study of Dickens's Autobiographical Novels, His Life, and Their Relationship to the Characteristic Themes and Style of His Fiction" (California, 1971).

2582 Ibe, Marcellinus Ukanwata. "The Educational Philosophy of Charles Dickens." *DAI* 37 (Jan. 1977): 4207A (Cincinnati). [*DavidC, GreatEx, HardT, NichN, OliverTw.*]

2583 Jablow, Betsy Lynn. "Illustrated Texts from Dickens to James." *DAI* 38 (June 1978): 7345A (Stanford). [Incl. *OliverTw.*]

2584 Jackson, R. "Dickens and the Gothic Tradition." *DAI* 40 (Autumn 1979): 15C (York). [Esp. late novels.]

2585 Jacobson, W. S. "A Commentary on Dickens's *The Mystery of Edwin Drood*" (Birmingham, 1975-1976).

2586 Jameson, Daphne A. "The Primary Narrators of Charles Dickens's Early Novels." *DAI* 40 (Feb. 1980): 4606A-4607A (Illinois).

2587 Janowitz, Katherine Eva. "Inviolable Goodness: The Idyllic Mode in the Novels of Charles Dickens." *DAI* 39 (May 1979): 6776A (Columbia). [*BarnR, GreatEx, MEDrood, NichN, OCShop, Oliver-Tw., PickP, SBoz.*]

2588 Johnson, Lyndon Eric. "The Status of a Fictive World with Examples from the Novels of Charles Dickens." *DAI* 38 (Dec. 1977): 3516A (Notre Dame).

2589 Jones, Elizabeth Falk. "Ends and Means of Fictions: *Hard Times* and *Mansfield Park*." *DAI* 39 (May 1979): 6776A-6777A (SUNY, Stony Brook).

2590 Kadragic, Alma. "Nature in the Novels of Charles Dickens." *DAI* 34 (May 1974): 7234A-7235A (CUNY).

2591 Kanner, Selma Barbara. "Victorian Institutional Patronage: Angela Burdett-Coutts, Charles Dickens and Urania Cottage, Reformatory for Women, 1846-1858." *DAI* 33 (Sept. 1972): 1114A (UCLA).

2592 Kauffman, Linda Sue. "Psychic Displacement and Adaptation in the Novels of Dickens and Faulkner." *DAI* 39 (Dec. 1978): 3573A-3574A (California, Santa Barbara). [Esp. *BleakH, LittleDor.*]

2593 Kaufman, Robert Frederick. "The Relationship between Illustration and Text in the Novels of Dickens, Thackeray, Trollope and Hardy." *DAI* 35 (Jan. 1975): 4433A-4434A (New York). [Incl. *BleakH, OliverTw, OurMF.*]

2594 Kelty, Jean McClure. "The Humanitarian Implications of Dickens's Creative Vision." *DAI* 31 (Dec. 1970): 2882A (Case Western Reserve).

2595 Kennedy, George Edward, II. "The Anatomy of Redemption: The Religious and Moral Implications of the Novels of Charles Dickens." *DAI* 37 (Mar. 1977): 5852A (New York).

2596 Kennedy, George William. "Domestic Ritual in the Novels of Charles Dickens." *DAI* 34 (Feb. 1974): 5107A (SUNY, Buffalo).

2596a Kennedy, V. J. "Language, Character and Society in Balzac and Dickens, with special Reference to *Le père Goriot, Oliver Twist, Illusions perdues,* and *Great Expectations*" (East Anglia, 1978).

2597 Kiernan, Gene Master. "Charles Dickens and His American Audience —1842: A Study in Ethos." *DAI* 32 (May 1972): 6588A (Ohio State).

2598 Kirschner, Ann Gail. "The Return to Paradise Hall: Orphans of Victorian Fiction." *DAI* 39 (Mar. 1979): 5487A (Princeton). [Incl. *BleakH.*]

2599 Klammer, Thomas P. "The Structure of Dialogue Paragraphs in Written English Dramatic and Narrative Discourse." *DAI* 32 (May 1972): 6405A-6406A (Michigan). [Incl. *GreatEx.*]

2600 Klotz, Kenneth. "Comedy and the Grotesque in Dickens and Dostoevsky." *DAI* 34 (Nov. 1973): 2631A (Yale). [Incl. *BleakH, OCShop, OliverTw.*]

2601 Knight, Harry Lionel. "Dickens and American Literature." *DAI* 33 (Feb. 1973): 4421A (Brown). [*AmerN, DavidC, GreatEx, MEDrood, OCShop.*]

2602 Knight, Theodore Olney. "The Novelist As Essayist: A Study of Narrative Voice and Strategy in Charles Dickens's *Sketches by Boz.*" *DAI* 36 (Sept. 1975): 1144A (SUNY, Buffalo).

2603 Koenig, Marie-Jeanette. "Charles Dickens: Artist of the Grotesque." *DAI* 38 (Oct. 1977): 2141A (SUNY, Binghampton). [*MChuz, OCShop, OurMF, PickP, SBoz.*]

2604 Krugman, Laura. "The Child in the Novels of Charles Dickens." *DAI* 32 (June 1972): 7001A (Yale). [Esp. *DavidC, GreatEx, OurMF.*]

2605 Kucich, John Richard. "Dickens and Excess." *DAI* 39 (March 1979): 5487A (SUNY, Buffalo). [*BleakH, GreatEx, OCShop, TaleTwoC.*]

2606 Kurata, Marilyn Jane. "The Eye Altering Alters All: Dickens and Hardy as Pre- and Post-Darwinian Writers." *DAI* 37 (Apr. 1977): 6500A (Wisconsin). [Incl. *GreatEx, LittleDor, OurMF.*]

2607 Kutzer, Marybeth Daphne. "Poor Jo: Middle-Class Ideas of Working-Class and Poor Children in England, 1837-1859." *DAI* 40 (Jan.

1980): 4054A (Indiana). [Incl. *OliverTw.*]

2608 Kylander, Ellen Childs. "The Fate of Dickens's *Edwin Drood:* A Century of Commentary and Criticism." *DAI* 38 (Apr. 1978): 6143A-6144A (Illinois).

2609 Lange, Bernd-Peter. "Das Problem der Charakterentwicklung in den Romanen von Charles Dickens." *EASG* 1969: 66-67 (Freie Univ. Berlin).

2610 Lankford, William T., III. "Prisoners and Children: Forms of Growth in Dickens's Novels." *DAI* 36 (Jan. 1976): 4512A-4513A (Emory). [*DavidC, GreatEx, OliverTw.*]

2611 Lapides, Robert D. "The Dialectics of Survival: A Typological Study of Dickens's Characters." *DAI* 32 (Apr. 1972): 5743A (New York).

2612 Larson, Janet Louise Karsten. "Designed to Tell: The Shape of Language in Dickens's *Little Dorrit.*" *DAI* 36 (Feb. 1976): 5320A (Northwestern).

2613 Lecker, Barbara G. "Dickens and Work" (London, 1973).

2614 Lehr, Dolores. "Charles Dickens and the Arts." *DAI* 39 (May 1979): 6778A (Temple). [*BleakH, GreatEx, LittleDor, MChuz, NichN, PictIt.*]

2615 Lesser, M. J. "Town and Townscape in Balzac's *Comédie humaine* and Dickens's Novels" (Manchester, 1973-1974).

2616 Levenson, Geraldine Bonnie. " 'That Reverend Vice': A Study of the Comic-Demonic Figure in English Drama and Fiction." *DAI* 38 (July 1977): 283A-284A (British Columbia). [Incl. *OCShop, OliverTw.*]

2617 Linehan, Thomas More. "Social Criticism and Fictional Form in Three Dickens Novels" (Chicago, 1974).

2618 Linfield, Nicholas Guys. "The Languages of Charles Dickens." *DAI* 30 (June 1970): 5449A-5450A (Texas). [*BleakH, DSon, MChuz, OurMF, SBoz.*]

2619 Loe, Thomas Benjamin. "The Gothic Strain in the Victorian Novel: Four Studies." *DAI* 35 (Oct. 1974): 2231A (Iowa). [Incl. *GreatEx.*]

2620 Lopez, Toni Ann. "The Victorian Novel: A Perceptual-Conceptual Compromise." *DAI* 38 (Nov. 1977): 2812A (Florida State). [Incl. *GreatEx, HardT.*—Method partly derived from Northrop.]

2621 Lovenheim, Barbara Irene. "The Apocalyptic Vision in Victorian Literature." *DAI* 31 (Feb. 1971): 4127A (Rochester). [Esp. *BleakH, OliverTw, TaleTwoC.*]

2622 Luhr, William George. "Victorian Novels on Film." *DAI* 39 (June 1979): 7358A (New York). [Incl. Cukor's 1935 *DavidC.*]

2623 Lukacher, Ned. "The Marginal Literary Machine: Texts and Contexts for a Revisionary Reading of the 19th Century." *DAI* 39 (Apr. 1979): 6121A-6122A (Duke). [Incl. narcissism, pantheism, metaphor of machine in *DSon.*]

2624 Lund, Michael Curtis. "Indifferent Monitors: Character and Narration in Thackeray and Dickens." *DAI* 34 (May 1974): 7195A-7196A (Emory). [Incl. *BleakH, DSon, GreatEx.*]

2625 Lundgren, Bruce Raymond. "Dickens and the Rhetoric of Romance." *DAI* 33 (Aug. 1972): 728A-729A (Western Ontario). [*DSon, GreatEx, HardT, MChuz, NichN, OCShop, OliverTw, OurMF, PickP.*]

2626 Maack, Annegret. "Der Raum im Spätwerk von Charles Dickens." *EASG* 1970: 69-71 (Marburg). [Rev. in 1961.]

2627 McClintick, Michael Lloyd. "The Comic Hero: A Study of the Mythopoeic Imagination in the Novel." *DAI* 35 (July 1974): 409A (Washington State). [Incl. *PickP.*]

2628 Macdonald, N. M. "The Presentation of Oppression in the English Novel from Godwin to Dickens" (Cambridge, 1977).

2629 McGowan, John Patrick. "Dickens's Comic Vision of History." *DAI* 39 (Sept. 1978): 1595A-1596A (SUNY, Buffalo).

2630 McGowan, M. T. "Pickwick and the Pirates: A Study of Some Early Imitations, Dramatisations and Plagiarisms of *Pickwick Papers*" (London, 1974-1976).

2631 McKee, Patricia. "The Disappearance of Desire: Studies of Six Novels of Dickens and Hardy." *DAI* 39 (Nov. 1978): 2956A (Brandeis). [Incl. *BleakH, LittleDor, OurMF.*]

2632 MacPike, Loralee. "The New Curiosity Shop: Dostoevsky's Dickens." *DAI* 37 (July 1976): 284A-285A (UCLA). [*Insulted and Injured.*]

2633 Maddox, James Hunt. "The Survival of Gothic Romance in the Nineteenth-Century Novel: A Study of Scott, Charlotte Brontë, and Dickens." *DAI* 32 (July 1971): 442A (Yale). [Incl. *BleakH, GreatEx.*]

2634 Madgwick, Gordon Alexander. "Charles Dickens—Gadfly for Educational Reform." *DAI* 31 (Apr. 1971): 5161A-5162A (Maryland).

2635 Magnet, Myron James. "Dickens and the Nature of Society: *Nicholas Nickleby* and *Barnaby Rudge.*" *DAI* 39 (Nov. 1977): 2813A (Columbia).

2636 Magnuson, Gordon Arnold. "Narrator Voice and Moral Vision in Six Novels of Charles Dickens." *DAI* 40 (Sept. 1979): 1483A-1484A (Arkansas). [*DSon, HardT, LittleDor, MChuz, OliverTw, OurMF.*]

2637 Marcus, David D. "The Theatre of the Mind: The Shifting Functions of Stylization in Dickens's Early and Middle Novels" (California, 1973).

2638 Margolin, Tamar Dvorkin. "Dickens and Mendele: A Study of Their Novel Openings." *DAI* 37 (Apr. 1977): 6465A-6466A (Cornell). [Incl. *BleakH, LittleDor, OurMF.*]

2639 Marlow, James Elliot. "A Rhetorical and Thematic Analysis of Charles Dickens's *Our Mutual Friend.*" *DAI* 33 (Apr. 1973): 5685A-5686A (California, Davis).

2640 Marsyla, Sandra Lee. "The Unheroic Hero: A Study of Mythical Echoes and Their Effect upon the Technically Ineffective Heroes of Charles Dickens's Fiction." *DAI* 33 (Jan. 1973): 3594A (Kent State).

2641 Marten, Harry Paul. "The Visual Imagination: A Study of the Artistic Relationship of Charles Dickens and William Hogarth." *DAI* 31 (May 1971): 6017A (California, Santa Barbara).

2642 Martin, Ernest Lowell. "The Maturity of Dickens's *Martin Chuzzlewit.*" *DAI* 38 (Sept. 1977): 1412A-1413A (Emory).

2643 Maxwell, Richard Collender. " 'Close and Blotted Texts': Dickens and the City as Language" (Chicago, 1976).

2644 Mengel, Nanette Vonnegut. "Coherence in Dickens's Novels: A Study of the Relationship between Form and Psychological Content in *Pickwick Papers, Martin Chuzzlewit* and *Our Mutual Friend*." *DAI* 35 (Dec. 1974): 3754A-3755A (California).

2645 Metz, Nancy Aycock. " 'To Understand Such Wretchedness': Dickens and Public Health." *DAI* 38 (Dec. 1977): 3486A-3487A (Michigan). [*BleakH, HsldWds, OurMF.*]

2646 Michasiw, Barbara Lorene. "The Heroines of Charles Dickens: Their Meaning and Function." *DAI* 37 (Apr. 1977): 6505A (Toronto). [*DSon, DavidC, BleakH, LittleDor, HardT, GreatEx, OurMF, MEDrood.*]

2647 Middlebro', Thomas Galbraith. "The Treatment of Industrialism in the Later Novels of Charles Dickens." *DAI* 34 (Aug. 1973): 735A-736A (McGill).

2648 Miller, Elliot Stuart. "The Victorian Domestic Realists." *DAI* 31 (Jan. 1971): 3557A (Ohio State).

2649 Miller, Michael G. "Dickens and the Law." *DAI* 36 (Apr. 1976): 6708A-6709A (Kentucky). [Esp. *DavidC, OurMF.*]

2650 Moranville, David Barry. "The Law and the Novel: Dickens's *Bleak House*." *DAI* 34 (Nov. 1973): 2643A (Kent State).

2651 Morgan, Mary Valentina. "The Shaping of Experience: A Study of Rhetorical Methods and Structure in Narrative Works by Chaucer, Fielding and Dickens." *DAI* 41 (Nov. 1980): 2126A (California, San Diego). [*BleakH.*]

2652 Morton, D. "A Study of the Anterior Character in the Works of Charles Dickens, George Eliot and Thomas Hardy" (Lancaster, 1977).

2653 Morton, Thomas Lionel. "Language and Reality in Dickens's Later Novels." *DAI* 38 (Mar. 1978): 5500A (Toronto).

2654 Moseley, Merritt Wayne, Jr. "Point of View in Dickens's 'Old Novels'." *DAI* 39 (May 1979): 6780A (North Carolina). [All except *DavidC, GreatEx.*]

2655 Mulderig, Gerald Patrick. "Studies in the Art of Nineteenth-Century English Biography." *DAI* 39 (Feb. 1979): 4960A-4961A (Ohio State). [Incl. Forster's *Life.*]

2656 Murphy, Mary Janice. "Dickens's 'Other Women': The Mature Women in His Novels." *DAI* 36 (Apr. 1976): 6709A-6710A (Louisville). [All except *BarnR, HardT, MEDrood, OliverTw, TaleTwoC.*]

2657 Murphy, Terry Wade. "Dostoevsky and Tolstoy on Dickens's Christianity." *DAI* 34 (Mar. 1974): 5922A-5923A (Kent State).

2658 Myers, Victoria Louise. "Humorous and Melodramatic Techniques of Characterization in the Novels of Dickens, Collins, and Reade." *DAI* 36 (Mar. 1976): 6087A-6088A (Illinois). [Incl. *BleakH, GreatEx, OutMF.*]

2659 Nash, Leslie Lee. "David Hero: Dickens's Portrait of the Artist." *DAI* 39 (Mar. 1979): 5529A-5530A (Ohio).

2660 Nebolsine, Arcadi. "Poshlost." *DAI* 33 (Nov. 1972): 2336A-2337A (Columbia). [Incl. *BleakH* and Dostoevski.—Method derived from Curtius, Spitzer, Auerbach.]

2661 Nelson, Carolyn Christensen. "Patterns in the Bildungsroman as Illustrated by Six English Novels from 1814 to 1860." *DAI* 33 (Jan. 1973): 3597A (Wisconsin). [Incl. *DavidC.*]

2662 Noffsinger, John William. "Character in Early Dickens." *DAI* 36 (Nov. 1975): 2852A (Virginia).

2663 Noonan, William Francis. "The Comic Artist in the Novels of Charles Dickens." *DAI* 35 (May 1975): 7263A (Ohio State).

2664 Nord, Thomas Edward. "Dickens's Memento Mori: *Our Mutual Friend.*" *DAI* 36 (Sept. 1975): 1531A-1532A (Wisconsin).

2665 North, Douglas McKay. "Inheritance in the Novels of Jane Austen, Charles Dickens, and George Eliot." *DAI* 31 (Apr. 1971): 5419A (Virginia). [Esp. *OurMF.*]

2666 Nunn, Robert Carl. "Remembering, Forgetting and Uncanny Repetition in *Dombey and Son, David Copperfield, Great Expectations* and *Our Mutual Friend.*" *DAI* 37 (Apr. 1977): 6506A (Toronto).

2667 O'Keefee, Anthony Joseph. "The Development of Formal Integrity in the Early Fiction of Charles Dickens." *DAI* 39 (Sept. 1978): 1598A (Pennsylvania).

2668 Okray, Peter Albert. "Charles Dickens: The Making of a Novelist."

DAI 32 (Dec. 1971): 3322A (Wisconsin). [Early Novels.]

2669 O'Mealy, Joseph Howard. "Charles Dickens's Sense of His Past." *DAI* 36 (Mar. 1976): 6118A (Stanford).

2670 Oppenlander, Ella Ann. "Dickens's *All the Year Round:* Descriptive Index and Contributor List." *DAI* 39 (May 1979): 6781A (Texas).

2671 Orsini, Daniel Joseph. "Balzac, Dickens, and the Ornament of Faith." *DAI* 35 (May 1975): 7264A-7265A (Brown). [Incl. *GreatEx, LittleDor.*]

2672 Osborne, Esther Euraleen. "Charles Dickens and the Middle Classes." *DAI* 31 (June 1971): 6563A-6564A (Howard). [*DSon, HardT, OurMF.*]

2673 Osborne, Marianne Muse. "The Hero and Heroine in the British Bildungsroman: *David Copperfield* and *A Portrait of the Artist as a Young Man, Jane Eyre* and *The Rainbow.*" *DAI* 32 (Jan. 1972): 4013A-4014A (Tulane).

2674 Owen, W. J. B. "A Study of Non-Standard English in Charles Dickens's *Martin Chuzzlewit*" (London, 1972-1973).

2675 Page, H. M. "The Critical Fortunes of *Little Dorrit*, 1855-1975" (Birkbeck, 1978).

2676 Palmer, William Joseph. "The Involved Self: Affirmation in Dickens's Novels." *DAI* 30 (June 1970): 5454A (Notre Dame).

2677 Parker, Sandra Ann. "Dickens and the Art of Characterization." *DAI* 30 (Mar. 1970): 3915A (Case Western Reserve).

2678 Parra, Nancy. "Dickens and His Heroines" (Chicago, 1973).

2679 Passow, Emilie Scherz. "Orphans and Aliens: Changing Images of Childhood in Works of Four Victorian Novelists." *DAI* 40 (Nov. 1979): 2698A (Columbia). [Incl. *DSon.*]

2680 Pearson, Ann Bowling. "Setting in the Works of Charles Dickens." *DAI* 32 (Dec. 1971): 3323A-3324A (Auburn).

2681 Perry, Donna Marie. "From Innocence through Experience: A Study of the Romantic Child in Five Nineteenth Century Novels." *DAI* 37 (Dec. 1976): 3599A (Marquette). [Incl. *GreatEx, DavidC.*]

2682 Petersen, Bruce Thorvald. "No Shadow of Another Parting: Dickens's Concept of the Family." *DAI* 41 (July 1980): 264A-265A (Indiana). [Esp. *BleakH, DavidC, DSon, GreatEx, LittleDor, PickP, TaleTwoC.*—Method partly derived from Erikson.]

2683 Petlewski, Paul John. "Order to Disorder: A Study of Four Novels by Charles Dickens." *DAI* 34 (May 1974): 7201A (Florida). [*HardT, MEDrood, OliverTw, TaleTwoC.*]

2684 Plourde, Ferdinand J., Jr. "Time Present and Time Past: Autobiography as a Narrative of Duration." *DAI* 30 (July 1969): 334A-335A (Minnesota). [Incl. *DavidC.*]

2685 Pope, Katherine Victoria. "Coversion as Theme, Style, and Purpose in *Martin Chuzzlewit*." *DAI* 32 (Oct. 1971): 2100A (Rice).

2686 Popowski, David J. "Preliminary Sketches: The Short Tale in Dickens and Thackeray." *DAI* 35 (Jan. 1975): 4450A-4451A (Bowling Green State).

2687 Power, Martin. "Dickens as City-Novelist: A Study of London in Dickens's Fiction." *DAI* 34 (June 1974): 7719A (McGill).

2688 Pratt, Branwen Elizabeth Bailey. "Dickens and Love: The Other as the Self in the Works of Charles Dickens." *DAI* 33 (Feb. 1973): 4430A (Stanford).

2689 Preston, Edward Arnold. "The Theme of Escape in the Novels of Charles Dickens." *DAI* 41 (Oct. 1980): 1616A (North Carolina).

2690 Putnam, Margaret Scobey. "The Primacy of the Past: *The Mill on the Floss, Great Expectations,* and *The Mayor of Casterbridge*." *DAI* 38 (June 1978): 7347A-7348A (Texas).

2691 Qualls, Barry Vinson. "Carlyle and Dickens: The Function of the Victorian Prophet." *DAI* 34 (Dec. 1973): 3354A (Northwestern). [*BleakH, LittleDor, GreatEx, OurMF.*]

2692 Quigley, Genevieve Lois Smith. "A Study of Dickens's Novels: Their Function as Models for the Apprentice Writer." *DAI* 32 (May 1972): 6447A-6448A (Michigan).

2693 Quinn, Martin Richard. "Dickens and Shaw: A Study of a Literary Relationship." *DAI* 35 (May 1975): 7323A (Pennsylvania State).

2694 Quirk, Eugene Francis. "Dickens's Men of Law: Dickens's Changing

Vision of English Legal Practice." *DAI* 34 (Aug. 1973): 738A (Illinois). [All novels except *BarnR, MChuz.*]

2695 Raina, Badri N. "Charles Dickens: The Dialect of Self." *DAI* 37 (Dec. 1976): 3648A (Wisconsin). [*DavidC, DSon, GreatEx, MChuz, OCShop, OliverTw, OurMF.*]

2696 Ray, Laura Krugman. "The Child in the Novels of Charles Dickens." *DAI* 32 (June 1972): 7001A (Yale).

2697 Rice, Thomas Jackson. "Charles Dickens as Historical Novelist: *Barnaby Rudge* (1841)." *DAI* 32 (May 1972): 6448A (Princeton).

2698 Rickert, Marilou. "The Fallen Woman in the Victorian Novel." *DAI* 40 (Feb. 1980): 4610A-4611A (Colorado). [Incl. *DavidC, DSon.*]

2699 Rignall, John M. "Balzac, Dickens and Keller: The 'Young Man from the Provinces' and the Bildungsroman: A Comparative Study of Vision and Technique" (Sussex, 1972).

2700 Roberts, Neil J. "Studies in the Social Criticism of Dickens and George Eliot" (Cambridge, 1973).

2701 Robison, Roselee Irene. "Innocence in the Novels of Charles Dickens." *DAI* 30 (Apr. 1970): 4424A-4425A (Toronto).

2702 Rodolff, R. C. "A Study of Four Victorian Novel-Endings: *David Copperfield, Villette, The Newcomes* and *The Mill on the Floss*" (London, 1975).

2703 Romanofsky, Barbara Ruth. "A Study of Child Rearing Practices in the Middle Novels of Charles Dickens." *DAI* 38 (Feb. 1978): 4853A (CUNY). [*DSon, DavidC, BleakH, HardT, LittleDor.*]

2704 Romig, Evelyn Matthews. "Women as Victims in the Novels of Charles Dickens and William Faulkner." *DAI* 39 (Sept. 1978): 1600A (Rice). [Incl. *BleakH, DavidC, GreatEx, LittleDor, OurMF.*]

2705 Ronald, Margaret Ann. "Function of Setting in the Novel: From Mrs. Radcliffe to Charles Dickens." *DAI* 31 (Apr. 1971): 5373A (Northwestern). [Incl. *BleakH.*]

2706 Roopnaraine, Rupert. "Reflexive Techniques in *The Pickwick Papers.*" *DAI* 33 (Oct. 1972): 1739A (Cornell).

2707 Rose, Phyllis D. "The Domestic Ideal in Dickens's Novels" (Harvard, 1970).

2708 Rosner, Mary Isobel. "Novel Beginnings: A Rhetorical Analysis of Overtures in Nineteenth-Century Fiction." *DAI* 39 (Aug. 1978): 903A (Ohio State). [Incl. *BleakH, MChuz.*]

2709 Rotkin, Charlotte. "Deception in Dickens's *Little Dorrit.*" *DAI* 41 (Oct. 1980): 1617A-1618A (Columbia).

2710 Roulet, Ann Edelen. "Dickens: The Controlling Voice of the Artist." *DAI* 32 (Dec. 1971): 3267A-3268A (Case Western Reserve). [*BleakH, DavidC, DSon, MChuz.*]

2711 Rubin, Stanley S. "The Crowd in Dickens: The Limits of Self Space, Consciousness, and Realism in the Novel" (Harvard, 1972).

2712 Sadoff, Dianne Fallon. "Waste and Transformation: A Psychoanalytic Study of Charles Dickens's *Bleak House* and *Our Mutual Friend.*" *DAI* 34 (Nov. 1973): 2653A-2654A (Rochester).

2713 Saks, Irene J. "Charles Dickens and the Self-Made Man." *DAI* 36 (Sept. 1975): 1535A (CUNY).

2714 Sanzenbacher, Richard C. "The Marvelous in Selected Novels of Charles Dickens." *DAI* 40 (July 1979): 277A (Bowling Green State). [*BleakH, GreatEx, OCShop, OliverTw.*]

2715 Sargent, Robert Bradford. "The Machinery of Justice in the Novels of Charles Dickens: Legal Process and the Counter Sytem of Natural Justice." *DAI* 33 (May 1973): 6325A (New York).

2716 Saunders, John Karen. "Charles Dickens: 'Sweet Day-Dreams and Visions of the Night'." *DAI* 38 (Dec. 1977): 3521A-3522A (SUNY, Stony Brook). [Early novels plus *BleakH, DSon, GreatEx.*]

2717 Savage, Robert Bartlit. "Artist-Audience Collaboration in Dickens's Serials." *DAI* 37 (Dec. 1976): 3650A (Ohio).

2718 Sawchuk, Mariette Timmins. "The Pilgrimage of Charles Dickens: A Study of Dickens's Evolving Vision of the Relationship between Conduct and Fate." *DAI* 35 (June 1975): 7878A-7879A (Stanford).

2719 Schachterle, Lance Edward. "Charles Dickens and the Techniques of the Serial Novel." *DAI* 31 (Apr. 1971): 5424A (Pennsylvania).

2720 Schäfer, Ursula. "Die Übertreibung als Strukturelement in den Romanen von Charles Dickens." *EASG* 1970: 66-67 (Tübingen). [Rev. in 1961.]

2721 Schlicke, Paul Van Waters. "Comic Characterization in Dickens's Early Fiction." *DAI* 32 (Apr. 1972): 5806A (California, San Diego).

2722 Schramm, David Eugene. "Theme and Action in the Novels of Charles Dickens: A Developmental Study." *DAI* 32 (Oct. 1971): 2103A (Washington Univ.). [All the novels except *MEDrood*.]

2723 Schreyer, Alice Altbach. "The Make-Believe of a Conclusion: Studies in Mid-Victorian Novel-Endings." *DAI* 37 (Jan. 1977): 4376A (Emory). [Incl. *GreatEx*.]

2724 Schuster, Charles Irwin. "Dickens and the Testimony of Appearances." *DAI* 38 (Oct. 1977): 2146A (Iowa). [*BarnR, BleakH, DSon, NichN, OurMF, PickP*.]

2725 Scott, Wayne Henry. "Shifting Masks and Multiple Plots: A Study of *Martin Chuzzlewit*." *DAI* 34 (July 1973): 286A-287A (Case Western Reserve).

2726 Scribner, Margo Parker. "The House of the Imagined Past: Hawthorne, Dickens, and James." *DAI* 41 (July 1980): 247A (Arizona). [Incl. *BleakH, GreatEx, LittleDor*.]

2727 Secor, Marie Jeanette. "Dickens's Rhetoric: A Study of Three Bildungsromans." *DAI* 31 (Mar. 1971): 4732A-4733A (Brown). [*DavidC, GreatEx, OliverTw*.]

2728 Seiple, Jo Ann Massie. "Charles Dickens and the Self-Denying Woman." *DAI* 40 (Jan. 1980): 4061A (East Texas State). [*BleakH, HardT, OurMF*.]

2729 Seiter, Richard David, ed. "Wilkie Collins as Writer for Charles Dickens's *Household Words* (1850-1859), and *All the Year Round* (1859-1870): A Selection of His Short Stories, Essays, and Sketches with Headnotes and Critical Introduction." *DAI* 31 (Oct. 1970): 1771A (Bowling Green State).

2730 Ser, Cary Douglas, ed. "*Sketches by Boz*: A Collated Text." *DAI* 40 (Jan. 1980): 4013A (Florida).

2731 Serlen, Ellen. "The Rage of Caliban: Realism and Romance in the Nineteenth-Century Novel." *DAI* 36 (Aug. 1975): 911A (SUNY, Stony Brook). [Incl. *BleakH.*]

2732 Shatto, S. "A Commentary on Dickens's *Bleak House*" (Birmingham, 1973-1974).

2733 Sheff, Pamela Haftel. "The Allegorical Vision: A Study of Charles Dickens's Later Novels as Allegories" (Harvard, 1975).

2734 Shelden, Michael Carl. "The Appointed Time: Dickens and the Free Trade Millennium." *DAI* 40 (Jan. 1980): 4062A (Indiana). [*BleakH, Chimes, HardT, LittleDor.*]

2735 Simpson, Joel Stewart. "Structural Innovation in *L'Éducation sentimentale* and *Middlemarch:* Their Quest Patterns and Background Strategies Compared to Those Used by Balzac and Dickens." *DAI* 38 (July 1977): 249A-250A (Brown). [Incl. *GreatEx, LittleDor.*]

2736 Sipe, Samuel M., Jr. "Manipulation and Creation in Dickens's Fiction." *DAI* 34 (Aug. 1973): 790A (SUNY, Buffalo). [Esp. *GreatEx, MChuz, OurMF.*]

2737 Skinner, J. L. "Changing Interpretations of Don Quixote from *Hudibras* to *Pickwick*" (Cambridge, 1972-1973).

2738 Skom, Edith Rosen. "Fitzjames Stephen and Charles Dickens: A Case Study in Anonymous Reviewing." *DAI* 39 (Apr. 1979): 6149A-6150A (Northwestern). [*LittleDor, TaleTwoC.*]

2739 Slater, Judith Fairbank. "The Development of Impressionistic Techniques in the Novels of Dickens." *DAI* 32 (July 1971): 400A-401A (Ohio State). [*BleakH, DavidC, GreatEx, HardT, OurMF, TaleTwoC.*]

2740 Smith, David Lee. "*Dombey and Son* and Dickens's Early Novels: A Study in Mixed Modes." *DAI* 36 (Dec. 1975): 3737A (North Carolina).

2741 Snyder, Philip Jay. "Stories and Storytellers in Dickens." *DAI* 41 (Nov. 1980): 2128A (Minnesota). [*BleakH, DavidC, GreatEx, OCShop, PickP.*]

2742 Sparbel, Mary Lou. "The Vanishing Garden: Dickens's Use of Pastoral in the Early Novels." *DAI* 35 (May 1975): 7270A (Illinois).

✓2743 Stark, Myra Carol. "The Home Department: The Uses of Children in the Novels of Charles Dickens." *DAI* 31 (May 1971): 6073A (New York).

2744 Stein, Sondra Gayle. "Woman and Her Master: The Feminine Ideal as Social Myth in the Novels of Charles Dickens, William Thackeray and Charlotte Brontë." *DAI* 37 (Feb. 1977): 5149A (Washington Univ.). [Incl. *DSon, HardT.*]

2745 Stern, Michael David. "The Sociological Imagination and the Form of Fiction: Social Structure in the Novels of Dickens, Trollope, and Eliot." *DAI* 38 (July 1977): 250A-251A (Yale). [Incl. *LittleDor.*]

2746 Stwertka, Eva Maria. "Created Images of Author and Reader in Seven English Novels from 1747 to 1953." *DAI* 36 (May 1976): 7446A-7447A (St. John's). [Incl. *OurMF.*]

2747 Swanson, Roger M. "Guilt in Selected Victorian Novels." *DAI* 30 (July 1969): 342A (Illinois). [Incl. *GreatEx.*]

2748 Tannacito, Dan John. "Transformal Structures: Studies of Anatomy-Romance and Novelistic Romance as Prose Fictional Genres." *DAI* 33 (Mar. 1973): 5144A (Oregon). [Incl. *OurMF.*]

2749 Tarantelli, Carole Beebe. "The Working Class in the 'Social Problem' Novel: 1830-1855." *DAI* 36 (Nov. 1975): 2857A-2858A (Brandeis). [Incl. *HardT.*]

2750 Thomas, Deborah Allen. "Fancy and Narrative Technique in Three Forms of the Short Fiction of Charles Dickens." *DAI* 33 (Nov. 1972): 2397A (Rochester).

2751 Thomas, Gillian M. "The Miser in Dickens's Novels and in Nineteenth Century Urban Folklore" (London, 1972).

2752 Thomas, Sr. Marilyn. "Church, City, and Labyrinth in Brontë, Dickens, Hardy, and Butor." *DAI* 39 (July 1978): 299A-300A (Minnesota). [Incl. *MEDrood.*]

2753 Thorn, Arline R. "The Waif as a Literary Type in the Nineteenth Century Novel." *DAI* 32 (Apr. 1972): 5753A (Illinois). [Incl. *DavidC, GreatEx.*]

2754 Thro, Arlin Brooker. "The Dickens Melodrama: Gentle Goodness and Passion in Dickens's Novels" (California, 1974).

2755 Thurin, Susan Molly Schoenbauer. "Marriageability: A Study of the Factors Entering the Marriage Choice in Eight English Novels." *DAI* 40 (Oct. 1979): 2080A (Wisconsin, Milwaukee). [Incl. *DavidC.*]

2756 Thyssel, Mary G. " 'This Attendant Atmosphere of Truth': Setting as Technique in the Novels of Dickens." *DAI* 33 (July 1972): 332A (Iowa). [Esp. *BleakH, DSon, GreatEx, LittleDor, OurMF.*]

2757 Timmerman, John Hager. "Feet of Clay: Concepts of Heroism in the Works of Carlyle, Dickens, Browning, Kierkegaard, and Nietzsche." *DAI* 34 (Mar. 1974): 5933A (Ohio). [Incl. *BleakH, DavidC, DSon, HardT, LittleDor.*]

2758 Ullman, Michael Alan. "Dickens's Haunted Heroes: A Study of the Emotional Lives of Major Characters in Seven of Dickens's Works." *DAI* 37 (Apr. 1977): 6517A-6518A (Michigan). [*BleakH, CCarol, DSon, "GS'sExpl," GreatEx, LittleDor, OurMF.*]

2759 Van Boheemen-Saaf, Christine. "The Mediating Function of Form: A Structural Study of *Tom Jones, Bleak House,* and *Ulysses.*" *DAI* 39 (Sept. 1978): 1526A-1527A (Rice).

2760 Van Hall, Sharon K. "The Foe in the Mirror: The Self-Destructive Characters in Charles Dickens's Novels." *DAI* 36 (Nov. 1975): 2860A (Illinois). [*DSon, HardT, LittleDor, MChuz, MEDrood, OliverTw, OurMF, TaleTwoC.*]

2761 Vaux, Sara Catherine Anson. "The Fool and the Two Kingdoms: Radical Revaluation in *King Lear, Little Dorrit,* and *The Brothers Karamazov.*" *DAI* 35 (Oct. 1974): 2245A (Rice).

2762 Vogler, Richard Allen. "Cruikshank and Dickens: A Review of the Role of Artist and Author." *DAI* 34 (Jan. 1974): 4221A (UCLA).

2763 Wadden, Anthony T. "The Novel as Psychic Drama: Studies of Scott, Dickens, Eliot, and James." *DAI* 31 (Mar. 1971): 4737A (Iowa). [Incl. *GreatEx.*—Method partly derived from Jung.]

2764 Wallins, Roger Peyton. "The Emerging Victorian Social Conscience." *DAI* 33 (Oct. 1972): 1699A (Ohio State).

2765 Walsky, Joan Ross. "Thespians and Theater: Performance in the Novels of Charles Dickens." *DAI* 33 (Oct. 1972): 1747A (Rutgers). [*BleakH, DSon, GreatEx, HardT, LittleDor, OliverTw.*]

2766 Watson, J. L. "The Development of Figurative Methods in the Language of Charles Dickens" (Otago, N.Z., 1973).

2767 Weiser, Irwin Howard. "Alternatives to the Myth of the Family: A Study of Parent-Child Relationships in Selected Nineteenth-Century English Novels." *DAI* 37 (May 1977): 7147A-7148A (Indiana). [*BleakH, DavidC, GreatEx, LittleDor, OliverTw, OurMF.*]

2768 Whitlock, Roger Dennis. "Charles Dickens and George Eliot: Moral Art in the 'Age of Equipoise'." *DAI* 35 (July 1974): 484A (Washington). [Incl. *GreatEx, HardT, OurMF.*]

2769 Whittington, Norma Jackson. "Journeys and Journeying in Dickens." *DAI* 31 (Feb. 1971): 4138A (Southern Mississippi).

2770 Wild, David W. "The Emergence of Literacy: 1780-1860." *DAI* 33 (Nov. 1972): 2349A (Washington). [Esp. *GreatEx, PickP.*]

2771 Wilkins, Michael K. "The Development of Dickens's Treatment of High Society, with Special Reference ot the Period 1833-1852" (London, 1970).

2772 Williams, Kristi Fayle. "The Idealized Heroine in Victorian Fiction." *DAI* 37 (July 1976): 346A (Brown). [*DavidC, LittleDor, OCShop, OurMF.*]

2773 Winslow, Joan Dorothy Salo. "Dickens's Sentimental Plot: A Formal Analysis of Three Novels." *DAI* 35 (Nov. 1974): 3017A-3018A (California). [*LittleDor, OCShop, OliverTw.*]

2774 Wolfe, Charles Keith. "Charles Dickens and the 'Theatrum Mundi'." *DAI* 31 (May 1971): 6076A-6077A (Kansas). [Esp. early novels.]

2775 Yelin, Louise. "Women, Money, and Language: *Dombey and Son* and the 1840s." *DAI* 38 (July 1977): 293A (Columbia).

2776 Zasadinski, Eugene Henry. "The Social and the Private: Conflicting Worlds in *Pickwick Papers*." *DAI* 40 (Nov. 1979): 2671A-2672A (St. John's).

MISCELLANEOUS

I. Educational and Audio-Visual Aids

See also "Fellowship News and Notes" regularly in *Dkn*. Films are 16mm sound unless otherwise noted.

I.a. Life, Collections, etc.

2777 *The Changing World of Charles Dickens,* dir. John Irvin. Learning Corp. of America. Film (28 min). [Dramatized episodes from novels for ages 9-14.—Note also 2778.—Rev.: *Booklist* 67 (15 Mar. 1971): 591.]

2778 *The Changing World of Charles Dickens.* Learning Corp. of America. 2 filmstrips (291 fr), 2 cassettes (21 min), guide. [Gr. 9-coll.— Based on 2777.—Rev.: Gloria K. Barber, *Previews* 5 (Nov. 1976): 31.]

2779 *Charles Dickens.* Great Writing through the Ages Ser. Learning Corp. of America. Film (30 min).

2780 *Charles Dickens: An Introduction to His Life and Work.* Seabourne Enterprises and Charles Dickens Fellowship. Film or videocassette (27 min). [Based on 2905.—Rev.: *Landers Film Revs* 24 (Nov.- Dec. 1979): 61-62.]

2781 *Charles Dickens: His World, His People,* by Stella Mary Newton. Visual Pubs. 2 filmstrips (72 fr). [Rev.: *Booklist* 68 (1 May 1972): 763-764.]

2782 *Dickens: Victorian England.* Novelists and their Times Ser. Teaching Resources Films. Filmstrip (75 fr) with record or cassette (18 min). [Gr. 7-12.—Rev.: D. R. Bernstein, *Previews* 5 (Apr. 1977): 22.]

2783 *Illustrations to the Novels of Charles Dickens,* notes Michael Brooks. Bucdek Films. 22 slides. [See *Victorian St Bull* 1 (Sept. 1977): 1.]

2784 *The Life and Works of Charles Dickens.* [London: Sunday Times, 1970.] 30x40" color wallchart. [Rev.: M[ichael] S[later], *Dkn* 66 (Sept. 1970): 224.]

2785 *Teaching Aids for Forty Enriched Classics,* ed. Harry Shefter. New York: Washington Square Press, 1975. [Objective tests, questions, vocab. st.—Incl. *GreatEx, OliverTw, TaleTwoC.*]

I.b. Individual Titles

A Christmas Carol

2786 *A Christmas Carol.* Brunswick Prods. Filmstrip (55 fr).

2787 *A Christmas Carol.* Encyclopaedia Britannica Ed. Corp. Filmstrip (64 fr), cassette (14 min), guide.

2788 *A Christmas Carol.* Listening Lib. 2 filmstrips (150 fr), 2 cassettes (48 min), guide. [Rev.: Marilyn W. Greenberg, *Previews* 7 (Feb. 1979): 22-23; B[eth] A[mes] H[erbert], *Booklist* 74 (1 July 1978): 1687.]

2789 *A Christmas Carol.* Pendulum Press. Cassette with activity book, answer key, book (illus. cartoon version), poster.

2790 *A Christmas Carol.* Teaching Resources Films. 4 filmstrips (181 fr) with 2 records or cassettes (60 min), guide. [Gr. K-3.—Rev.: Janet G. Conover, *Previews* 4 (Nov. 1975): 23.]

2791 *A Christmas Carol.* United Prods. 4 filmstrips (512 fr), 2 records (47 min).

David Copperfield

2792 *David Copperfield.* Brunswick Prods. Filmstrip (55 fr).

Great Expectations

2793 *Great Expectations.* Listening Lib. 3 filmstrips (208 fr), 3 cassettes (75 min), guide. [Rev.: Margaret F. Coughlin, *Previews* 8 (May 1980): 34; E[llen] M[andel], *Booklist* 76 (1 June 1980): 1431.]

2794 *Great Expectations.* Films, Inc. 2 filmstrips (208 fr), 2 cassettes

(42 min), guide. [From David Lean's 1946 film.—Rev.: Brenda G. Epperson, *Previews* 7 (Mar. 1979): 22, E[llen] M[andel] , *Booklist* 76 (1 Sept. 1979): 53.]

2795 *Great Expectations.* Popular Science Audio-Visuals. Filmstrip (43 fr).

2796 *Scenes from Great Expectations.* Encyclopaedia Britannica Ed. Corp. Filmstrip (79 fr), cassette or record (20 min), guide. [Rev.: B[eth] A[mes] H[erbert] , *Booklist* 73 (1 June 1977): 1509.]

"A Holiday Romance"

2797 *Magic Fishbone.* Listening Lib. Filmstrip (66 fr), cassette (15 min), guide. [Gr. K-3.]

Oliver Twist

2798 *Oliver Twist.* Ed. Dimensions Corp. Filmstrip (85 fr), record. [From David Lean's 1948 film.]

2799 *Oliver Twist.* Films, Inc. 2 filmstrips (372 fr), 2 cassettes (38 min), guide. [From David Lean's 1948 film.—Rev.: Thomas McChesney, *Previews* 8 (Dec. 1979): 37.]

A Tale of Two Cities

2800 *Charles Dickens's A Tale of Two Cities.* Jam Handy Co. 15 transparencies with 24 overlays. [Gr. 9-12.—Rev.: Evelyn Barrow, *Previews* 2 (Nov. 1973): 41-42.]

2801 *A Tale of Two Cities.* Brunswick Prods. Filmstrip (69 fr), 4 cassettes (narr. Michael Clarke-Lawrence), Monarch Notes, book.

2802 *A Tale of Two Cities.* Films, Inc. 3 filmstrips (504 fr), 3 cassettes (52 min), guide. [From Jack Conway's 1935 film.—Rev.: Brenda G. Epperson, *Previews* 7 (May 1979): 28.]

2803 *A Tale of Two Cities.* Pendulum Press. Cassette, answer key, 2 books.

2804 *A Tale of Two Cities: A Review of the Novel,* prod. Sharon Honea. Current Affairs Films. Filmstrip (55 fr), cassette (13 min), guide.

[Rev.: E[llen] M[andel] , *Booklist* 76 (1 Mar. 1980): 993.]

II. Adaptations for Special Readers

Bleak House

2805 *Bleak House,* adap. Margaret Tarner, illus. Kay Mary Wilson. London: Heinemann Ed., 1976. vi, 122 pp. [Upper students.]

A Christmas Carol

2806 *A Christmas Carol,* adap. A. Sweaney, illus. Rosemary Parsons. Hong Kong: Oxford UP, 1975. 59 pp. [Foreign readers.]

David Copperfield

2807 *David Copperfield,* adap. Norman Wymer, illus. Anne Rodger. London, etc.: Collins, 1978. 96 pp. [Foreign students.]

Great Expectations

2808 *Great Expectations,* adap. Rosemary de Courcy. London: Futura, 1975. 208 pp. [Young readers.]

2809 *Great Expectations,* adap F. Page, illus. Priscilla Keung. Hong Kong, etc.: Oxford UP, 1973. 127 pp. [Foreign students.]

2810 *Great Expectations,* adap. Ronald Storer. London: Oxford UP, 1979. 96 pp. [Foreign students.—Rev.: Johannes Hedberg, *MSpr* 73, iii (1979): 289-290.]

Hard Times

2811 *Hard Times,* adap. Viola Huggins, illus. Scoular Anderson. London, etc.: Collins, 1979. 127 pp. [Foreign students.]

2812 *Hard Times,* adap. Roland John. London: Longman, 1975. 108 pp. [Foreign students.]

Oliver Twist

2813 *Oliver Twist,* adap. Doris Dickens. London: Collins, 1980. 191 pp. [Young readers.]

2814 *Oliver Twist,* adap. Josephine Page, illus. Frank Po. Hong Kong, etc.: Oxford UP, 1973. 125 pp. [Foreign students.]

2815 *Oliver Twist,* adap. Ronald Storer. Oxford, etc.: Oxford UP, 1979. 95 pp. [Foreign students.]

2816 *Oliver Twist,* adap. Norman Wymer, illus. Scoular Anderson. London, etc.: Collins, 1979. 48 pp. [Foreign students.]

Our Mutual Friend

2817 *Our Mutual Friend,* adap. Margaret Tarner, illus. Kay Mary Wilson. London: Heinemann Ed., 1978. vi, 106 pp. [Foreign students.]

A Tale of Two Cities

2818 *A Tale of Two Cities,* adap. Andrea M. Clare, illus. Dick Cole. Belmont, Cal.: Fearon Pub., 1973. 92 pp. [Learning disabled, educable mentally handicapped, or emotionally disturbed readers.]

2819 *A Tale of Two Cities,* adap. Patti Krapesh, illus. Charles Shaw. Milwaukee: Raintree, 1980. 48 pp. [Young readers.]

2820 *A Tale of Two Cities,* adap. Alan Robertshaw, illus. Tom Barling. London: Pan, 1978. 108 pp. [Young readers.]

III. Scripts of Plays Chiefly for Schools

III.a. Life, Collections, etc.

2821 Beech, Marjorie. *Young Mr. Dickens.* Macclesfield: New Playwrights' Network, [1977]. 72 pp.

2822 Frederick, Leo Brooke. "Boz: Extracts from the Play Based on the Life and Loves of Charles Dickens." *Thought* (Delhi) 25 (6 Jan. 1973): 13-14.

2823 Hardwick, Michael and Mollie, adaps. *Plays from Dickens.* London: John Murray, 1970; rpt. 1978. vii, 87 pp. [Incl. 2842, 2843, 2847, 2852, 2853, 2856.—Rev.: Elwyn Jenkins, *Crux* 13 (Oct. 1979): 61.]

III.b. Individual Titles

A Christmas Carol

2824 *A Christmas Carol,* adap. Lynne Goldsmith. New York: Scholastic Book, 1970. 29 pp.

2825 "A Christmas Carol," adap. Walter Hackett. *Plays* 36 (Dec. 1976): 83-95. [Orig. in Dec. 1962 no.; rpt. 30 (Dec. 1970): 83-95 and 33 (Dec. 1973): 77-89.]

2826 "A Christmas Carol," rev. adap. Walter Hackett. *Plays* 34 (Dec. 1974): 85-95. [Classroom or radio-style.—Orig. in Dec. 1966 no.; rpt. 32 (Dec. 1972): 81-90.]

2827 *A Christmas Carol,* adap. Michael Hardwick. London: Davis-Poynter, 1974. 43 pp.

2828 *A Christmas Carol,* adap. Lewy Olfson, in *A Treasury of Christmas Plays,* ed. Sylvia E. Kamerman (Boston: Plays, 1975), 423-437. [Round-the-table or microphone.—This coll. prev. pub. 1958, 1972.]

2829 *A Christmas Carol,* adap. Kenneth Robbins, music and lyrics Mark Ollington. Manhattan, Kan.: Modern Theatre for Youth, 1978. 40 pp. [Without music.]

2830 *A Christmas Carol,* adap. Lyn Stevens. Elgin, Ill.: Performance, 1972. 86 pp.

2831 "A Christmas Carol," adap. Adele Thane, in *On Stage for Christmas: A Collection of Royalty-Free, One-Act Christmas Plays for Young People,* ed. Sylvia E. Kamerman (Boston: Plays, 1978), 408-428. [Rpt. from *Plays,* 38 (Dec. 1978): 61-72—Coll. also incl. 2839.]

2832 *A Christmas Carol,* adap. Michele L. Vacca. Dolton, Ill.: On Stage, 1975. 67 pp.

2833 *A Christmas Carol,* adap. Guy R. Williams. London: Macmillan, 1973. 50 pp.

2834 *A Christmas Carol: Scrooge and Marley*, adap. Israel Horovitz. New York: Dramatists Play Service, [1979] . 52 pp.

2835 *The Dickens Christmas Carol Show,* adap. Arthur Scholey, music Norman Beedie. New Orleans: Anchorage Press, 1979. 67 pp. [Rev.: Susanna Hill, *Speech and Drama* 29 (Spring 1980): 20; Olwen Wymark, *Drama* no. 136 (Apr. 1980): 68-69.]

2836 "Mr. Scrooge Finds Christmas," adap. Aileen Fisher. *Plays* 35 (Dec. 1975): 73-83.

2837 *Scrooge: A Christmas Play*, adap. Warren Graves.   Toronto: Playwrights Co-op, 1979. 47 pp.

2838 *Scrooge the Miser,* adap. Eric Jones-Evans, new ed.   Southampton: G. F. Wilson, 1973. 42 pp. [Prev. ed. 1962.]

2839 "Whatever Happened to Good Old Ebenezer Scrooge?," adap. Bill Majeski. In 2831, pp. 47-64. [Rpt. from *Plays* 36 (Dec. 1976): 1-10.]

David Copperfield

2840 *David Copperfield,* adap. Guy R. Williams. London: Macmillan, 1971. 42 pp. [First part of novel.—Rev.: J[ohn] G[reaves] , *Dkn* 67 (Sept. 1971): 178.]

2841 "The Fall of Uriah Heep," adap. Joellen Bland. *Plays* 31 (Mar. 1972): 85-96.

Dombey and Son

2842 "An Adventure in the Streets." In 2823, pp. 33-38.

Great Expectations

2843 "Miss Havisham's Revenge." In 2823, pp. 15-23.

2844 *Pip and the Convict*, adap. Guy R. Williams. London: Macmillan, 1971. 19 pp. [Rev.: J[ohn] G[reaves] , *Dkn* 67 (Sept. 1971): 178.]

Hard Times

2845 *Issues in Interpretation* 1, ii [1976?]. [On adap. of chap. 1 for oral interpretation with versions and comments by Robert S. Breen, pp. 3-4, Ronald Q. Frederickson, pp. 4-6, Judith C. Espinola, pp. 6-7, M. Lee Potts, pp. 8-10, Elbert R. Bowen, pp. 10-11, Ronald C. Cribbs, pp. 11-13, Robert Parisien, pp. 13-15, Philip C. Rossi, pp. 15-17.]

Nicholas Nickleby

2846 *Nicholas Nickleby,* adap. Guy R. Williams. London: Macmillan, 1972. 38 pp. [Rev.: Celia Boyd, *Young Drama* 1 (Feb. 1973): 49-50.]

2847 "Nicholas Turns the Tables." In 2823, pp. 1-13.

The Old Curiosity Shop

2848 "The Conspiracy," adap. Adele Thane. *Plays* 30 (Feb. 1971): 85-86.

Oliver Twist

2849 *Oliver Twist,* adap. Joellen Bland. Denver: Pioneer Drama, 1979. 56 pp.

2850 "Oliver Twist," adap. Joellen Bland. *Plays* 39 (Mar. 1980): 67-79. [Rpt. from 30 (Nov. 1970): 85-96 and in 34 (Mar. 1975): 85-96.]

2851 *Oliver Twist,* adap. Brian Way. Boston: Baker's Plays, 1977. 72 pp. [Orig. pub. in his *Three Plays for Open Stage,* 1958.]

2852 "School for Thieves." In 2823, pp. 39-47.

The Pickwick Papers

2853 "Bardell v. Pickwick." In 2823, pp. 49-87.

A Tale of Two Cities

2854 "A Tale of Two Cities," adap. Adele Thane. *Plays* 29 (Jan. 1970): 81-95.

2855 "A Tale of Two Cities," adap. Walter Hackett. *Plays* 37 (Nov. 1977): 84-96. [Round-the-table.]

2856 "The Worst of Times." In 2823, pp. 25-31.

IV. Recordings

Recordings that accompany visual aids are included in "Educational and Audio-Visual Aids," above. Recordings for radio broadcast and recordings of entire dramatic or musical adaptations are included in "Stage, Screen, Radio, and Television Performances," below. Recordings are 12" 33 1/3 rpm unless otherwise noted.

IV.a.i. Recordings: Life, Collections, etc.

2857 *Charles Dickens,* prod. Ivan Berg. Jeffrey Norton Pub. 41005. Cassette. [Biog. sketch and readings from works.—Rev.: Sr. G[ilmary] S[peirs], *Booklist* 74 (15 June 1978): 1631.]

2858 *Charles Dickens Cassette Library,* narr. Patrick Horgan. Listening Lib. CXL518. 6 cassettes, guide. [Selections from novels.—Rev.: Aaron L. Fessler, *Previews* 5 (Feb. 1977): 23 (gives contents); B[eth] J[o] K[napke], *Booklist* 73 (15 Apr. 1977): 1286.]

2859 *Charles Dickens 1812-1870: A Dramatized Biography,* narr. Michael and Mollie Hardwick. Ivan Berg Associates (Audio Pub.) HM-014. Tape. [Rev.: A[lan] S. W[atts], *Dkn* 73 (Sept. 1977): 174-175.]

2860 *Christmas Tales,* narr. Grant Sheehan. Talking Book Records TB1734. 16 2/3 rpm record.

2861 *Dickens Duets,* narr. Frank Pettingell. Spoken Arts SA741 or SAC7127. Record or cassette. [Rev.: Roy Blatchford, *TES* 20 Jan. 1978: 31.]

2862 *Portraits from Dickens,* narr. Anthony Jacobs. CMS Records CMS-634. Record. [Rev.: *Booklist* 69 (1 Dec. 1972): 348.]

2863 *The Public Readings,* narr. Roy Dotrice. Argo ZDSW707/13. 7 records. [Rev.: Mary Postgate, *Gramaphone* 56 (Jan. 1979): 1330-1331 (gives contents).]

IV.a.ii. Recordings: Individual Titles

Bleak House

2864 *Bleak House,* narr. Norman Barrs. National Lib. Service for the Blind
   RC10464. 7 cassettes.

A Christmas Carol

2865 *A Christmas Carol.* Audio Book Co. Cassettes.

2866 *A Christmas Carol.* Jabberwocky. Cassette.

2867 *A Christmas Carol,* narr. Roy Dotrice. Argo ZSW584/5. 2 records.
   [Rev.: Philip Collins, *TLS* 27 Jan. 1978: 90; Colin Evans, *TES* 8
   Sept. 1978: 25; Jenny Fowler, *Gramaphone* 55 (Dec. 1977): 1142;
   A[lan] S. W[atts], *Dkn* 74 (May 1978): 115.]

2868 *A Christmas Carol,* narr. Patrick Horgan. Listening Lib. AA3386/88
   or CX386/88. 3 records or 3 cassettes. [Rev.: William S. Forshaw,
   Booklist 70 (15 Mar. 1974): 791; J[ames] L. L[imbacher], *Previews* 3 (Nov. 1974): 44.]

2869 *A Christmas Carol,* narr. Leonard Rossiter. Listen for Pleasure TC-
   LFP80101/2. Cassette. [Rev.: Mary Postgate, *Gramaphone* 57
   (Jan. 1980): 1202.]

2870 *A Christmas Carol,* dir. Howard Sackler, narr. Paul Scofield. Caedmon CDL 51135. Cassette.

2871 *A Christmas Carol; Mr. Pickwick's Christmas,* narr. Ronald Colman
   (first piece), Charles Laughton (second piece). MCA 15010. Record.

David Copperfield

2872 [From *David Copperfield*], narr. Bransby Williams. On *Authors and
   Actors,* vol. 2. Rococo ROC-4014. Record.

Dombey and Son

2873 *Dombey and Son,* narr. Michael Clarke-Lawrence. National Lib. Service for the Blind RC10486. 14 cassettes.

Great Expectations

2874 *Great Expectations.* Books on Tape 1075. 11 cassettes. [Rev.: Linda Hillegass, *Previews* 7 (Nov. 1978): 31.]

2875 *Great Expectations.* DAK. Cassette.

2876 *Great Expectations,* narr. Patrick Horgan. Listening Lib. AA3382-83 or LX382-83. 2 records or 2 cassettes. [Rev.: William S. Forshaw, *Booklist* 70 (15 Jan. 1974): 529.]

2877 *Great Expectations,* adap. and dir. Robert Lewis. Cassette Classics Lib. 3 cassettes.

"A Holiday Romance"

2878 *Two Tales.* Mulberry 29356. Cassette. ["Magic Fishbone," "Captain Boldheart."—Rev.: Margaret Bush, *Previews* 3 (Nov. 1974): 44.]

Oliver Twist

2879 *Oliver Twist.* Library IV Ser. Jabberwocky. Cassette. [Gr. 7-12.— Rev.: E. Reed, *Booklist* 73 (15 Mar. 1977): 1112.]

2880 *Oliver Twist,* narr. Anthony Quayle. Caedmon TC1484 or CDL51484. Record or cassette. [Chaps. 1-2, 8-9.—Rev.: P[atrick] G[ardner], *Booklist* 74 (15 June 1978): 1631.]

2881 *Oliver Twist,* adap. J. K. Ross, narr. John Allen. Columbia CR-21509. Record. [Rev.: Barbara S. Miller, *Booklist* 69 (1 Mar. 1973): 628.]

The Pickwick Papers

2882 *The Pickwick Papers.* DAK. Cassette.

2883 *The Pickwick Papers,* narr. Brendan Burke. Amer. Foundation for the Blind TB3505. 20 records.

2884 *The Pickwick Papers,* dir. Howard Sackler, narr. Lewis Casson and Boris Karloff. Caedmon CDL 51121. Cassette.

Pictures from Italy

2885 *Pictures from Italy,* narr. Vida More.   National Lib. Service for the
     Blind RC 8740. 4 tape cassettes.

A Tale of Two Cities

2886 *A Tale of Two Cities.* Jimcin Recordings 0-19. 8 cassettes.

2887 *A Tale of Two Cities,* narr. Michael Clarke-Lawrence. Listening Lib.
     A1630. 2 16 2/3 rpm records.

2888 *A Tale of Two Cities,* narr. James Mason. Caedmon TC2079. 2 re-
     cords or 2 cassettes. [Selctions.—Rev.: J[ames] L. L[imbacher],
     Previews 5 (Sept. 1976): 35; V[irginia] M[cKenna], *Booklist* 73
     (15 June 1977): 1590.]

IV.b. Recordings: Musical Settings and Scores

Dickens's Works

David Copperfield

2889 "David Copperfield," music Herbert Stothart. On *The Film Music of
     Herbert Stothart.* Tony Thomas Prods. TT-ST-1/2. 2 records.
     [For George Cukor's 1935 film.]

Oliver Twist

2890 "Fagin's Romp"; "Finale," music Arnold Bax. On *Great British Film
     Scores,* Bernard Herrmann cond. National Philharmonic Orch.
     London SPC-21149. Record. [For David Lean's 1948 film.]

IV.c. Recordings: Critical and Popular Discussions

2891 Dyson, A. E. and Angus Wilson. *Dickens.* Approach to Literary Criti-
     cism Ser., A6. BFA Ed. Media F12006. Cassette. [Note also 2129.]

2892 Hardy, Barbara and Michael Slater. *Dickens: Hard Times and Social
     Criticism; Great Expectations and Dickens's Art.* Audio Learning
     11. Tape or cassette, supp. booklet by John Sutherland and Keith
     Walker. [Rev.: A[lan] S. W[atts], *Dkn* 73 (Sept. 1977): 174-175.]

2893 Highet, Gilbert. *The Mystery of Edwin Drood.* J. Norton Pub. 23295. Cassette.

2894 Morris, Robert. *Dickens and Great Expectations.* Center for Cassette St. 28427. Cassette. [Rev.: James L. Limbacher, *Previews* 2 (Jan. 1974): 73.]

2895 Ross, Angus. *Charles Dickens, Poet and Entertainer: Pickwick Papers, Bleak House, Great Expectations, Dombey and Son, Our Mutual Friend.* Cassette Curriculum 3800/5. 6 cassettes.

2896 Wilson, Angus. *Charles Dickens.* J. Norton 23075. Reel or cassette. [Recorded from 1967 radio talk.]

2897 —. *The English Novel Today: Dickens to Snow.* J. Norton 23074. Reel or cassette. [Recorded from 1960 radio talk.]

V. Novels and Stories Based upon Life and Works

2898 Busch, Frederick. *The Mutual Friend.* New York: Harper; Hassocks: Harvester Press, 1978. 222 pp. [Chap. 2 orig. pub. *IowaR* 9 (Winter 1978): 1-23; excerpt from chap. 4 in *NYT* 25 Dec. 1977: D11.—Rev.: *Charles A. Brady, *Buffalo Evening News* 13 Aug. 1978; *Mitzi M. Brunsdale, *Houston Post* 18 June 1978; Jeffrey Burke, *Harper's* 256 (June 1978): 89-90; Daniel Coogan, *America* 139 (26 Aug. 1978): 113; Valentine Cunningham, *NewSt* 97 (2 Feb. 1979): 158; Paula Deitz, *OntarioR* no. 9 (Fall-Winter 1978-1979): 99-102; Nicholas Delbanco, *New Republic* 178 (25 Mar. 1978): 26-27; *Monica Dickens, *Boston Globe* 12 July 1978; *Robert Finn, *Cleveland Plain Dealer* 28 May 1978; Mollie Hardwick, *B&B* 24 (Jan. 1979): 20-21; Aidan Higgins, *Hibernia* 8 Feb. 1979: 25; Peter Kemp, *Lstr* 101 (11 Jan. 1979): 61-62; *Jeffrey L. Lant, *St. Louis Globe-Democrat* 8-9 July 1978 and *Providence J* 20 Aug. 1978; William S. Levison, *LJ* 103 (15 May 1978): 1979; Ruth Mathewson, *New Leader* 61 (22 May 1978): 3-4; *Jo Modert, *St. Louis Post-Dispatch* 23 July 1978: C4; Tom Paulin, *Enc* 52 (May 1979): 72-73; *K. McCormick Price, *Denver Post* 21 May 1978; Roger Sale, *NYTBR* 9 Apr. 1978: 10, 33-34; Albert J. Solomon, *Best Sellers* 38 (July 1978): 100; *Bookviews* 1 (Apr. 1978): 38; *Ch* 15 (Dec. 1978): 1365; *Washington Star* 7 May 1978; also rev. in 981.]

2899 Hardwick, Michael and Mollie. *The Gaslight Boy: A Novel Based on Yorkshire Television's Series, Dickens of London.* London:

Weidenfeld and Nicholson, 1976; New York: Dell, 1977. 191 pp. [See also 2906.—Rev.: Neil Hepburn, *Lstr* 96 (9 Dec. 1976): 745.]

2900 McHugh, Stuart Dickens. *Knock on the Nursery Door: Tales of the Dickens Children.* London: Michael Joseph, 1972; New York: Transatlantic, 1973. 157 pp. [Life in D household 1841-1858.— Rev.: T. J. Galvin, *LJ* 98 (1 June 1973): 1844.]

2901 Markham, Marion M. "What Really Happened to Scrooge." *Blackwood's Mag* 314 (July 1973): 20-27.

2902 Paustovsky, Konstatin. "An Incident with Dickens." *Sputnik* 12 (Dec. 1970): 143-144.

2903 Wilkie, Katherine E. *Charles Dickens: The Inimitable Boz.* New York: Abelard-Schuman, 1970. 188 pp. [For young adults.—Rev.: Michael Cart, *LJ* 95 (15 Oct. 1970): 3641; Polly Longsworth, *NYTBR* 6 Sept. 1970: 16; *Kirkus Revs* 38 (1 Mar. 1970): 254-255; *Publishers Weekly* 197 (1 June 1970): 67.]

VI. Stage, Screen, Radio, and Television Performances
Including Published Scores and Scripts

See also in Subject Index under Adaptation and the following announcements of other productions: *Dkn* 66 (May 1970): 188, 193; 68 (Jan. 1972): 50; 70 (Jan., May 1974): 53, 112; 72 (Sept. 1976): 182-183; 73 (Sept. 1977): 197-198; 74 (Sept. 1978): 187-188.

VI.a. Performances: Life

2904 *The Boy from the Blacking Factory,* adap. Tom Vernon. [BBC Radio 4, 19 Dec. 1976.]

2905 *The Charles Dickens Show,* dir. Piers Jessop. Color film (60 min). Dist. International Film Bureau, Chicago. [Described in *EJ* 63 (Jan. 1974): 29.—See also 2780.—Rev.: Nina May Walsh, *Previews* 3 (Dec. 1974): 12; Ana Laura Zambrano, *DSN* 6 (Mar. 1975): 24-27; *Dkn* 69 (Sept. 1973): 175.]

2906 *Dickens of London,* prod. and dir. Marc Miller, adap. Wolf Mankowitz. [Thirteen-part serial on ITV starting 28 Sept. 1976; later on PBS.—See also 1252, 2899.—Rev.: *Jack E. Anderson, *Miami Herald* 28 Aug. 1977; A[nthony] B[urton], *Dkn* 73 (Jan. 1977):

39-42; *Robert W. Butler, *Kansas City Star* 28 Aug. 1977; *Bill Carter, *Baltimore Sun* 26 Aug. 1977; J[ohn] G[reaves], *Dkn* 72 (Sept. 1976): 172; Anthony Holden, *STimes* (London) 3 Oct. 1976: 39; Diana Loecher, *CSM* 29 Aug. 1977: 2; *Owen McNally, *Hartford Courant* 29 Aug. 1977; John J. O'Connor, *NYT* 25 Sept. 1977: B27 with Edgar Johnson's comments on inaccuracies; Pit, *Variety* 6 Oct. 1976: 52; Stanley Reynolds, *Times* (London) 6 Oct. 1976: 11; John Romano, *TV Guide* 25 (3 Sept. 1977): 20-22; Lorna Sage, *TLS* 12 Nov. 1976: 1425; Richard F. Shepard, *NYT* 26 Aug. 1977: C21; David Wheeler, *Lstr* 96 (18 Nov. 1976): 652; *Obs* 26 Sept. 1976: 24; *Raleigh News and Obs* 30 Aug. 1977.– Note also Mankowitz's remarks at D Fellowship dinner, *Dkn* 72 (May 1976): 124 and Irene Howlett's ltr. to ed., 73 (Sept. 1977): 162.]

2907 *Emlyn Williams as Charles Dickens.* [Note also film (120 min) dist. Arthur Cantor, New York.–Rev. of film: *Choice* 18 (Apr. 1981): 1114.–Note also Charles Dickens, narr. Emlyn Williams. Argo TA507/8. 2 records.–Rev. of records: Jane Gregg, *Speech and Drama* 20 (Summer 1971): 50-52; C[elia] W[hite], *Records and Recording* 14 (Feb. 1971): 106; Margaret Willy, *English* 20 (Spring 1971): 19.–Note also interview by *Patricia Rice, "His Life is Intertwined with Dickens," *St. Louis Post-Dispatch* 23 Dec. 1976. –Rev. of performance: Clive Barnes, *NYT* 4 Nov. 1970: 41; Andy Boyle, *Plays and Players* 7 (Apr. 1975): 28; Thomas Lask, *NYT* 7 Jan. 1976: 49; Charles Lewsen, *Times* (London) 5 Feb. 1975: 11; John C. Mahoney, *Los Angeles Times* 14 Nov. 1975: D19; Sheridan Morley, *Punch* 268 (12 Feb. 1975): 281; Benedict Nightingale, *NewSt* 89 (14 Feb. 1975): 218; John Peter, *STimes* (London) 9 Feb. 1975: 37; M[ichael] S[later], *Dkn* 71 (May 1975): 105; see also 2277 and *Dkn* 66 (Sept. 1970): 194.]

2908 *The Great Inimitable Mr. Dickens*, dir. Ned Sherrin, adap. Ned Sherrin and Caryl Brahms. [BBC-2 TV biog., 2 June 1970.–Rev.: Nancy Banks-Smith, *Guardian* 3 June 1970: 8; Henry Raynor, *Times* (London) 3 June 1970: 7.]

2909 *These Garish Lights*, adap. Philip Collins. [BBC Radio 4, 7 Sept. 1975.–Rev.: A[nthony] B[urton], *Dkn* 72 (Jan. 1976): 35.–For a report of Collins's centenary readings, see *Dkn* 66 (May 1970): 190-191 and his ltr. to ed., 67 (Jan. 1971): 42.]

VI.b. Performances: Individual Titles

Bleak House

2910 *Bleak House,* play adap., dir. Mike Alfred. [Shared Experience road co. prod.—Rev.: Paul Allen, *Plays and Players* 25 (Apr. 1978): 39; Ned Chaillet, *Times* (London) 7 Apr. 1978: 13; John Elsom, *Lstr* 99 (27 Apr. 1978): 548-549; Irene Howlett, *Dkn* 74 (Sept. 1978): 178-179; Benedict Nightingale, *NewSt* 94 (14 Apr. 1978): 504; Eric Shorter, *Drama* no. 127 (Winter 1977-1978): 65-67.]

A Christmas Carol

2911 *An American Christmas Carol,* dir. Eric Till, adap. Jerome Cooper-smith. [On ABC-TV 16 Dec. 1979.—Rev.: *Mark Bretz, *St. Louis Globe-Democrat* 14 Dec. 1979; J[ames] B[rown], *Los Angeles Times* 15 Dec. 1979: B3; *Tom Shales, *Washington Post* 15 Dec. 1979; Arthur Unger, *CSM* 12 Dec. 1979: 19.—Note also *Stacy Jenel Smith's interview with Henry Winkler, *San Francisco Examiner* 12 Dec. 1979.]

2912 *A Chirstmas Carol.* National Recording Co. D-9493. Cassette. ["Old time radio programs."]

2913 *A Christmas Carol,* [adap. for NBC radio "Richard Diamond, Private Detective."] On Amer. Forces Radio and TV Service RU32-1(X-70)66A. Record. [Intended for US Armed Forces Radio only.]

2914 *A Christmas Carol,* adap. Alan Dinehart and Alan Young, music Buddy Baker, lyrics Tom and Francis Adair. Disneyland Records 3811. Record.

2915 *A Christmas Carol,* adap. Sr. Marcella Marie Holloway, music Sr. Mary Ann Joyce. Denver: Pioneer Drama Service, 1975. 24 pp. (book); 21 pp. (score).

2916 *A Christmas Carol,* adap. and with Charles Ludlam. [Ridiculous Theatrical Co. (N.Y.) prod. during Dec. 1979.—Rev.: Mel Gussow, *NYT* 4 Dec. 1979: C9; Erika Munk, *Village Voice* 17 Dec. 1979: 115; *Marilyn Stasio, *New York Post* 15 Dec. 1979; David Sterritt, *CSM* 24 Dec. 1979: 15.]

2917 *A Christmas Carol,* mime by Marcel Marceau. [BBC-TV, 27 Dec. 1973.—Note also 1257.—Rev.: A[nthony] B[urton], *Dkn* 70 (Jan. 1974): 53.]

2918 *A Christmas Carol,* music and libretto Thea Musgrave. [Premiere by Virginia Opera Assn. at Centre Theatre (Norfolk) 7 Dec. 1979, cond. Peter Mark, dir. David Farrar.—Note also NPR broadcast 16 Dec. 1979.—Rev.: Harold Blumenfeld, *Opera J* 13, ii (1980): 15-18 (slightly diff. version in *St. Louis Post-Dispatch* 16 Dec. 1979: E5); Carl Dolmetsch, *Opera* 31 (Feb. 1980): 150-152, 170; Robert Jacobson, *Opera News* 44 (29 Mar. 1980): 150-152; Leighton Kerner, *Village Voice* 31 Dec. 1979: 61; *Robert Merritt, *Richmond Times-Dispatch* 9 Dec. 1979; *Tim Morton, *Norfolk Virginian-Pilot* 9 Dec. 1979; Andrew Porter, *NY* 55 (24 Dec. 1979): 84-87; Peter J. Rosenwald, *Horizon* 22 (Dec. 1979). 64-68, 70-71; Patrick J. Smith, *Times* (London) 12 Dec. 1979: 11 and (a diff. rev.) *Musical America* (supp. to *High Fidelity*) 30 (Apr. 1980): 31-32; Annalyn Swan, *Newsweek* 94 (17 Dec. 1979): 88, 90.]

2919 *A Christmas Carol,* narr. Laurence Olivier. Center for Cassette St. 39014. [Radio drama orig. broadcast 1953.]

2920 *A Christmas Carol,* narr. Michael Redgrave. [ABC-TV animated prod., 21 Dec. 1971.—ABC Media Concepts 27456. Color film (26 min). —Rev.: A[nthony] B[urton], *Dkn* 70 (Jan. 1974): 53; John Coleman, *NewSt* 84 (22 Dec. 1972): 953; Avi Wortis, *Previews* 1 (Feb. 1973): 15-16.—Note also *TV Guide* 19 (18 Dec. 1971): 19-22.]

2921 *A Christmas Carol,* dir. John Salway, narr. Paul Honeyman, illus. John Worseley. [Anglia TV prod.—Rev.: Leonard Buckely, *Times* (London): 24 Dec. 1970: 11.]

2922 *A Christmas Carol,* David Willcocks cond. Bach Choir and Jacques Orch. Classics for Pleasure CFP 180. Record. [With traditional carols interspersed.—Rev.: Celia White, *Records and Recording* 15 (Jan. 1972): 91.]

2923 *Comin' Uptown,* dir. Philip Rose, adap. Philip Rose and Peter Udell, music Garry Sherman, lyrics Peter Udell. [Opened Winter Garden Theatre (N.Y.) 20 Dec. 1979.—Rev. (starred items in *New York Theatre Critics' Revs* 40 [31 Dec. 1979] : 59-62): *Clive Barnes, *New York Post* 21 Dec. 1979; *John Beaufort, *CSM* 26 Dec. 1979; *Gerald Clarke, *Time* 114 (31 Dec. 1979): 44; Brendan Gill, *NY* 55 (7 Jan. 1980): 57; *Walter Kerr, *NYT* 21 Dec. 1979: C5; Hobe [Morrison], *Variety* 26 Dec. 1979: 56; *Christopher Sharp, *Women's Wear Daily* 21 Dec. 1979; John Simon, *New York* 13 (14 Jan. 1980): 71; Sally R. Sommer, *Village Voice* 31 Dec. 1979: 71; *Douglas Watt, *New York Daily News* 21 Dec. 1979; *Edwin Wilson, *Wall Street J* 28 Dec. 1979: 7.—Note also *Dennis Cunningham on WCBS-TV 20 Dec. 1979; Nan Robertson, *NYT* 27 Nov. 1979: C7; *Joel Siegel on WABC-TV 20 Dec. 1979; Carol Lawson's interview with Rose, *NYT* 27 June 1979: C28.]

2924 *Scrooge,* dir. Ronald Neame, screenplay Leslie Bricusse. Film. [Rev.: James Arnold, *St. Anthony Messenger* 78 (Feb. 1971): 8; Michael Billington, *ILN* 257 (5 Dec. 1970): 27; Vincent Canby, *NYT* 20 Nov. 1970: 29; J[ay] C[locks], *Time* 96 (7 Dec. 1970): 73 and Bing Crosby's ltr. to ed., 97 (4 Jan. 1971): 4; Jerry Cotter, *Sign* 50 (Dec. 1970): 41; Brian Davis, *Monthly Film Bull* 38 (Jan. 1971): 13-14; Tatiana Balkoff Drowne, *Films in Review* 21 (Dec. 1970): 644-645; Gordon Gow, *Films and Filming* 17 (Jan. 1971): 48; Barbara Hardy, *Dkn* 67 (Jan. 1971): 41-42; Philip T. Hartung, *Commonweal* 93 (25 Dec. 1970): 327; Kimmis Hendrick, *CSM* 16 Dec. 1970: 8; Pauline Kael, *NY* 46 (28 Nov. 1970): 175-176; Alex Keneas, *Newsweek* 76 (14 Dec. 1970): 104-105; Arthur Knight, *SatR* 53 (5 Dec. 1970): 44; Derek Malcolm, *Guardian Weekly* 5 Dec. 1970: 16; Richard Mallett, *Punch* 259 (2 Dec. 1970): 806; Tom Milne, *Obs* 29 Nov. 1970: 29; Robert L. Patten, *DSN* 1 (Dec. 1970): 18-22; Margaret Ronan, *Senior Scholastic* 97 (14 Dec. 1970): 17; Gene Shalit, *Look* 34 (15 Dec. 1970): 28-32; Bruce Stewart, *Month* 231 (Mar. 1971): 90; Louise Sweeney, *CSM* 20 Nov. 1970: 6; John Russell Taylor, *Times* (London) 27 Nov. 1970: 13; *Films and Filming,* 17 (Dec. 1970): 26-27 (pictorial); *Playboy* 18 (Feb. 1971): 34.—Note also soundtrack for film on record Columbia S-30258 and *Scrooge,* adap. Elaine Donaldson (New York: Cinema Center Films; Nashville: Aurora Press, 1970), 128 pp.]

2925 *The Stingiest Man in Town,* prod. and dir. Arthur Rankin, Jr., and Jules Bass, adap. Romeo Muller, music Fred Spielman, book and lyrics Janice Torre. [Animated prod. on NBC-TV 23 Dec. 1978.— Rev.: Carol Burton Terry, *San Franciso Chronicle* 23 Dec. 1978: 27; see also *TV Guide* 26 (23 Dec. 1978): 4-5.]

David Copperfield

2926 *David Copperfield,* [adap. for Favorite Story Radio ser.]   On Amer. Forces Radio and TV Service RU33-6, 3B. Record. [Intended for US Armed Forces Radio only.]

2927 *David Copperfield,* dir. Delbert Mann, screenplay Frederick Brogger and Jack Pulman. Film. [Theatre showing in Great Britain, then on NBC-TV 15 Mar. 1970.—Rev.: Michael Billington, *ILN* 256 (3 Jan. 1970): 29; Russell Campbell, *Monthly Film Bull* 37 (Feb.

1970): 23-24; John Coleman, *NewSt* 79 (2 Jan. 1970): 24-25; James Doussard, *Louisville Courier-J* 17 Mar. 1970: B2; Jack Gould, *NYT* 16 Mar. 1970: 87; Penelope Houston, *Spec* 224 (10 Jan. 1970): 54; Lawrence Laurent, *Washington Post* 16 Mar. 1970: D9; Diana Loercher, *CSM* 18 Mar. 1970: 16; Derek Malcolm, *Guardian Weekly* 10 Jan. 1970: 20; S[ylvia] M[atheran] de P[otenze], *Criterio* 43 (26 Nov. 1970): 850; Terrence O'Flaherty, *San Francisco Chronicle* 18 Mar. 1970: 40; Cecil Smith, *TV Times* (supp. to *Los Angeles Times*) 15 Mar. 1970: 2 and *Los Angeles Times* 16 Mar. 1970: D1, D27; John Russell Taylor, *Times* (London) 1 Jan. 1970: 6 and (a diff. rev.) 3 Jan. 1970: III; John Walker, *Films and Filming* 16 (Mar. 1970): 42-43; see also Michael Billington, "A New Deal for David Copperfield," *ILN* 256 (3 Jan. 1970: 20-23; *Films and Filming* 16 (Feb. 1970): 32-33 (pictorial). —Note also 507.]

2928 *David Copperfield,* dir. Jean-Claude Penchenat. [Théâtre du Campagnol and Théâtre du Soleil prod.—Opened 4 Nov. 1977 at Cartoucherie (Vincennes).—Rev.: Béatrix Andrade, *NL* 3 Nov. 1977: 11; Guy Dumur, *Nouvel observateur* 21-27 Nov. 1977: 93 and Sylvère Monod's ltr. to ed. 5 Dec., p. 28; Matthieu Galey, *NL* 17 Nov. 1977: 28; Renate Klett, *Theatre heute* 19 (Jan. 1978): 32; Jean Mambrino, S. J., *Études* 348 (Mar. 1978): 375-376; Judith G. Miller, *ETJ* 30 (Oct. 1978): 408-409; Richard Monod, *Travail théâtral* no. 30 (Jan.-Mar. 1978): 116-121 and (a diff. rev.) *FMonde* no. 136 (Apr. 1978): 59-60; Sylvère Monod, *EA* 31 (Jan.-Mar. 1978): 118-119 and (a diff. rev.) *Dkn* 74 (May 1978): 116; Renée Saurel, *TM* 33 (Feb. 1978): 1307-1324; Raymonde Temkine, *Europe* no. 588 (Apr. 1978): 217-219.—Note also C[aroline] A[lexander], *L'Express* 24 Oct. 1977: 63-64.]

2929 *David Copperfield,* adap. Hugh Whitemore. [BBC-TV1 serialization.—Rev.: Alan Coren, *Times* (London) 9 Dec. 1974: 11; J[ohn] G[reaves], *Dkn* 71 (May 1975): 104; *Bob Lundegaard, *Minneapolis Tribune* 10 Jan. 1977; John Nickerson, *Senior Scholastic* (Teacher's Ed.) 109 (13 Jan. 1977): 18-19.]

Great Expectations

2930 *Great Expectations,* dir. Joseph Hardy, screenplay Sherman Yellen. [On NBC-TV 22 Nov. 1974; re-released for theatre showing.—Rev.: A[nthony] B[urton], *Dkn* 72 (Sept. 1976): 165-166; Maryvonne Butcher, *Tablet* 230 (24 June 1976): 85; Philip French, *Times* (London) 16 Jan. 1976: 11; Gordon Gow, *Films and Filming* 22 (Mar. 1976): 35-36; Philip Jenkinson, *Punch* 207 (21 Jan. 1976): 131; Lois A. Markham, *Scholastic Teacher* (Jr./Sr. High Teacher's Ed.) Nov.-Dec. 1974: 43; Sylvia Millar, *Monthly Film Bull* 42 (Dec. 1975): 261; J. J. O'Connor, *NYT* 22 Nov. 1974: 79; Dilys Powell, *STimes* (London) 18 Jan. 1976: 36; David Wilson, *NewSt* 91 (16 Jan. 1976): 78; Ana Laura Zambrano, *DSN* 6 (Mar. 1975): 27-28 and responses by Charles I. Schuster and Michael Riley with Zambrano's reply, 6 (Sept. 1975): 75-78. —Note also Edith Efron's interview with stars, *TV Guide* 22 (16 Nov. 1974): 17-18, 20, 22.]

2931 *Miss Donnithorne's Maggot,* music Peter Maxwell Davies, text Randolph Stow. [Music-theatre for mezzo-soprano and chamber orch. based on life of one of models for Miss Havisham.—Pub. London, etc.: Boosey and Hawkes, [1977]. [vi], 58 pp.—Premiered 9 Apr. 1974, Adelaide Festival, with Mary Thomas and the Fires of London, cond. Davies; 23 Apr. 1974, Elizabeth Hall (London).—Rev.: Fred R. Blanks, *Musical Times* 115 (May 1974): 413 (Adelaide performance); Michael Chanan, *Music and Musicians* 22 (July 1974): 51-52 (London); Paul Griffiths, *Musical Times* 115 (June 1974): 496-497 (London); Peter Heyworth, *Nuova rivista musicale italiana* 8 (Apr.-June 1974): 285-286 (London).—Note also Randolph Stow, "Om *Miss Donnithorne's Maggot,*" *Nutida Musik* 18, i (1974-1975): 6.]

2932 *Miss Havisham's Fire,* music Dominick Argento, text John Olon-Scrymgeour. [Opened New York City Opera 22 Mar. 1979, cond. Julius Rudel.—Pub. New York and London: Boosey and Hawkes, [1979]. 40 pp.; libretto of *Miss Havisham's Wedding Night,* earlier one-act version, also pub. Boosey and Hawkes, rpt. *DSN* 10 (Dec. 1979): 106-113.—See also 147.—Rev.: Harold Blumenfeld, *St. Louis Post-Dispatch* 6 May 1979: E5; Duane DeVries, *DSN* 10 (Dec. 1979): 103-105 (illus.); Thor Eckert, Jr., *CSM* 5 Apr. 1979: 19; Margaret Ganz, *DSN* 10 (Dec. 1979): 115-118 (illus.); Manuela Hoelterhoff, *Wall Street J* 30 Mar. 1979: 4; Robert Jacobson, *Opera News* 43 (June 1979): 39-40; Harriet Johnson, *Washington Post* 24 Mar. 1979: B5; R[obert] T. J[ones], *Musical America* (supp. to *High Fidelity*) 29 (Aug. 1979): 28; Leighton Kerner, *Village Voice* 9 Apr. 1979: 71; Robert J. Landry, *Variety* 28 Mar. 1979: 104; K. Oppens, *Opernwelt* 20, vi (1979): 48-49; Andrew Porter, *NY* 55 (9 Apr. 1979): 125-129; Alan Rich, *New York* 12 (16 Apr. 1979): 91; Harold C. Schonberg, *NYT* 24 Mar. 1979: 12; Laurence Shyer, *TJ* 31 (Dec. 1979): 553-554; Patrick J. Smith, *Opera* 30 (June 1979): 587-588; Stephen Vasta, *World of Opera* 1, vi (1979): 11-13; Bert Wechsler, *Music J* 37 (Sept.-Oct. 1979): 53; *Boosey and Hawkes Newsletter* 11 (Spring-Summer 1979): 1, 11 (survey of revs.).—Note also Peter C. Davis, *NYT* 18 Mar. 1979: B1, B21; Hans Heinsheimer, *Opera News* 43 (24 Mar. 1979): 34-35.]

2933 *Miss Havisham's Wedding Day,* dir. Ronald Mason, adap. Carolyn Sally Jones. [On BBC Radio 4, 11 Feb. 1980.]

Hard Times

2934 *Hard Times,* dir. John Irvin, adap. Arthur Hopcraft. [Four-part NET prod. (also available on 4 videocassettes (240 min) from WNET/13 Media Services, New York) later on Granada TV.—Rev.: Anthony Burton, *Dkn* 74 (Jan. 1978): 48-50; Michael Church, *Times* (London) 26 Oct. 1977: 9; G[erald] C[larke], *Time* 109 (16 May 1977): 57; Benny Green, *Punch* 273 (2 Nov. 1977): 855; Joseph Hone, *Lstr* 98 (3 Nov. 1977): 585-586; Michael Irwin, *TLS* 4 Nov. 1977: 1295; Mick [Larry Michie], *Variety* 18 May 1977: 102; Richard North, *Lstr* 98 (17 Nov. 1977): 652; John J. O'Connor, *NYT* 11 May 1977: C22 and (a diff. rev.) 22 May, p. B31; Dennis Potter, *STimes* (London) 30 Oct. 1977: 37; Jay Sharbutt, *St. Louis Post-Dispatch* 20 May 1977: D6; W[illiam] W[ard], *Booklist* 74 (1 Jan. 1978): 764; James Wolcott, *Village Voice* 30 May 1977: 76; **Raleigh News and Obs* 18 May 1977.—Note also S[ara] D. T[oney], *Humanities* (NEH) 7 (May 1977): 1, 8 and WNET's pamphlet *The World of Dickens's Hard Times: A Guide for the Viewer* by George Ford and Steven Marcus and their essay based on it, *NYT* 8 May 1977: B29, B41.]

2935 *Hard Times,* adap. Hugh Thomas. Musical. [Performed Oxford's Playhouse, Nov. 1971.—Rev.: M[ichael] S[later], *Dkn* 68 (Jan. 1972): 50.—New prod. at Belgrade Theatre, Coventry, Nov. 1973. —Rev.: *Dkn* 70 (Jan. 1974): 52.]

Little Dorrit

2936 *Little Dorrit,* dir. Jane Morgan, adap. Betty Davies. [Six-part BBC Radio 4 ser., beginning 13 Apr. 1980.]

"Mugby Junction"

2937 *L'Embranchement de Mugby,* dir. Brigitte Jacques, trans. Pierre Leyris, adap. François Regnault and Brigitte Jacques. [At Centre Beaubourg (Paris).—Rev.: Béatrix Andrade, *NL* 18 Jan. 1979: 12; Florence Delay, *NRF* no. 315 (1 Apr. 1979): 103-105; Patrick De

Rosbo, *NL* 25 Jan. 1979: 29; Guy Dumur, *Nouvel observateur* 29 Jan. 1979: 87.]

2938 *The Signalman,* adap. Peter Packer and Nathan Zucker, in *Story into Film,* ed. Ulrich Ruchti and Sybil Taylor (New York: Laurel-Leaf Lib., 1978), 183-225. [Story and script on facing pp.—Note also "Charles Dickens and 'The Signalman'," pp. 178-182; biog. note on and interview with Zucker (who also directed the 1955 TV prod.), pp. 227-236; prod. credits, p. 226.]

Nicholas Nickleby

2939 "Arthur Schwartz Does Songs for Nickleby Musical." *Variety* 9 July 1975: 71. ["Arthur Cantor plans to produce the show next winter. . . ."]

2940 *The Life and Adventures of Nicholas Nickleby,* dir. Trevor Nunn and John Caird, adap. David Edgar. [Royal Shakespeare Co. prod., Aldwych Theatre (London) 5 June-26 July 1980; re-opened Nov. through New Year's.—Rev.: Ned Chaillet, *Times* (London) 23 June 1980: 9; Jay Cocks and Erik Amfitheatrof, *Time* 116 (24 Nov. 1980): 96-97, 99; Richard Dunn, *DSN* 11 (Sept. 1980): 86-89; John Elsom, *Lstr* 104 (3 July 1980): 29; René Elvin, *RDM* no. 9 (Sept. 1980): 747-748; Margaret Ganz, *DSN* 11 (Sept. 1980): 81-84 (incl. playbill); Frank Giles, *STimes* 20 July 1980: 16; W. J. Igoe, *Month* 261 (Sept. 1980): 315; Peter Jenkins, *Spec* 244 (28 June 1980): 25; Peter Keating, *TLS* 27 June 1980: 733; Bernard Levin, *Times* (London) 8 July 1980: 14; Robert Merry, *Chicago Tribune* 6 July 1980: F17; Sheridan Morley, *Punch* 279 (2 July 1980): 30; Benedict Nightingale, *NewSt* 99 (27 June 1980): 979; J. C. Trewin, *ILN* 268 (Aug. 1980): 98; Lynne Truss, *TES* 27 June 1980: 21.—Note also interview with Roger Rees by Sheridan Morley, *Times* (London) 11 June 1980: 9; for photos, see *Plays and Players* 27 (June 1980): 10-11.]

2941 *Nickleby and Me,* dir. Ned Sherrin, music Ron Grainer, adap. Caryl Brahms and Ned Sherrin. [Opened Theatre Royal (London) 7 Dec. 1975.—Rev.: Jonathan Hammond, *Plays and Players* 23 (Feb. 1976): 33-34; Harold Hobson, *STimes* (London) 28 Dec. 1975: 29; Charles Lewsen, *Times* (London) 17 Dec. 1975: 10; Sheridan Morley, *Punch* 269 (24 Dec. 1975): 1208; Victoria Radin, *Obs* 21 Dec. 1975: 22; M[ichael] S[later], *Dkn* 72 (Jan. 1976): 37.]

2942 *Smike,* adap. Roger Holman, Simon May, Clive Barnett, words and

music Holman and May. London: ATV Music, 1976. 76 pp.
(book); 104 pp. (score). [Pop musical.—Further adap. for BBC2-
TV prod. 26 Dec. 1973 by Paul Ciani and John Morley (this prod.
recorded on Pye NSPL 18423).—Rev.: Clive Gammon, *Spec*
232 (5 Jan. 1974): 19; Peter Lennon, *STimes* (London) 30 Dec.
1973: 34.]

The Old Curiosity Shop

2943 *Mister Quilp*, dir. Michael Tuchner, screenplay Louis and Irene Kamp,
music Anthony Newley. [Videocassette available from Reader's
Digest Films.—Note also *Quilp: A Musical Adaptation of Charles
Dickens's The Old Curiosity Shop.* New York [and London]:
Morris, 1975 (songs enclosed separately in cover): "Quilp"; "Some-
where"; "Happiness Pie"; "The Sport of Kings"; "Every Dog Has
His Day"; "When a Felon Needs a Friend"; "Love Has the Longest
Memory."—Rev. (starred items excerpted in *Film Rev Digest
Annual* 1976: 219-221): Michael Billington, *ILN* 264 (Jan. 1976):
67; Geoff Brown, *Monthly Film Bull* 42 (Oct. 1975): 220; David
Castell, *Films Illustrated* 5 (Dec. 1975): 124; *Charles Champlin,
Los Angeles Times 19 Nov. 1975; John Coleman, *NewSt* 90 (21
Nov. 1975): 651; *Bruce Cook, *Newsweek* 86 (24 Nov. 1975):
113; Roger Ebert, *Chicago Sun-Times* 25 Nov. 1975: 50; Richard
Eder, *NYT* 8 Nov. 1975: 22; *Philip French, *Times* (London) 21
Nov. 1975: 14; B. Glasser, *Independent Film J* 29 Oct. 1975: 8;
*Sylviane Gold, *New York Post* 8 Nov. 1975; Gordon Gow, *Films
and Filming* 22 (Nov. 1975): 35-36; Benny Green, *Punch* 269 (26
Nov. 1975): 1007; Barbara Hardy, *Dkn* 72 (Jan. 1976): 36-37;
*Howard Kissel, *Women's Wear Daily* 7 Nov. 1975; Murf [A. D.
Murphy], *Variety* 22 Oct. 1975: 34; Dilys Powell, *STimes* (Lon-
don) 23 Nov. 1975: 36; Judith Ripp, *Parents' Mag and Better
Homemaking* 50 (Dec. 1975): 19; Margaret Ronan, *Senior Scholas-
tic* (Teacher's ed.) 107 (16 Dec. 1975): 22; Richard Schickel,
Time 106 (8 Dec. 1975): 71-72; *John Simon, *New York* 8 (17
Nov. 1975): 106, 108; *David Sterritt, *CSM* 5 Dec. 1975; Pat
Strachan, *Films in Rev* 26 (Dec. 1975): 633-634; *David A.
Tilyer, *Film Information* Nov. 1975; William Wolf, *Cue* 15 Nov.
1975: 33.—Note also pre-release notice by Iain McAsh, *Film Rev*
24 (Sept. 1974): 10.]

2944 *The Old Curiosity Shop*, adap. William Trevor. [BBC-TV serial,
started Dec. 1979; also on PBS.—Rev.: Philip Collins, *Lstr* 103
(24 Jan. 1980): 113 (from BBC Radio 4, with comments by
Trevor); Andrew Davies, *TES* 28 Dec. 1979: 15; Stuart Hood, *TES*
1 Feb. 1980: 21.—Note also teacher's guide, *Amer Educator* 3

(Fall 1979): 27.]

Oliver Twist

2945 *The Further Adventures of Oliver Twist*, by David Butler and Hugh Leonard. [Serial on ATV (U.K.).—Rev.: Benny Green, *Punch* 278 (12 Mar. 1980): 436 (see also Miles Kington, "Please Sir, We Want Some More," p. 409); Frances Farrer, *TES* 9 May 1980: 31.]

2946 *Oliver!*, dir. Robin Midgley and Larry Oaks, words and music Lionel Bart. [Albery Theatre (London) prod. opened 21 Dec. 1977.—Rev.: David Castell, *Films Illustrated* 4 (Jan. 1975): 171; Bernard Levin, *STimes* (London) 22 Jan. 1978: 37; Sheridan Morley, *Punch* 274 (11 Jan. 1978): 70; Rosalind Wade, *ContempR* 232 (May 1978): 266-268; Irving Wardle, *Times* (London) 29 Dec. 1977: 5.—Note also release of 1968 film, *Oliver!* dir. Carol Reed.—Rev.: Benny Green, *Punch* 267 (18 Dec. 1974): 1080; I. Rubanova, *Sovetskii ekran* 12 (June 1971): 15.]

Our Mutual Friend

2947 *Our Mutual Friend*, dir. Peter Hammond, adap. Julia Jones and Donald Churchill. [Seven-part serial on BBC2-TV starting 1 Mar. 1976; later on PBS.—Note also background for this prod. by Ian McEwan, "Beneath the Victorian Veneer," *Radio Times* 20 Feb.-5 Mar. 1976: n.pp.—Rev.: A[nthony] B[urton], *Dkn* 72 (Sept. 1976): 164-165; *Owen Findsen, *Cincinnati Enquirer* 16 Apr. 1978; *Judy Flander, *Washington Star* 15 Apr. 1978; *Hugh Gallagher, *Albuquerque J* 16 Apr. 1978; Peter Lennon, *STimes* (London) 7 Mar. 1976: 38; *Dave Montoro, *Florida Times-Union* (Jacksonville) 16 Apr. 1978; John J. O'Connor, *NYT* 14 May 1978: B31; Michael Ratcliffe, *Times* (London) 2 Mar. 1976: 9; James Wolcott, *Village Voice* 17 Apr. 1978: 54; *Baltimore Sun* 13 Apr. 1978; *Syracuse Herald Amer* 16 Apr. 1978.]

Pickwick Papers

2948 *Pickwick Papers*. [Twelve-part serial on BBC Radio-4.—Rev.: Steve Race, *Lstr* 98 (1 Dec. 1977): 726.—Brief notice: Eric Korn, *NewSt* 94 (9 Dec. 1977): 825.]

A Tale of Two Cities

2949 *Chicago Radio Theatre's Production of Charles Dickens's A Tale of Two Cities*, adap., prod., dir. Yuri Rosovsky. All-media Dramatic Workshop. 2 stereo cassettes (107 min).

The Village Coquettes

2950 "There's a Charm in Spring," music Margaret Judd. London: Bosworth, 1970. 4 pp. [Squire Norton's song set for sop. and alto with piano acc.]

VII. Other Miscellanea

2951 Armour, Richard. "Charles Dickens"; "*David Copperfield.*" *It All Started with Freshman English* (New York: McGraw-Hill, 1973), 55-56; 85-97. [2nd rpt. from his *Classics Reclassified*, 1960.]

2952 Barry, James D. "An Autobiographical Fragment by David T. D. Copperfield." *CEA* 39 (May 1977): 22-27.

2952a Brigden, C. A. T., illus. *Characters from Charles Dickens*, orig. drawn J. Clayton Clark. Rochester, Kent: John Hallewell, 1978. [55 pp.] [Brief descriptions of 25 characters excerpted from novels with pen and ink drawings on facing pp.]

2953 Coren, Alan. "A Dingley Dell Situation." *Punch* 227 (28 Nov. 1979): 984-985.

2954 Davies, Robertson. "Dickens Digested." *One Half of Robertson Davies* (New York: Viking Press, 1978), 107-115. ["Ghost story."]

2955 Davis, Russell. "Wery Hard Times." *STimes* (London) 9 July 1978: 16. [Parody of *OCShop.*]

2956 Doyle, Paul A. " 'The Man Who Liked Dickens' on Television." *EWN* 12 (Autumn 1978): 1-3. [Robert Tallman's adap. of Waugh's story.]

2957 Ewart, Gavin. "Dickens and I." *London Rev of Books* 20 Nov. 1980: 8. [Prose-poem.]

2958 Cancelled.

2959 Garfield, Leon, concluded by. *The Mystery of Edwin Drood*, intro. Edward Blishen, illus. Anthony Maitland. London: Deutsch, 1980. 327 pp. [Rev.: Brigid Brophy, *London Rev of Books* 6 Nov. 1980: 9-10; Margaret Drabble, *Lstr* 104 (23 Oct. 1980): 552-553; Stefan Kanfer, *Time* 116 (27 Oct. 1980): 100, 103; Hilary Spurling, *TES* 3 Oct. 1970: 25; J. I. M. Stewart, *TLS* 3 Oct. 1980: 1087.]

2960 Graves, Robert. "*Pickwick Papers* Rewritten," intro. A. S. G. Edwards. *MHRev* no. 25 (Jan. 1973): 9-30. [Chaps. 1-3 abrg., here 1st pub.]

2961 Hartmann, Otto Julius. "Das Hereinwirken der geistigen Welten in das künstliche Schaffen." *Kommenden* 32 (25 June 1978): 17-20. [Spiritualism; incl. *MEDrood*, J. F. Oberlin.]

2962 Hume, Alex Hope. *Strew Roses in the Abbey: Presenting an Ode to the Memory of Charles Dickens (1812-1870) Written in 1870, the Year of His Death and Interment in Westminster Abbey*, [ed. S. Bedale Hume]. [Brisbane: Fortitude Press, 1970.] xxiii, 30 pp.

2963 Luciani, Albino (later Pope John Paul I). "A Charles Dickens: Siamo agli sgoccioli"; "Ai quattro del Circolo Pickwick: Le cantonate e la scala di Mohs." *Illustrissimi: Lettere del Patriarca*, 4th ed. Collana Messaggero, 1 (Padua: Edizioni Messaggero, 1978), 13-19; 95-102. [Hortative.—1st ed. 1976, orig. pub. *Messaggero di S. Antonio* 1971, 1972.—Note also *Illustrissimi: Letters from Pope John Paul I*, trans. William Weaver (Boston, Toronto: Little, Brown, 1978), 3-8; 65-71; note also U. K. ed. trans. Isabel Quigley (London: Collins, 1978); Span. trans. José Legaza et al. (Madrid: Biblioteca de Autores Cristianos, 1978); Germ. trans. Wolfgang Bader and Hans Heilkenbrinker (Zurich and Vienna: Neue Stadt, 1978).—Brief notice: *Dkn* 75 (Spring 1979): 56.]

2964 MacKendrick, Russ. "Christmas Carol Time." *NYT* 11 Dec. 1977: B47. [On 1912 bronze medal by John Conway.]

2965 Onwhyn, Thomas, illus. *Illustrations to Nicholas Nickleby*. Ilkley, Yorks: Ilkley Lit. Festival, 1973. [Facs. rpt. in portfolio of 38 engravings of 1839 from orig. proofs at D House.]

2966 Prenen, Harry. "Tafelgedicht ter gelegenheid van het virede lustrum."

Dutch Dkn 7, xvi (Dec. 1978): 4-9. [Toast-poem for D Fellowship, Haarlem.]

2967 Price, R. G. G. "Inside David Copperfield." *Punch* 270 (4 Feb. 1976): 198-199. [Satirical obscenity trial.]

2968 Sagoff, Maurice. "Oliver Twist." *Shrinklits: Seventy of the World's Towering Classics Cut Down to Size*, illus. Roslyn Schwartz, rev. enl. ed. (New York: Workman, 1980), 33. [1st ed. 1970.]

2969 Waterhouse, Keith. "The Crachit Factor." *Punch* 275 (20 Sept. 1978): 428-429.

2970 —. "Dave Copperfield." *Punch* 276 (6 June 1979): 972-973.

2971 Wolkomir, Richard. "Charles Dickens's Great Mystery." *Psychic* 4 (Apr. 1973): 16-17. [*MEDrood* completed through medium Thomas P. James.]

Unsigned

2972 "The Pickwick Papers, by Charles Dickens." *National Lampoon* 1 (Aug. 1976): 77, 81. [One of a group of "Obligatory Sex Scenes" after various hands.]

APPENDIX

23   *Bleak House,* ed. Duane DeVries. [Contents: Ed., "Background Material," 833-920 (discarded titles, number plans, excerpts from D's ltrs., speeches, and other writings); "Selected Bibliography," 1073-1080; William F. Axton, 1041-1051 (from 160); Trevor Blount, "The Graveyard Satire of *Bleak House* in the Context of 1850," 966-975 (from *RES,* 1963); John Butt, "*Bleak House* in the Context of 1851," 931-949 (from *NCF,* 1955 and rev. for *Dickens at Work,* 1957); G. K. Chesterton, 988-992 (from 2282); Leonard W. Deen, "Style and Unity in *Bleak House,*" 1012-1014 (from *Criticism,* 1961); Robert A. Donovan, "Structure and Idea in *Bleak House,*" 1015-1032 (from *ELH,* 1962); John Forster, 976-984 (from *Life of Charles Dickens,* 1872-1874); Joseph I. Fradin, "Will and Society in *Bleak House,*" 1052-1071 (from *PMLA,* 1961); Robert Garis, 1032-1041 (from 755); George Gissing, 987-988 (from 2335); Humphry House, 923-931 (from *Dickens World,* 1942); Jack Lindsay, 992-995 (from 2371); J. Hillis Miller, 995-1011 (from 2384); Raymond Williams, "Social Criticism in Dickens: Some Problems of Method and Approach," 949-965 (from *CritQ,* 1964).]

24   *Bleak House,* ed. George Ford and Sylvère Monod. [Contents: Eds., "Introduction," ix-xiii; "Introductory Note on Law Courts and Colleges," xvi-xx; "A Note on the Text," 773-813 (working plans, running headlines, textual history); "Textual Notes," 815-880; "The Genesis and Composition of *Bleak House,*" 881-895 (chronology, excerpts from D's ltrs., originals of characters and places); "Backgrounds," 897-929 (items on pollution by anon. authors and by Thomas Carlyle, D, Hector Gavin, R. H. Horne, Henry Mayhew, Thomas Miller, and W. H. Wills and George Hogarth; on government by anon. authors and by Thomas Carlyle; on law courts, inquests, and police by anon. authors and by D); "Bibliography," 985-986; "Anonymous Review of *Bleak House* in the *Examiner,*" (1853), 937-941; George Brimley, "A Review of *Bleak House* in the *Spectator,*" (1853), 933-937; G. K. Chesterton, "Characters in *Bleak House,*" 942-946 (from 2282); A. O. J. Cockshut, "Order and Madness in *Bleak House,*" 960-963 (from *Imagination of Charles Dickens,* 1961); H. M. Daleski, "Transformation in a Sick Society," 970-974 (from 509); George Ford, "A Note on *Bleak*

House and Kafka," 946-947 (from 2330); W. J. Harvey, "The Double Narrative of *Bleak House*," 963-970 (from *Character and the Novel*, 1965); J. Hillis Miller, "The World of *Bleak House*," 947-959 (from 2384); Ian Ousby, 974-984 (see 1451).]

205 Beckwith, Charles E., ed. *Twentieth Century Interpretations of A Tale of Two Cities*. [Contents: Ed., "Introduction," 1-18; "Chronology of Important Dates," 114-117; "Selected Bibliography," 120-122; A. O. J. Cockshut, 104-109 (from *Imagination of Charles Dickens*, 1962); Earle Davis, 29-43 (from *Flint and the Flame*, 1963); Sergei Eisenstein, 100-104 (from 614); John Gross, 19-28 (from *Dickens and the Twentieth Century*, ed. Gross and Pearson, 1962); Jack Lindsay, 52-63 (from *Life and Letters*, 1949); William H. Marshall, "The Method of *A Tale of Two Cities*," 44-51 (from *Dkn*, 1961); George Orwell, 96-100 (see 2393); George Bernard Shaw, 95-96 (from "Preface" to *Man and Superman*, 1903); G. Robert Stange, "Dickens and The Fiery Past: *A Tale of Two Cities* Reconsidered," 64-75 (from *EJ*, 1957); Taylor Stoehr, "The Style," 76-93, 110-113 (from 1890).]

438 Collins, Philip, ed. *Dickens: The Critical Heritage*. [Contents: Ed., "Authorship of Anonymous Items: Evidence for Attributions," 623; "Bibliography," 625-628; Robert L. Patten, "The Sales of Dickens's Works," 617-622; plus 168 items, chiefly contemporary revs. of the novels, by anonymous authors and by J. E. E. D. Lord Acton, Matthew Arnold, Alfred Austin, W. E. Aytoun, Walter Bagehot, George Brimley, B. R. Brough, Robert Buchanan, Charles Buller, C. S. Calverley, J. M. Capes, Thomas Carlyle, Henry Fothergill Chorley, Thomas Cleghorn, Wilkie Collins, John Wilson Croker, E. S. Dallas, D, John Eagles, George Eliot, Cornelius C. Felton, Edward Fitzgerald, Richard Ford, John Forster, William Forsyth, E. B. Hamley, James Hannay, Abraham Hayward, Arthur Helps, Matthew Davenport Hill, John Hollingshead, Thomas Hood, R. H. Horne, William Dean Howells, William Howitt, R. H. Hutton, Francis Jacox, Henry James, John Cordy Jeaffreson, Francis Lord Jeffrey, Charles Kent, G. H. Lewes, T. H. Lister, Arthur Locker, Samuel Lucas, Justin McCarthy, W. C. Macready, Theodore Martin, Harriet Martineau, David Masson, John Stuart Mill, Mary Russell Mitford, Mowbray Morris, Margaret Oliphant, Coventry Patmore, Samuel Phillips, Edgar Allan Poe (see 1550), Thomas Powell, W. B. Rands, Henry Crabb Robinson, John Ruskin, George Augustus Sala, Lord Shaftesbury, Edith Simcox, Richard Simpson, James Spedding, A. P. Stanley, James Fitzjames Stephen, James Augustine Stothert, George Stott, Hippolyte Taine, W. M. Thackeray, Anthony Trollope (see 2433), Queen Victoria, A. W. Ward, Samuel Warren, Edwin P. Whipple.]

848 Gross, Konrad, ed. "Dickens." *Der englische Soziale Roman im 19. Jahrhundert.* [Contents incl.: Trevor Blount, "The Ironmaster and the New Acquisitiveness," 255-268 (from *EIC*, 1965); W. Walter Crotch, "Dickens's Instinct for Reform," 219-230 (from *Dkn*, 1905); William Kent, *"Hard Times* from a Socialist Standpoint," 231-236 (from *Dkn*, 1928); Ingeborg Leimberg, 269-308 (see 1157); Raymond Williams, "Social Criticism in Dickens: Some Problems of Method and Approach," 237-254 (from *CritQ*, 1964).]

1440 Olmsted, John Charles, ed. *A Victorian Art of Fiction: Essays on the Novel in British Periodicals.* [Contents of vol. 1 incl.: Ed., "Introduction," xiii-xxxv; "Charles Dickens and His Works," 325-344 (from *Fraser's Mag*, 1840); H. F. Chorley, *"Martin Chuzzlewit,"* 431-433 (from *Athenaeum*, 1844); Thomas Cleghorn, "Writings of Charles Dickens," 451-473 (from *North British Rev*, 1845); Richard Ford, *"Oliver Twist,"* 277-296 (from *Quarterly Rev*, 1839); T. H. Lister, "Dickens's Tales," 269-274 (from *Edinburgh Rev*, 1838); J. W. Marston, *"The Battle of Life; a Love Story,"* 533 (from *Athenaeum*, 1846).—Vol. 2 incl.: Ed., "Introduction," xiii-xxii; D, "Curious Misprint in the *Edinburgh Review*," 349-352 (from *HsldWds*, 1857); David Masson, *"Pendennis* and *Copperfield:* Thackeray *and* Dickens," 3-35 (from *North British Rev*, 1851); James Fitzjames Stephen, "The Licence of Modern Novelists," 301-333 (*LittleDor;* from *Edinburgh Rev*, 1857) and "The *Edinburgh Review* and Modern Novelists," 343-346 (from *Saturday Rev*, 1857).]

1458 Page, Norman, ed. *Dickens: Hard Times, Great Expectations, and Our Mutual Friend: A Casebook.* [Contents: 43 items from essays, reviews, and books, 8 by D, 3 by anon. reviewers, incl. background material from D, John Forster, R. H. Horne, Henry Mayhew.—On *HardT:* John Butt and Kathleen Tillotson, "The Problems of a Weekly Serial," 50-69 (from *Dickens at Work*, 1957); John Forster, " 'No thesis can be argued in a novel'," 30-31 (from *Examiner*, 1854); George Gissing, "Dickens and the Working Class," 37 (see 2335); Humphry House, "A Novel of Sociological Argument," 45-50 (from *Dickens World*, 1941); David Lodge, 69-87 (see 2373); John Ruskin, "The Critic of Society," 34 (from *Cornhill Mag*, 1860 and *Unto This Last*, 1862); George Bernard Shaw, "Dickens's Portrait of England," 38-45 (see 1749); Richard Simpson, "The Limitations of Dickens," 31-32 (from *Rambler*, 1854); Hippolyte Taine, "The Two Classes," 33 (from *Rev des deux mondes*, 1856 and *History of English Literature*, 1859); Edwin Whipple, "A Reply to Ruskin," 35-36 (from *Atlantic Monthly*, 1877).—On *GreatEx:* G. K. Chesterton, "A Heavier Reality," 102 (from 2283);

H. F. Chorley, " 'The imaginative book of the year'," 94-96 (from *Athenaeum*, 1861); E. S. Dallas, "A Return to Humour," 99 (from *Times*, 1861); John Forster, "Character and Comedy," 100-101 (from *Life of Charles Dickens*, 1872-1874); Barbara Hardy, "The Dickensian Feast," 130-140 (see 884); Martin Meisel, "The Problem of a Novel's Ending," 125-129 (from *EIC*, 1965); Julian Moynahan, "The Hero's Guilt: The Case of *Great Expectations*," (from *EIC*, 1960); Margaret Oliphant, "A Product of Fatigue," 99-100 (from *Blackwood's Mag*, 1862); Robert B. Partlow, Jr., "The Moving I: A Study of the Point of View in *Great Expectations*," 118-124 (from *CE*, 1961); Edwin Whipple, "Dickens's Best Plot," 98 (from *Atlantic Monthly*, 1861).—On *OurMF*: H. F. Chorley, "A Carefully-Wrought Novel," 150 (from *Athenaeum*, 1865); Philip Collins, "The Trained Teacher and Social Mobility," 172-184 (from *Dickens and Education*, 1963); E. S. Dallas, "An Astonishing Fertility," 151-152 (from *Times*, 1865); John Forster, "A Lack of Freshness," 156-157 (from *Life of Charles Dickens*, 1872-1874); Henry James, "Dickens Exhausted," 152-156 (from *Nation*, 1865); Arnold Kettle, "Dickens and Class," 160-171 (from *Dickens and the Twentieth Century*, ed. Gross and Pearson, 1962); Jack Lindsay, "The Symbolic Dust-Heap," 158-159 (from 2371); Kenneth Muir, "Image and Structure in *Our Mutual Friend*," 184-195 (from *E&S*, 1966); Norman Page, "The Problem of Speech," 195-202 (see 1457).]

2064 Wall, Stephen, ed. *Charles Dickens: A Critical Anthology*. [Contents: K. J. Fielding, "The Number Divisions of Dickens's Novels," 528-536 (from *Dkn*, 1958); Ed., "Select Bibliography," 539-540; plus 135 items from essays, revs., ltrs., and books, 53 by D, one by an anon. reviewer and others by the following (for reasons of space, only the authors in "Part Three: Modern Views" have titles and pp.): Matthew Arnold; W. H. Auden, "From 'Dingley Dell and the Fleet'." 458-468 (from *Dyer's Hand*, 1962); Walter Bagehot; John Bayley, "*Oliver Twist:* 'Things as They Really Are'," 442-458 (from *Dickens and the Twentieth Century*, ed. Gross and Pearson, 1962); John Butt and Kathleen Tillotson, "From 'Dickens as a Serial Novelist'," 379-391 (from *Dickens at Work*, 1957); Louis Cazamian (see 370); G. K. Chesterton (see 2283); Philip Collins, "From 'Dickens and His Age'," 468-472 (from 427); Wilkie Collins; George Dolby (from 2312); Fëdor Dostoevski; George Eliot; T. S. Eliot (see 617); Ralph Waldo Emerson (see 621); Edward Fitzgerald; E. M. Forster; John Forster; Robert Garis, "From 'Action and Structure in the Dickens Theatre'," 492-499 (from 755); André Gide; Henry Gifford, "Dickens in Russia: The Initial Phase," 509-519 (from *FMLS*, 1968); George Gissing (see 2335); Graham Greene, "From 'The Young Dickens'," 359-363 (from

Lost Childhood and Other Essays, 1951); Barbara Hardy, 478-490 (from 884); W. J. Harvey, "From 'Character and Narration'," 499-509 (*BleakH;* from *Character and the Novel,* 1965); Thomas Hood; R. H. Horne; Humphry House, "From 'The Changing Scene'," 323-348 (from *Dickens World,* 1941) and "The Macabre Dickens," 351-357 (see 2348); R. H. Hutton; Aldous Huxley; Henry James; Louis James, "From *Fiction for the Working Man 1830-1850*" (*BleakH;* 1963); Francis Lord Jeffrey; Benjamin Jowett; Franz Kafka; Arnold Kettle, "From '*Oliver Twist*'," 358-359 (from *Introduction to the English Novel,* 1951); George Lear; G. H. Lewes; Robert Liddell, "From *A Treatise on the Novel,*" 350-351 (*BleakH;* 1947); T. H. Lister; Percy Lubbock; Georg Lukács, "From *The Historical Novel,*" 432-433 (1962); Otto Ludwig; Steven Marcus, "From 'The Myth of Nell'," 490-492 (from *Dickens: From Pickwick to Dombey,* 1965); Harriet Martineau; David Masson; John Stuart Mill; J. Hillis Miller, "From '*Martin Chuzzlewit*'," 391-405 (see 2384); Sylvère Monod, "Dickens's Language and Style in *David Copperfield,*" 519-527 (see 1356); Margaret Oliphant; George Orwell (see 2393); V. S. Pritchett, "From '*Edwin Drood*'," 349-350 (from *Living Novel,* 1946); Randolph Quirk, 409-422 (see 1595, 2407); John Ruskin; George Saintsbury; George Santayana; George Bernard Shaw (see 1749); James Fitzjames Stephen; Leslie Stephen; Harry Stone, "From 'Dickens and Interior Monologue'," 422-432 (from *PQ,* 1959); A. C. Swinburne (see 2429); Hippolyte Taine; W. M. Thackeray; Lionel Trilling, 363-374 (see 2016); Anthony Trollope; Dorothy Van Ghent, "From 'On *Great Expectations*'," 375-379 (from *English Novel: Form and Function,* 1953); Raymond Williams, "The Industrial Novels: *Hard Times,*" 405-409 (from *Culture and Society 1780-1950,* 1958); Angus Wilson, "The Heroes and Heroines of Dickens," 433-442 (from *Dickens and the Twentieth Century,* ed. Gross and Pearson, 1962); Virginia Woolf; William Wordsworth.]

2082 Watt, Ian, ed. *The Victorian Novel: Modern Essays in Criticism.* [Contents incl.: John Butt, "The Serial Publication of Dickens's Novels *Martin Chuzzlewit* and *Little Dorrit,*" 70-82 (from *Pope, Dickens and Others,* 1969); Robert Alan Donovan, "Structure and Idea in *Bleak House,*" 83-109 (from *ELH,* 1962); T. S. Eliot, 133-141 (see 1849); Humphry House, "The Macabre Dickens," 40-46 (see 2348); J. Hillis Miller, "*Our Mutual Friend,*" 123-132 (from afwd. to New American Lib. ed., 1964); V. S. Pritchett, "The Comic World of Dickens," 27-39 (from *Lstr,* 1954); G. Robert Stange, 110-122 (see 1849); Kathleen Tillotson, "Introductory," 3-26 (incl. *DSon;* from *Novels of the Eighteen Forties,* 1954); Raymond Williams, "The Industrial Novels," 142-164 (incl. *HardT;* from *Culture and Society 1780-1950,* 1958).]

2331 Ford, George H. and Lauriat Lane, Jr., eds. *The Dickens Critics.*
[Contents: Ed. (Lane), "Introduction: Dickens and Criticism," 1-
18; Emile Chartier, "Imagination in the Novel," 171-180 (from
Rev de Paris, 1940 and *En lisant Dickens,* 1945); G. K. Chesterton,
109-121, 122-125 (see 2283); T. S. Eliot, 151-152 (see 617);
George H. Ford, "*David Copperfield,*" 349-365 (from intro. to
Riverside ed., 1958); George Gissing, "Dickens's Satiric Por-
traiture," 76-94 (from 2335); Graham Greene, "The Young Dick-
ens," 244-252 (from intro. to *OliverTw,* 1950 and *Lost Childhood
and Other Essays,* 1951); Humphry House, "The Macabre Dick-
ens," 190-197 (see 2348); Aldous Huxley, "The Vulgarity of Little
Nell," 153-157 (from *Vulgarity in Literature,* 1930); Henry James,
"The Limitations of Dickens," 48-54 (from *Nation,* 1865 and
Views and Reviews, 1908); Edgar Johnson, "*The Christmas Carol*
and the Economic Man," 270-278 (from *ASch,* 1952 and *D: His
Tragedy and Triumph,* 1952); Arnold Kettle, "Dickens: *Oliver
Twist,*" 252-270 (from *Introduction to the English Novel,* 1951);
George Henry Lewes, "Dickens in Relation to Criticism," 54-74
(from *Fortnightly Rev,* 1872); Jack Lindsay, "Final Judgment,"
233-243 (see 2371); David Masson, "Dickens and Thackeray,"
25-37 (from *British Novelists and Their Styles,* 1859); Alice Mey-
nell, "Charles Dickens as a Man of Letters," 95-108 (from *Atlantic
Monthly,* 1903); J. Hillis Miller, "*Dombey and Son,*" 366-373
(from 2384); Robert Morse, "*Our Mutual Friend,*" 197-213 (from
PR, 1949); George Orwell, "Charles Dickens," 157-171 (from
2393); Edgar Allan Poe, 19-24 (see 1550); V. S. Pritchett, "The
Comic World of Dickens," 309-324 (from *Lstr,* 1954 and
Avon Book of Modern Writing, 1955); John Ruskin, "A Note on
Hard Times," 47-48 (from *Cornhill Mag,* 1860 and *Unto This
Last,* 1862); George Santayana, "Dickens," 135-151 (from *Dial,*
1921 and *Soliloquies in England,* 1922); George Bernard Shaw,
125-135 (see 1749); G. Robert Stange, 294-308 (see 1849); James
Fitzjames Stephen, "*A Tale of Two Cities,*" 38-46 (from *Saturday
Rev,* 1859); Lionel Trilling, 279-293 (see 2016); Anthony Trol-
lope, "Charles Dickens," 74-76 (from 2433); Dorothy Van Ghent,
"The Dickens World: A View from Todgers's," 213-232 (from *SR,*
1950); Rex Warner, "On Reading Dickens," 181-189 (from *Cult
of Power,* 1947); Angus Wilson, "Charles Dickens: A Haunting,"
374-385 (from *CritQ,* 1960); Morton Dauwen Zabel, "*Bleak
House:* The Undivided Imagination," 325-348 (from intro. to
Riverside ed., 1965 and *Craft and Character in Modern Fiction,*
1957).]

ADDENDA

Secondary Sources

add1   Baker, William. "Dickens, David Copperfield and the King's School." *Cantuarian* 43 (1979): 100-101.

add2   Bentley, Nicholas. "A First Edition Mystery: Some Fancy Forensic Spadework." *Antiquarian Book Monthly Rev* 4 (Feb. 1977): 48-50. [*Travelling Letters, Written on the Road,* pub. N.Y. 1846, later incl. in *PictIt.*]

add3   Chatterjee, Visvanath. "Saratchandra and Dickens." *Aspects of Literature* (Calcutta: Progressive Pubs., 1978), 183-189. [Rpt. from *Sarat Centenary Souvenir,* 1975.]

add4   Dello Buono, Carmen Joseph, ed. *Rare Early Essays on Charles Dickens.* Rare Early Essay Ser. [Norwood, Pa.] : Norwood Eds., 1978. 208 pp. [Contents: A. St. John Adcock, "Dickens," 189-202 (from *Famous Houses and Literary Shrines of London,* 1929); Alfred Ainger, "Mr. Dickens's Amateur Theatricals: A Reminiscence," 28-55 (from *Lectures and Essays,* II, 1905); J. H. Balfour Browne, "*Bleak House* (Dickens)," 137-148 (from *Essays Critical and Political,* I, 1907); Percy Fitzgerald, "Charles Dickens as an Editor" and "Charles Dickens at Home," 57-87, 88-135 (from *Recreations of a Literary Man,* 1883); Harry Furniss, "Charles Dickens—As an Actor," 159-186 (from *Some Victorian Men,* 1924); Thomas Powell, "Charles Dickens," 1-26 (from *Living Authors of England,* 1849); Ernie Trory, "Dickens in the Soviet Union," 205-208 (from *Mainly About Books,* 1945); Claude C. H. Williamson, "The Humour of Dickens," 151-157 (from *Writers of Three Centuries,* 1920).]

add5   Favell, Christine. *At the Time of Charles Dickens.* London: Longman, 1977. 64 pp. [Primary school text.]

add6   Herman, Barry E. "Fagin the Villain or Fagin the Villainous Jew." *Judaica Post* 7 (Sept.-Oct. 1979): 962-964. [Fagin on commemorative stamps issued by Botswana and by Barbuda.]

add7   Jablkowska, Róża. "Kunszt potocznego jezyka w setna rocznice śmierci Karola Dickensa (1812-1870)." *Jezyki obce w szkole* no. 71 (1970): 257-263. [Colloquial lang.]

add8   Martin, Jean-Paul. "Le cauchemar de l'histoire (Dickens, *A Tale of Two Cities*, 1859)," in *Recherches sur le roman historique en Europe, XVIIIe-XIXe siècles.* Centre de Recherches d'Histoire et Littérature au XVIIIe et au XIXe Siècles, 10; Annales Littéraires de l'Univ. de Besançon, 233 (Paris: Belles Lettres, 1979), II, 133-162.

add9   Persico, Gemma. *Educazione et società nell'Inghilterra vittoriana: Per una rilettura di Hard Times.* Quaderni de pedagogia, 2. Catania: Edigraf, 1978. 32 pp.

add10   Swales, Martin. "The German Bildungsroman and 'The Great Tradition'." *CCrit* 1 (1979): 91-105. [Incl. *DavidC, GreatEx.*]

add11   Vasilev, Aleksandar. "Carls Dikens—voenen Korespondent v Balgarija." *Balgarski zurnalist* 8 (1974): 42-43. [Claims D as war correspondent in Bulgaria.]

Reprints

Dickens's Works

Miscellanea

add12   "In Memoriam," in *Thackeray the Humorist and the Man of Letters: The Story of His Life and Literary Labours. . .*, by Theodore Taylor [i.e., John Camden Hotten] (1864; rpt. New York: Haskell, 1971), 224-231. [Orig. in *Cornhill Mag,* Feb. 1864.]

Dissertations

add13   Mounajjed, O. "Développement du thème de l'enfance dans les romans de Charles Dickens" (Paris III, 1978).

add14   Sadrin, Anny. "L'Être et l'avoir dans les romans de Charles Dickens" (Paris III, 1980).

Miscellaneous

III. Scripts of Plays Chiefly for Schools

A Christmas Carol
add15 *Scrooge,* adap. James Leisy. Delaware Water Gap, Pa.: Shawnee
Press, 1978. 96 pp. [Musical.]

SUBJECT INDEX

Adaptation (cont'd)
  —Stage (cont'd)
    —*NichN* 2940
    —*OliverTw* 736, 2041
    —Biography 2907
  —Television 121, 1707, 2956
    —*CCarol* 2911, 2920, 2921, 2925
    —*DavidC* 2929
    —*GreatEx* 2930
    —*HardT* 2934
    —*NichN* 2942
    —*OCShop* 2944
    —*OliverTw* 2945
    —*OurMF* 2947
    —Biography 2906, 2908
  —sa   Audio-Visual Aids
Address, Forms of: su   Style
Adolescent: *see* Child
Advertisements: su   Publishing
Affective Criticism: *see* Reader's Response
Ainsworth, William Harrison 1300, 2315
Alberta, University of 2180
Alienation: su   Society
Allegory 115, 780, 2479
  —*BleakH* 1375, 1478
  —*DavidC* 1375, 2052
  —*DSon* 1556
  —*GreatEx* 130
  —*HardT* 1556, 1986
  —*OCShop* 626, 1375
  —Late Novels 2733
  —sa   Symbolism
America 9, 274, 349, 392, 421, 433, 493, 545, 776, 820, 888, 898, 1012, 1036, 1037, 1217, 1333, 1377, 1379, 1409, 1675, 1726, 1885, 2112, 2222, 2349, 2439, 2472, 2597
  —*MChuz* 631, 1499
  —Architecture 165
  —Boston 548
  —Illinois 532
  —Institutions 469

America (cont'd)
  —Literature 750, 898, 996, 2545, 2601
  —New York: *see* general entries under America
  —Ohio 679, 681
  —Philadelphia 2012
  —Pittsburgh 946
  —Reception 168, 272, 438, 785, 2085
    —*OurMF* 938
  —Shakers 357
  —West Point 357
  —sa   Biography (1842), (1867)
Amis, Kingsley 223
Analogy: su   Style
Andersen, Hans Christian 279, 1474, 2542
Animals 2677, 2594
  —*BarnR* 1853
  —*BleakH* 223
  —*MChuz* 1734
  —Birds
    —*BleakH* 484
  —Dogs 1826, 2111, 2291
  —Mythic 1564
Animation 643, 1769, 1957, 2594, 2736
Anthologies etc. 1-3, 7-9, 2240-2243, 2245, 2246
  —*PickP* 2257
Appearance and Reality 115, 2724, 2736
  —*BleakH* 1415, 1451
  —*GreatEx* 183, 515
  —*LittleDor* 1403
  —*MChuz* 2725
  —*OurMF* 1394
  —*PickP* 748
  —Deception
    —*LittleDor* 2709
  —Disguise 1611
    —*HardT* 1284, 1736
    —*OurMF* 1343
  —Hypocrisy
    —*HardT* 811

Appreciative Criticism 110, 251, 289,
  302, 360a, 412a, 512, 535a, 546,
  628, 698, 768, 778, 783, 838, 927,
  998, 1027, 1093, 1139, 1142, 1149,
  1172, 1334, 1352, 1370, 1473,
  1628, 1684, 1806, 1821, 1928,
  1933, 2007, 2011, 2044, 2045,
  2061, 2274, 2287, 2300, 2321,
  2388, 2401, 2420, 2429, 2444
  —*BleakH* 835
  —*CCarol* 466, 973, 1672, 2031
  —*CrickH* 404
  —*DavidC* 1143, 1518
  —*GreatEx* 477, 1374
  —*OurMF* 928
  —*PickP* 555
  —*TaleTwoC* 1626
Archetype: *see* Genre—Fable and Fairy
  Tale; Myth
Architecture 2614
  —America 165
Arctic 1642
Ardizzone, Edward: su Illustrators
Argentina
  —Centenary Events 628
Arnold, Matthew 1199
Art 630, 955, 1291, 1629, 2149,
  2614
  —*PictIt* 2467
  —Barrow 344
  —Daumier 896
  —D's collection of 2445
  —Frith 708, 1421, 2125
  —Hogarth 970, 1272, 1274, 1701,
    2574, 2641
  —Hunt 1912
  —Landseer 1162
  —Millais 247
  —Miller 1018
  —Royal Academy 1664
  —Scheffer 1715
  —Stanfield 246, 1321, 2267
  —sa other arts and Pre-Raphaelite
    Brotherhood
Artist (Theme) 1897, 2663
  —*DavidC* 971, 1425, 1987, 2659

Artist (Theme) (cont'd)
  —*LittleDor* 1150, 1403
  —*MH'sClock* 1699
  —*OurMF* 1881
Artistic Development (D's) 146, 455,
  509, 527, 582, 592, 749, 798, 855,
  882, 955, 1523, 1728, 1896, 2128,
  2580, 2609, 2686, 2710, 2727
  —*NicbN* 364
  —*PickP* 2510
  —*SBoz* 543, 845
  —Early Novels 2667, 2668
  —Late Novels 814
Auctions and Sales 358, 1426, 1427,
  1428, 1784, 1785, 2186, 2198,
  2233, 2234, 2445
Audio-Visual Aids 2777, 2778, 2779,
  2781, 2782, 2783, 2784, 2858,
  2861, 2862, 2863, 2891, 2895,
  2896, 2897, 2907, 2912, 2914,
  2922, 2924, 2934
  —*BleakH* 2864
  —*CCarol* 2786, 2787, 2788, 2789,
    2790, 2791, 2865, 2866, 2867,
    2868, 2869, 2870, 2871
  —*CStories* 2860
  —*DavidC* 2792, 2872, 2889
  —*DSon* 2873
  —*GreatEx* 2793, 2794, 2795, 2796,
    2874, 2875, 2876, 2877, 2892,
    2894
  —*HardT* 2892
  —"*HRom*" 2797, 2878
  —*MEDrood* 2893
  —*OCShop* 2943
  —*OliverTw* 2798, 2799, 2879,
    2880, 2881, 2890
  —*PickP* 2871, 2882, 2883, 2884
  —*PictIt* 2885
  —*TaleTwoC* 2800, 2801, 2802,
    2804, 2886, 2887, 2888
  —Biography 2780, 2857, 2859
  —Surveys 2170
Auerbach, Erich 2660
Austen, Jane 851, 2546, 2589
Australia 401, 1138, 1146

Family (cont'd)
  —*HardT* 742
  —*NichN* 187
  —*TaleTwoC* 977, add8
  —Idealization 2707
  —Incest 808
    —*LittleDor* 1691
  —Late Novels 2521
  —Uncle
    —*PickP* 1170
  —sa   Child; Parent and Child
Fantasy: su   Genre; also Genre—
  Fable and Fairy Tale; Myth; Super-
  natural
Farina, Salvatore 1090
Fate: *see* Providence and Fate
Faulkner, William 109, 218, 609, 853,
  1043, 2447, 2466, 2592, 2704
Feeling 882
  —*DSon* 563, 1824
  —Melancholy
    —*OCShop* 1301
Feminist Criticism 331, 366, 381,
  1395
  —*GreatEx* 619
  —sa   Woman
Fiction (Theme) 883, 2102, 2741
  —*DavidC* 153
  —*LittleDor* 1691
  —*MChuz* 1674
Fiction, Theory of (D's) 442, 1269,
  2470
Fictitiousness 1058, 1882, 2588
  —*DavidC* 425, 675
  —*HardT* 2139
  —*LittleDor* 123, 342
  —*OliverTw* 1332
  —*PickP* 1077, 2706
  —*SBoz* 822, 1332
  —Characters
    —Gamp, Sarah 359, 2036
    —Pickwick 359, 2036
Fielding, Henry 1646, 2532
Fields, Annie and James 380, 1675,
  2349
Fildes, Luke: su   Illustrators

Film 322, 375, 614, 980a, 1135,
  1882, 2183, 2222
  —sau   Adaptation; Audio-Visual
  Aids
Fire: su   Imagery
Fitzgerald, F. Scott 722
Flaubert, Gustave 2735
Fogazzaro, Antonio 1090
Fonblanque, Albany 283
Food and Drink 485, 1118, 1128,
  1217, 2081, 2448, 2596, 2597
  —*DSon* 2080
  —*GreatEx* 884
  —*HardT* 2080
  —*MChuz* 201, 1995
  —*PickP* 2010, 2080
  —Recipes 921
  —sa   Christmas
Ford, George 133
Form: *see* Structure
Forster, John 278, 282, 283, 316,
  317, 318, 442, 479, 516, 520, 521,
  522, 524, 624, 656, 657, 912, 1664,
  1985, 1998, 2032, 2156, 2416,
  2655
Foucault, Michel 1697a
France 1365
  —Centenary Events 1355, 2002
  —Conferences and Festivals 2182,
  2193
  —Reception 692, 1350, 1367
  —Translation 222, 768, 1024,
  1350, 1367, 1638
    —*BleakH* 1023
Frederic, Harold 1203
Freedom and Confinement 592, 1201,
  1609, 2131, 2558, 2610
  —*BleakH* 223, 1610
  —*DSon* 1659
  —*MChuz* 1570
  —*OCShop* 1659
  —*OliverTw* 696
  —Escape 2689
  —Prison 770
    —*LittleDor* 202, 447, 603, 849,
    1004, 1529, 1659

India (cont'd)
   —*NicbN* 1108
   —Centenary Events 512, 2212
   —Literature 2212
   —Mutiny of 1857 1437
Individual and Society: su   Society
Industrialism 139, 277, 323, 428,
   2514, 2770
   —*BleakH* 239, 1204
   —*DavidC* 1105
   —*DSon* 647, 992, 1163
   —*HardT* 256, 489, 503, 660, 773,
      856, 861, 909, 913, 1104,
      1311, 1319, 1429, 1438, 1805,
      1903, 2119
   —*HsldWds* 194
   —*NicbN* 1319
   —*OCShop* 647
   —*OliverTw* 1903
   —*OurMF* 1588
   —*PickP* 992
   —Early Novels 370
   —Late Novels 2647
   —sa   Economics; Railway
Influence of
   —Bentham 804
   —Browning 1900
   —Bulwer-Lytton 390, 1585
   —Bunyan 215, 536
   —Carlyle 189, 389, 701, 802, 804,
      1058, 1070, 1258, 1438, 1588,
      1727, 1776, 1948, 1950, 2691
   —Cervantes 567, 740
   —Chesterfield 1239
   —Collins 1191, 1358
   —Defoe 1067
   —Fielding 1646
   —Goldsmith 347
   —Hawthorne 1891
   —Hogarth 970, 1272
   —Holbein 942
   —Hood 453
   —Hugo 1300
   —Irving 351, 352
   —Jerrold 1776
   —Jonson 587

Influence of (cont'd)
   —Milton 505
   —*Portfolio* 1974
   —Punch 215
   —Rogers 140
   —Scott 362, 1413
   —Shakespeare 397, 875, 961,
      1308, 1376
   —Sheridan 1398
   —Smith 1227
   —Tennyson 1051
   —Wordsworth 639
   —sa   Comparative Criticism;
      Sources of
Influence on
   —American Literature 750
   —Babits 1194
   —Baroja 586, 963
   —Beckett 1695
   —Bergman 1135
   —Brontë 232
   —Carroll 767, 902a
   —Collins 175, 1191, 1994
   —Conrad 1459
   —Dostoevski 1039a, 1086, 1141,
      2122, 2561
   —Eisenstein 1531
   —Eliot, George 823
   —Eliot, T. S. 633
   —Faulkner 609, 1043
   —Frith 2125
   —Genre
      —Autobiography 771
   —German Literature 607, 1446
   —Gissing 388, 816
   —Griffith 614, 1531
   —Harte 750, 1372
   —Howells 752, 2545
   —Hungarian Literature 1161
   —Indian Literature 2212
   —James 231, 1587
   —Japanese Literature 1294
   —Joyce 2103
   —Kafka 929, 1842, 1952
   —Lawrence 805
   —Lawson 779, 1237

Mexico (cont'd)
—Reception
  —*CCarol* 1448
Mill, John Stuart 763, 771, 1685
Millais, John Everett 247
Miller, Alfred Jacob: su   Illustrators
Milton, John 505
Miser: su   Characters—Types
Mitton, Thomas 97
Modern Language Association of
  America 278, 2222
Money: su   Economics
Monod, Sylvère 768, 1023, 1024,
  1638
Morality 214, 537, 592, 798, 802,
  845, 884, 1019, 1034, 1060, 1080,
  1169, 1269, 1559, 1584, 1585,
  1917, 2062, 2157, 2379, 2384,
  2479, 2490, 2507, 2513, 2592,
  2595, 2636, 2648, 2676, 2718,
  2768
—*BarnR* 1539, 1634
—*BleakH* 1266, 1451, 1553, 1742,
  1813, 2133
—*CCarol* 135, 926
—*DavidC* 1207
—*DSon* 1150, 1241, 1329, 1539,
  1556, 2118
—"*GS'sExpl*" 1971, 2028
—*GreatEx* 163, 329, 694, 1150,
  1207, 1326, 1338, 1339, 1660,
  1725, 1849, 2092
—*HardT* 1180, 1556
—*LittleDor* 342, 945, 1004, 2016
—*MChuz* 187, 200, 201, 1259,
  2642
—*OCShop* 626, 1539
—*OliverTw* 510, 620, 696, 1134,
  1613, 1659, 1967, 1982
—*OurMF* 842, 1089, 1703
—*PickP* 1035, 1627
—Altruism 2564, 2728
  —*BleakH* 611
—Benevolence 955
  —*LittleDor* 1468, 1988
  —*OCShop* 1468

Morality (cont'd)
—Benevolence (cont'd)
  —*PickP* 1468, 1843
—Conscience
  —*BarnR* 1239
—Duty
  —*DavidC* 230
—Early Novels 370
—Egoism
  —*DSon* 859
  —*GreatEx* 859
  —*MChuz* 1259
  —*TaleTwoC* 859
—Excess 2605
—Orderliness 340
—Work 2519
—sa   Good and Evil; Religion
Morley, Henry 283
Motion Pictures: *see* Film
Mudie's Library 844
Music 501, 1682, 2370, 2614
—*HMan* 1056
—*LittleDor* 833
Myth 115, 384, 955, 1564, 1984,
  2640
—*BleakH* 722
—*DavidC* 1250, 1937
—*GreatEx* 535
—*MChuz* 505, 1069, 1921, 2725
—*PickP* 2627
—*SBoz* 845
—sa   Genre—Fable and Fairy Tale;
  Genre—Fantasy; Supernatural
Mytton, John 1915

Nabokov, Vladimir 1147
Names and Naming 292, 780, 2557
—*BleakH* 1597
—*DavidC* 899, 1937
—*HardT* 1140, 1677
—*MEDrood* 684
—*OurMF* 1064, 1089
Narrator 115, 365, 575, 853, 883,
  1080, 1107, 1584, 1917, 2493,
  2543, 2552, 2624, 2636, 2654,

Optimism and Pessimism (cont'd)
  2124, 2621, 2676, 2740
  —*BleakH* 1733, 1813
  —*GreatEx* 1116
  —*HardT* 856
  —*LittleDor* 782, 1151, 1244,
    1468, 1733
  —*OCShop* 1468
  —*OurMF* 1470, 1733
  —*PickP* 1468
Order and Disorder 340, 2683
  —*DavidC* 2477
  —*LittleDor* 949
  —*OurMF* 519
  —Late Novels 1674a
Orphan: su   Child
Orr, William Somerville 174
Orwell, George 199, 387, 1324, 2073
Overs, John 1815, 1816
Oxenford, John 1846

Painters: *see* Art
Palmerston, Henry John Temple 98
Parent and Child 851, 1170, 1405,
  1536, 1984, 2017, 2384, 2575,
  2656, 2701, 2703
  —*BleakH* 2178
  —*DavidC* 2042
  —*DSon* 834, 1308, 1824
  —*GreatEx* 538, 717, 1523, 2105
  —*HardT* 1308, 1834
  —*MChuz* 1921
  —*NichN* 1709
  —*OCShop* 1308
  —Daughter 2451, 2438, 2566
    —*DSon* 2554
  —Father 1643, 2451, 2512, 2538, 2566
    —*LittleDor* 1691, 1705
  —Mother
    —*DSon* 2554
  —sa   Child; Family
Parody of Criticism
  —*BleakH* 677
Parody etc. (of D) 1372, 2951
  —*CCarol* 2901, 2969

Parody etc. (of D) (cont'd)
  —*DavidC* 2952, 2967, 2970
  —*OCShop* 2955
  —*OliverTw* 2968
  —*PickP* 2953, 2972
Past: su   Time
Pastoral: su   Nature
Pater, Walter 771
Pavese, Cesare 1871
Perception
  —*BleakH* 1451
Pérez Galdós, Benito 1176, 1177,
  1706, 1760, 2159
Perkins Institute for the Blind (Boston)
  1032
Personal Recollections of D 502, 655,
  2273, 2278, 2308, 2309, 2310,
  2311, 2411
Perugini, Kate (Dickens) 2428
Pessimism: *see* Optimism and Pessimism
Peyrouton, Noel C.: su   Collections
Philadelphia 2012
  —Dickens Fellowship 1781
  —Free Library 2232
Philanthropy: su   Society
Philosophical Criticism 359, 371, 613,
  2036, 2588
  —*CCarol* 786
  —*HardT* 150, 890
  —*LittleDor* 1468
  —*OCShop* 1468
  —*PickP* 1077, 1468
  —Hegel
    —*LittleDor* 676
  —Marx 594, 595, 924, 992, 1074,
    1075, 1087, 1317, 1687, 1765,
    1953a, 2352, 2452
    —*BleakH* 1410
    —*GreatEx* 1697
    —*LittleDor* 1455
    —*MChuz* 1947
  —Sartre
    —*OurMF* 1470
  —sa   Utilitarianism
Phrenology: su   Science
Picaresque: su   Genre

Reception (cont'd)
 —Hungary 1041, 1091
 —Iceland 935
 —Italy 1544
 —Mexico
  —*CCarol* 1448
 —Netherlands 1071
 —Norway 299
 —Poland 1095, 1113, 2099
 —Romania 2046
 —Russia 144, 721, 2202, 2231,
  2458, add4
 —sa   America; Surveys of Criticism
Recordings: *see* Audio-Visual Aids
Redemption: su   Self
Reed College (Dunedin) 1232
Reed, Carol 1652
Referentiality: *see* Fictitiousness
Reform: su   Society
Regeneration: su   Self; Society
Reich, Charles A. 719
Religion 247, 423, 714, 1315,
  2080, 2093, 2129, 2132,
  2154, 2245, 2540, 2595,
  2601, 2657, 2660, 2671,
  2688, 2963
 —*BattL* 347
 —*BleakH* 536
 —*CCarol* 941, 1505
 —*DavidC* 724, 1524
 —*GreatEx* 2063
 —*HardT* 836, 873
 —*LittleDor* 185, 202, 907, 2761
 —*MChuz* 505, 2685
 —*MEDrood* 474, 2752
 —*OCShop* 1539
 —*OliverTw* 696
 —*TaleTwoC* 674
 —Bible 2576
 —Biblical Allusions 2487
  —*DavidC* 2052
  —*GreatEx* 1725
  —*HardT* 2104
 —Catholicism
  —*PictIt* 2467
 —Clergy 1603

Religion (cont'd)
 —Deadly Sins 1198
 —Dissent 503
 —Evangelicalism 1559
  —*BleakH* 275, 1002
  —*LittleDor* 275, 1002
 —Original Sin
  —*DavidC* 1516
  —*DSon* 1516
  —*OCShop* 1516
 —Protestantism
  —*BarnR* 1539
 —Puritanism 2379
  —*DavidC* 1562
 —Secular
  —Late Novels 2496
 —Shakers 357
 —Symbolism 955
 —Unitarianism
  —*DSon* 1539
Research
 —In Progress (1971) 1307
 —Opportunities 164, 1497
 —Trends 113
Revolution: su   Society
Reynolds, G. M. 1303, 1521
Rhetoric: *see* Style
Richardson, Samuel 396
Rochester: *see* Kent
Rockingham Castle (Northants) 419
Rogers, Samuel 140
Romance: su   Genre
Romania
 —Centenary Events 332
 —Reception 2046
Romanticism 613, 802, 897, 1150,
  1893, 1897, 1958, 2222, 2516,
  2611, 2625, 2671, 2682, 2701
 —*BleakH* 1742
 —*CStories* 1513
 —*DavidC* 763
 —*DSon* 944
 —*LittleDor* 2499
 —*MChuz* 1136
 —*OCShop* 944
 —*SBoz* 944

Symbolism (cont'd)
  —*OCShop* 111
  —*OurMF* 125, 1089, 1174, 1768,
    1914
  —*PickP* 1627
  —Beacon
    —*GreatEx* 1233
  —Clock 2540
  —Cucumber
    —*NichN* 1430
  —Gibbet
    —*GreatEx* 1233
  —Inheritance 770
  —Journey 2769
  —Religion 955
  —Sex 294
  —Ship
    —*GreatEx* 1233
  —Storm
    —*DavidC* 1052
  —Water 770, 1650
    —*DavidC* 538
    —*LittleDor* 672
    —*OurMF* 672, 1445, 1515
  —sa   Allegory; Imagery
Synopses: *see* Plot—Encyclopedias and
  Companions
Széchenyirol, Istvan 739

Tauchnitz 518
Taylor, Meadows 994
Teaching of
  —*DavidC* 1205
  —*GreatEx* 528, 680, 1182, 1884, 2785
  —*HardT* 517, 1182, 1852
  —*OliverTw* 769, 1614, 2785
  —*TaleTwoC* 528, 2785
  —D 565, 2144
  —Novels 161
  —Social Conditions 643a
  —Writing 2692
  —sa   Student Aids
Technique, General
  —*TaleTwoC* 864, 977
  —Laughter

Technique, General (cont'd)
  —Laughter (cont'd)
    —*OurMF* 1754
  —Short Fiction 1756
Tennyson, Alfred 791, 886, 1051,
  1744
Tense: su   Style
Ternan, Ellen 705, 1015
Texas, University of 354, 772
Texts
  —Book Titles
    —*HardT* 179
  —Readings (D's) 291, 435, 436,
    456
  —sa   Editions
Textual Criticism
  —*BleakH* 24, 1368, 2079
  —*DSon* 42
  —"GS'sExpl" 196
  —*GreatEx* 1669
  —*LittleDor* 64, 2079
  —*MEDrood* 65
Thackeray, William Makepeace 260,
  348, 411, 1472, 1506, 1639, 1747,
  1855, 1926, 1992, 2116, 2167,
  2168, 2317, 2464, 2500, 2523,
  2546, 2624, 2686, 2744, add12
Theatre: *see* Drama and Theatre
Theses
  —Bibliography 959, 1688
  —sa   Dissertations
Thompson, T. J. 1481
Thoms, William John 1188
Thornton, Charles Irving 392
Time 365, 575, 699, 714, 1650,
  2101, 2480, 2540
  —*BleakH* 1665
  —*Chimes* 2096
  —*CCarol* 1546
  —*DavidC* 574, 2684
  —*DSon* 647
  —*GreatEx* 1218, 1940, 2051
  —*HardT* 956
  —*LittleDor* 945, 1663
  —*MH'sClock* 1218
  —*MEDrood* 818

Warren, Samuel 1868
Waste: *see* Society—Sanitation
Water: su   Symbolism
Watson, Lavinia and Richard 419
Waugh, Evelyn 1315, 1612, 2956
Webster, Benjamin 2049
Well (D's at Gadshill) 891
Wellcome Institute of the History of
    Medicine 759
Weller, Christiana 1481
Welles, Orson 685
Wells, H. G. 2075
West, Nathanael 1542
Whitehead, Charles 553
Whitstable 686
Wilkie, David 396
Williams, Raymond 1464
Wills, William Henry 459, 1187, 2260
Wilson, Angus 1209
Winchester School 2199
Wisbech and Fenland Museum 44
Woman 340, 412, 910, 1013, 1253,
    1254, 1369, 1900, 2017, 2034,
    2093, 2222, 2410, 2431, 2489,

Women (cont'd)
    2646, 2656, 2678, 2704, 2728,
    2744
    —*BleakH* 1347
    —*CStories* 1970
    —*DavidC* 1200, 1371
    —*DSon* 156, 968, 2165
    —*LittleDor* 907, 2155, 2709
    —*PickP* 1627
    —Fallen 195, 1047, 1061, 2517,
        2698
        —*DavidC* 892, 1964
        —*DSon* 1964
        —*OliverTw* 1964
    —Idealization 934, 1611, 2772
    —Spinster 195
    —sa   Feminist Criticism
Woollcott, Alexander 376
Word and Phrases: su   Style
Wordsworth, William 530, 639, 853,
    2499
Work 2613
    —Morality 2519

WORKS

AllYR
    —General Criticism 636
    —Comparative Criticism
        —Mayhew 969
    —Contributors 518, 1969, 2325,
        2670
        —Collins 2729
    —Editions 518
    —Language (Theme) 534
    —Law
        —Capital Punishment 470
    —Letter Book 415
    —Politics 739
    —Publishing 536a, 844, 1924
    —Science
        —Paleontology 1744
    —Serialization 2494
    —Uncollected Works 1899

AmerN
    —General Criticism 621, 776, 898
    —Comedy and Humor 1333
    —Editions 18-20, 267, 269, 2223
        —First 271
    —Education
        —Deaf and Dumb 1032
    —Influence on
        —Melville 1125
    —Publishing 273
    —Reception 1378
        —America 267
    —Setting 689

BarnR
    —Animals 1853
    —Characters
        —Chester, Sir John 408, 1239

"HRom" (cont'd)
—Genre (cont'd)
—Fable and Fairy Tale 2013

"HTree"
—Christmas 1968
—Genre
—Romance 1968

HsldWds
—General Criticism 636, 1187,
1836
—Body
—Beard 1184
—Comparative Criticism
—Mayhew 969
—Reynold's *Mysteries of Lon-
don* 1303, 1521
—Contributors 1185, 1186, 1969,
2325
—Collins 2729
—Ollier 383
—Oxenford 1846
—Wills 459, 1187, 2260
—Genre
—Detective and Crime Fiction
1931
—Industrialism 194
—Language (Theme) 534
—Law
—Police 1452
—Politics 739
—Pre-Raphaelite Brotherhood 530,
630
—Publishing 459, add4
—Science 1323
—Paleontology 1744
—Setting 829
—Society
—General Reform 194
—Individual 1303
—Uncollected Works 1899

LazyT
—Characters
—Serious Stationer 339

LifeL
—Editions 62

LittleDor
—General Criticism 2016
—Adaptation
—Radio 2936
—Appearance and Reality 1403
—Deception 2709
—Artist (Theme) 1150, 1403
—Authority 1691, 1763
—Characterization 1004, 2709
—Grotesque 1399a
—Characters
—Aunt, Mr. F's 2137
—Bishop 1603
—Blandois 1004
—Chivery, John 601
—Clennam, Arthur 849, 1659,
2461
—Dorrit, Amy 1380
—Dorrit, Frederick 833
—Dorrit, William 603
—Maggy 2137
—Meagles 1988
—Merdle 1811, 1912, 2172
—Rigaud 1916
—City 672, 2120
—Comedy and Humor 1655, 1733,
2137
—Satire 925, 1179
—Comparative Criticism
—Balzac's *Cousine Bette* 1151
—Blake 1150
—Eliot's *Mill on the Floss* 645
—Gissing 2449
—Lee's *Gilbert Massenger* 1762
—Wordsworth 2499
—Composition and Revision 2079
—Courtship and Marriage 601, 853
—Crime 1966
—Critical Methods 922
—Disease 191
—Economics 1318
—Money 1380, 1702a, 1844
—Editions 63, 64

FOREIGN LANGUAGE INDEX

NAME INDEX

Samuels, Allen 393, 1494, 2052
Sanders, Andrew 104, 390, 420, 543, 958, 1223, 1441, 2182
Sanders, Charles Richard 802
Santayana, George 2064, 2331
Sargent, Robert B. 2182
Saurel, Renée 2928
Schachterle, Lance 636
Schantz, Enid 1527
Schantz, Tom 1527
Schickel, Richard 2943
Schiffman, Joseph 1830
Schiller, Justin G. 27
Schlicke, Paul 1080, 1733, 2101, 2217
Schmidt, Dorey 648
Schmoll, Peter 517
Schnitzer, Jean 614
Schnitzer, Luda 614
Scholey, Arthur 2835
Schonberg, Harold 2932
Schrock, Ruth 237, 2093
Schuster, Charles I. 1034, 1881
Schwartz, Roslyn 2968
Schwarzbach, F. S. 390, 543, 570, 845, 1111, 1112, 1659
Scofield, Paul 2870
Scollins, Richard 60
Scott, Patrick 2217
Seehase, Georg 1620, 1786
Sehgal, Nayantara 2212
Selva, Mauricio de la 813
Senelick, Laurence 294, 1410
Sergeant, Howard 1489
Seydoux, Marianne 393
Seymour, Robert 80, 2258, 2365
Seymour, William Kean 295, 1786
Shaftesbury, 7th Earl of 438
Shales, Tom 2911
Shalit, Gene 2924
Sharbutt, Jay 2934
Sharp, Christopher 2923
Sharp, Richard 91
Sharples, Edward 802, 1438
Shaw, Charles 2819
Shaw, George Bernard 205, 1458,

Shaw, George Bernard (cont'd) 2064, 2331
Shaw, Harry Edmund 1704
Shayer, D. R. G. 1150
Sheehan, Grant 2860
Shefter, Harry 2785
Shelston, Alan 64, 1150
Shenker, Israel 1027
Shepard, Richard F. 2906
Sherman, Garry 2923
Sherrin, Ned 2908, 2941
Shippey, T. A. 65
Shorter, Eric 2910
Shyer, Laurence 2932
Siegel, Joel 2923
Simcox, Edith 438
Simon, John 2923, 2943
Simpson, Donald H. 1137
Simpson, Richard 438, 1458
Sinai, Camille 1544
Skelton, Susan 853
Slater, Michael 5, 9, 24, 42, 64, 67, 102, 104, 251, 478, 576, 802, 846, 1221, 1223, 1356, 1438, 1477, 1489, 1491, 1496, 1559, 1683, 1821, 2093, 2181, 2186, 2217, 2220, 2784, 2892, 2907, 2935, 2941
Smith, Angela 292
Smith, Anne 596, 660
Smith, Cecil 2927
Smith, F. Seymour 1786
Smith, Grahame 509, 1917, 2157, 2217
Smith, Harry B. 2262
Smith, Patrick J. 2918, 2932
Smith, Sheila M. 127, 154, 743, 1053, 1104
Smith, Stacy Jenel 2911
Smith, Timothy d'Arch 354, 1777
Snow, C. P. 1896
Soetaert, Ronald 1029
Solomon, Albert J. 2898
Sommer, Sally R. 2923
Sorfleet, John R. 798, 802
Spanberg, Sven-Johan 643
Spector, Robert D. 853